SHERWOOD ANDERSON'S MEMOIRS

Books by Sherwood Anderson

WINDY MCPHERSON'S SON (1916)

MARCHING MEN (1917)

MID-AMERICAN CHANTS (1918)

WINESBURG, OHIO (1919)

POOR WHITE (1921)

THE TRIUMPH OF THE EGG (1921)

MANY MARRIAGES (1923)

HORSES AND MEN (1923)

A STORY TELLER'S STORY (1924)

DARK LAUGHTER (1925)

THE MODERN WRITER (1925)

TAR—A MIDWEST CHILDHOOD (1926)

SHERWOOD ANDERSON'S NOTEBOOK (1926)

A NEW TESTAMENT (1927)

HELLO TOWNS (1929)

PERHAPS WOMEN (1931)

BEYOND DESIRE (1932)

DEATH IN THE WOODS (1933)

NO SWANK (1934)

PUZZLED AMERICA (1935)

KIT BRANDON (1936)

PLAYS: WINESBURG AND OTHERS (1937)

HOME TOWN (1940)

Sherwood Anderson's Memoirs

New York

HARCOURT, BRACE AND COMPANY

first edition

PRINTED IN THE UNITED STATES OF AMERICA

Publisher's Note

When he died Sherwood Anderson had almost completed his memoirs. The plan was complete, but some of the later sections had to be revised or fitted into the general structure. It was found necessary to omit some passages of a fragmentary nature. Mrs. Sherwood Anderson and the publishers wish to thank Mr. Paul Rosenfeld for his generous assistance in making selections from the incompleted sections, and for helping to prepare the manuscript. They also wish to thank Mr. Roger Sergel, Mr. Lewis Galantiere, Mr. Ferdinand Schevill, and Mr. Stanley Young for reading and advising on the manuscript.

Contents

BOOK V. INTO THE THIRTIES

BOOK VI. LIFE, NOT DEATH—

SHERWOOD ANDERSON'S MEMOIRS

This Book

When I read of the lives of genuinely great men, how they have struggled and suffered; of Keats and Chekhov in their losing fight against disease, de Maupassant and Van Gogh struggling against insanity, Herbert Spencer fighting against poverty; of Charles Darwin and his trip to the tropics in the *Beagle* and his long months of horrible illness, his determination and perseverance; John Brown in his mad stroke for justice to the American Negroes, Abraham Lincoln in the White House during the four terrible years of our Civil War, Dostoievsky in the hour in which he faced a firing squad and in the years in a Siberian prison camp; when I read about these men and many others in the long, often tragic story of man's passionate devotion to some art, some science or idea of justice, and then look back on my own career as an American story teller, I have to consider my life a most fortunate one.

Fortunate despite the fact that I cannot rank myself among the heroes. There has been something of struggle but little enough of the heroic in my life. For all my egotism I know I am but a minor figure. Yet I had something of these men's devotion in my frame, and now when I come to the point of summing up, of looking not forward but backward on events and people that have affected my life, I am compelled to exclaim—

"Oh thou fortunate one!" Lucky to have been born an American in what well may turn out to have been America's happiest period, to have been born poor and in a small town where community life was intimate and close, to have had to work as a laborer both in factories and on farms, thus to have known whence came the food that nourished my body and what toil went into its production, to have had the mother and the invariably picturesque father I had; lucky in my brothers; on the whole in my loves of women, in having been born with a talent; lucky in all my circumstances, in the friends I have made, even in my enemies—

But wait—where are my enemies? Have I indeed any?

If I am hated anywhere perhaps I am too great an egotist to know of it. Perhaps my entire feeling about myself flows from this egotism.

Once when we were both young men in Chicago, Ben Hecht and I spoke of this possibility over a glass of beer. "Yes, you are lucky and will always feel yourself lucky," he said. If I were to fall into a river, he suggested, I wouldn't get wet.

"Man, it's because of your profound egotism. It is colossal. When you are snubbed, you do not know it. When someone condemns your work, you simply put him down as a fool. Some of us have to go through terrible times of doubt of our talents, but you never have to. You will sail blithely through life, often doing terrible things to others without at all knowing what you are doing. Friends will stand by you. When you are pressed someone will always come to your rescue. You will always be loved more than you deserve. Your egotism . . . Why, man, it is so colossal that you will always be going about wearing an air of modesty and even of humility. You will even believe that you actually are humble. Lord God, man, but you are a lucky one!"

No doubt I am not quoting Ben exactly. He always was a very flowery talker. That however is the substance of what he said in the Chicago restaurant, and I have often since wondered if it was the truth.

Yet—what's wrong with this egotism? If a man doesn't delight in himself and the force in him and feel that he and it are wonders, how is all life to become important to him? The interest in the lives of others, the high evaluation of these lives, what are they but the overflow of the interest he finds in himself, the value he attributes to his own being?

But of this fortune— There was a secretary I once had, who worked with me for several years. She was about to get married. She came to say good-by. A little smile played about the corner of her mouth. She stood hesitatingly at the door of the room in which we worked together. It was while I was still half a man of business.

"Mr. Anderson—"

"Yes?"

"There is something I have long been wanting to say but I hardly know how."

"What is coming?" I had begun asking myself. "Why, go ahead, go ahead, child. Don't be afraid," I said.

The glance of her eyes had become wicked.

"You will remember, Mr. Anderson, that you employed me out of a business office. You call me a child, but I am past thirty. We were both employed in that same business office. I happen to know what you did there."

"Well?"

"I just wanted to say that I did not and do not in the least blame you for what you did and do. There is an old saying that business is business, and it is quite true. It is a shark's game."

"Well, so it is—"

"You see, since I have been with you—you know how many letters I have taken for you—to your clients—to your friends—I wanted to say, before I left you—you see, you have continually been saying to these men with whom you do business—'I am no business man.' You are always playing the innocent. You put on an air. You make yourself appear naïve. Please, Mr. Anderson, don't keep it up until you believe it yourself!"

She closed the door. She entered into the sacred bonds of matrimony. I thought she would probably do all right as a wife.

I have always, from the beginning, been a rather foxy man, with a foxiness which at times approached slickness. If ever by chance you get into a horse trade with me, be a little careful.

This slickness. It is the curse of the world. It is in too many of our diplomats, our statesmen, governors, politicians. Business is lousy with it. It invades the world of art, is in families, in groups of so-called friends, it is everywhere.

"How can I use this man or woman? What can I make this one do for me?"

We do it under the cloak of friendship. You do it and I do it. It is a disease. When I was a boy I heard it on all sides.

Go it, boy. Be on the alert. Watch your chance, then push forward. Oh, onward and upward, over the shoulders of others, trample them down.

It has grown stronger, the cry, since the first World War. Could that be helped? Some psychic wound, some inflation, chilling, hardening would seem the inevitable result of having to take part in such wars.

Why, lives were thrown away like worn-out shoes. Men had to renounce too much of their self-esteem. Killing and being killed became mechanical. Is there any wonder that so much of present-day writing, of story telling, is concerned with death? Death in the morning, in the afternoon; death at night; death of animals, of men; death in poetry, in prose?

In peace-time there is a chance that life here on these streets, new life ever pushing up from the wombs of women, will touch us, enter into us, take us out of, interest us in, restore us to, ourselves. Not always, however. Sometimes I think we Americans are the loneliest people in the world. To be sure, we hunger for the power of affection, the self-acceptance that gives life. It is the oldest and strongest hunger in the world. But hungering is not enough.

A curious sickness overcame me. Then one night I began writing. It was a little tale of something seen or felt, something remembered out of my experience of people.

The act did something for me. I kept writing little tales of people. I put them through experiences I had myself been through and suddenly there came a new revelation. It was this—that it is only by thinking hard of others that you can attain self-knowledge.

Man cannot think clearly of self, cannot see himself except through others. The self you seek, the true self you want to face, to accept, perhaps to love, is hidden away.

It is in the man you just met in the street. It is in the eyes of a child. It is in a tired old woman, in a thief. It is everywhere in others.

There are shades of things to be caught, a little the story of lives to be put down, the eternal challenge, something by which you can breathe.

My luck has held. I have found work that engrosses me all my days and continually enlarges my horizon. Whether or not I have succeeded in permanently curing myself of the slickness I so hated in myself, I have, at least, found the road to health.

My life has been so rich and crowded that I want to tell something about it before the bell rings. It began just at the right hour and I hope it may not carry on too far. Physical life doesn't so much matter—the ability to win foot races, hit a baseball, ride a horse over jumps—

but I would like to quit living just before that terrible time when the brain, the imagination, ceases from activity.

Still, whose life is this? What is your own life? I am one thing in my own consciousness, another as you see me, still another as I seem to Jane Grey or Tom Smith or John Emerson. Is there even such a thing as a life of one's own? Is it not some illusion, some limitation in ourselves that makes us feel there is? It seems to me that all lives merge.

And do I want in any case to write about this apparent life of my own? When one writes of self one inevitably makes a hero of self. No, I want to use my own life only as a kind of springboard. What difference when I was born, what women I made love to, what friends I betrayed? What is interesting is the woman loved, the friend betrayed, the friend to whom I was loyal. My ambition to become rich, to be a big man as we in our town thought of big men when I was a boy, that is to say, a money maker, did pass: I became interested in people—and I want to make my book, my rambling house of a book, a book of people.

But here is something I must also explain. It happens that I have met, in the course of the life I just have briefly outlined, a good many so-called "notable" men and women, famous writers, painters, singers, actors, publishers. Whom have I not met? I have remained a restless man, ever on the move. As writer, I came into writing at a time when new paths were being made. Often nowadays my name is coupled with that of Theodore Dreiser, Sinclair Lewis, Edgar Lee Masters, Carl Sandburg, Eugene O'Neill and others as, shall I say, a "pioneer"? Naturally I am interested in these men met, women met, so-called notable men and women with many of whom I have formed friendships. But—this fact may disappoint you who have happened to pick up this book—these notable ones are not and have not been my central interest. Some of them may appear in the pages of my book and others may not; and if they do appear it will be but incidentally—for, in my writing, I have always written of "obscure" people. It is these who have given me life.

There is still another desire. I would like to write a book of the life of the mind and of the imagination. Facts elude me. I cannot remember dates. When I deal in facts, at once I begin to lie. I can't help it. I am by nature a story teller. No one ever taught me. Like such men as Erskine Caldwell, Ring Lardner and others I've known, I'm a natural.

Once, many years ago, I sat down to write the story of my own boyhood in a Middle-Western town. I couldn't do it.

When, for example, I wrote of my own father and mother I depicted people my brothers and my sister could not recognize.

"Anyway," I said to myself, "I have made a picture of my father and mother—" They were my father and mother as I felt them.

I remember once, a good many years ago, going on a fishing trip with several men friends. Marco Morrow, later Senator Arthur Capper's right hand man out in Topeka, Kansas, publisher of Arthur's *Topeka Capitol* and a lot of farm papers, was of the party, and Frank Dunn, then publisher of the *Chicago Post,* was along. There were half a dozen of us, all except myself newspaper men and we were staying at a fishing lodge somewhere far up in Minnesota.

The point is that the proprietor of the lodge was a man who took my fancy. He was one of the sort of men I am always making up stories about. Such stories became very real to me. All sorts of odd absurd things happened at the table up there in the fishing lodge.

Well, our host had a certain quality. Everything he said had to me a certain delightful naïveté. I began to invent speeches for him.

And then later one night in Chicago at a dinner table I began to report some of the man's absurd and amusing remarks. I was going good. I had the whole table laughing at some of the remarks made by that man of the Minnesota lakes and woods when a man at the end of the table caught my eye.

It was Marco Morrow and there was a look of astonishment in his eyes.

I was just about to launch forth on a new anecdote when he spoke.

"Ladies and gentlemen," he said, "we have here with us this evening the champion liar of the world. He has been telling you stories of happenings in a fishing lodge up in Minnesota. He has been using me as a stooge for some of his stories. He forgot that I was here, listening. You see I was also one of this party of which he has been speaking. Not one of all these happenings with which he has been amusing you really happened."

Marco rose in his place at the table and bowed to me.

"Go ahead, you liar," he said. "Don't let me stop you. Don't let the truth get in your way." Just the same and although Marco did rather take the wind out of my sails that evening (I had forgotten that he was one of the party and I had convinced myself that all the stories I was telling that evening were true)—just the same, I swear that, although I may have been inventing some, I had really got the quality of our host at the fishing camp. If he had not said some of the things I made him say he should have said them.

What I am here trying to do comes to the same thing. I believe in the imagination, its importance. To me there is a certain music to all good prose writing. There is tone and color in words as in notes in music. Persons also have a certain tone, a certain color. What care I for the person's age, the color of his hair, the length of his legs? When writing of another being I have always found it best to do so in accordance with my feeling. Besides, men do not exist in facts. They exist in dreams. My readers, therefore, those who go along with me, will have to be patient. I am an imaginative man.

Besides, I shall tell the tale as though you, my readers, were personal friends. We are walking together, let's say on a country road. The road follows a stream and the day is pleasant. We are unhurried. We stop at times to sit on rocks beside the stream. We arise and walk again and I talk.

I keep talking, love to talk. I am telling you that this thing happened to me, that that thing happened.

Do you wish I would stop talking, let you talk? Why then, dear readers, go write your own books.

BOOK I

WHAT A MAN'S MADE OF

1. The Age

As I remember it, the town of Clyde itself was a fair and a sweet town. There was something of New England— It was in the so-called Western Reserve in the state of Ohio. There were many little white frame houses. All the residence streets were lined with great spreading maples. And at the back of his yard, every citizen with any pretensions had a barn.

The modern world had not come into full flower. Why, look, it is the far-famed horse and buggy age! Of course I shall be accused of nostalgia for speaking of it! But wasn't it Dean Swift who spoke of the man coming back from the world ruled by horses to a world ruled by men, and having a terrible time readjusting himself?

There were always horses tied to hitching-posts along the main street of the town. Sparrows grew fat from the droppings. There were old lady horses with sad eyes, and worn-out geldings: perhaps too many male horses early robbed of malehood.

There were horse races in our main street on winter afternoons, the streets cleared for them, and on winter nights, dances in country barns. Maple trees shedding their winged seeds on spring days when a breeze sprang up, creeks near town where boys went to swim. The terrible passionate curiosity of the young male concerning the young female. Old men, young men already failures in life—inspired ones, who from the beginning accepted failure, embraced it . . . But look! Young fellows of the local baseball team, having won a game from some neighboring town, having got a keg of beer, are going off to Ames's wood, down past the old stave factory, to drink there in the darkness, under trees, to sing ribald songs.

The achievement of a kind of drunkenness. It doesn't all come from the beer. There is the night with shining stars. The keg of beer we have got is sitting on a little platform made of logs or on a stump. We are at the wood's edge, with pasture lands between us and the town. Young men sprawling, lads sprawling. In the pastures nearby, in bright moonlight, cows are grazing. Thoughts weave themselves in and out among spoken thoughts from the others, among the songs. —Now some fellow is boasting of his virility. We have poor little street-tarts in our town. They lie with men and boys under hedges—as they lay with them in the towns told about in the Old Testament, in Greek and Roman towns, in English towns, in French. How but for them do we get our education as young males?

One of the gang is talking. Already we have begun thinking of ourselves as a gang. Suddenly a thought emerges. "Why is it that those among the young men and boys of this town who listen to our elders, remain virtuous, go early to bed, do not associate with our town roughs, or smoke or drink or swear—surely all of them headed onward and upward—everyone says so—why is it that they are almost always such bum ball-players?"

There is that big fellow Jim, lying there on the grass, boasting now. He is very strong. He carried the keg of beer to the wood on his shoulder. Jim belongs to a poor family of the town and already has been arrested for stealing chickens. A doctor of the town, who is a rabid ball-fan, got him out of it by appearing and paying his fine. He carried the keg of beer right down through Main Street, past stores, past people walking, while the rest of us sneaked through alleyways, not wanting it known that we were to share it with him. He is a pitcher with marvelous control. He is a curve ball pitcher. It was his work that enabled us to beat the neighboring town—and last night, when any athlete, to do good work, should have been early to bed, Jim was out with one of our town tarts.

Why, oh, why, in that town of the American Northwest where Sinclair Lewis spent his boyhood, were there no such evenings among other young men and boys! What a different book *Main Street* might have been had a circus ever come to his town, had his town baseball team ever whipped a team from a neighboring one—had springs but come—winter nights under the stars—had he but kissed some high-school girl on a dark porch, her father right inside the house, pretending to read a book in there, thus putting one over on papa. Poor Lewis, he missed a lot! And Henry Mencken, with his trick of making all small-town and country people into one pattern— But of that, more perhaps later. We are in the wood now and Jim is boasting.

"But where did you take her?"

"To the graveyard," he says. Our town graveyard has a national hero buried in it. There is a bronze monument. The United States government put it up . . . But surely, when he, our national hero, was a lad here in this town, he did not go off with other boys for such evenings as this? He did not listen to such ribald songs, hear such talk as is going on here?

Jim laughs. What envy there is in the rest of us! "Oh that I could be such a one." There is the feeling that his boast may not be a boast. There is a nice grass plot about the statue of our national hero. It is on a small hill. "Do you suppose they were lying there, in the moonlight, on the grass, under the monument?"

A butcher's son is sprawling near our mighty virile one. He rolls over on his back and looks up at the stars. He has an ambition, wonderful, gigantic. "Before I die," wistfully he says, "I intend to be with one of every nation on earth."

This scene, and in the distance the lights of the town. The eternal puzzle of life beginning in a boy. "There is this life here, that I am at this moment leading, with these fellows. In spite of all talk, this talk of women, of man's adventures with women, now going on here, in spite of all this, it's a kind of good warm flow." On the ball field during the afternoon, there was a certain play made. You had nothing to do with it. You were playing in the right field and but one fly ball came your way during the game. You muffed that. At bat you did nothing. There was a ball shot down through the infield, very hot, a hard hit one, and little Shorty Grimes raced over. He got it with one hand, turned a quick pivot. He shot it to second . . . a double play. All of the bases full, our side but one run ahead. At that moment you felt something . . . Something of Shorty's quick and so beautifully graceful movement was also in your own body. You felt no jealousy, no envy. There was a strange gladness in you.

The puzzle about all of this as you lie out there under the trees, beneath the stars, the lights of the stars in the distance! There is your own mother. She works hard, is fairly killing herself with work to keep her sons alive. What of her? Suppose she were here now, heard as you did these tales of triumphant sin, heard those songs sung?

That thought put aside as being a bit too uncomfortable. "There is the woman's world, her life, and there is our man's life. There is a world and a time of youth, and a world and a time of maturity. Maybe sometime I may become mature, a man in a man's world. But now I am a boy. There is this happiness, the warm feeling I now have for these others out here with me at the edge of the wood. For everything its time and place."

2. The Family

The first of the many houses in which we Andersons lived that has stayed clearly in my mind was the little brick house, now gone. It was the first in which we lived in Clyde, but father and mother must have lived in several others before we came to the town. "It looks as though they had moved whenever the rent came due," my brother Irwin once said. I have no notion of where my mother and father married. It may have been in the village at Morning Sun, in Ohio, where my older brother Karl was born. Karl and my sister Stella both beat me in the race into the world. When father married my mother he might have been a quite prosperous young man. Mother had been a bound girl, the daughter of a strange old peasant woman who had been married four times, had children by each husband—children that when she got a new man she got bound out by a custom of her time to live as a kind of semi-servant until they grew to manhood and womanhood. Our mother had been bound out to some farming family in the southern part of the state of Ohio, and our father, then no doubt something of a young dandy, had found her there. She must have been quite lovely. A picture of her, taken at that time, stands on my desk before me as I write.

And what a life she was to lead after the picture was taken, after she had stood up before some preacher to make her vows to be a faithful wife to my father.

She was all of that. She was game. Surely later she must have known of some of my father's surreptitious adventures in the field of love but if she ever complained, I at least never heard her and so I must leave that phase of her character to the still night hours, husband and wife lying together in their bed. Married men should know what I mean.

After Morning Sun and the coming into the world of Karl and Stella our little family moved to Camden, Ohio, where my turn came. Then to another village called Caledonia, Ohio. Some faint memories of that place remain in me. I had learned to walk and even a little to go adventuring and, offended no doubt by something Karl and Stella may have done (they may have grown weary of my tagging at their heels and ordered me to go home), decided to run away from home.

I could not have gone far, perhaps into some nearby meadow. The town of Caledonia was very small. It was one of the sort of towns, once described by George Ade as "a town dividing two farms." However, I had decided to leave home and town forever. The wanderlust that was to be in me always had already asserted itself.

But I have written of that adventure in a book of childhood tales called *Tar,* told of how I grew hungry and, no doubt having seen sheep, cows, and horses grazing in the fields, decided to eat grass, and of how, as I went on all fours nibbling at the grass and clover tops a bee, disturbed on his clover top, stung me on the lips so that I went howling home.

There is also a faint memory of a flood in a stream that must have passed close to our house, the yellow spring flood waters spreading out and covering the nearby fields, and another of a trip taken, holding mother's hand, to father's harness shop, and of the pungent smell of leather in the little shop.

There was a small pot-bellied stove, red hot. Its door was open. A great piece of iron turned yellow by the heat lay on the coals. It was for heating the water in a tub in which leather was put to be softened. My father grasped the hot iron in a pair of tongs and threw it into the tub. A great cloud of steam flew up. The iron was of a sort used at that time for coupling freight cars together and how father had got it is still a mystery to me.

Later (it must have been several years later) I questioned mother.

I was remembering how the glowing iron hissed and seemed to scream, as if with pain, when thrown into the tub of water. By the time I questioned mother I must have become aware of the way in which freight cars were coupled together.

"Was he ever a railroad man? Was he ever an engineer?"

"No, child, no." Mother was never one for long explanations. She was not a talker and was always very busy. There were too many children about for her to spend much time in answering questions.

"But if he did not work on the railroad, what right had he to it?" I may have been half hoping that my father had, at some time, been connected with the running of trains. Railroad men would have become half heroes to me. I would have resented having my dream destroyed and I began to picture in my mind my father's snitching the piece of iron from a car on some railroad siding. It is possible that I had already begun to snitch fruit from trees in the yards of neighbors. I may have wanted to find out if father was also one given to snitching.

Why, what have we here, a little moralist? There is something wrong here.

I do remember continually questioning mother about the mystery. I had burned my hand on our kitchen stove. For some reason the heated iron, thrown into the tub of water, had made a great impression on my child's mind. I wondered if putting the iron into the stove to be heated had hurt it as touching the hot stove in our kitchen had hurt me. It had seemed to hurt. It had seemed to scream with pain.

"But if he was never a railroad man, what right had he to it?"

"I don't know, child. Now run away and play."

We had traveled north. The town of Clyde is some twenty miles south of Sandusky, on Put-in Bay, the bay from which Admiral Perry once sent the stirring message, "We have met the enemy and they are ours!"

But as I write, other vague memories of the earlier little towns crowd in on me. There was a fire in Caledonia, people running in the streets at night, fire apparatus from the larger neighboring town of Marion coming to our little town in flat cars, the freight engine, hauling the cars, screaming as it neared the town. Mr. Warren Harding, who was to become President, may have come with the Marion fire fighters. There is a tradition that he and my father once played together in the same cornet band. He would have been a joiner as father was. What a shame that father did not live to demand and get a government job under his presidency.

As the fire raged I went abroad in the night with my brother Karl and my sister Stella, and it is a sharp remembrance, with the blazing buildings, the sparks flying far up into the night sky, the people running from houses into roadways with household goods, the great piles of such goods in the streets, chains of people passing pails of water from hand to hand, others wetting blankets taken from their beds to spread over the roofs of houses so that the flying sparks would not set them afire. Our own house in that place must have been out of the path of the fire but the memory of it is fixed sharply in my mind.

Then an adventure of another kind. I was with my sister Stella, some two years my elder. We had wandered away from the side of our house along a country road. We came to a rail fence by a field, and there, in the field before us, something was going on that was strange and even terrifying to us.

A mother pig lay in the field near the fence and tiny pigs were coming from her. It was a thing that my sister and I could not understand and the sight curiously absorbed and, at the same time, frightened us.

"Oh, look! There is another. They are alive. They are little pigs." But how could that be, life coming thus from life? The mother pig kept groaning as if in pain.

How long my sister and I stayed there by the fence I do not know. No doubt we stayed but a few minutes, as we were both frightened by what we had just seen, but I do remember my sister's taking my hand and our running along the road toward our house. Afterwards when we had got safely home she made me promise I would not tell mother of what we had seen and that I would not question her.

"But why mustn't I tell?"

"I don't know, but you mustn't, you mustn't."

It was as though already we had eaten of the fruit of the tree of the knowledge of good and evil. And I do not believe that it could have been the promise to my sister that kept me from questioning our mother. It was something else. It was the newly discovered strangeness about the life in animals. It got into my dreams. Horses were coming from horses, pigs from pigs, and cows from cows. There was this amazing multiplication of life going on. It is impossible for the man, writing of all this, to be quite sure of what could have been in the child's mind. I do know that he wanted very much to ask his mother about it all but for some mysterious reason did not dare.

It must have been soon after the incident of the birth of the litter of pigs that we began our march northward to the town of Clyde. Father had gone broke and his harness shop was gone and, knowing my father as I came to know him later, I am sure it must have been a bitter dose for him to take. Later I was to hear many explanations of his failure.

We had moved northward to the town of Clyde, father now become a maker of harnesses for farm horses, a mere workman in another man's shop. I do not remember the railroad journey or our arrival in the new place. I do know that in the old place, at Caledonia, and in my own place, Camden, Ohio, he was a man who would be long remembered.

They would remember him as a great teller of tales, and as a man always ready whenever a parade was to be held to close his shop and go off for the day, to take the train over to Marion and play in the band. They would also remember him for the parts he took in the amateur theatricals in Morning Sun, in Camden, in Caledonia and in neighboring towns—now of a comic Irishman, now of a German, now of the farmer of such plays of the times, the comic figure of all such amateur plays, whiskers on chin and straw in mouth. He would never have missed anything of that sort nor would he have missed the gathering of men at the back of the town saloons, political parades, or speech makings.

As for the business of running a harness shop, the spring plowing season being on, farmers clamoring for harnesses ordered for farm horses—is a man to be a slave? Of what is a man made?

The brick house in Clyde indeed was very small. How we all managed to live in it is still a mystery to me, for other children continually were coming. More children coming and father often without work. In Clyde he soon lost his place in the harness shop. It may have been due to one of the periods of depression, the two men who owned the shop, the brothers Irwin, compelled to retrench, no more work coming in, no new harness being sold, or it may have been father's fault, his work neglected, he running off to some reunion of Civil War veterans or perhaps gone into one of his periods of drinking when he could not work.

But, at any rate, there is a winter of hardship fixed in my mind, mother struggling to in some way take father's place as the family breadwinner. She had father paint a sign on cardboard and hang on the front door of our house. It said that mother would take in family sewing. I do not believe that any sewing ever came to her.

I remember my resentment. It may have been that mother was again big with child and could not work. She would already, during that for us so terrible winter, have begun taking in family washing but, the new child being on the way, would have had to give up that work while we became objects of charity, neighbors bringing food to our door, we children half unaware of the terror of actual hunger and yet, even as small children, vaguely conscious of our mother's fright and sadness, the tears often coming suddenly to her eyes so that we all began to cry loudly in sympathy with her. There would be the strange long periods of silence in the house, myself, with the two other children, Karl and Stella, going along neighboring railroad tracks on winter days and picking up pieces of coal dropped from trains to keep the one stove in our house going, we all, in winter evenings, huddled about the stove in the little kitchen, no lamp burning, as there would have been no oil for it, and then the crawling into bed in the darkness, all of us in the one bed, frightened by something we had seen in mother's eyes and huddled together for safety and warmth.

Father would have been much from home during that winter. It was our hardest one. Painting the sign announcing mother's willingness to become a seamstress may have set off the artist in him. It may have been that winter that he became a sign painter, going off somewhere seeking jobs.

But I have written much of my father in another book of mine, *A Story Teller's Story,* of his many vagaries and, I trust, a little of his charm, and must not too much repeat, although (it may be because so many of my father's characteristics are also mine) he will always be a tempting subject to me. And what I am wondering as I write is whether during that, our hardest winter, mother was carrying my brother Earl. For I am quite sure there was in me already a resentment of the fact of her pregnancy, a resentment that must have also been in my brother Karl and my sister Stella. At the time we could hardly have known by what mysterious process our mother had become pregnant but also there may have been a vague realization of the father's having to do with it. My sister and I had seen the little pigs born of the mother pig in the field. After the event, it was never spoken of between my sister and myself but it would have been remembered. It is quite possible that Karl and perhaps Stella were already going to school and would have seen the obscene drawings I was later to see scrawled on the schoolhouse fence and on the walls of the boys' privy. They may have been laughed at for the notion of children dropped into houses from the sky by birds.

I am also wondering if the same resentment of renewed pregnancy is not in all children born in all families among the poor? At any rate, it was a resentment that my brother Earl, the last but one of the seven children mother bore, felt all his life. All through his life and until his premature death he continued to feel himself an unwanted child.

But I will not here attempt to tell of my brother Earl's strange fate. Here I only want to suggest that the end of his life when I went to him as he lay paralyzed and dying, and after the long years when he kept himself hidden away from the rest of us in the little workman's boarding house in the city of Brooklyn, in the room that my brother Karl, when he went to him after the stroke that laid him low, found filled with paintings, paintings under his bed, paintings packed away in his closet, paintings everywhere, no one of which had been sold or even shown to others—when I sat beside him as he lay dying and unable to speak, he took a pencil into his hand and wrote the words: "I was unwanted. You others did not want me to be born and mother did not want me."

As I said, I will write of Earl's strange life in another and later part of this book. Here I am only thinking of the dim awareness and resentment of a mother's pregnancy in small children in a destitute family. It was sharp in me. It is the feeling that comes thus to a small child, seeing the sudden new shapelessness of a mother, sensing without quite knowing of, the coming event—is it jealousy of a mother's love which must again be more widely distributed? I only know the feeling as a part of the experience of that particular winter, along with resentment that other children of the neighborhood could be more warmly clad, that they did not have to go to the railroad to search for coal with half-frozen fingers, that they could have new shoes when the soles of my own and my brother's and sister's had become loose so that our toes stuck out, that they lived in warmer houses and their fathers seemed to have a kind of dignity our father could not achieve; I only know that along with these resentments was this other and sharper one, so that when the child was born I hated it also, and when I had been called into a room to see it lying so small and red in the bed beside mother I crept away into a little shed at the back of the house and had a good long and lonely cry.

3. A Small Town Street

For what seems to him long years, a child's life goes on in a single street of his town or a block of his city. How vividly the streets along which a boy runs or walks are remembered, the houses that border them, the vacant lots between houses, the fields at the edge of town, some small stream that flows past, the streets at night in summer or on a winter night when smoke curls up out of the chimneys of small houses! In our street, it was the house of the saloon keeper that I remember first. The saloon keeper, a quite tall German man, had a young wife. He left his house at daybreak and returned late at night. He went silently, with bent head, along the street. There was a picket fence at the front of his house and his wife and their one child were seldom seen. What an isolated life they seemed to lead. The wife of the saloon keeper did not go in and out of the other houses in the street, and his one child, a boy of about my own age, seldom came out from behind the picket fence.

Could it have been that the saloon keeper, his wife and child, were socially ostracized because of the business in which he was engaged? It was an age of temperance societies and there were two churches on our street. To sell liquor, to own a saloon, was to be, I am sure, the devil's servant. Once, filled with curiosity, I ventured across the street to the picket fence before the saloon keeper's house and there was his boy child. He was always very well dressed. He did not go bare-footed even in the summer. His hair was neatly combed, his face seemed always newly washed and once I heard one of the Moffatt boys, a stone hurler and my brother Karl's friend, call the saloon keeper's boy a sissy.

"He is a sissy, a mother's darling," the Moffatt boy said.

The boy was sitting on the grass in the saloon keeper's front yard. He had some colored marbles and was playing with them. I pressed my face into an opening between two of the pickets.

"Hello," I called.

How strange! The boy quickly arose. He gathered up his marbles and ran. He ran toward the kitchen door of the saloon keeper's house.

"Mamma, Mamma," he cried.

Well, he was indeed a sissy. Think of calling your mother mamma. "No boy not a sissy would do that," my brother Irwin said.

My brother Irwin, named for our father, was very pugnacious and, even when little more than a babe, was always getting into fights. He was a climber of trees, a climber onto the roof of our house. He was a thrower of stones at windows of houses. He had thrown a stone at a little girl passing in the street and mother had caught him in the act. She cut a switch from a bush and holding him by the collar of his shirt switched his behind. He cried lustily.

"Ouch! Ouch!" he cried, but the moment mother had released him his cries died in his throat and he ran away.

He ran through our back yard. He climbed a fence. He had something on his mind. There was a boy child of his own age who lived several houses away along our street and Irwin had gone to fight with him. He had already been in several fights with the boy, whose name was Crowley, and had gone to seek another. Whenever mother switched him (she did not strike hard; her whippings did not hurt much), he sought out the Crowley boy and pummeled him. It was a way to re-establish his self-respect. He had been held helpless in the hands of mother. He had shed tears in the presence of his brothers and had been humiliated before us. The pummeling of the Crowley boy until he also shed tears and ran howling to his mother gave him back something he had lost.

The stone throwers along our street were older than my brother Irwin and myself. The two younger boys of our family, Earl and Ray, were still babies. Now our hardest winter had been got through and spring had come. Before this house there was a great maple tree with a huge trunk that stood just at the sidewalk's edge, and on spring days my sister Stella would be sitting under it. She was minding the two babies as they crawled about the yard at her feet.

Sometimes the stone throwers of the street assembled under the maple. They were all larger boys than Irwin and myself, but sometimes, when the early spring darkness began to descend, Karl went forth to join the throwers' army, and sometimes, slipping away from the house unobserved, Irwin and I tagged along.

We were told by the older boys to go on home. We were pushed and occasionally slapped. We were reminded that the stone-throwing contest carried on with some boys from the neighboring street was not an affair for babies. But, though compelled by the older boys on the street to return to our own yard, we did not stay there. We crept back to the scene of the battle.

There was a running back and forth through back yards. There was a hiding behind fences. Stones were hurled. The forces from our street were led by the older of the two Moffatt boys. There were cries and shouts. It was all very exciting, but, unlike my younger brother Irwin, I was frightened. I wanted to return to the safety of our own yard but Irwin would not. Already, although he was as yet in skirts, had not yet attained to the glory of pants, he yearned to be one of the embattled stone throwers, and in his little fist was clutched a stone. Once, on a summer evening, when we were lurking thus on the edge of the battle, in the half darkness, in some neighbor's back yard, and when one of the stones hurled by a real stone thrower had crashed through the window of a house so that both armies were fleeing from the field, Irwin did throw a stone (it may have been merely a handful of gravel) at a figure dashing past us in the half darkness as we crouched behind the bush. He had hit the running boy in the face and he stopped running and came to us.

What a moment and how magnificent my younger brother! The boy might have been twelve or thirteen. He seemed a giant to me. He grasped my brother by the collar of his shirt just as mother did when she switched him, but now Irwin did not cry although I was near to tears. The larger boy held my brother and shook him. It was evident that he was not one of our street's forces but an enemy. He was holding my brother firmly. He laughed.

"Why, you little bastard," he said, and "Oh, you go to hell," my brother replied.

It was, I thought, magnificent. Such bravery! Such defiance in the very hands of the enemy! I did not know the meaning of the word bastard but knew it was a swear word, one of the words for saying which we Anderson boys occasionally had our mouths washed with soap. My brother had defied one of the enemy and he had won a victory. The bigger boy let go his hold on Irwin's collar and laughed again. In the distance we could hear the voice of a woman, no doubt of the woman the window of whose house had been broken by the flying stone. She was scolding in a loud voice and the enemy boy, still laughing, continued his flight into the darkness while Irwin and I went on home, my own breast filled with pride at my brother's bravery.

The street grew longer. On Sundays, horses hitched to buggies, phaetons, and even to farm wagons, stood tied at sheds back of the two churches and in the street before the churches. Neither our father nor our mother went to church and I do not remember any of us children going to Sunday School while we lived in that street. We were perhaps too poor and had no fit clothes. Mother's pride would have kept us at home.

But we had begun to prosper a little. Now father had become a house painter. He had begun to speak a new language. There was much talk of the fine art of mixing house paint, of how the brush should be held in the hand. At that time there was a great passion for what was called "graining." The trick was to make pine look like oak, oak like cherry, cherry like walnut. Father had acquired an outfit of graining tools and practiced on the doors and walls of our house. He spread a dirty brown mixture over a panel of one of the doors and got out his tools. He advanced upon the door, made certain flourishes with his hand. The point was to imitate the grain of some particular wood.

"You see, it is pine, it will become oak. See how perfectly the grain of oak is reproduced. There is not another man in Ohio could do so perfect or beautiful a job of graining."

Now father was always coming home covered with paint. I was also, when later he sometimes took me with him to help paint some farmer's barn. There was paint in his hair, on his eyebrows and mustache. It was on his hands, on his face. His clothes were yellow, then brown, then green, then red.

It must have been about this time that our mother began her career as a washwoman. She had worked all of her life, even from childhood, for others, a childhood and young girlhood of washing dishes, milking cows, waiting on tables, a kind of half servant in a house of strangers to her own blood, only, after marriage and the coming of her children, to become a washwoman. And I remember keenly a kind of shame that began to grow in the breasts of us children when we were sent off to bear home baskets of dirty clothes or to return them washed and ironed.

We did not go, on these trips, through the streets but kept as far as possible to the alleyways. If we went through the streets and heard someone coming we quickly turned into a yard before some house and set the basket down. We tried to pretend we had nothing to do with it. It was shame to us that mother should have to do such work. She was no longer strong and she coughed a good deal.

Of course it is possible that the feeling of shame in us that our mother should be brought down to so low a position in the town life was due to remarks made by other children on our street. The same may have come at first into the minds of the two older children, Karl and Stella, and may have been transmitted to us younger ones through them. At any rate, it was there and I am sure that even then we had begun asking ourselves the unanswerable question:

"Why is it that this one is born into life in a big house, with a carriage at the door, with no thought of where food comes from, with warm clothes to wear, all of life to be lived in luxury, while we others, outside in the cold, often in ragged clothes, like little animals, are compelled to hunt our food from day to day? Why is it? Why is it?

"Why does our mother have to wash the dirty clothes soiled by other people?"

It was not, I am sure, hatred of seemingly more fortunate ones that was growing in us. It was not even envy. It was a kind of shame, and I am quite sure that at a very early age it took the form (at least it did in me) of despising our father.

It was a feeling that was to stay in me, as the hardship of our mother's life continued, down to the very day of her death, and to grow into a kind of hatred. Our mother, I felt, was not made for the life she was compelled to live. She was a woman delicately built and whom I thought beautiful and I am quite sure that, even as a child, I began to want for her the things in life she was never to have.

Am I running too far ahead now? I do not know. I do know that it was only after I had become a mature man, long after our mother's death, that I began to appreciate our father and to understand somewhat his eternal boyishness, his lack of the feeling of responsibility to others, his passion for always playing with life, qualities which, I have no doubt, our mother saw in him and which enabled her, in spite of the long hardship of her life with him, to remain always a faithful, and for anything I ever heard her say, a devoted wife.

And if in my own life, after many attempts at living as laborer, soldier, follower of race horses, factory hand, and business man, I became at last a writer, a writer whose sympathy went out most to the little frame houses, on often mean enough streets in American towns, to defeated people, often with thwarted lives, it is, I am sure, all due to this feeling toward our mother that had begun to grow in me as a small child. It must have been in several of us in the form of a feeling of responsibility to our mother, in my brother Karl, who was later to become an outstanding American painter, member of the National Academy, a man of note in the world of American painters.

I am back now in the little street, the first of the American small town streets that were to stay always so sharply in my mind, up and down which my imagination was always to play, searching for the key to the secret of lives. Karl, who must have been a boy of twelve or thirteen while we lived in that particular street, had been out searching for work to help a little lift the load from mother, and had got a job. In a frame house near the street's head, near where it led into the town's main thoroughfare, there was a certain creature. It was half man. It had the body of a baby and the head of a man. Its arms and legs were helpless rubbery things. It went about, was wheeled about the town and to neighboring towns in a baby carriage, a boy pushing the carriage. It was the job of my brother, for which he was paid twenty-five cents a day, to push the baby carriage.

The thing in the baby carriage was frightening to children. It sat propped up in the baby carriage. It talked. It grew violently angry and used profane words. It wheedled. It begged. It sold lead pencils and packages of pins and needles.

It abused those who would not give. It swore at them, called them vile names. It was petulant. It was greedy.

I remember well the time when I first saw the thing in its carriage. I ran. There was a strange new fear in me. I ran away and as I ran I cried.

The thing in the baby carriage lived in a house. There was, I believe, an old mother and another woman, perhaps an aunt. It had to be fed with a spoon. At night it was carried into the house and put into bed. The women washed it. They fed it.

No doubt it swore at them. No doubt it also grew petulant and abused them.

People sympathized with it. Even the poor gave it nickels, gave it dimes. People bought from it lead pencils and needles they did not want.

It rode free on trains. It was lifted, in its baby carriage, into the baggage car of trains. It went to other towns, my brother wheeling it about the streets of the towns.

It was curiously greedy about money, was always afraid it would be robbed. It imagined its being robbed and having no power to resist the robbers. While my brother was wheeling it through streets it suddenly began to swear violently. It went into paroxysms of weeping.

My brother took it to our county-seat town and there was a certain house there it wanted to visit. It wanted to see the women of that house, wanted to be fondled by them. The women of that house gave it money. They took it into their arms. They let it fondle their necks and their breasts.

They, perhaps, felt it a pitiful outcast like themselves. If it was vile, they also felt themselves vile.

They held it. They fondled it. They gave it money.

My brother wheeled it about. He went with it to town. He was a sensitive and a delicate boy, but he went.

He went for money. He went to take some of the load from mother. He must often have been sickened by it. But he felt he must do it.

4. Through the Corn

The corn fields began just back of the big old frame house. The house seemed big to us. The neighbors said it was haunted, that a Mamma Culver was occasionally in the habit of riding through it at midnight on a ghostly white horse. She was said to ride right through the door and walls. They spoke of the clanking of chains, of the heavy feet of the white horse on the floors, of groans and sighs. We heard none of this while we lived there. Mamma Culver astride her white horse did not bother the house but I have no doubt that it was because of her reputed inclination to take these nightly rides through the walls of the house that we Andersons had gotten it at a low price.

You went down through corn fields to the town reservoir and Racoon Creek that fed the town reservoir. You went through corn fields to the Mamma Culver swimming hole . . . and what things I learned there! I learned to really swear. There I found out many things (most of them I am sure not true) about the town girls. Young men and boys came. I learned to swim, to dive.

One young man was subject to fits. He was in the pool, formed by damming the creek. He was near me when one of the fits came upon him but I was not brave. I was horribly frightened and swam and scampered rapidly away.

They dragged him out on the grassy bank of the pool. His legs and arms jerked. He made strange noises. A white froth came to his lips.

I had run naked to hide in the bushes. The fit went on for a long time and my own body began to tremble. The young man, who had fits, got suddenly to his feet and, dressing in silence, walked silently away.

I was in the bushes, hiding in the bushes. I put my hands over my eyes so that I could not see, but the sight of the man having the fit aroused my curiosity. I kept taking my hands away. When the young man had left, going along a path up a small hill beside a wheat field, I stayed hidden in the bushes. Then some of the boys dipped my shirt and pants into the pool. They tied them into hard wet knots and I had to use my teeth and hands in the effort to loosen them. There were several boys in the pool, some my own age, the others much older, and coming out of the pool they gathered about me. They had soft mud in their hands and with it spattered my naked body.

They sang a song full of vile words, the chorus of which consisted of two words repeated over and over.

"Chaw beef,

"Chaw beef," they sang. There were other lines and verses to the song. There were words I had never heard before. Some of the boys kept running to the creek's edge to get more handfuls of the mud. There were small stones mixed with the mud and the stones stung my flesh. The song suggested other humiliating things that might be done to me and presently I became so angry that I cried. I struck out at one of the boys but he dodged away and laughed at me. I was angry at myself for crying. They kept pelting me with mud filled with the stones and singing this song.

"Chaw beef,

"Chaw beef."

I rushed at them. I struck out. I was sobbing now. There was one boy, a quite innocent one who stood aside from the others at the creek's edge. He had taken no part in my torture, was fully dressed, was a small and rather sickly-looking boy, but as I rushed away from the others, clutching my wet clothes, I gave him a violent shove sending him backward into the pool. The boy could not swim. He was a sickly little fellow and the others were pursuing me, still throwing the mud and stones, and I learned later that it was only by chance that one of the older boys saw the pale, sickly one about to drown in the pool and pulled him out. So there it was, the innocent one made to suffer and come near losing his life because of the boys' cruelty to the other, myself thus tortured and striking, not one of my persecutors, but an innocent bystander. I ran away into the bushes. I was compelled to dress in the wet clothes with the mud still clinging to my body, but presently I would grow older and bigger and ioin the others in pelting some other new boy.

The corn fields were everywhere. Piety Hill, where we had now come to live in the old frame house, was then a little separated from the town by a creek and by a stretch of low swampy land. You got to it by a kind of viaduct, a sidewalk on stilts. It was at the edge of the farm lands. But the people of the hill were far from pious. Across the street from us, when we moved to the hill, lived the McNutt boys, and the McNutt boys were tough. They swore and fought with one another and with the older boys along the street. Their father, who was rarely at home, traveled with a circus. He was a trapeze performer.

The McNutt boys caught us.

They made us play circus with them. They played the part of circus clowns and had long flat paddles with which they continually beat us. When the beating hurt and we cried they also had a song they sang.

> "Cry Baby,
> Cry Baby,
> Go home and get weaned,
> Go home and get weaned," they sang.

I saw the corn fields plowed in the spring. I saw how the land rolled up under the plows. I saw the muscles working across the breasts of the horses as they pulled at the plows and long afterwards, in the little book of verse called *Mid-American Chants,* I tried to sing of the corn fields.

> All about me the corn—in the night the fields mysterious and vast voices of Indians—names remembered—murmurings of winds—the secret meaning of my own young boyhood and manhood.

> I lived there—I dreamed there—I was suckled face downward in the black earth of the cornfields. I remember as though it were yesterday how I first began to stand up.

I sang the ugliness of life, the strange beauty of life pressing in on the mind of a boy.

I saw the new corn push up out of the rich black earth around our house. I saw the crows come to pull up the young sprouts and get the softened kernels of corn down under the earth. I saw men and boys come to the fields with shotguns. I saw them put up scarecrows.

The black crows seemed to laugh at them. There was a sentinel crow who sat on one of the arms of the scarecrow and when the men and boys came with guns he gave a warning cry. The flock of crows flew away into the trees at the field's edge. They sat on the limbs of the trees and laughed at the men and boys with their guns. It seemed a kind of game, and how shrewd and wary the crows seemed.

I saw the young corn push up higher and higher. Men and boys drove teams of horses up and down the rows plowing the young corn. The horses were muzzled, they could not tear the broad leaves of the young corn.

And now the corn had grown higher than a boy's head. It was a forest. It was a place in which to hide from the McNutt boys and other boys along the street. I went along the corn rows under the corn. There was a soft light down there under the tall corn. What sights, what warm delicious smells, smell of the earth, smell of the young pumpkin vines planted in the corn rows. It was a place for adventure. Rabbits scurried away along the rows. I could lie on the warm earth under the corn and see the life of insects, hear the soft sound of broad green leaves rubbing across each other as the summer winds blew over the fields. It was a place for lovely thoughts. Something in me began to sing now. I even fancied that the rustling leaves of the corn were whispering to me.

And now it was the time for the cutting of the corn. The tall corn stalks were set up in shocks. They became armies standing at attention in the fields. They were not fighting armies. They stood in rows ready to feed a nation of men. Men came to husk out the corn. I saw the piles of yellow gold on the brown earth. There was something to make the heart glad—the corn field, the corn field.

I went through the fields with a boy named Jimmy Moore, later in life to become a forester in the American Far West. He lived alone with his mother in a house at the end of the street on Piety Hill. It was the last house along the street before the farms began. He became my first boyhood friend. We went through the corn fields to Coon Creek. We followed the windings of Coon Creek and presently were in a little valley between low wooded hills. Pawpaws grew there. We undressed and played in the creek. We ran naked and ran among the trees. We pretended we were monkeys and tried to swing from branch to branch of nearby trees. We kept falling but we arose and tried again. We went to lie in the grass beside the creek. In the distance we could see a man in the corn field, cultivating the young corn. There were big white clouds moving slowly across the summer sky. We saw a coon come down to the creek. We were very quiet as we watched him. There were berry bushes growing near the creek and the coon reached up with his little fingered paws and picked the berries.

In the quiet of that place something began. There was Jimmy

Moore, lying beside me in the grass at the creek's edge. He was another boy. He saw what I saw. He was not my brother, had been born of another mother and another father. He did not live in my body but in his own body. While I was having thoughts, dreaming dreams, lying there beside him, he was also having thoughts, dreaming dreams. Sometimes they were my thoughts and my dreams and sometimes he went off on his own. Such days, such moments, long remembered, were the beginning of wonder about others, of questions beginning in the mind.

What is this other like? What is he thinking?

A curiosity about others, outside self, that was to become a growing passion, beginning on a summer afternoon, lying naked beside the boy Jimmy Moore, beside a creek, and watching in silence a little animal picking and eating berries. The little animal was very clean. He washed the berries in the creek before he ate them.

I discovered a passion in myself. I had begun going to school. The presence of others, boys and girls, in the schoolroom and in the school yard frightened me. When another boy spoke to me I was shy and afraid. I hurried away from him without answering his greeting. I often walked alone now from our house on Piety Hill. You walked across the dam, passed the engine house, went up a little hill and along another corn field and there you were at the fair grounds.

It was a time when trotting and pacing horses were in their full glory and in our town, as in all American towns of that time, there were men who devoted their lives to the development of such horses.

At the race track, on spring and early summer mornings, there would be one-eyed George Crosby, and Frank Harvey, a tall silent man with his bay stallion, and Tom Whitehead who had a whole stable of race horses and even went away to the races on the grand circuit.

There was the little bay gelding, Dr. Fritz, the great black stallion Solarian (a dangerous one that), and Dr. Robinson's gelding was there. They declared that that one was crazy. If you did not blindfold him he would suddenly go through fences. He was mad with speed. He never let up. Turned at the head of the race tracks in the home stretch he would put the last ounce of his great strength and courage into every stride, would keep going so, would not stop until he dropped dead.

And there was our hotel man, Frank Welker. He did not drive but had another drive for him. His little black mare was very tiny. When she was going at speed she drew her lips back from her teeth. She seemed always to be laughing. There was a boy, myself, hanging over the low fence in the infield by the judges' stand. How his heart beat. There was something in the sustained rhythmic swing of the legs and bodies of the horses going at speed that touched some secret hunger in him. And morning after morning, when the horses were in training, he cut away from his father's house alone and raced through the corn fields past the water works and the engine house to the fair grounds to catch what he could of the glorious sight before he was compelled to go off to school. He stood by the low fence trembling. He leaned far over the fence. Tears sometimes came into his eyes and a lump into his throat. It was his first love. Oh, how the beautiful, the courageous and the aristocratic creatures stirred him. He grew sick with envy of the drivers in their high-wheeled carts whirling about the half-mile track, their hands on the reins. With all his heart he longed to hold the reins over some such beautiful beast and a heavy sadness came into his heart when the first school bell rang and he had to go, with dragging, reluctant feet, away from the racing track and toward the distant schoolhouse.

5. Experiments

The stage was a little strip of lawn by the railroad station in our town. Two railroads, one running east and west, the other north and south, crossed at our railroad station. They made common use of the same station building, the same telegraph operator, ticket agent, express and baggage masters. The little strip of lawn, beside the north- and south-bound tracks, had as a back drop the walls of an old flour mill and grain elevator and there were always a few empty freight cars on a railroad siding along the wall of the building. From the building a continual soft grinding noise went on but it was not loud enough to disturb the actors on the stage. An old blind horse went round and round inside the mill, turning the machinery.

As in all American towns of the time the railroad station was a magnet that continually drew our people. There was a passenger train going away into the mysterious West at some twenty minutes after seven in the evenings and, as six o'clock was our universal supper hour (dinner took place at high noon), we all congregated at the station to see the train arrive and depart, we boys gathering far down the station platform to gape with hungry eyes at the locomotive.

Oh, how we all longed to be grown men and railroad engineers.

I might have been twelve or thirteen. It was during the time I was peddling newspapers, the *Cleveland Plain Dealer* and the *Toledo Bee,* and was at the station to meet all trains.

And what a proud position! I was on familiar speaking terms with the ticket agent, the telegraph operator, the baggage man, and with Skinny Letson, the express agent. I was even privileged to call him Skinny.

"Why, hello, Skinny. How's tricks?"

It was pretty grand. I even knew by name some of the train conductors and the brakeman, and when north- and south-bound trains had to wait, to pick up passengers from the east- and west-bound trains, I climbed aboard. I went shouting my wares through the cars.

It was that fact—that the afternoon train, north-bound from Springfield, Ohio, to Sandusky on Lake Erie, often had to wait for passengers to get off the train from Cleveland—that put the idea of becoming a playwright and an actor into my head.

I daresay I had been reading dime novels when the inspiration for my play struck me. And there was the stage all ready for it. There was the tiny strip of green lawn beside the I B & W railroad tracks that could be used as a stage, the back drop was the old combined flour mill and grain elevator with two or three empty box cars parked beneath its wall, and as an audience there were the passengers of the north-bound train waiting at the junction, the passengers climbing out of the cars on fair spring, summer, and fall afternoons to stretch and to stroll up and down on the station platform.

I even saw the great John L. Sullivan, the national ring hero of the day, on the platform. He was walking up and down, an unlighted cigar in his mouth and a tiny dog in his arms. The conductor of the train had told our ticket agent; the ticket agent had told Skinny Letson; the express agent had told me and I had told the other boys who were hanging about. It was a spring day and school had closed for the afternoon. We boys, a growing crowd of us, followed the great man up and down the station platform.

And was he not truly a great one? When we had all congregated and stood open-mouthed, gaping, he took a dollar bill from his pocket. He lighted the bill with a match and then with the blazing bill lighted his cigar.

"Why, what a man! What a man!"

But to the play. The play's the thing. I had got Toughy McClary in with me as partner in my theatrical venture and as fellow actor. Toughy was our local Huckleberry Finn. He was a boy of my own age who had no visible father or mother to bother him. He did not go to school. He hunted. He fished. He slept sometimes in Frank Harvey's livery barn, sometimes even in a house. Someone in the town would take him in for a meal and for a night.

He managed to live. He went about. He was always wearing some larger person's cast-off clothes, the legs and arms of the pants and coat rolled up, but he was a free soul. He ran no errands. No one said to him, "Do this, do that." He did as he pleased. And he was, as I was, eager to make money. He wanted it to buy powder and shot for a muzzle-loading shotgun he had in some way acquired, to improve his fishing equipment, to buy food.

As I was the one who had devised our play, naturally I chose for myself the hero's part. We did our rehearsing on the lawn before the warehouse when there was no one about. We were two desperate bad men of the Far West. On fine afternoons, when the north-bound train had to wait for its connection with the west-bound train and when the passengers had alighted and were walking up and down before the little strip of lawn, we emerged from behind the freight cars by the grain elevator wall, he from behind one car and I from another. We walked slowly toward each other. We were both armed. We had whittled out our notion of bowie knives from sticks of wood and had them stuck in our pants tops.

And now Toughy recognized me, his mortal enemy, walking toward him across the lawn.

"Well," he cried. "So it's you, you cur, you rat. Now I will taste of your heart's blood."

I do not answer him. I laugh.

"Ha, ha," I laugh.

And now we have both drawn our knives and are prepared to rush upon each other. We are beginning to get the attention of our audience. They stop walking up and down. They stand watching.

"So you would drink my heart's blood, would you? Come on. If you have courage, show it now."

And now we have sprung upon each other. We struggle desperately. We pant and groan, and when we have become quite sure of the absorbed attention of our audience, with a skillful movement of my arm and hand I suddenly disarm him. I send his knife flying away on the grass and while he is still half stunned by my amazing display of skill, I pounce upon his knife.

And now I am in possession of both weapons. I have him at my mercy. And he, realizing his situation, springs a little away from me.

But he is no coward. He folds his arms across his chest. He stands erect. He defies me.

"So, you would attack an unarmed man, you cur? I always knew you for a coward and a rat," he says.

But I am also no coward. I am a true man and there is a noble heart beating in my breast. Holding the two knives in my open hand I now approach him.

"I would scorn to attack an unarmed man," I say. "Here, take your choice of these weapons."

But what is this evil look that now comes into the eyes of Toughy? He is gazing at the weapons in my open hands. Suddenly with a cat-like spring he leaps forward and snatches both of the weapons. He does not hesitate. In his eyes is the gleam of the killer. In possession of both of the weapons he now leaps upon me. He strikes and strikes again. He stabs me to the heart and falling upon the grass I expire in agony while Toughy, cap in hand, runs among the passengers gathering in nickels and dimes.

Why, our play was an immediate success. In modern terms it was a smash hit. It was in for a long run, had from the beginning gone over big, but alas—it was my mother who broke it up. When she heard of it she called me aside into a bedroom in our house. She said I would have to give up my play.

"But mother—"

Oh, the nickels and dimes!

"But it is too much like begging," she declared.

"But mother—"

She was, however, adamant. I had to chuck it. My first effort in the field of art was killed dead as a doornail.

Begging indeed! But what can the budding artist do when he is up against a woman, particularly when that woman is his mother?

There was a Sunday afternoon when I went off into the woods alone. I went past our town reservoir and up past Coon Creek and, climbing a little hill, sat under a tree. This happened at the period of my own life when a boy's voice suddenly changes, when he becomes shy about his own body, then the body of the female begins to have a strange significance to him.

I sat under the tree alone on the summer afternoon and it seemed to me that I held my own life in the palm of my hand. Periods of a strange weakness had been coming upon me for weeks and now another came. I felt faint and ill. It seemed to me that I held my own life in my hand and that it slipped out of my grasp.

It became like a bird I had been holding in my hand and that had suddenly escaped and that was flying away from me. It was a clear, sunshiny day, and there were no clouds in the sky. I remember sharply every detail of the scene, how a little wind played across a distant ripening wheat field, how single leaves in nearby trees fluttered crazily when the wind came in little puffs. I remember a man riding a horse slowly along a distant road.

I was convinced that my life was flying away from me. It was going, going, going. It became very small, far out there in the clear, blue sky. It became a mere speck against the blue of the sky.

Have I somewhere in some of my books or stories spoken of this odd experience of young boyhood? Surely I have. It is all very sharp in my mind. I never reread my own stories or books. I have the notion that it is bad luck to do so. When a new book or story of mine is printed I read it once, shuddering to think how much I have missed of what I was trying for, and never read it again.

There was my own life going away from me on a summer day. I had the definite conviction that if it went quite out of sight out there, I would then be dead. My eyes clung with desperate intensity to the little dark spot against the distant blue.

And then my life came, slowly at first and then with a rush, back into my body. It seemed to fly back into me.

For a time, perhaps for an hour or two after this experience, I was very weak, and I have often wondered if others have had similar experiences during boyhood or girlhood. During the weak period, after the return of my life into my body, I fell into a dreamless sleep. It was oddly like the sleep that comes to people when they have become satiated with love-making, and when I woke I was well again.

But I must hurry through my stories of childhood and boyhood. There is a temptation to go on and on with them. The impressions gathered by a writer, let us say, in the first twenty years of his life, impressions of people, and events experienced during these formative years when the imagination is most alive, are bound to become source materials for him all his life, and often you have to go far back into childhood to recapture some of these impressions that become materials.

When I was a man past forty I wrote a story that became the title story to a book of short tales. The story I called "Death in the Woods" —to my mind it is one of the best, most solid of all my tales. I was a long time writing it and it would not come off.

There was a little old woman in the story as I finally wrote it, the wife of a brutal husband and the mother of an equally brutal son. I daresay that, when I was a boy, I saw many such women. They are women who are compelled, by fate, to spend their lives feeding the animal in both men and animals. They feed farm animals and dogs. They feed chickens. They feed the animal lust in men.

The little old woman of my story froze to death in the winter woods. She was very old, very small, very weary. She carried on her back a pack of dog meat, given her by a sympathetic small town butcher. She was accompanied on her journey home through the woods by several large hungry dogs.

When she was dead the dogs tore the pack from her back and in doing so tore the clothes from her body. She lay there frozen and naked in the winter roads. In death her slender old body had become strangely like the lovely body of a young girl—

A boy had come to me filled with excitement when I was perhaps twelve or thirteen.

It was winter. There was deep snow on the ground.

"Do you want to see something?"

He would not tell me what he had in store for me.

"You come tonight, when it is dark."

He was very mysterious. He was one of the boys of our neighborhood with whom I had been engaged in the young boys' search for some of the secrets of life.

Once during the summer before, he had come to me equally filled with excitement. There was, at that time, a place in the town where a sidewalk had been built over some low swampy land. The sidewalk was on stilts. It was a plank walk set up on posts sunk into the swampy ground. We crawled under the walk. We thought that when women came along the sidewalk we might be able to see, through cracks in the walk, up under their skirts.

Small boys are often like that. We were. We stayed for hours lying on wet grass under the sidewalk. I do not remember that there was any addition made to our knowledge of life.

I went to the boy's house at night, through the deep snow, and he was waiting for me. I had crept out of our own house and he was waiting in the barn back of his father's house.

"Come on. I'll show you. You'll see something you never have seen."

We went through several streets to where there was a house, at the edge of town. It was, as I remember it, an old brick house, set in a large yard that was surrounded by a sage apple hedge. There were many bushes and trees in the yard.

We crept into the yard and stood in the deep snow behind one of the bushes. My boy friend had not told me why we had come.

I was a good deal frightened. I was very cold. I kept questioning him but he would tell me nothing.

"You wait. You'll see."

We stood where we could look into a downstairs room of the house. Earlier it had been snowing but now the snow no longer fell and the sky began to clear. The house, near the window of which we stood in the soft winter darkness, was occupied by an old man and his wife.

They had taken a young girl, a niece, of about my own age, to live with them. She had come there from another town. I knew about her because I had already become the town newsboy and delivered a morning paper to that house.

I had seen the strange young girl through a window and once she had spoken to me.

That was also during the same winter. I had come to the house with the morning Cleveland paper and she had opened the door. She spoke to me.

"Hello."

"Why, hello."

We were both embarrassed. She was a straight-bodied slender little thing just a little beginning to grow into voung womanhood.

We had stood looking at each other.

"Come around to the kitchen door," she said. "I have something for you."

She gave me some cookies her aunt, the old woman, had baked. She had wanted to be friends. She was a strange girl in the town.

I had muttered some words of thanks and had hurried away but on other mornings, when I took the paper to the house, I had hoped to see her again.

I hadn't, but I had been dreaming of her. I had thought about her at night when I was in bed with one of my brothers. She had become increasingly beautiful to me.

I was there with that boy, at night, behind the bush, near the window. There was a room with chairs and a table. There was an old-fashioned stove of the sort called base-burners. There was an oil lamp, turned low.

I do not know how long we stood in the cold and the darkness but at last she came. The old aunt and uncle must already have gone to bed.

She had come into the room to undress before the stove. It was that my boy friend had, by some accident, seen on the night before.

She was there in the room before the glowing stove. She undressed slowly. When she was quite nude she began to turn her young body slowly before the stove. The stove had isinglass windows. She was slowly warming all of her body.

We stood there, quite close to the window, staring at her and then suddenly something happened to me—

Years later, many years later, a New York surgeon once took me with him to a hospital where he was doing an appendectomy on such another young girl, having got me into the operating room by passing me off as a visiting doctor.

I had wanted, for the sake of some story I was writing, to see such an operation. Perhaps I never wrote the story.

Anyway I was in the hospital, in the operating room, and there was a young and slender girl, quite nude, lying on the operating table.

I thought her body very beautiful. I could not bear to see the surgeon cut her body. I turned and hurried out of the room. The surgeon thought I was frightened by the thought of blood about to be shed but it wasn't that.

I wanted to grab the surgeon's arm.

"Don't. It's too beautiful. Don't cut it."

That was what I felt when as a young boy I stood in the snow back of the bush before that house—

Or was it something else I felt on that winter night? I don't know. I was standing there with the other small town boy. I was seeing something I had long thought I most wanted to see, a naked woman.

And then suddenly, for some obscure reason, I turned and struck my boy friend as hard as I could in the face with my fist.

I knocked him into the snow. The young girl was still warming her slender young body by the glowing stove. She was turning her young body slowly around before the stove.

I struck him in the face with all my might and then I ran. I kept running and for a long time couldn't go home. I just walked about alone in the winter streets of the town. I hadn't been angry with the other boy when I hit him with my fist and ran away. It may be that I didn't like what was in his mind and in my own mind. It may be that I really wanted to hit myself as hard as I could with my own fist. How do I know? In any case the figure of the girl by the stove has always been curiously confused in my mind with that of another beautiful young girl under the knife of a surgeon and of the old woman I once saw frozen in the winter woods, her ragged old clothes torn from her body by a pack of hungry dogs.

6. Discovery of a Father

You hear it said that fathers want their sons to be what they feel they cannot themselves be, but I tell you it also works the other way. A boy wants something very special from his father. I know that as a small boy I wanted my father to be a certain thing he was not. I wanted him to be a proud, silent, dignified father. When I was with other boys and he passed along the street, I wanted to feel a flow of pride: "There he is. That is my father."

But he wasn't such a one. He couldn't be. It seemed to me then that he was always showing off. Let's say someone in our town had got up a show. They were always doing it. The druggist would be in it, the shoe-store clerk, the horse doctor, and a lot of women and girls. My father would manage to get the chief comedy part. It was, let's say, a Civil War play and he was a comic Irish soldier. He had to do the most absurd things. They thought he was funny, but I didn't.

I thought he was terrible. I didn't see how mother could stand it. She even laughed with the others. Maybe I would have laughed if it hadn't been my father.

Or there was a parade, the Fourth of July or Decoration Day. He'd be in that, too, right at the front of it, as Grand Marshal or something, on a white horse hired from a livery stable.

He couldn't ride for shucks. He fell off the horse and everyone hooted with laughter, but he didn't care. He even seemed to like it. I remember once when he had done something ridiculous, and right out on Main Street, too. I was with some other boys and they were laughing and shouting at him and he was shouting back and having as good a time as they were. I ran down an alley back of some stores and there in the Presbyterian Church sheds I had a good long cry.

Or I would be in bed at night and father would come home a little lit up and bring some men with him. He was a man who was never alone. Before he went broke, running a harness shop, there were always a lot of men loafing in the shop. He went broke, of course, because he gave too much credit. He couldn't refuse it and I thought he was a fool. I had got to hating him.

There'd be men I didn't think would want to be fooling around with him. There might even be the superintendent of our schools and a quiet man who ran the hardware store. Once I remember there was a white-haired man who was a cashier of the bank. It was a wonder to me they'd want to be seen with such a windbag. That's what I thought he was. I know now what it was that attracted them. It was because life in our town, as in all small towns, was at times pretty dull and he livened it up. He made them laugh. He could tell stories. He'd even get them to singing.

If they didn't come to our house they'd go off, say at night, to where there was a grassy place by a creek. They'd cook food there and drink beer and sit about listening to his stories.

He was always telling stories about himself. He'd say this or that wonderful thing had happened to him. It might be something that made him look like a fool. He didn't care.

If an Irishman came to our house, right away father would say he was Irish. He'd tell what county in Ireland he was born in. He'd tell things that happened there when he was a boy. He'd make it seem so real that, if I hadn't known he was born in southern Ohio, I'd have believed him myself.

If it was a Scotchman the same thing happened. He'd get a burr into his speech. Or he was a German or a Swede. He'd be anything the other man was. I think they all knew he was lying, but they seemed to like him just the same. As a boy that was what I couldn't understand.

And there was mother. How could she stand it? I wanted to ask but never did. She was not the kind you asked such questions.

I'd be upstairs in my bed, in my room above the porch, and father would be telling some of his tales. A lot of father's stories were about the Civil War. To hear him tell it he'd been in about every battle. He'd known Grant, Sherman, Sheridan and I don't know how many others. He'd been particularly intimate with General Grant so that when Grant went East, to take charge of all the armies, he took father along.

"I was an orderly at headquarters and Sim Grant said to me, 'Irve,' he said, 'I'm going to take you along with me.' "

It seems he and Grant used to slip off sometimes and have a quiet drink together. That's what my father said. He'd tell about the day Lee surrendered and how, when the great moment came, they couldn't find Grant.

"You know," my father said, "about General Grant's book, his memoirs. You've read of how he said he had a headache and how, when he got word that Lee was ready to call it quits, he was suddenly and miraculously cured.

"Huh," said father. "He was in the woods with me.

"I was in there with my back against a tree. I was pretty well corned. I had got hold of a bottle of pretty good stuff.

"They were looking for Grant. He had got off his horse and come into the woods. He found me. He was covered with mud.

"I had the bottle in my hand. What'd I care? The war was over. I knew we had them licked."

My father said that he was the one who told Grant about Lee. An orderly riding by had told him, because the orderly knew how thick he was with Grant. Grant was embarrassed.

"But, Irve, look at me. I'm all covered with mud," he said to father.

And then, my father said, he and Grant decided to have a drink together. They took a couple of shots and then, because he didn't want Grant to show up potted before the immaculate Lee, he smashed the bottle against the tree.

"Sim Grant's dead now and I wouldn't want it to get out on him," my father said.

That's just one of the kind of things he'd tell. Of course the men knew he was lying, but they seemed to like it just the same.

When we got broke, down and out, do you think he ever brought anything home? Not he. If there wasn't anything to eat in the house, he'd go off visiting around at farmhouses. They all wanted him. Sometimes he'd stay away for weeks, mother working to keep us fed, and then home he'd come bringing, let's say, a ham. He'd got it from some farmer friend. He'd slap it on the table in the kitchen. "You bet I'm going to see that my kids have something to eat," he'd say, and mother would just stand smiling at him. She'd never say a word about all the weeks and months he'd been away, not leaving us a cent for food. Once I heard her speaking to a woman in our street. Maybe the woman had dared to sympathize with her. "Oh," she said, "it's all right. He isn't ever dull like most of the men in this street. Life is never dull when my man is about."

But often I was filled with bitterness, and sometimes I wished he wasn't my father. I'd even invent another man as my father. To protect my mother I'd make up stories of a secret marriage that for some strange reason never got known. As though some man, say the president of a railroad company or maybe a Congressman, had married my mother, thinking his wife was dead and then it turned out she wasn't.

So they had to hush it up but I got born just the same. I wasn't really the son of my father. Somewhere in the world there was a very dignified, quite wonderful man who was really my father. I even made myself half believe these fancies.

And then there came a certain night. He'd been off somewhere for two or three weeks. He found me alone in the house, reading by the kitchen table.

It had been raining and he was very wet. He sat and looked at me for a long time, not saying a word. I was startled, for there was on his face the saddest look I had ever seen. He sat for a time, his clothes dripping. Then he got up.

"Come on with me," he said.

I got up and went with him out of the house. I was filled with wonder but I wasn't afraid. We went along a dirt road that led down into a valley, about a mile out of town, where there was a pond. We walked in silence. The man who was always talking had stopped his talking.

I didn't know what was up and had the queer feeling that I was with a stranger. I don't know whether my father intended it so. I don't think he did.

The pond was quite large. It was still raining hard and there were flashes of lightning followed by thunder. We were on a grassy bank at the pond's edge when my father spoke, and in the darkness and rain his voice sounded strange.

"Take off your clothes," he said. Still filled with wonder, I began to undress. There was a flash of lightning and I saw that he was already naked.

Naked, we went into the pond. Taking my hand he pulled me in. It may be that I was too frightened, too full of a feeling of strangeness, to speak. Before that night my father had never seemed to pay any attention to me.

"And what is he up to now?" I kept asking myself. I did not swim very well, but he put my hand on his shoulder and struck out into the darkness.

He was a man with big shoulders, a powerful swimmer. In the darkness I could feel the movement of his muscles. We swam to the far edge of the pond and then back to where we had left our clothes. The rain continued and the wind blew. Sometimes my father swam on his back and when he did he took my hand in his large powerful one and moved it over so that it rested always on his shoulder. Sometimes there would be a flash of lightning and I could see his face quite clearly.

It was as it was earlier, in the kitchen, a face filled with sadness. There would be the momentary glimpse of his face and then again the darkness, the wind and the rain. In me there was a feeling I had never known before.

It was a feeling of closeness. It was something strange. It was as though there were only we two in the world. It was as though I had been jerked suddenly out of myself, out of my world of the schoolboy, out of a world in which I was ashamed of my father.

He had become blood of my blood; he the strong swimmer and I the boy clinging to him in the darkness. We swam in silence and in silence we dressed in our wet clothes, and went home.

There was a lamp lighted in the kitchen and when we came in, the water dripping from us, there was my mother. She smiled at us. I remember that she called us "boys."

"What have you boys been up to?" she asked, but my father did not answer. As he had begun the evening's experience with me in silence, so he ended it. He turned and looked at me. Then he went, I thought, with a new and strange dignity out of the room.

I climbed the stairs to my own room, undressed in the darkness and got into bed. I couldn't sleep and did not want to sleep. For the first time I knew that I was the son of my father. He was a story teller as I was to be. It may be that I even laughed a little softly there in the darkness. If I did, I laughed knowing that I would never again be wanting another father.

7. New Worlds

Something new and strange had come suddenly into our town life. Main Street was to be paved and a sewer was to be laid down. Why, here was something new indeed. Not so many years before we came to Clyde there had been no town water supply and as yet many families of the town got their water from wells.

Our small yellow house at the foot of its street by the cattail swamp had been supplied with water from the spring at the base of the great beech tree that stood at the edge of our tiny front yard. There was a barrel sunk in the ground and once we had a terrible tragedy at the spring. Someone had carelessly left the cover off the barrel and a small neighbor child, one of the children of Wyatt, the town drayman, a little thing just beginning to totter about, went down there and fell into the sunken barrel.

The child was drowned, and mother going for a pail of water found it, and I remember vividly the sight of mother, the tiny white body of the child in her arms, her own face white, the water running from the little child's clothes and leaving a dark trail in the dust of the roadway. Mother must have screamed for there were the Wyatts, running out of their house and also screaming.

It was a cry taken up along the little street, women running out of houses, cries and sobs, the whole street aroused. Someone had run for the drayman and presently here he came, standing up in his dray and lashing his horses, the dray followed by the buggy of a doctor.

The doctor was, however, too late and I perhaps remember the tragedy so clearly because it seemed to me at the time that mother was, in some way, the central figure among the screaming sobbing women gathered about the door of the Wyatt house. She had uttered one wild cry and then had remained silent, and having delivered the dead child into the arms of its mother, had come quietly back to our house to resume her place at the washtub.

Now Main Street, that had, in the winter, spring, and fall so often been a sea of mud, was to be paved like a sidewalk (how unbelievable that such a thing could be done), while a sewer was to be laid down and the little outhouses in the back yards were to go. That is to say the outhouses on the streets on which the more well-to-do people of the town lived. We would still keep ours. All the families on the streets where the more humble people lived would keep theirs. Some of these little outhouses were covered with vines and decorated with pictures. They were kept clean and neat. Others were horrible enough, particularly that of the town school when I was a boy there.

But forward with American progress. Italian workmen came in gangs to our town, brought there by a contractor. A strange language was heard up and down our streets. Now, a seemingly vast enterprise to us, the sewer and new brick pavement were being laid down all the way from the head of Main Street upon the hill near the fair grounds, down past the houses of lawyers, doctors, merchants and the stores of Main Street proper, across the Lake Shore tracks into lower Main (the section of the town we called "Canada," a place then of saloons and small stores), past the big flour mill by the I B & W tracks, lower down past the Wheeling and Lake Erie and so on to where our main street led into the Maumee Pike.

We Anderson boys were beginning to grow up. We went to school. All of us except the two younger ones had jobs. My older brother Karl had now apprenticed himself to the harness maker's trade and went every day to sit on his harness maker's horse in the Irwin Shop. There was my brother Irwin at his job at the doctor's, a job Karl and I had both had. He swept out the doctor's office. The doctor was an almost religiously clean man and was very large. As Karl and I had formerly done, Irwin was now compelled, when the doctor left his house in the morning, to walk around him.

"Boy, am I all right at the back? You had better take this brush and brush me off.

"Now come around in front. Look at my pants. Are all the buttons buttoned?"

Or it would be a summer day and Irwin had pumped water from the well for the doctor's bath. He has filled a large tub that sat in an arbor near the back door of the doctor's house and he has come out of his house for his bath.

He has thrown off his bathrobe and now he is sitting in the tub.

He is concealed from passers-by in the street by the grapevines that cover the arbor. He begins to shout, at first, for his wife.

"Annie, Annie," he calls and the cry can be heard far down the street. He wants Annie to come and scrub his back but she will not come. She stays hidden in the house, is perhaps even laughing at him.

And now there is another cry.

"Boy, boy, where are you? Come here, boy."

But Irwin has hidden himself away, as formerly Karl and I did but, at last, the doctor's cry of, "Boy, boy," keeping up so persistently, he does come and with a big brush scrubs the doctor's broad back.

I myself was running about from one job to another. I had suddenly become sharp and alive. I had determined that some day I would be a rich man. I wanted money for myself, for mother.—There were families in the town who lived in larger and more comfortable houses. In such families there was no fear of hunger. The children wore warm comfortable clothes. In the winter they had overcoats to wear. Boys of my own age even rose to the glory of boots with red leather tops. Such boys owned skates. They had gaily-colored sleds on which to slide down hill when the snows came in the winter. Back of such a house there would be, inevitably, a barn, and in many a back yard there was a pigpen with its fat pig, to be killed in the fall.

Sausage to be made, hams and bacon to be cured. In the cellar of such a house there would be bins of apples, of potatoes, turnips, cabbages. There were shelves often with hundreds of cans of fruit, put down in the fall by the woman of the house assisted by her hired girl.

The rooms in such a house were all warm in the winter. There was a great base-burner in what was called the "front" room. In the parlor there was an enlarged crayon portrait of the head of the house, a merchant, a lawyer, a doctor or a retired farmer. There were stoves in other rooms in such houses, even sometimes in bedrooms while, in our house on cold days we all clustered about the kitchen stove, the one fire in the house.

There was this to me seeming luxury in these other houses. In the barn back of the house there was a cow, driven during the summer to some pasture near the town's edge, and there were horses, to be hitched to family carriages on Sundays and on summer evenings, and to gay-looking sleighs in winter. I had begun driving the cows belonging to these more well-to-do families off to some pasture on the town's edge in the early morning and back to the barns back of the houses in the early evening. I got twenty-five cents per week per cow and oh what a creature the cow! She is so mild. She has such large soft eyes. For months she goes along patiently, being driven off in the morning to some distant pasture and back at night. She will stand patiently while she is milked. She becomes a mother and in a few weeks her son or daughter is taken from her. When this happens she will, for a day or two, be somewhat restless, will thrust her head up and bawl loudly but in a few days she forgets. She becomes again man's most valued and patient servant, a mere machine to turn out milk.

And then suddenly you are driving her off to Ames's field when something strange and startling happens to her.

She falls suddenly into the mood of love. It seizes her. Her huge bulk is shaken with it. Now suddenly she will bolt, throw her tail into the air and bawl loudly. Let us say you are leading her with a rope. Look out. She will charge through fences. Her hind legs fly high into the air. If you are leading her along a road that follows the crest of a hill she will drag you up and down hill. There is this huge bulk of cow weighing perhaps eight or nine hundred pounds, rampaging across country. It is late fall and it rains, and darkness is coming, and she has charged up and down hills and through several fences and then, having torn herself loose from the retaining rope, has disappeared into the darkness.

And you must get her home. You must find her. She is one of God's creatures who must have what she wants when she wants it. Let her have it and she becomes again man's most valued and patient servant.

The table at the Hurd house was piled high with food.

"Oh, come on—stay to supper," said Herman.

"Naw—I can't."

I had begun going to such houses. To that of my closest friend Herman, the son of a grocer, a bearded kindly man with a sharp-tongued wife, a leader in the local woman's temperance movement. There were several sisters, warm friendly healthy girls, some older, some younger than Herman.

"Sure you can."

My protests became feebler.

"Naw I can't."

"Yes you can now. Now you come on. Ma has made some pies."

Herman has been in the kitchen of the Hurd house. "Ma's made corn bread. Gee. There's some swell pie. There's chicken with dumplings. Pa's brought home a big watermelon from the store."

I let myself be persuaded, and how I feast. I have been told by mother that, when I am invited out to dine, I must not be a pig.

"You mustn't ever take the last helping on the dish.

"If there is pie, do not try to get the biggest piece as you are always doing here at home. Whatever you do you must not give people the impression you are starved."

And now, at the Hurd table, Herman's father, that man of the graying beard, with the small shrewd gray eyes, in which there is at the moment shy laughter, is urging me.

"Pass your plate, boy."

"No thank you, Mr. Hurd. I have had enough."

I am trying so hard, as mother is always saying, to act as an Anderson boy should.

"No thank you, Mr. Hurd."

But how glorious he is. He pays no attention to my protests but keeps piling high my plate.

He is a man known in the town as an agnostic, one who has his own notions of God and occasionally, on the long summer afternoons, when I am not busy at one of my jobs and when there is no school, he asks me to go with him to his farm, some miles out of our town, and I go eagerly.

We go in a wagon drawn by an old black mare named Topsy and as we go slowly along, past fields of tall corn and other fields in which the wheat has already been cut and shocked, he sometimes speaks of God.

"There is a God, boy. Don't doubt it," he says. "But he is not the God of the churches. He is in the field here, in that wheat stacked in that field there. He is in every growing stalk of corn. He is in the grass, in these weeds growing here beside the road. He is not, I am afraid, much in the churches. He is in you, in me, in the trees."

The kindly gray-bearded grocer becomes silent and as we jog along the country road toward his farm, little puffs of dust rising from under the hoofs of his old black mare, I am also silent, a kind of new wonder growing in me as I look at the fields and at the clump of woodland seen in the distance beyond some field. A kind of awe before the facts of life in meadows, in the corn and wheat fields, in men and women and even in the flies being whisked away from her sides by the tail of the grocer's old black mare, begins growing in me.

✦

I had got a new name. I was no longer "Sherwood" except at home. On the streets, in the stores, at the railroad station, I had become "Jobby."

I was the boy eternally seeking jobs. With what energy, what fire, what determination! Men stopped me on the street. "Go it, boy," they said. "Watch your chance."

I became an entrepreneur. I became the newsman of our town. I had a monopoly and for a time sold all newspapers that came there. I employed other boys, made a little money out of their work. I did not wait for spring and the coming of the new grass to get jobs mowing lawns. Even during winter months, I engaged jobs ahead for the next spring.

I engaged more jobs than I could do.—There was a man known as "Street Commissioner." Someone whispered to me in the street and I went to his house at night. He was not at home. I sat on his front step. He did not return to his house until after midnight but I was waiting. I got a job as water boy for the foreign workmen the pavement and sewer job brought us.

Jobs that could not be handled could be sublet or even sold. Grown men of the town patted my back. "Go it, kid. You're the stuff."

"I tell you that kid will get on."

And in the midst of this I had a period of illness about which I told no one. My illness seemed to me something of the mind. It might be, I thought, that I was going insane.

I was at the table with others of my family and from where I sat at the table could look out through a window.

There was a tree out there. It was a great walnut tree. It stood at the crest of a little hill and below it, at the foot of the hill, was a spring.

I was looking at the tree and it came out of the ground. It began to float. It went away into the distance.

It was becoming a tiny thing in a blue or gray sky. I gripped the edge of the chair on which I sat. Now the tree was becoming a tiny speck in the distance. I had the fixed notion that if the tree entirely disappeared, if I completely lost sight of it, I would die.

My life was in the tree. I did not know why this was true.

"If it disappears I will die."

It may be that I got a little pale. I sat rigid. Sometimes my mother or my father or one of my brothers spoke to me.

"What's the matter with you? Why don't you eat?

"Why are you sitting like a statue?"

I did not answer immediately. I waited.

"They do not know it but I am hanging onto my life."

And now the tree had become a very tiny speck in the sky. I waited trembling.

And then it came back. It came back with incredible speed. It was in the air above the ground. It was again in its place in the ground. A wind was playing in the branches of the trees. My life was again my own.

"What's the matter with you?"

"Nothing. I was only thinking."

I did not dare tell. I ached to tell my mother but I did not dare.

They will think I have gone insane.

There was an aunt, my mother's sister, who was for a time insane.

It happened when I was running with papers in the street, when I was mowing a lawn. My boy friend Herman swore at me.

"I have been shouting at you for five minutes. What's the matter with you?

"You're a nut."

There were buildings going away and coming back. People did it. Houses and trains did it. Once mother was in the yard, hanging clothes on a clothes line. She went away into the sky.

That time I cried out. I startled her, but afterwards I said that a bee had stung me.

I didn't want them to know. I didn't dare let them know.

I was in bed at night and the faces began to come. They crowded about me. Sometimes there was one face, sometimes many.

They were all the faces of women and girls. They came. There was a tall strong woman who held me close to her breasts. I could feel her warm breath in my hair. There were kind gentle faces, hard ugly ones, sneering faces, leering, ugly faces. Gradually in a year or two, perhaps between the ages of fifteen and seventeen, the trees, people, houses, trains, began to quit going away into the sky but the faces kept coming. They have been visiting me all my life.

Then another hard winter: now our father has a new occupation. He is going from door to door in the town and to nearby farmers, trying to sell books. One of the books is *The Memoirs of General*

Grant. Another is a book about the Civil War, about a soldier called Si Klegg. This was an occupation my father must have liked. It took him into many houses. He could sit and talk to people for hours.

But no, dear reader, I am not going to spin for you still another story about my father. How unscrupulously I have used all my family, particularly my father! Once I had a letter from a reader. "It may be true that your father would not work," it ran, "but you have sure worked him." In fact, I have used him so imaginatively, letting my fancy play over his figure, that none of my brothers seem able to recognize him in my writings. No, dear reader, my aim in this book is to tell another sort of story, the story of a mind groping, in the end perhaps reaching expression in an art, of what then happens to the work of art itself, how it in its turn must grope, trying to find its own life.

As I was saying, our father was selling books. And I was reading them. There was a passage in General Grant's *Memoirs* to be long remembered.

General Grant had been a failure in life but then war came and he was put in command of soldiers in a time of war.

With his regiment he was sent to a certain valley where there was an encampment of the enemy. He was marching at the head of his regiment, along a road up the side of a hill that would lead into a valley beyond. He was suddenly afraid. He trembled with fear. Would he be able to do the right thing when it came to the moment of battle?

Now he is doubting himself, is filled with fear. He rides at the head of his regiment over the brow of the hill and behold, the enemy has fled.

The experience taught General Grant something that, he says in his book, he always remembered, that when he was afraid of the other man, it was also likely that the other man was afraid of him. The thought made a deep impression on my boy's mind. What General Grant had said seemed to jerk open a door. All my life the simple thought so simply and directly put down was to be a help.

I read other books, any books I could get my hands on. I went fishing with a book under my arm, went to ball games and read in a book between innings. There being few books in our house, I went book borrowing through the town. The hunger in me found a quick response. Not that we had many intellectuals among us, but there were some, and a few book readers, book lovers. There was the town photographer who loaned me Bellamy's *Looking Backward* which sent me off into youthful dreams of a new and beautiful social system in which I might some day live. Other men and women, sensing my passion for books, called me into their houses, "Here, boy. You may read this. Take good care of it. Be sure to bring it back." It was Dickens or Thackeray, and even, now and then, a book of Balzac's.

There were pictures hung on the walls of some of the houses into which I went with boy friends. They were pictures of Emerson, Whittier, Longfellow, Hawthorne. The intellectual life of the northeastern Ohio town was dominated by New England—and there was none of Melville, the greatest of all our pre-Civil-War prose-men. An odd sort of problem got into my mind. I found a certain dryness, hardness, coldness in the pictured faces. My boy's mind connected them oddly with the town preachers, and we of our family were not churchgoers. Nevertheless these pictured book-writers were like the preachers—and in me there was this book passion—

I received a key from the superintendent of our town schools, an often violently angry, big-shouldered Irishman with a great black beard. We boys called him Faker Ginn: it was rumored that he went about peeping through keyholes to catch boys throwing spitballs when their teacher's back was turned. An unfair accusation, I am sure. The old style whipping sort of schoolmaster, he had many times tanned my backside. He hated having you make a fuss about it. You were a boy and did certain things. Punishment was necessary. "For God's sake try to take it like a man." Of course, he didn't say quite that.

There was the Irish schoolmaster then who had taken me into his office. This at the end of the school day. I could hear the other kids trooping down a flight of stairs, going into the great outdoors. "Better to get the strapping and have done with it," I would have been thinking. At least if he strapped me, he would not keep me after school.

"You know it's coming to you?"

"Yes sir."

"Then try to take it like a man."

"Yes sir."

He gave it to you vigorously, but if you could take it, it soon stopped.

But the key. There was an occasion when, after such a strapping, at the end of a school day, our schoolmaster took me by the hand.

"Well, that's done. Now you come with me." We went, myself fearfully, through streets to his house, and I remember that it was a brick house on one of our better residence streets. Silently we went along and when we had come to the house, we did not enter by the front door, or by the kitchen door where I had been many times to deliver the family wash, but to a hidden side door that led directly into the schoolmaster's study.

We went in and there the room was. I had never before been in such a room. There were books everywhere. Why, how could there be so many books in all the world? There were shelves of books on all four sides of the room going from the floor to the ceiling. The schoolmaster took a key from a bunch of keys and handed it to me. "It is the key to the outer door to this room." It was the place where he worked, but he was gone all day and often in the evening. I got dimly a sense of something I had never before thought of. In our family, there being seven children, we always living in four- or five-room houses, the rooms in the houses always small, there was not, could not be, such a thing as privacy.

There wasn't even the privacy of the toilet. There was the little house at the foot of the yard. Mother had tried to make flower gardens, to make grass grow, but her efforts had been unsuccessful. The soil in the yard was thin and gravelly. Only a few weeds succeeded in leading a short and meager life there.

There was the little evil-smelling house at the foot of the yard. It had two seats. You went in and shut the door. No privacy even there. "Can't I, at least here, be let alone?"

No. "I want in. I can't wait." It was one of my brothers.

That, compared with the schoolmaster's house— But, dear reader, I am not seeking to ring the changes on the hardships of youth in a house of poverty. After all, I am not a candidate for public office, and then besides, I am very grateful for these early years of poverty. So many men I have known have been so frightened all their lives by fear of poverty in old age. It is what has kept their noses to the grindstone while I have often walked free. It is true that I remember whole winters when there was no such thing as white flour in our house. There was, during a whole winter, no butter to spread on bread. Well, what of it? We got a little corn meal. More eating of corn bread would I'm sure make a better foundation for an American literature. The white bread we eat is to corn bread what Hollywood will be to real American dramatic literature when it comes.—I am thinking now entirely of the impression made on a boy's mind by a room, the sense coming to the boy in the room of the schoolmaster.

What? He has a room of his own? He may go into it, sit in here, be undisturbed? The others respect his desire for occasional privacy? A kind of catch in the boy's throat. Will such a thing ever happen to me? Will I also have a place, a room like this?

"Not surely with so many books. I could never read them all. I could never get at what the writers were trying to say."

There was the schoolmaster standing and looking down at me. I dare say I was barefooted, bare-legged, my feet dirty and dusty. It seems to me now, looking back to that moment, that there was a very beautiful rug on the floor. My imagination had built the little study of the small-town schoolmaster into a kind of palace. Now, in my fancy, the room becomes huge. Once, many years later, I was in the library of the Emperor Napoleon, in his palace at Fontainebleau. Now, in my fancy, the schoolmaster's study seems rather like that.

"There is this key. It is to be yours. I have a duplicate. Except to clean and dust, no one except myself ever comes into this room, and I get little enough time here. There is this door leading to a little side porch. If you come and I am not here it will not upset me.

"The idea is that you may come and go in this room as you please." I must, even at the moment, have known that I would never dare do it. "You do not behave yourself very well in school, but I do not know that it matters." Could the man have said such a wise thing to me? "It is possible that you may have a mind. There are few enough real minds in the world. I cannot help you much. It may be there are books here that will be of help.

"You are to come and go as you please. You are to take what books you want to read." I am sure the man said nothing about being careful to return the books, nothing of the danger of getting them dirty.

He went about the town, boasting of me.

"He has read more good books than any grown man of this town. He is educating himself thus. He is getting a better education than we could possibly give him in school."

8. Ohio Pagans

There were two young girls used to parade up and down the streets. They were small. They kept inviting the men and boys. One of the girls was the daughter of a man who went about exhibiting a stuffed whale.

He had the whale on a flat car. It was hitched to a freight train and hauled from town to town. How the whale was preserved I do not know. Perhaps it was but a papier-mâché whale.

He had a fence built about it and the people paid ten cents to climb up and look. He was always gone from home exhibiting his whale.

The other girl was the daughter of a drunken tailor. He had been in the Civil War, under General Sherman. He was the sort of drunkard who goes along, sober and quiet for a long time. Such a one accumulates money.

Then his day comes. He begins to drink, pours it in.

The tailor was a fat man with a bald head and watery blue eyes. He had been sitting, let us say, for three months crosslegged on his tailor's bench, sewing and sewing.

Suddenly, he jumps down, rushes off to a saloon, begins to drink.

And now he is drunk. He is reeling through the streets. He goes to a grocery and begins to buy groceries.

He has plenty of money and spends it with gusto.

"What, a sack of flour? Send six sacks. Send ten bushels of potatoes, two hundred pounds of sugar."

He keeps on buying, buys a wagon load, slaps his money on the counter.

He goes in search of me. He has the illusion that my name is Sherman, that I was named for his general. He thrusts a silver dollar into my hand. "Take it, my boy. You are named for a great man, the greatest one our country has produced." I do take the dollar. I do not tell him that my name is really Sherwood.

"Why not take it? It will soon all be thrown away," I tell myself—

The two girls, the daughter of the tailor and of the man of the stuffed whale, were always together. Every evening they were on the main street, going up and down, up and down.

They were with men. They were with young boys. The going up and down went on.

There was a dark graveyard in the town where a Union general was buried. The two girls went there with boys. There were green lanes and pastures at the edge of town. They were there.

They were walking up and down past lighted stores, past the town post office, past the railroad station. Our main street sloped gently down to where the railroad crossed it. The section beyond the railroad was called Canada.

The two girls went into Canada. They came out of Canada. They were looking, expecting. The men and boys of the town did not fail them.

It was in Canada it happened. It was Sunday night and the main street was dark. Many of the people of the town were in the churches but the two girls did not go to church. They walked up and down the dark main street where men and boys were gathered in groups.

The men and boys laughed.

"There they go, the Shetland ponies. Who will have them tonight?"

We crept along an alleyway back of the stores. I was with a bold boy, the son of a butcher. He had come to me.

"I have got it fixed," he said. "Will you come?"

I was terribly afraid. I was ashamed. I wanted to go and did not want to go. I was ashamed of my shame. I was ashamed that I was afraid.

I kept thinking of the bold boy who had invited me to go. I wanted to be as he was. He had gone right up to them, on Main Street, had asked them.

He had asked them what boy they wanted to come with him and the daughter of the man of the stuffed whale had spoken my name.

So he had come to me.

"She wants you to come. Will you?"

I had said I would.

But why did my heart beat so heavily? It would be for me really the first time and, although I was but a young boy, how often I had dreamed of it.

Did I dare? I walked along, through the alleyway with the butcher's son, so bold, I thought, so free from shame and fear. How I envied him.

We had got to the lower end of town and had crossed the railroad into Canada. Down there, all was silent, the stores dark, no men and boys standing about. We stood before one of the stores. It was an undertaking establishment, where coffins were sold.

Life and death, eh?

Would we take them to the cemetery? Well, now I was in for it. I would let the butcher's son manage.

They came, the two little things, and we walked along a dark street. I had not spoken to her, could not speak. There was a trembling sensation all over my body. My cheeks were hot. My mouth felt dry.

There seemed to be a strange silence over the town. I thought of my mother. Perhaps she had gone to church. She did occasionally. She would be sitting there, with the people, in her dress, the proud, silent mother I knew.

"But she could not know. How could she know?"

I do not think that I had much sense of sin, of doing a wrong.

"Would I be effective? Would I prove a good lover to the little girl who walked with me?"

This thought, no doubt, most in my mind, we went in silence and there was the butcher's son, with the daughter of the tailor walking before us.

They were not silent. They kept laughing and pushing each other about.

And then, suddenly, the little girl walking with me took my hand. She put her little hand in mine. She had asked the butcher's son to ask me. She wanted me. The thought gave me a little confidence.

We went along so until we came to where another railroad crossed the street of silent dark houses in which we had been walking. We turned down along the railroad, went along the tracks, stepping on the railroad ties. We went past a dark railroad station and came to where some empty freight cars stood on a railroad siding.

It was proposed that we crawl into one of the cars. The butcher's boy proposed it but the girls were afraid. They said an engine might come and take us away. They said they were afraid they would get their dresses dirty. They stood together, whispering and giggling.

So again we walked along the tracks. Again the daughter of the whale man walked with me. It had grown somewhat lighter. The moon was coming up.

We had got to the edge of the town and turned into a lane. It was a lane along which cows were driven from a farm back of a brick house at the edge of town to distant fields.

There was a field, where I, with other boys, had played baseball. The cows were driven there along the narrow lane.

There was a worm fence. There were little grass-covered recesses where the rails of the fence formed a V. The butcher's son with the daughter of the tailor went into one of the recesses and the daughter of the whale man led me into another.

It was a great moment.

I stood in silence. She was wearing the sort of little white undergarments called "panties" and she took them off. She hung them on the fence.

She was lying on the grass.

"Come on," she whispered.

And then it happened. I had let down my own short pants. I stood there. I was terribly frightened. I was excited. As I stood thus, my small buttocks exposed to the moonlight, there was a sudden swishing noise and a hand full of gravel gathered from the railroad tracks and thrown with violence struck my buttocks and I ran.

We had been followed. A young man living in a little house beside the railroad tracks along which we had come had seen us and, recognizing the Shetland ponies, had crept after us.

He had crept along the narrow lane at our heels. He had dodged from one V to another along the worm fence. He had seen my little buttocks shining in the moonlight. As he had come along the railroad tracks he had gathered a hand full of fine stones. So there I was under fire. I was wounded. A great wild cry came from my lips and clutching my pants to hold them up I ran.

I ran and I kept running but as I ran I did think of the daughter of the whaleman and of her white panties on the fence. Perhaps I did not want her to lose them. There is this sense of property we all have. It is bred into us early in life.

And so, as I ran along the lane, I kept crying to her.

"Get your pants," I cried. Her name was Lily.

"Get your pants, Lily. Get your pants, Lily."

It was on my lips. I could not stop it. It was a hysteria. Even when

I had left her and the others far behind and was in the big field where with others I had played baseball and later when I had got into a wood and was running under trees in the moonlight I kept crying the words.

"Get your pants, Lily. Get your pants, Lily."

It was the cry that was my undoing. It was taken up by all the boys of the town.

It was a desperate time for me. Men and boys cried the words at me in the streets. When there were women or girls about, clerks in the stores to which I had been sent on errands by my mother whispered it to me across the counters.

"Get your pants, Lily. Get your pants, Lily," they whispered.

It was a time of dreadful fear, of shame. Did my father, my mother, my sister, my brothers know? "I will run away," I told myself. I had read *Huckleberry Finn*. I decided I would go to Cairo, Illinois. I would be a bootblack on the streets there. I would become acquainted with some river pilot and he would take me as an apprentice, a cub.

I got boards and, going into an empty barn back of a vacant house on our street, made myself a bootblacking box. I hid it there. I decided I would save money, would peddle newspapers to people's houses until I had got together a small stake and then, on some dark night, I would disappear from the town.

However, I did not go. There was our mother, still alive, and not to make too much a point of my loyalty to her, there was my friend Herman, who when taken into my confidence, laughed me out of going.

"Aw, they'll soon forget all about you and Lily," he said. "Don't be such a chump."

"And then besides," he suggested, "I don't believe anyone ever has his shoes shined in a town like that.

"They sure don't in this town," he said.

Gradually the cry—

"Get your pants

"Get your pants" died away.

As for Lily and how she felt about it all, I did not know. Perhaps she did not care. Perhaps she and the daughter of the tailor were like the son of the butcher who was only amused by my fright and my flight. At any rate, I do not remember that I ever again spoke to the daughter of the whale man. She and the tailor's daughter continued on summer evenings to walk on Main Street.

They walked up and down, up and down, but when I saw them on the street I dodged. I hurried into an alleyway at the back. I got off the street for the night.

Then came my real adventure. I was on the main street, a slender boy of fourteen now, standing with a certain man of the town.

He was a railroad brakeman, at home for the day. He was one who liked to talk and brag of his adventures on the railroad and had found in me a good listener.

There were tales of storms at night, nights of sleet and snow when a brakeman must go out and run over the tops of moving freight cars, of the constant facing of death, of wrecks, of fights with bums and car thieves.

The man was leaning against a store front, spreading it on, and I stood all attention, excited by his tales, when a young girl, strange in the town, passed along the street.

There was a certain look in her eyes. There was a little smile on her lips as she went past us; the brakeman stopped telling his tales and punched me with his forefinger.

"Did you see that?" he asked. He declared that the strange girl had made eyes at me.

"Kid, you could get her if you dared, if you had the nerve."

He took a paper dollar from his pocket.

"I'll bet you this that you do not dare."

"Dare what?" I asked.

"Dare to go after her now, here in the street. Go up to her, walk with her, make a date with her."

The strange girl was plump and pretty. She would be of about my own age. She walked with a certain light grace. She had dark brown eyes, dark brown hair. When she had passed us she began to walk more slowly. She turned to look back.

There was a woman who had been my schoolteacher walking along. There was a druggist standing in the door of his drugstore.

"See, she is looking back.

"I'll bet you do not dare.

"See, here is this dollar. I'll tell you what I will do. You go after her, walk away with her and the dollar is yours."

The railroad brakeman was laughing at me. He was goading me because of my cowardice. I grew angry. I half ran along the street.

I was with the strange girl. I was beside her. I spoke rapidly, in a frightened voice. I thought, "If she does not consent to let me walk with her the brakeman will laugh at me, the druggist will laugh."

There were others in the streets, clerks, housewives, going to the stores. Two schoolboys I knew walked along on the opposite side of the main street.

"If she turns me down they will laugh at me."

I was with the girl, walking with her. She went along without speaking. She was smiling. There was something bold in the tilt of her little head, in her eyes, in the curl of her lips as she smiled.

"Sure you may go with me," she said at last.

"Did you not see me making eyes at you?

"I think you are a handsome boy. Come on, walk with me."

And now I was walking with her, filled with excitement. What did it matter who saw me, who laughed at me.

She came from a little village some twenty miles to the north. She told me that she lived there with her grandfather and her grandmother. Her father had run away from her mother and then her mother had died.

She told me all of this in a rush of words. There was another old man, her grandfather's brother, who lived in my town and she had come to him on a visit.

He was an old man I knew. He was a teamster. He was a burner and hauler of lime. He hauled lumber and brick for building houses. He was a rather silent, stoop-shouldered old man, the owner of a team of well-groomed, huge draft horses. He lived in a brick house on a street at the town's edge and I had often seen him driving his team through the streets. He was the owner also of a bus for hauling passengers, and once he had been hired to take the baseball team, of which I was a member, to a neighboring town.

He had been dressed in his Sunday clothes on that occasion but, as on other days, when he was hauling brick or lime and was covered with white dust, he was silent.

How strange it seemed to go into that house. The teamster, it developed, lived with his old wife on the second floor, the first floor having been let and, when I had, in the afternoon, escorted the strange girl to the house, she had told me that the first floor was occupied by the teamster's daughter.

She was, in fact, standing at the front door of the house that afternoon when I, with my new conquest, came along the street. The teamster's daughter was a tall woman of perhaps forty. She stood at the front door of the house and when the girl and I came along the street and stopped at the gate leading into the yard of the house, she began to laugh.

"So you have got you one? You have got what you wanted?" she said, looking at the girl and laughing.

She said that and, still laughing, with a curious high shrill laughter, went into the house and the girl tried to explain.

"She is my cousin," she said. "She is a great joker."

The cousin, it seemed, was married to a railroad brakeman. He was one who worked with the railroad brakeman who had goaded me into pursuit of the girl.

The girl looked at me and also laughed. Already she had invited me to come to her that evening.

"I think . . . I am not sure but just the same I am pretty sure that when her man is away, she does as she pleases with other men," she whispered.

How boldly she looked at me as she said it.

"And so, you and I . . . we can do as we please. If she knew she wouldn't dare tell.

"And anyway she wouldn't care."

The new girl had said that to me. She said it boldly, leaning toward me. She had laughed. When she had whispered the words to me, in the open street, at the gate before the house, in the afternoon, in the full light of day, with neighbors in that part of the town to which I came every day to deliver my newspapers, when she had said it, she had leaned forward, her round sun-burned face near my face, so close, I had thought she was about to kiss me and had drawn a little away.

And that had made her laugh again. She had boldly spoken of that too.

"Ha. You thought I was going to kiss you, here in the street and you were afraid.

"Well, you come tonight at eight. I will be upstairs. My grandfather and my grandmother go to bed at seven."

She had pointed to a wooden stairway, the lower steps of which could just be seen at the back of the house.

"You come up the stairs. I will be waiting for you."

It had been, for me, a terrific adventure. I was a good deal frightened. I thought that the hours until eight o'clock would never pass.

There were my evening papers to be delivered. The train bringing them arrived at five, but what if it should be late? I ran about with the papers debating with myself. At one moment I determined I would not go to her. She was too bold. In her laughter there was something too strong, too reckless.

"I will be getting myself into trouble," I thought. Although I was but fourteen I had already heard many stories of boys and young men caught by girls and women.

Suddenly there was a child expected. That was it. It all began out of a kind of blind eagerness you could not control. You were with a girl and it happened. And then, before you realized what you were in for, you were caught, forced into a marriage. On a certain street of the town, near the street in which I lived, there was a family of girls. There were six girls in that family and three of them had got men in that way.

It was a risk. It was something terrible. The girl was too bold. I had no doubt at all of what was about to happen.

Something in the eyes of the girl had told me. It was also in the way she walked, in the way she laughed. But how lovely she was. I thought her beautiful. She had a slender young body. She was the sort of young girl you sometimes see who develops young. What a lovely soft, sun-burned skin she had. She had golden brown hair and little strands of it had been blown about her face as I had walked with her. She had kept putting up her plump little hand to brush it into place.

She had indicated to me, so boldly, that she liked me.

"When I saw you on the street talking to that man, I knew at once that I wanted you to come with me."

She had said things like that, boldly laughing as she said them.

There was in me a kind of new terror, a heavy beating of the heart. How strange it seemed, being at home, at the table that evening, my father and mother, my brothers and sister, with them not knowing what had happened to me, what was about to happen. I could not eat. They were all, even my mother, suddenly as strangers to me.

They were like people far off, seen through the wrong end of a telescope. They were speaking of ordinary things, about getting wild strawberries, the price of food, what someone met in the street, in some strange world of ordinary affairs, had said to one of them and what had been said in reply.

He said and I said.

I did not sleep well last night.

I had a headache or a toothache.

My father, I remember, smelled of paint on this night. He had gone back to painting and was painting Mrs. Edward Smith's house. His mustache dropped down over his mouth and there were spots of white paint on it. As he took bites of food he kept brushing the mustache aside with his hand. Crumbs of food clung to his mustache. He wiped it with his hand and then wiped his hand on his pants leg.

My mother was reproving him for this.

What a strange world, far off, unreal.

Or was it unreal that at last I was up there in a room, on the second floor of the brick house in which lived the teamster and burner of lime, with the new and beautiful girl?

It all seemed unreal to me.

"Why should such good fortune come to me?"

It was so obvious something was about to . . . I had been there in that room with her for perhaps a half hour.

It was a stuffy little room with a woven rag carpet on the floor, two rocking chairs by a small table on which was a coal oil lamp, turned low, and a couch against the wall; and there were two doors besides the one leading to a back porch and the wooden stairway by which I had come up. The two doors led into two bedrooms, one occupied by the old teamster and his wife, and one by the granddaughter.

The old teamster and his old wife were both in bed and asleep. They both snored. I thought they must both be having troubled dreams. Little broken sighs and muttered words came from the room. I had been met at the door by the new girl. The door to the porch was standing open when I climbed up and she stood in the doorway waiting. She put a finger to her lips.

"Sh . . . They are asleep. Don't talk loud. They might wake up."

She had led me into the room and had seated me on the couch and immediately she put her arms about my neck and kissed me.

"Do you like me?

"Oh, I like you."

She had jumped up and had gone into her own room, whispering to me that she had something to show me. She had been dressed in a tight-fitting little flowered cotton dress but when she came back into the room to me she was dressed as I had never seen a woman dressed.

She had put on some sort of loose gown cut very low at the neck so that her hard firm little round breasts could be plainly seen. It was such a dress as I was to see later on women of fashion; and, the few occasions when I was to enter such places, on the women in certain houses where women were for hire.

The little plump thing came immediately to me. Was it possible that she was about to give herself without my having to ask! The thought thrilled me. There was the great difficulty—you had to ask. You had to be sure to say certain words, make the proposal. Here was something new in all my experience with girls. Well, I had been with other boys to boy and girl parties. They had played kissing games. There was one game you played in which you were called into a darkened room. The game was "post office."

There was a girl hidden in the room and your name was announced. There was a letter for you in the post office. You went in and there the girl was. She giggled and you pursued her about the room and at last caught her. You gave her a little pecking kiss.

She was a nice girl, that was it. You didn't attempt to go too far with her. Nice girls didn't go too far.

To be sure there were always stories being told by braggart boys. Oh, how much of the talk among the boys I knew was concerned with girls. There was the butcher boy, a dark-skinned lad with stiff black hair, with his ambitions.

"You'll see what I am going to do when I get to be a man."

He was going to travel all over the world, go to China, Japan, India. He was going to visit every nation in the world.

"I am going to have me a woman of every nation in the world."

"And a Negro woman too?"

"Yes sir. You bet." It was something wonderful to think about.

I thought I had got into something like a strange new world. It was Paradise. I had become a man. I was one who had been singled out by a strange new kind of girl.

Her words were like bells ringing. Was I in a dream? Here were doors being thrown open to me. Life was suddenly becoming wonderful, glorious.

She thought perhaps we had better go out and walk. "We will find some nice place."

The grandmother or the grandfather might awaken. There was that aunt who lived downstairs. It would be just like her to poke her nose in.

We went together out of the house, walked along a street, crossed a bridge over a creek, climbed over a fence and went across a field. It was a moonlight night. It was a night I would remember all my life.

There was this new strange aliveness. Something in her had swept away my timidity. It seemed to me that night that every leaf on every tree in a strip of woods into which we went stood out separate and apart from every other leaf, that every blade of grass in the meadow we crossed stood out separate and apart from every other blade. We were there in the little strip of woods for what seemed to me a long time. We were lying quietly together there.

Then we were walking again. We went into a graveyard. She said she wanted to lie with me on a grave. The idea did not shock me. There was something about her that was all youth and life, defying old age and death. She plucked a flower off the grave on which we had been lying and put it in the lapel of my coat.

We went back to the house of the teamster. We sat on the wooden stairs. There was a little garden back of the house with a grassy path. We went to lie there.

There was dew on the grass but she did not mind.

We were exhausted. We talked softly, the little back yard back of the brick house with its vegetable garden and the grassy path that led to an outhouse at the end of the garden was, no doubt, in the daytime, or when seen under ordinary circumstances, commonplace enough, but on that night it was, to me, utterly lovely.

I wanted to sleep, to lie with her arms about me and sleep. I spoke of it to her.

"It would be nice if we could do that, if we could lie here together like this forever."

Was it love? I was with her on the next night, and the next and the next. There was a night when it rained.

It did not matter. We were on the couch in the room upstairs. I could hear the snoring of her grandfather and her grandmother. I could hear the aunt, that tall strong-looking woman, moving about downstairs.

Finally, one day, my girl went away to that other town where she lived with another old grandfather and grandmother, and I worked and saved money to hire a horse and buggy to go there to her.

When I was with her I was happy, in a kind of paradise, but when I had left her, in the daytime, when I was going about with other boys and girls, when I was with my brothers or my sister, I said nothing of my adventure.

I became afraid.

"She will be having a child and I will have to marry her."

I made great plans for my life. I was going to be a business man and grow rich. I who lived with my father and mother, my brothers and sister in a little yellow house on one of the poorer streets of the town. I wanted to build a great house for my mother. She was not strong and worked too hard. I wanted to buy her beautiful clothes. There was in the town a certain woman whose husband had invested money in the enterprises of a man named Rockefeller and who, every year, while doing nothing, got richer and richer. She had got two beautiful horses and in the afternoon rode about in her carriage.

I wanted such a team and such a carriage for my mother.

I still wanted to become a driver of race horses. Sometimes I thought, "I will become a business man and get rich," and again I thought, "No, I will become a famous race horse driver."

I was in the town. I was on the streets, was with boy friends. I was at a party at the house of some nice girl.

She who had been so free with me would be free with others.

There was that aunt, and it was said that when her husband was away from town, at his job on the railroad . . .

But she had been so generous to me, so wonderful.

And yet . . .

I grew more and more afraid.

"No, I must not go to her. I must not. I must not."

One day I was walking in the street and there was her aunt. She stopped me on the street.

"Have you been to see her again?

"When are you going again?

"You had better look out," she said and laughed.

She went away laughing along the street and I grew white with fright.

"I mustn't. I mustn't any more."

If it happened my mother would have to know, my sister, my brothers. I came at last to the taking of a resolution.

"I'll cut it out. Now I am going to cut it out."

I waited, in fear. She was in my dreams. She had become a terror to me but nothing happened; and when a month, two months, three months had passed and there was no word from her I began to be proud.

I became the conquering one. I walked proudly. The other boys of the town might talk. But who among them had known, had been privileged to know, such an adventure as mine!

9. Horses, Bicycles and Men

Now our family was soon to break up. Our mother, after the long struggle to keep our house all together, had at last been struck down by disease.

It came upon her suddenly. We were living in the little yellow house by the swamp land (now, I believe, drained) and there had been a bitterly cold winter during which she continued to toil as a washwoman, running constantly in and out of the house, her clothes wet with the warm wash water in the tub by the kitchen stove and often freezing on her body as she went to hang the washed clothes on the clothesline strung across the back yard, her bony hands growing thinner and bonier, her gaunt body continually more gaunt.

This must have been the winter when I was sleeping in the livery stable with the man Ed, and as to where our father was at that time I do not know. During all of this period his figure becomes strangely vague and meaningless to me. It may be that seeing his wife disintegrating under her hard lot and knowing himself a good deal to blame, he had simply run away, as I myself, alas, so often have done.

There would have been places enough for him to go. He had made acquaintances far and wide through the surrounding country and was always welcome, for either long or short visits, at many lonely farmhouses. He would pay his way by story telling and, perhaps, as at one such farmhouse where I once stayed with him for two or three days—he having taken me with him on one of his jaunts—there would be a woman (she might be a maiden woman in the house or perhaps a widow; he had, it seemed, a preference for widows) to whom he was secretly making love, creeping to her—as I was on this occasion conscious of, having followed him along the upstairs hallway from the bedroom where I slept.

At any rate, I am quite without any memory of his presence in our house when mother was suddenly struck down. There was a cold that immediately ran into pneumonia and in a few days our mother was dead.

With mother gone my older brother Karl, having discovered in himself a natural talent for drawing—he had won a prize at our county fair for a drawing of our town high school building and had even made an oil painting from a photograph of our father's mother which stood on an easel in our little dark parlor—had gone away, first to the town of Mansfield, Ohio, where he had a job designing gravestones, and then to Cleveland where he became what was called a "spot-knocker."

It was an occupation that, I dare say, needs an explanation. There were certain men who went through the Middle-Western towns selling what were known as "crayon portraits." You handed such a one a photograph, usually of some dead person in the family, and, for a certain sum, ten, fifteen, perhaps even twenty dollars, you were to receive what was called a free-hand, life-size crayon portrait of the deceased, this in an ornate golden frame. You were told that you paid nothing for the free-hand crayon drawing. The unknown artist was but a passive figure in the march of commerce. You were only paying for the golden frame. But you could not have the drawing without the frame.

It was something to set up on an easel in your front parlor. It was a portrait of a dead child or perhaps of a grandfather. You were very sad about the death in your family and wanted your sadness known so you draped the portrait in a black cloth. The small photograph you had given the agent was taken away to the city and by some mysterious process, perfectly understandable to photographers, it was thrown up into the desired life size.

It was then that the spot-knocker took hold. He made certain strokes across the enlarged photograph to make it look like a large free-hand drawing. He went over it with his stick of crayon, a line drawn here, a dash of black put there, shadows put under the eyes, a kind of fixed stare given to the eyes, and there you were. A good spot-knocker could turn you out some ten or twelve of these creations in a day and he was paid a dollar each. It was a good job for our brother Karl and he could now send money home as well as put aside a little each week for the art education for which he hungered and which he was presently to begin in the Art Institute in the city of Chicago where I was later to join him.

As for myself, I was growing rapidly. At home we were again on the edge of actual want, and so I had taken a job as groom of livery-stable horses in Frank Harvey's livery stable.

What a come down for me. Here I had been dreaming of some day becoming a driver of fine race horses, another Ed Greer or a Budd Doble, famous race-horse drivers of the day, and instead spent my days cleaning the mud off tired, old livery-stable horses, wheeling out manure and washing buggies, and my nights with a man named Ed, both of us sleeping under horse blankets in a little room at the front of the long barn.

It was another sickness that finally drove me out of this place. The time was late in February, but a warm, summery day had come and we were storing hay, hauled from some nearby farm, in the loft of the barn. The hay was being passed up from a farmer's hayrack through an opening at the front of the barn, facing the street, and Ed, who was very strong, gathered up great forkfuls and running a few steps into the loft pitched it at my feet. It was my job to carry the forkfuls to the rear of the barn.

Ed was too strong for me. He was too quick. He kept piling the hay at my feet and laughing at me.

"Hurry up, kid. What's the matter with you? Are you bushed? Hurry! Hurry!"

Ed kept laughing at me, and the farmer and his hired man, at work on the hayrack, put their heads in at the opening through which they had been pitching the hay and also laughed.

"Bushed, eh? What's the matter with you, kid? Why don't you clear that hay away? Are you bushed?"

It was the old cry of the workman, proud of his own strength and glorying in the weakness of a boy, and I became furiously angry. I ran under the great forkfuls of hay that kept coming faster and faster. I ran, I stumbled and fell. Tears came into my eyes.

"I'll show them. I'll show them."

I set my jaws and worked harder and harder. The sweat rolled from my body.

And then at last the hayrack was empty and, in the darkness of the rear of the barn loft, I drew my arms across my eyes to wipe away my angry tears and went to join the men.

"I'll not let them know I was angry because they would only laugh," I thought. I was determined also not to let them know I had been crying. The empty hayrack was being driven away from the front of the barn and another huge load was being driven up by the farmer's hired man.

The men did not, however, immediately go to work on the new load. They went off together to a nearby saloon while I sat waiting on the floor of the loft and presently they returned and Ed had brought a glass of beer for me. He climbed with it into the barn loft while the farmer and his hired man climbed up to the second load of hay.

"Here, you drink this," Ed said, handing the glass of beer to me.

The farmer and his hired man had come to put their heads in at the opening at the front of the loft. They were laughing. The farmer poked a finger into the ribs of his hired man and they both shouted with laughter.

So they thought I was just a kid who could not drink beer.

"I'll show them," I thought.

How was I to know that a crude joke had been concocted in the saloon, that they had got the bartender to fill the glass half full of raw whiskey? Although I had never until that moment tasted beer, I stood up and with a great gulp swallowed the mess.

It was a horrid sickness. It began almost at once. Ed had taken the glass from my hand and I had taken my place, preparatory to doing my part in the storing away of the hay. It began. The men kept laughing but now I did not mind. I carried one, two, three, of the heavy forkfuls of hay to the rear of the loft. I began to stagger. Something down inside of me seemed rolling and tumbling about. The walls of the barn loft seemed whirling about my head in the dim light. They danced about me. I became faint and fell.

"I must not let them know.

"Now, see, they are laughing again. If they can drink beer so also can I. I will not be overcome."

A kind of desperate inner struggle began in me. I grew faint and my legs would no longer hold me erect. The sweat poured from my body. I fell and arose, fell and arose. It seemed to me that if I did not at once get out of the loft I would choke.

"I cannot breathe in here," I thought. "I must have air."

In a kind of drunken stupor I ran, continually falling and arising, toward the opening at the front of the loft. I pitched through the opening, fortunately upon the load of hay. I could still hear the men laughing. The crude workingmen's joke had proved a great success.

I lay sprawled thus upon the load of hay and then all consciousness left me and I was helpless in their hands.

When I woke it was night and I was lying on straw in an empty horse stall, having been thrown there by the men. I was on a pile of litter, half manure and, while in my unconscious state, had been ill. I had thrown off the poisonous mess they had got into me and now stood on my feet. Fortunately I had been wearing overalls over my clothes and these I took off and threw onto the barn floor.

I staggered thus, weak and sick, and with a great hatred for all men in me, out to the floor of the barn and there, dimly seen by the light of a lantern hung to a wooden peg, were the patient livery horses, each in his own stall, the long-suffering, patient beasts seen in the dim light.

I had a queer impulse. It must have been late in the night when I came out of my stupor, and a thousand red demons seemed to lodge in my head and were now beating with little hammers on my brain. But, following some obscure impulse, I went from one to another of the livery horses, touching each with my hand. And then I went out into the night, leaving Ed, no doubt by now sound asleep on his cot in the little stable office. He it was, I was very sure, who had concocted the joke on me.

"Well, I am not that low. I do not need to be with such a man any more. Even though I have no other job I do not need to be near him, hear any more of his senseless boasting, sleep in the same room with him."

Even on that night, as a boy, I must have come to the conclusion that the animals that are the servants of men are infinitely finer and better than many of the men that a boy would have to deal with in living his life. It was a conviction that was to stick with me through life. It was very strong in me that February night as I went out of the livery stable determined not to return. It was even stronger in me, for the moment, than the fear that our poor sick mother would in some way find out what had happened to me. It was a conviction that was to be of great help to me later, strengthening in me a contempt that was to become a part of my nature.

There was something strange happening to our town that must have been happening at about the same time to thousands of American towns: a sudden and almost universal turning of men from the old handicrafts toward our modern life of the machines.

I was to see it happen. I was to be part of it. It meant the end of the old craftsmen of the towns, the shoemakers, the harness, wagon, buggy, furniture and clothing makers. All the little shops scattered through the towns, shops in which men fashioned things with their hands directly out of the raw materials furnished by nature, were to disappear with amazing rapidity. It was a strange time and, as I now look back upon it, it seems to have all happened almost in a day. It was a kind of fever, an excitement in the veins of the people, and later when I tried to write of it, using not a particular individual but rather an American town as the central character of my story, it became to me strangely dramatic.

There was a kind of blind faith in what we were all doing, a belief that the machine would solve an old, old problem for men, lifting the load of heavy brutal toil off men's shoulders, making a new life of ease and comfort for all. This, however, all mingled with a feeling of doubt and fear among the older men of the towns.

This feeling of change was in our own little house. It was in all the houses along our street. It was in all of the houses in every street of every town. Men proclaimed it while others protested. It was the end of the old workman.

It ran all through our Middle West. Here and there, in towns nearby, oil and gas began to spurt out of the ground.

In the nearby city of Cleveland a Mr. John Rockefeller was at work, planning and scheming. His plans reached down into our town. There was a certain E. M. Harkness who ran a little variety store on our main street. He sold calicos, thread, needles and pins. We called him "Em." He was of the Harkness family that put money in with the Rockefellers and I remember, years later, when I once went to Yale University, when I spoke there, how I walked past the great Harkness memorial building at Yale, thinking of our Em, hurrying down to our main street in the early morning to open his little store.

And what an amazing period. What a place, our Middle West, to have been boy and man in this America in my time—our Em to go off later in his own private yacht, sailing over the world, to visit many far countries and cities.

The Harkness Memorial—really I do not suppose that our Em built it. It may have been a brother or a cousin. Some such brother or cousin, no doubt, had written a letter to our Em.

"You scratch up a thousand or two thousand. You put it in with this John D. Rockefeller. He's going to get there."

Stories of quick fortunes made were running through the towns of the Middle West, huge fortunes to be made overnight, suddenly a new idea abroad in the towns. A little investment could make much money for you. It would pile up and up while you stood aside doing nothing.

"Look, here's the machine that will do the work of a hundred, of two, or even three hundred men."

And all of this very puzzling to the old workman, to the men who had worked all of their lives with their hands, fashioning things for others to use out of the raw materials of nature. You got a little money for all your labor. If you were a frugal man you saved a little. Money was a medium of exchange. You got so and so many dollars and cents for building a chair, a table, a set of farm harness. You took the money to the grocer to get food, to the tailor who made you a suit of clothes or an overcoat against the cold of winter.

But look, money was also something more than a medium for the exchange of goods. It was power. It had a life of its own. You bought certain pieces of paper called stocks. There was something going on, away off somewhere. A mysterious thing happened. Some man or group of men you had never talked to, never seen, declared what was called a stock dividend. You had ten shares of stock and then suddenly you had twenty, thirty, a hundred shares. Dividends began to pour in. Without lifting a hand you were suddenly rich, or, as more commonly happened, disaster came. You put a mortgage on your house, your farm, your little business. John Jones was getting suddenly and mysteriously rich. Why not you?

And here all sorts of scheming, shrewd men who understood what you did not understand. In Ohio towns Cal Brice, in New York Jim Fiske, Commodore Vanderbilt, Daniel Drew, Jay Gould, and others. There was a new kind of man, jugglers, sleight-of-hand men, pitching millions of dollars into the air, catching them between their legs, behind their backs, your own hard-earned dollars mixed in with all of the others.

"Now you see it, now you don't. The hand is quicker than the eye."

A kind of gigantic pea and thimble game going on in a big, national way, many little men puzzled, frightened, but full of a strange new hope.

"John Jones made it. Now look at him. He used to work down in the flour mill for a dollar a day. There he is, he and his family, driving about now in a new carriage."

Fairy stories of sudden acquired wealth whispered in the streets, men and women whispering together in their beds at night hoping for a college education for the children. In the daytime, in small town hotel lobbies, on trains, in saloons, new fairy tales being told. There was a sudden flood of new inventions. Gadgets and more gadgets.

"Why, Jack, I bet you can sell a million of that. Look, Jack, you make ten cents on every one you sell. It will go like hot cakes.

"The thing to do, Jack, is to organize a company and sell stock."

And then the modern world suddenly invaded our town with a rush. We got a bicycle factory.

It was set up in an old building along the Lake Shore railroad tracks, a building that had once been occupied by a piano factory that had failed. It was revamped, new machinery shipped in, great lathes and other machine tools that were a town wonder arriving on freight trains and set up in the factory, crowds of men and boys going there every day to hang about the factory doors and to peer in at the windows. There were machines with great iron legs, like the legs of elephants; and delicate, complicated-looking machines. We small-towners stood about staring and speaking in low, awed voices.

"Why, look at that one. Gee, it will take some man to run a machine like that!"

For the new men that were to come among us there was something of the same reverence that we had long felt for railroad engineers.

And there was other excited talk on the streets. Many men were to be hired in the new factory. It was said that men were to get two dollars a day for only twelve hours' work. It seemed unbelievable to us. Why, what a fortune!

And then the new men coming in, the trained machinists, kings among men to us, men who could guide great rods of steel across a lathe, cutting, it was said, to the thousandth fraction of an inch.

"It is all bunk I tell you. You can't do that."

"Yes, you can. You'll see."

Dreams of a new era of prosperity, money rolling in, the stores along the main street refurbished, dreams of something happening to our town such as presently was to happen to the towns of Akron,

Youngstown, and to many other small American towns. In the quiet old city of Detroit, Henry Ford, no doubt, already at work in his little Detroit bicycle shop, experimenting with his horseless carriage.

In our town, swaggering among us now on the street in the evening, these new men, the trained mechanics. They seemed millionaires to us. It was even whispered that some of them got as much as three, even four dollars for a day's work.

And they did not seem to have to work hard. Their work was what we called a "snap." Such a man was like a railroad engineer who merely sat up there in his engine pulling certain levers, the engine doing the work while like a lord he traveled from town to town, surveying the world.

"I tell you what, knowledge is a great thing. Education's the thing."

We boys, now growing toward young manhood, gathered in groups at night and sat on the express trucks by the darkened railroad station. We walked down the dark railroad tracks to the factory. Who among us would get a job? There were great plans made.

"No, I am not going to work in any factory. I am going to be a railroad mail clerk. I want to see the world."

A railroad mail clerk went to distant cities, maybe as far west as Chicago, maybe even east to New York. Once such a railroad mail clerk had come to our town. He was on vacation from his job and was on a drunk. He had gone about our town boasting about all the far places he had seen. His words had stirred longings in us.

One boy was determined to be a jeweler. (He was going away to a school where he would learn to repair watches.) Another dreamed of becoming a dentist; while my own dream, never, alas, to be realized, was clear enough. It was true I had been through the sad experience of groom in the livery stable and had had the name of "livery-stable chambermaid" shouted at me by other boys, but I still clung desperately to the hope of becoming a race-horse driver and had even, during the summer before, gone off (my sister protesting) for some months with Tom Whitehead's string of trotting and pacing horses.

But now I return to the factory gate. I was one of the fortunate ones who got a job. Fall had turned to winter and all the race horses were in their winter barns. I was doubly lucky, for my new job as a factory hand did not take me into the main factory building. In the early morning I went in with the others and punched the time clock. The winter days had come and as we worked a twelve-hour day it was still dark as we factory hands hurried through the street. I went through the factory and through a rear door and along an elevated platform to a small brick building where bicycle frames were painted.

They were not really painted. They were dipped into tanks of black enamel. We in the little building, some four or five of us, for the most part boys, caught the frames on hooks and plunged them down into the black liquid. The shining black liquid in the tanks was said to be highly inflammable and there were signs everywhere forbidding our smoking. It also stank horribly, making our nostrils smart and our eyes water.

We stood over the tanks letting the frames drip and softly brushing away the enamel that tended to gather in lumps as it dried. We ran with the frames to certain steel ovens where we hung them up to be baked. We worked eagerly, with a kind of desperate eagerness, until all the ovens were filled, and then we rested.

My luck held. The boss in the new place was one Rice, a short, compact little man with broad shoulders, a dark, leathery skin and a huge black mustache. He sang all day long. He had been a carriage painter and it was his particular job to superintend our work and to put golden stripes on the bicycle frames when they came shining and black from the ovens.

He was very skillful and we all admired him. Grasping in his short, stubby fingers a peculiar long-haired brush, he made a quick sweeping stroke the whole length of the round steel tube that made up a section of the bicycle frame. He never missed. The golden lines he drew with such amazing speed were always perfect. They were of the same thickness from end to end of the frame.

We boys stood about admiring as he worked. Even when our boss had been off on one of his occasional sprees and the brush trembled in his hand, the line drawn was nevertheless perfect.

"Here, you try it," he said, handing the brush to one of us and, one by one, we did try. But in every case we made but a straggling, wavering line that must at once be erased with a rag, a failure that always delighted our boss.

He crowed. He danced a jig on the floor.

"Why, you do it like this. It is very simple," he said. He made another of the long sweeping strokes with the brush and again the line was perfect. He began to stroke his mustache. He strutted before us.

"Every man to his trade," he said. He began to speak at length of his years of work at the carriage-painting trade. He told us of the carriage he had once finished for a rich banker and of another job that he did on a carriage built for the governor of the state.

"This dipping of bicycles in tanks of enamel—it is all right for you boys but for a real workman like me, bah!" He walked over and spat in one of the tanks of enamel.

"It does not take a real workman to do such a job as you boys are doing." He began to curse the man who owned the bicycle factory, a round fat little man who occasionally strutted out of the factory door and into our little building. This man who now owned a bicycle factory had come from a town where our boss, Rice, had worked as a finisher of fine, hand-built carriages. Our boss recited to us the factory owner's history.

"What does such a man know of real workmanship?" he asked, his voice filled with contempt. The manufacturer of bicycles had gone away from his town as a young man. He had attended a business college. He had a rich father who had given him his start. Everything the man touched turned to gold. Such a man did not have to have brains. His luck would always put him through. Our boss had heard that the bicycle manufacturer, already making money hand over fist out of bicycles, was thinking of going into the making of horseless carriages. He declared that the idea was a crazy one but that, nevertheless, and because our big boss was going into it, it would succeed. Everything he went into did succeed.

There was one thing, however, that the manufacturer could not do. He could not make our boss dip bicycles into tanks. To be sure, he striped them. That was all right. It was a job that took some skill. Boys like us could not do it. He had told the bicycle manufacturer what he would do and what he would not do. The carriage-making trade was going to the devil. Now everyone was crazy about bicycles and presently, no doubt, they would be really crazy about the stinking horseless carriages that were now about to come into vogue. The old carriage-making trade was shot and the bicycle manufacturer had written to our boss telling him to come to our town to work in the factory and he had come.

He declared that he had known the bicycle manufacturer when they were both boys. The manufacturer had shown him into the little shop where he was now our boss. It was already equipped. Our boss had looked about. He had seen the tanks filled with the black, evil-smelling enamel.

"For God's sake, you do not expect me, a workman like me, to stand over one of these tanks, dipping bicycle frames into that stuff. If you do, you are barking up the wrong tree. I will see you in hell before I will lower myself to a job like that."

Our boss kept repeating to us over and over the conversation he declared he had had with the manufacturer. He repeated it to us every day.

But the manufacturer had known what he was up against. He had found out he was dealing with a real man, a real workman. The manufacturer was smart all right. He had reassured our boss. He would get boys like us to do the dirty work. Our boss could be a striper, nothing else. When there were no bicycle frames to stripe he could just be boss.

The signs everywhere in our little shop forbidding us to smoke irritated our boss. He placed one of us on guard, by a paint-spattered window facing the main factory—this against the possible sudden appearance of the manufacturer—while all the others hung out the windows at the back of the little shop. Pipes and cigarettes were lighted.

It was this dark and merry paintshop boss, with the big mustache, who later gave me the notion for the figure of Sponge Martin, the old gaffer of the mythical town of Old Harbour on the Ohio River, where the equally mythical character of Bruce Dudley of the novel *Dark Laughter* had certain adventures.

Not that my actual paintshop boss, in my first factory job, had any such background as the one I gave my Sponge Martin. It is true that the man had a little, wiry-looking wife and that they seemed, when I saw them together, to be two people entirely capable of always enjoying each other, but there was no daughter in a questionable house in Cincinnati and as for their fondness for sawdust piles at night by the slow-flowing Ohio, that was all imagination.

I do know that our actual paintshop boss occasionally, on a Saturday night, invited some of us youngsters to go on a spree with him.

"You boys meet me down town tonight, at Body Adair's place. You come on. We'll lift a few. We'll have a good time." He would dance little jigs on the floor all Saturday afternoon as we finished the week's work.

"Saturday night and supper on the table. It is the happiest time in a workman's life," he sang.

We would often join him in the evening, although I was, as yet, too young to be admitted to the fellowship of the men in Body's place and could only hang about in the street outside. But I could hear our little boss singing in there, and would wait for him to come out. Something curious happened by the time he came out. When he had taken a certain number of drinks he became suddenly silent. He could be singing and dancing before the others but, after several drinks, he appeared overcome with sadness. This night he stood for a moment looking at the men he had invited to drink with him. Once when we were alone together in the paintshop in the evening he tried to explain to me his peculiar behavior on similar occasions.

"I get proud," he said. "I am in the saloon drinking with the others and then I get proud."

There was something on his mind he wanted to tell me about. He began to give me advice. I was not to stay long in the factory.

"Here we paint these bicycles," he said. "Well, you see, we do not paint them. We dip them in these goddamn tanks filled with this stinking stuff. It is true that I do not myself dip them into the tanks. I stripe the damn things. You see how it is, there are thousands and thousands of them, all striped just alike."

Sometimes, he declared, his work in the shop drove him to the edge of insanity. He wanted to begin to make flourishes on the frames of the bicycles with his striping brush. He spoke at length of his former occupation. He had been a partner in a small carriage-building firm and at that place, he said, they made each carriage a little different than the one before.

"We could keep planning and scheming how to make them better and better," he said. He spoke of what a carriage-finishing job had meant to him, a certain shining velvety finish to be achieved, often after infinite labor, a coat of varnish to be put on and to be rubbed and rubbed, and then another and another coat with more of the patient rubbing.

And then there was the striping of such a job. He could let his fancy play a little. He did not have to stripe hundreds of carriages all alike.

"I tell you, boy, you get out of here as soon as you can. I am getting old now and I have to do what I can."

There was a new tone of sadness in his voice. He walked with hanging head up and down in the little shop before me.

"I have got my old woman and the kids," he said sadly.

He had a son, a young boy who had lost his leg. The boy had been catching rides on freight trains, slipping off and on with other boys and had slipped and fallen under a freight-car wheel. The boss spoke of him. He would have to be taken care of, and there was a big doctor's bill to be paid.

"They've got me trapped, kid, but you are young. I have told you how the carriage-building business is going to hell. You have seen a few of these new horseless carriages here on the streets of our town. There will be more and more of them. Our own big boss will be making them pretty soon.

"And it will be the same as with these goddamn bicycles, all alike, all alike."

The little boss came to stand before me. He was very serious, very earnest.

"If you are smart you will get into something where everything keeps changing, where you can never be satisfied with what you do, always wanting to make it better and better."

It was on the night when we were alone in the shop that he tried to explain to me what sometimes happened to him when he was out with the boys on a Saturday night.

"I get proud," he said. "At first I am proud and then I am sad. I am with the boys, there in Body Adair's place or somewhere else. I have been dancing and singing. I have been cutting up shines for them. You know how I do sometimes here in the shop. It is because I am trying to conquer the sadness in my heart.

"I am in a saloon with the others and a strange new feeling comes over me. I begin to wonder if any of them can know how I hate striping these bicycles, all alike, all alike, the same lines drawn on every frame, day after day, week after week, me, who was once a master workman. I get to thinking about our big boss here. Hell, boy, I knew him when he was just a snot-nosed kid. He doesn't know a damn thing about how I feel. He thinks he pays me well and that settles everything. He thinks I am getting old and that, for old times' sake, since we were boys in the same town, he is taking care of me.

"As though that mattered!" The little boss was getting excited.

"So I am in the saloon and I am thinking of him and of all the others. I am thinking of the men I am with, drinking with, in Body Adair's place, and how they do not any of them give a damn and I get a little crazy. I am scared that I will begin to cry and so I run."

What happened to our boss on these occasions was that he suddenly emerged from the saloon doors. He would rush out into the middle of the street and begin to run, perhaps lose his hat, his arms and legs flying wildly, the men and boys shouting at him.

"Go it, man! Go it!" they shouted.

Some of the people were curious.

"Why is he running?" they asked. But as he had done the same thing on several other Saturday evenings there was always some town wit who could explain.

"Oh, it's nothing. He is going rabbit hunting," the wit explained.

"He wants a rabbit for his Sunday dinner. He doesn't shoot rabbits. He runs them down."

Our boss would run through our main street and out of sight into the darkness. On the evening in the shop when he tried to explain it to me he said he just kept running until he could not run any more.

"It is a kind of running fit I have. It is like dogs sometimes have," he said. "I run until I cannot run any more and then I lie down. I am alone in the darkness and sometimes I lie there and cry. Then I get up and go home to my old woman. I start all over again. Sometimes I tell my old woman about it and she understands. She is the only one who does understand."

10. My Sister Stella

The bicycle was an accepted fact. It was continuously being improved and even the girls had begun to ride. Two or three of the more daring ladies had even put on bloomers.

"Did you see that? Now what do you think of that?"

"Great God, what next?"

"What, do you mean to tell me that the whole town will be lighted by the turning of one switch, by the pulling of a lever?"

"But I tell you they already have one at Fremont, only eight miles away. I was there. I saw it. I will get the horse and buggy and we will drive there so you can see it."

"Well, it is too bad. There is John Becker, who goes about every day with his horse and a little cart, cleaning the street lamps, and when evening comes and there is no moonlight, hurrying about to light them. Poor John, he will lose his job."

It was at Fremont that I first saw a town all lighted by electric lights. How isolated our lives in the town had been and what an adventure to go off to another town, to Fremont, our county-seat, eight miles to the west, or to Bellevue, an equal distance to the east. We boys got aboard freight trains and stole rides to these towns.

What a wonder! "Do you mean to tell me they pull just one switch—"

When would these wonders end? Not only for me but for plenty of grown men and women in such towns as ours who had never been out of the town, had never been on a railroad train, the great world outside our little main street remained a vast unknown mystery.

To be sure there were always a few men coming and going. Occasionally one of our merchants went as far away as Toledo or Cleveland, and there would be traveling salesmen, occasionally, rarely, one perhaps from as far away as Chicago or New York, who would spend the night at one of our two hotels. Such men were looked upon almost as world travelers, gaping crowds of us standing about listening as such a one talked in the stores, or talked sitting, on a summer evening, with his chair tilted back against the front wall of our Empire House, speaking so freely of faraway places and of strange mechanical wonders to come.—As he talked Frank Welker, the hotel proprietor, usually walked up and down playing with a pile of silver dollars. He had formerly been the proprietor of a gambling house, but had reformed. He made the silver dollars dance up and down like single cards in a pack of cards. He seemed fabulously rich to us boys.

Now we were rushing pell-mell into the modern world. Soon now the roads, east and west, north and south would all be paved. Cars would be moving up and down them at fifty, sixty miles an hour.

The horse to go soon now. Something fine taken out of the daily lives of many men. Barns back of houses to become garages. The radio, the movie, the airplane. Who could foresee death rained down out of the sky from airplanes on cities and towns, foresee the machines throwing more and more men out of employment? Progress. Progress.

A restlessness came upon me, a restlessness that was to keep coming all the rest of my life. There was our house, with mother gone now. It had begun to seem strangely empty and meaningless to me.

What had happened at home was something which must have happened in many families such as ours, families with several boys and one girl. Our family life had been disorganized by our mother's death and there was Stella, our one sister, compelled suddenly to serve as a mother.

For us boys there had been the life of the streets. We three older boys, Karl, Irwin and myself, had run about. We got jobs. It seems to me now, as I look back upon that time, that the men and women of the town were infinitely kind to us.

Men were speaking words of encouragement, no doubt many of them often the same men who sat with our father at night in some saloon. Those same men, knowing also of our father's total lack of any feeling of responsibility for his children, liking and even loving him for his gift as a talker, a little understanding him, as we could not until long years later, would at the same time have had an almost fatherly feeling toward his sons.

It was in the Irwin brothers, the brothers who had discharged father because of his drinking and his irresponsibility and into whose shop Karl was taken to learn the harness-making trade; it was in the fat doctor for whom Karl, Irwin, and myself all at different times worked; it was in the hardware man; the grocer; the superintendent of the town school; it was even in the saloon keepers.

"Do not think too badly of your father. He is what he is. He cannot be different. He is a good fellow. He's all right. Some day you will understand him better than you do now."

The man unable to say what he felt, feeling, no doubt, the confusion and perplexity of his own life in relation to his own children, a little, perhaps, envying father's ability to throw all off and give himself to the moment, living so much in a world of his own invention—the man himself, being a saloon keeper and bearing the odium connected with that trade, wondering if his own sons also felt shame of their father.

"Some day you'll understand him better than you do now." Prophetic words—

But I must return to my sister and her peculiar plight. She had been very ambitious. She had graduated from the town high school at a very early age. She had been, always, at the top of her class.

At the time a young girl just coming into womanhood, there was about her a shining kind of beauty. She had shining black hair, shining black eyes. Like my older brother Karl, and unlike the rest of us, she had a clear beautiful skin.

She had dreamed of going away somewhere to college, of working her way through college. In secret she wrote verses. Perhaps she might be able to win a scholarship in some college.

But now, with our mother's death, all had to be given up. Now she must stay at home, all day and every day, in our little house, while we older boys roamed the streets.

We were getting along. We were working. A little money was coming in. We could buy new suits of clothes, usually on the installment plan, five or ten dollars down, a dollar a week. We could go to parties, walk about through the streets at night with gangs of boy friends, stopping to sing before the house in which some girl lived. It was a custom among us in our town in that time.

We could go in the winter to sleigh-ride parties, to spellings down in some country schoolhouse. Some of the more prosperous parents of one of the boys of the several gangs to which Karl, Irve and myself belonged would own horses and surreys. We could go with one such on a moonlight summer night for drives into the country with girls. Life having for each of us young males a certain gaiety—youth—what did having to work matter? What did a little hardship matter?

Stella always at home, being mother now to the two small boys left on her hands by mother's death. They would have been as yet very small children.

Long days of it, nights of it, with her confined so.

It must have seemed to her that all life, all opportunity in life was slipping away.

We, her brothers, unconscious of all this, the casual hardness of boys in us.

For her no going about on spring, fall, and summer evenings with crowds of young girls of her own age, no courting by town boys, no parties organized, no walks home from church on summer evenings with young girls of her own age.

She read a good deal and it must have been about this time that she began the writing of verses. The verses gave an impression of deep dissatisfaction with life, of feelings of loneliness, of feelings that her life had come to an end. I remember that our father had been very fond of quoting Poe, and that no doubt had influenced Stella. There was a raven croaking also at her.

> Shall I see the lost Lenore?
> Quoth the raven "Nevermore."

Stella's lost Lenore would at the time have been a job teaching school.

Suddenly an old woman, my mother's mother, descended upon us. She was an old woman I later wrote much about. She is in a book of mine called *A Story Teller's Story*. It may be that in that book I have romanticized her a little, as writers do, but not much. She was something terrific. One of her eyes had gone dead and she was in her late eighties, but she was as strong as a horse. Once I saw her in the top of a cherry tree picking and eating cherries. She had climbed up there. I have always attributed some of my own health to her strong old body.

She had come to our house without an invitation, having no doubt heard of our mother's death, knowing she would find in our house certain young males, wanting herself to be at the head of such a household of growing young men. Having come, she was determined to remain.

As to just what really happened between my sister and my grandmother I have no way of knowing. My sister was a highly imaginative girl as she was later a woman. There was in her something that is in most writers of tales. Such a writer begins to tell a story, based perhaps upon some foundation of fact, and then his imagination goes to work.

There was the determined old woman in our house and there was my sister, and a contest had begun between them. They were both, I fancy, determined to be the female head of the house. It was a woman's war. In my sister, young as she was, there had already grown up a kind of pride. She had undertaken something. A sacrifice had been made. She who had been so bright in school, who had stood always at the head of her class, who had planned a career for herself, had got now this mother feeling for us. There was our house to be managed, we three older boys in some way to find the money. It was understood that we would go on, that we would pull it off. She must have felt that it was a kind of sacred duty to be performed, herself to take the place of our dead mother.

I am sure we had not asked her to do it.

"I have given up my own career. I have made this sacrifice. Life has wronged me so. You shall not take the wrong from me. Now I desire to be wronged."

All of this, I am quite sure, was unconsciously in her mind.

And there was this old woman. She so very strong, very determined.

She would have gone about the house muttering words. She was always doing that. She was one who aroused fear.

One afternoon my sister took two of us, my brother Irve and myself, into a little shed that stood just by our kitchen door. She was very nervous and excited. She was dry-washing her hands and there were tears in her eyes when she spoke to us.

The old woman was somewhere in the house. She was going about in there muttering words. Our house seemed haunted by her presence.

"It has to end. It cannot go on," my sister said. Her face was flushed and tears stood in her eyes. She swore that the old woman, who had come into our house, had threatened to kill her.

It had happened, she said, but a few hours before. She was standing in the kitchen, was at work in there and the old woman had come in to her. There was a large kitchen knife lying on the table.

In the woodshed my sister sat on a bench. She put her hands over her face. A shudder ran through her body. The old woman had been going about town. She had been making inquiries. My sister had wanted to be a schoolteacher. "Go and be one," the old woman had shouted to her. She had begun by trying to persuade my sister and then she had begun to threaten and it had ended, my sister declared, by her coming into the kitchen intent upon killing her.

The old woman had picked up the knife from the table. She had walked to where my sister stood. She had raised the knife to strike.

My sister got more and more dramatic as she told the tale. She rose from the bench. It developed that, for weeks, she had been saving money, a little at a time. She had it wrapped in a pocket handkerchief and, as my brother and I stood listening to her tale, she unwrapped it and handed it to me. There was, she said, enough money to buy a railroad ticket for grandmother.

"She can go back to the place from which she came. No one asked her to come here. It is that old woman or it is me," she declared. There was enough money saved to send the old woman back to our aunt, our mother's sister, who lived on a farm somewhere in southern Ohio.

"She is in the house there. If she stays I cannot stay.

"It is now three and there is a train leaving at five," my sister said.

My sister got up from the bench. There was a determined look in her eyes. "You two will have to be men."

She was no longer crying. She stood erect before us. "You will have to choose," she said. We were to go, the two of us, to the old woman, our grandmother. We were to explain to her, order her to pack and be gone. We were to tell her that, if she did not go, we would call the police. As she said all of this, giving us thus our instructions, my sister put the money into my hands. She stood, with her slender girlish figure very erect and pointed toward the house. "Go," she said.

There was in her at the moment a suggestion of the actress playing some tragic role. Years later when I saw the actress Ada Rehan in a tragic role I thought of my sister Stella. She declared that she would never again enter our house while the old woman was there.

We did go. Accompanied by my brother Irve I marched into the house and found the old woman sitting in a chair and as I delivered our ultimatum, my voice trembled. As my sister had suggested I spoke of the police and for a time, after I had made my speech, there was silence.

It was a silence that awoke fear. We stood and she sat and there was her one old eye looking at us. The other eye was always closed. We did not know whether or not sight was lost in it.

"She is not going to do it," I thought. A kind of terror took possession of me and now, for a time, I believed the tale of the knife, as told by my sister. The one eye of the old woman was, I thought, filled with hatred. I wanted to turn and run away, but presently, after staring at us so for several minutes, the old woman arose.

She packed in silence and in silence marched to the station, my brother Irve and I marching silent behind her and, at the station, I bought the railroad ticket and put it into her hand. There was nothing said, no good-bys but, when at last the train came and she had got aboard and my brother and I stood on the station platform and she sat by an open window, her one old eye still staring at us—was it really hatred or sadness I saw in the old woman's eye?—as the train pulled out I saw her thin old lips begin to move. She was saying words but, because of the sound made by the train, we could not hear. Was she muttering curses or was she pleading with us?

At any rate she had gone and, when we had seen the last of her, I became suddenly sad and, as my brother and I walked homeward, I remember that there was a sudden skepticism in us both.

"Do you really believe the story of the knife?" my brother asked. "You know," he added, "the threat to kill, do you believe in it?"

I said I did not know.

For a time we went on living so, my sister more or less the female head of the house, myself playing the part of the dominant male.

And the male head made the most of his growing privilege: to hurry out of the house, after the evening meal, to get set with some girl, hear from her lips some of the scandals of the town, go with a crowd of other young males on courting expeditions among the so-called "nice" girls, some of the "nice" girls a little angry and jealous (they couldn't go sit in the darkness on back porches of houses with young male toughs). To jump on a freight train and go to a neighboring town, eight miles away, play pool in a poolroom there, flirt with girls of that town.

Your sister compelled to stay at home, evening after evening, wash the evening dishes, put the smaller children to bed.

Perhaps no young male courting her. What was the use? She was attractive, even beautiful, but, as she said, there were always the children about, always to be taken care of, watched over.

It was early on a Sunday evening, still light outside, the church bells ringing and I was upstairs in our house. I had been off with several boys for a Sunday afternoon tramp in the woods but now I had other plans. I had put on my new suit, combed my hair, had shined my shoes.

There was always the Sunday night hunt. Well, you did not go to church. You roamed about with other boys until time for people to emerge from church and then you went there. You stood, with other boys, at the edge of a sidewalk, under the maple trees until the girls appeared, and then they appeared and you stepped forth.

"May I see you home, Miss Grey?"

It was a critical moment. If she refused to let you walk with her—"turned you down," a hoot, a cry from the other young males.

"Yah! Yah! You got turned down."

There was a new young girl in town, one with blue eyes and soft yellow hair and she had smiled at me as girls do. She would be going to church. Would I dare?

Yes. I was determined. I'd risk it. I'd take a chance.

I had gone from the room where I slept with two of my brothers and into my sister's room. There was a glass in there. My necktie must be just right, my hair arranged just right. I was standing before the glass in my sister's room when she came in.

My sister went to sit on the bed.

"You are going to try to get a girl," she said and there was something, a certain tone in her voice that made me turn to look at her.

Why, what was this? Her cheeks were flushed and there was the suggestion of tears about to flow.

"Why, I don't know. I was just going out. Why?"

My sister hesitated. Her head was bowed and she was looking at the floor.

"I had thought," she said, "it is going to be a fine night."

She had turned. She threw herself face down on the bed. She was crying and I had gone to her.

I felt curiously awkward and ashamed. Perhaps, at the moment, for the first time there had come to me a realization of what her life was like. She was so young. She was beautiful. Our mother's death had thrown upon her young shoulders all of this responsibility.

There we were, a family of boys. There had been another girl child, born shortly before mother's death, but it had lived but a few weeks. We could not afford a servant and our grandmother had been sent away.

Stella had wanted that. She had not wanted the old woman about. There had been a contest between the old and the young woman.

They had both wanted the position as female head of the house.

There had been this struggle between them and my sister had won. She had this quick imagination. It had been her story that the old woman had threatened to kill her, had gone muttering about the house with a large kitchen knife in her hand, muttering threats that had led to her being sent away.

My sister had won but she was now paying for her victory. She was a little upset now by her victory. She was there on the bed, her shoulders shaking. She was crying.

I stood over her. I was embarrassed. I wanted to take her in my arms, comfort her, but she was my sister.

You did not do it in such families as ours. You did not hold your sister in your arms. Well, you teased her. You came suddenly up behind her and pinched her. You pulled her hair. You even occasionally wrestled with her. It was thus you expressed your affection.

My sister had stopped crying. She sat again on the edge of her bed. She wiped her eyes. We were alone together in the house, the other boys having gone out into the town streets. Although I did not yet know it, my sister had arranged with a neighbor woman who was to come for the two younger boys for the evening. She had made certain plans but she had not consulted me. We two were to go off somewhere together.

"What is it, Stella? What do you want? What's the matter?"

She sat there before me, a little hesitant, suddenly shy.

"It isn't anything."

"Yes it is. Now you tell me."

It came out with a rush. It was the story of her loneliness.

"I wanted to get away, far away somewhere, from this house. I wanted to go, with you or someone, away from here."

It was growing dark outside the house, and as I stood in the room, my sister's room in our house, she sitting before me on the bed, her face flushed, her eyes still red from weeping (she was trying to smile now), there was a certain shyness.

Can it be that I, at the moment, realized what my sister wanted?

She wanted to pretend, for the one summer evening, that I was something I wasn't, that I was not her brother, that I was just a young male, any young male, come to court her.

She did not say that.

"Oh, I just wanted to be with you. I thought, perhaps . . . well, I thought we might go off somewhere together, away from this house, away from this street.

"It is going to be a moonlight night," she said. "We could take a walk in the country. Do you mind?"

It was very strange. There I was, out in the half darkness of the summer night with my sister. We had walked together in silence along a country road, we had climbed fences and crossed fields. We were in woodland paths, beside a creek. It was quite dark and she had reached out and had taken my hand into hers, when we had stopped on a little hill I had, for just a moment, held her in my arms and we had kissed.

It was all very strange. The whole evening with my sister, the only time during our life together in the same house when we were really close to each other, was passed in a strange silence. There was a game being played and I had, for the evening, given myself to it.

I had and I had not. I am quite sure now, as I think back on that strange evening with her, myself the young male, eager for the female, my sister eager for the young male, she being shut out from something she wanted, being as she was half young female poet.

She was, for the evening, pretending that I was something I was not, that I was not her brother. Once, as we walked along together, when we were in a little meadow beside a wheat field (the whole scene curiously vivid in my mind as I write of it after these years) she suddenly drew close to me.

We had stopped by a rail fence, and as I stood, somewhat embarrassed, leaning against the fence she came close. Her hand reached up and caressed my cheek. Her hand caressed my hair. She spoke in a soft whisper. There was a little breeze playing across the field of ripening wheat so that the mind seemed to be playing a game. The wheat field was like a little yellow lake with waves running across it.

"It's beautiful, isn't it, James?" my sister whispered but I was silent and for just a moment (a strange awkward shy moment) she put her arms about my neck and drew my face down to her face.

"Do you love me, James?" she whispered again and then she kissed me quickly on the cheek and drawing quickly away she laughed. It was an embarrassed, nervous little laugh. She did not tell me who "James" was.

We came back across the fields and along a country road and to our house, my sister and I speaking now quite freely of things concerned with the family. She was talking rapidly now, speaking of certain plans she had for our younger brothers, plans that were never fulfilled. She had become again my sister, our sister. She had been playing a little game with the life she felt herself shut out from, but now she had given up the game.

And so we came back to our house and I left her at the door and went away, half hoping, I dare say, that I would still be in time to try for the new girl at the door of the church.

As to whether or not I was in time for that, I can't remember, the memory of my sister and her mood on that evening crowding out all other memories; but I am quite sure that the feeling of strangeness and of a queer unreality that was to be the whole story of my sister's life must have stayed with me so that no doubt, for the rest of that evening and before I returned to our house to crawl into bed with my brother Irve, I must just have walked about alone trying to get some understanding of what had happened between us.

Later for a time things cleared for her. She had the college hunger. It had been eating at her for years and when we, her brothers, began a little to prosper, an arrangement was made. We all, that is to say Karl, Irve and myself, chipped in what we could and the younger boys were for a time farmed out, were put to live with a neighbor named Musgrave while Stella, at last free, got her wish.

She was entered as a student in the University of Chicago and although now we did not live together, I occasionally saw her.

As for myself, I had become a young blade. I had got into the advertising agency and begun to prosper.

For me also there had been the education myth, that education was to be got at by certain years spent in college. You did that and then, emerging, you were prepared for life.

And now my sister was a student in the university. She became a kind of fixture there. The years passed and it went on and on. About every college and university there are such women. They stay until they become old women, they remain students for life.

It was happening so with my sister and at last, after several years, some of my brothers having already married, they also having a struggle, it was agreed between us that she would have to quit, to go to work.

It was put up to me to tell her and I did. I remember the occasion. "I will have her downtown," I said to myself. "I will buy her a dinner with wine."

And so she came and we were both embarrassed, but at last, as we sat thus at a table in one of the more fashionable restaurants of the city, I told her of our decision.

"Now I guess, Stella, it will have to end," I said.

I spoke of her former ambition to be a schoolteacher.

"Now you should be ready for that," I said. It was an embarrassing moment for me.

She began to abuse me. She felt then, as she did later, that having stood by her younger brothers, having, as she said, sacrificed all of young girlhood and womanhood, it was up to us, her older brothers, to stand by her.

"But you cannot always go to college. You have been there now, six, seven, perhaps eight years. It is not fair to the others."

She got up from her place at the table and I remember sharply my own embarrassment over the scene that followed. She spoke in a shrill voice. Could this be the sister of my childhood, Stella the dark-eyed gentle one?

Many people in the restaurant had turned and were looking at us. She began to berate me bitterly, in a loud voice, and then, throwing up her head, she turned and with her open hand, slapped me in the face.

It was, for me, a terrible moment. She walked out of the restaurant and I stood there staring at her retreating figure. A man, the head waiter in the place, had come up to me. "We cannot have such things going on in here," he said.

I said nothing. Paying the bill I left. I was bitterly angry. "She can go to the devil. I am done with her," I thought; but, after some weeks, when I had heard nothing from her, I got a letter.

She had asked my forgiveness. She had indeed become a schoolteacher and had taken a job in a town somewhere down in the state.

In the letter she said that she had been through a great change. She had found God, she said.

God, she said, had come to her in the form of his son.

"I have had a visitation from Jesus," she said. In her letter she described the scene. It was at night, she was in her bed. She had been thinking of her brothers, blaming us, had been filled with a great bitterness against us, but, while all of this was going on in her, as she lay in the darkness in her room in a boarding house in the town, there had come a great light into the room.

She said it was Jesus Himself and that he had taken her into his arms. He had caressed and comforted her but he had also told her of the wrong she had done to us. It was Jesus, she said, who had told her to write the letter, asking my forgiveness for the scene she had made in the restaurant.

Later, my sister got married. She remained devoutly religious. She had returned to the city but I did not see her often and, when occasionally I did see her, she was profoundly changed. Sometimes, on such occasions, she spoke of her marriage, saying that it had been a mistake, that it wasn't the fault of her husband but that, after the visitation she had had, she should have devoted her life to religion.

"It is too bad I am not a Catholic. I should have been a nun," she said and putting her face in her hands she wept. Without saying so she gave me to understand that not her husband, not any man, could ever understand how she felt.

"You are all carnal," she said, "while I, who have been touched by the hand of Jesus Himself . . ."

She could not go on and I, being on all such occasions deeply embarrassed, saw her less and less.

And then she died and, with my several brothers, all now grown to manhood, I went to her funeral.

It was held in a little Protestant church and when we, her brothers, had all filed in . . . we sat in the front row of seats in the little church . . . the preacher began to speak.

He spoke, telling of what was, to us, her brothers, a strange enough story of my sister's life. He said that having at an early age lost her father and mother and having, as all in the church could see, several brothers, she had devoted her life to them.

One by one the preacher began and told the story of our lives. There was my older brother. He had, by my sister's efforts, been sent to study painting in Europe. She had done it, he said, by patient toil, by saving money, by sacrificing herself. She had, by bitter hard work, by much self-sacrifice educated us all. This one had been sent to college, that one set up in business. The story went on and on.

We, her brothers, turned occasionally to stare at one another.

BOOK II

AMERICAN MONEY

1. Chicago

Fear.

Something huge, not understandable. Streets thirty miles long, perfectly flat. Buildings and houses you dream about in distorted dreams.

Boats crowded in the narrow river. Mills. Factories. Smoke, dirt, a low black swampy land, a wind-riven land, a climate so terrible in its extremes of heat and cold that only strong people can survive, really live.

Men, men, men. To the east, reaching up, Michigan. To the west, Wisconsin, Minnesota, the Northwest. Chicago lying where the long tongue of the Great Lakes reaches farthest down into the land. And to the south, smooth as a billiard table—fat land. No such corn land anywhere in the world. Innumerable droves of great sleepy hogs, eating the corn. Cattle off the dry western lands, coming in lean and bony, getting fat and sleek, eating corn.

Railroads coming in, all the real railroads. Railroads everywhere.

I was a raw boy just out of my Ohio town when I first came to Chicago. What city man, come out of a small town, can forget his first hours in the city, the strangeness and terror of the tall buildings, the human jam?

I walked through the crowded streets with my brother. He was but a year or two older, but suddenly, what a gulf between us. This was not his first city. He had been away from our town for two or three years: in Cleveland, and in Chicago for at least a year. He seemed unimpressed. The bigness did not overwhelm him.

We were not in our family very demonstrative. "Hello, kid," "Hello." We walked through the flowing human stream, got aboard a street car. He was silent. He read a newspaper.

So he had me on his hands. Work had been hard to find in our little town. I had taken the great step, separated from my boyhood friends, from familiar streets, fields at the edge of town where I went with other boys to hunt rabbits or walk.

I was little more than a boy. It was too big for me, too terrible. Could people live in such streets, in such houses? Crowded together so?

You who have seen only the famous Michigan Boulevard, the North Side, Lincoln Park, Jackson Park, do not know Chicago. Why talk?

There is the huge Northwest Side, the West Side, the South Side.

Millions of people of all nationalities packed in close, packed in among slaughterhouses, factories, warehouses, mills.

Long stretches of vacant lots. Five-, six- and eight-storied apartment buildings, standing in the midst of acres of black weeds.

Brutal murders going on. Everything unfinished. Hope—hopelessness. Nothing to do but get drunk as often as possible.

I remember nights when I walked the streets of Chicago—half drunk, hopeless—swimming in a sea of ugliness.

Then suddenly—a glimpse of the Chicago River—that great sewer. A sewer nothing. You wait. The Chicago River will some day become one of the lovely rivers of the world of cities. Sometimes it is unbelievably beautiful—from the bridges—the gulls soaring above, the strange, lovely chrysoprase river—the cries and oaths.

There is something inevitable about Chicago. So many people in one great flat place—where a real city had to be. A city not in the least like New York, Boston, Philadelphia, Baltimore.

Beside it Cleveland and Detroit are villages—grown suddenly to look like cities. From the first Chicago had to be, will always be while the land lasts, a real city, like New York, London, Paris.

A real city does not care too much what you, a mere man, think of it. "Here I am. Go to hell."

Los Angeles, Cleveland, Seattle, such places give themselves away too much. They are whistling in the dark.

A city to be a real one has to have something back of it. Land, a lot of it. Rich land—corn, wheat, iron, rivers, mountains, hogs, cattle. Chicago back of it has the Middle West—the empire called Mid-America. Corn, hogs, wheat, iron, coal, industrialism—a new age moving across a continent by railroads, moving unbelievable quantities of goods across a vast place, in the center of which Chicago stands.

Through Chicago. You'll be routed that way, going most anywhere.

✦

It became the city of my own young manhood. Chicago is unformed, it is terrible. There is something terrible about the making of every great city. Who can tell what it will be? Leopold and Loeb? Carl Sandburg, Edgar Lee Masters, or Clarence Darrow?

And Chicago is still making. Yet when it is formed it will not be another New York, Paris, London. It will be Chicago. Here I am. Go to hell. In its very terribleness it is at moments beautiful in a way apparent only when you have lived there a long time. When you have been sick of it to the very marrow and accepted it, then at last, walking hopeless, endless streets—yourself hopeless—you begin to feel its beauty, its half-wild beauty. The beauty of the loose and undisciplined, unfinished and unlimited. Something half wild and very alive in yourself is there, too. The city you have dreaded and feared is like your own soul.

It remained my city after I had begun to comprehend the distinctiveness of the great city, almost as great as that of individuals, nations, trees, peoples, hills.

There I saw the first woman who rejected me—felt what men feel when they are so rejected. There I first made ink flow, sang my first song. There after many efforts I wrote a sentence I could bear reading the next day.

There I first heard the sound of men's voices—related to streets, houses, cities—saw my first real actor walk upon a stage, heard music first, saw painting.

When I visit any other great city of the world I am a guest. When I am in Chicago I am at home. It is a little what I am. I am more than a little what Chicago is. No man can escape this city.

I am not proud of it. Chicago will not be proud. But it is a real city —my city.

Take it or leave it.

There it is.

And, God helping me, here am I—

2. We Share

I was a laborer working in a huge cold storage warehouse just across the river in Chicago's North Side, all day handling barrels filled with apples and crates of eggs. We piled the barrels and crates high in great rooms at a low temperature. Most of the men who worked with me were heavy-shouldered Swedes, and Poles and Finns. We worked in the warehouse ten hours a day and I received two dollars a day. At that time I was living in a cheap tenement on the West Side.

With me were my sister Stella and my younger brothers. We had but two or three rooms in an unheated apartment building, and in the winter huddled about a small coal stove. My older brother Karl, who had become an illustrator, continually sent us money to help us along. I walked back and forth from my work to save my car-fare.

To get to my tenement I was compelled to walk through a red-light district. Women came to the doors of the houses and invited me to enter. I dreaded these encounters but at the same time wanted them. By going three or four blocks out of my way I could have avoided the encounters. I didn't. I wanted the temptation while I dreaded it. I had no money with which to enter.

At this time I was injured at my work and was in bed for some weeks. I had a friend, John Emerson, who later with his wife, Anita Loos, became a well-known producer of moving pictures. John and I had both been boys in the same village and had both come to Chicago. He was at that time, if I remember, a clerk in the wholesale department of Marshall Field and Co. How generous he was with me during my time of illness. In fact during my whole life he has helped me over many a bad spot in the road. But at this time of illness he came at the end of each week and left me half his own meager salary.

When I had recovered from my illness I was constantly disturbed thinking of women. Passionately I wanted a woman of my own. I had got out of bed but was still not strong enough to go to work. I walked the streets at night filled with the hunger. I followed chance-met women for blocks along a street. Yet I could not have found courage within myself to speak to one of them, had the opportunity offered— At last, occasionally, I went to the women of the town.

I remember sharply one such adventure. I had walked for hours through the night, too restless to go home and to bed. It is true that, at the time, I was doing hard laborious work all day but I was very strong. I was in a street of drab little frame houses clustered about a factory. There was a huge bakery where bread was made. An elevated railroad ran through the street.

A woman spoke to me and I followed her up a stairway into a small dismal room. There were two small children lying on a bed.

Was I to make love to her there, in that room, in the presence of the sleeping children?

I sat on a rickety chair in the room. It was in a little frame house just opposite the factory. There was only a dim light in the room. The factory was working at night. Through a window I could see men and women at work over there.

I began to ask her questions and she explained, saying she had been deserted by her man. She said she worked through the day getting a woman of the house to come for her children but could not make enough to feed and clothe them and herself, pay her rent, etc.

And so, at night she saw men.

"It is all right. I have it fixed with the woman here."

There was a little alcove to the room and she put the sleeping children on the floor in there. She arranged a curtain across the face of the alcove.

"It is all right," she said. "Come on."

I told her I couldn't.

"It is all right. Here is your money."

She wouldn't take it.

"No," she said. "You have come up here, now you must go to bed with me.

"I'll not be an object of charity," she said.

I remember later that night, walking about in the streets, filled with shame. I cried. An odd thing happened. As I walked about so, overcome with shame, not necessarily of shame for myself or her but of all society, all mankind, it seemed to me that I wanted to be something higher and nobler than my nature would let me be.

"Why was I ever born as I am?" I cried.

I was walking about thus when, under a street lamp, beside the sidewalk I saw something that, when I pounced upon it, turned out to be a woman's purse. There were five one dollar bills and some small change. There were some other small trinkets.

At that time I was still working as a laborer. I was making two dollars for a day of ten hours. My sister and two young brothers had come to live with me. I had to save carefully to get money enough to be with a woman.

Money. Money.

What a strange thing it is. It seemed to me that if I went back to that woman, gave her the money I had found, the act would in some small way remove a little of my own feeling of shame.

And so I did go back to her. I had some difficulty finding her house but at last did find it. Fortunately the door to the street was unlocked and I went in, lighted matches, found my way up a stairway to her room and knocked.

She seemed annoyed.

"Well, what do you want?" she asked when she opened the door. I could see into the room as she had turned up a bud of light. She had put the two children back into the bed and had been lying with them.

I put the purse in her hand.

"Here, I found this," I said and turning, hurried away down the stairs.

3. Money! Money!

In the warehouse I didn't have to work on Saturday afternoons. On Saturday nights John and I often walked together for hours. This whole matter, my relation with my friend John, is something that has puzzled me all my life.

The bond between us was an old one. We lived together when I first came to Chicago. His sister kept a rooming house there, on a street in Chicago's vast West Side. I had for him a rather intense boyish admiration. He seemed very talented.

He had something of the same sort of talent that Robert Benchley later developed. He'd begin a kind of hesitating explanation of something, assume a highly amusing nervousness, lose the trend of his discourse, fumble in his pockets, make little laughter-creating side remarks. I used to laugh at him until my body ached, as later I was to laugh at Benchley.

He was never a strong boy or young man, but he had a quick shrewd mind. He always managed to get along. When there was something he wanted, a certain job, an advancement in the job he had, he would set about accomplishing his end with a cold, shrewd, patient determination that filled me with admiration.

There was a certain man, let us say, at the head of a company where he wanted a place. He would begin to study the man, search out his prejudices.

Let us say he was to have an interview with some man regarding an advancement. He sat at a desk and wrote out what he planned to say, walked up and down the room, read it aloud to me, kept changing and improving it. He always ended by getting what he wanted.

He had a strange power over women. He was not handsome. Was always thin and pale. We were both, as I presume most young men of a certain age are, intent upon sex.

Oh, how I at that time wanted a woman, any woman. But adventures did not happen to me. They happened however to John. Women were always attaching themselves to him. I knew it had happened at home, while we were boys, in our home town. It kept on happening.

I kept seeing him with attractive-looking women.

"But do they give themselves to you?"

He laughed.

"Yes."

I knew it was true. There is something that, when you see a man and woman together, tells you the story.

We used to speak of it.

"You are too serious," he said.

"You want them to be in love with you. You are yourself always falling in love. It means too much to you."

It was quite true. At the time I could see no future for myself. It seemed to me that I must go on forever being just a laborer.

I was continually falling in love. I saw a woman walking in the street, followed her at a distance. Had she noticed me, turned and spoken to me, I would have been frightened.

On the other hand John, for all his continual illness, was bold and successful.

"You are too serious. You want love. There is too much taking of responsibility involved in that. You frighten women by the intense way you look at them.

"As a matter of fact the women you see me with often like and respect you more than they do me."

It was apparent that, when John wanted to be with a woman, he simply asked her. If she refused that was that. He went on to another. There was something essentially vulgar in many women. They liked his casual way with them. It in some queer way left them free.

It seemed to me that there was in him at bottom a contempt for the individual.

It wasn't in me. John spoke of that on several occasions. I kept wondering why he wanted to bother with me, why, apparently, he clung to my friendship.

Sometimes he spoke of that.

"I can see that you think I'll be a successful person in life while you probably will not," he said. We would be walking in the streets at night. He put an arm about my shoulder.

"It may be that you will always be the only man I'll ever love," he said. "To get along, get what you want, or think you want, from life, you have to be ruthless, have to use people, make them serve your purpose."

He said that he knew he would never be tempted to do that with me.

"There is in some way a different foundation to our two lives. You believe in people, their good intentions, while I do not." These conversations between John and myself usually took place at night when we walked in Chicago West Side streets.

We were in Halsted Street or in Madison Avenue. Often we walked along for blocks in silence. Sometimes we walked with John's arm about my shoulder and occasionally we passed men who turned to laugh at us.

I know now that they thought we were two fairies but, at that time, I had never heard of homosexuality. Only at moments I was a little embarrassed when we walked thus. Something in the eyes of people we passed, something in their thoughts of us walking so, made me uncomfortable.

Sometimes we went into bars or into small restaurants. We ate and drank, John always paying the bill. Already he had begun to earn more money than I then thought I ever could earn. He embarrassed me by always paying the bills. I wanted to be with him. Vaguely I think I felt that he was something I wanted to be, a man who, in spite of physical handicaps, would get on, make his way, make people give to him what he wanted from life.

Yet on such occasions I would go along absorbed in the people seen. There was a tired-faced young woman, evidently half ill, going along with packages in her arms. There was a droop to the corners of her mouth, her eyes looked tired. I began to make a quick imagined picture of her life. She was, let us say, a stenographer working all day in an office, or a clerk who worked in a store. All day she had been standing and now was very tired.

She had a sick mother at home and a brother who drank. As she passed us I had noticed a small scar, as from an old cut, just above one of her eyes.

One night her brother had come home drunk and quarrelsome and when she had tried to quiet him, get him into bed, he threw something at her. It was some hard object he had picked up in a room in their little cheap apartment.

Or there was a tired prostitute standing in a dark hallway. I got but a momentary glimpse of her face but about her also I made up a story. These stories, often commonplace enough, of the imagined lives of people passed swiftly through my mind as I walked with John.

Or something, something more intense, a little hard to explain would happen when we were together. Let us say we had gone into a little restaurant. John wanted a cup of tea. He could not drink coffee, beer or any hard liquor. It upset his insides. He was a little angry about it.

"If I only had your physique.

"I am always being ill. I get so tired sometimes."

There was a young woman who came to wait on us and, occasionally, when our eyes met something happened between her and me. I had again, as she came toward us, made a picture of her life but this time the thing had really happened. What I had imagined about her, the picture I had made of her life so swiftly, was true. This I knew and she knew. She knew when our eyes met. It was almost as though the woman and myself had lived together in great intimacy for years. There was nothing about her I did not know.

But how shall I explain all of this? There is, sometimes, this sudden half mystic bond suddenly set up between people, deep knowledge of each other, something deeply felt, something known. All my life it has been happening to me.

It is love. What else can it be called? It is one of the thousands of marriages people make. It is something that is always happening between people, but they dare not, or will not, know it. When men and women dare let themselves know it there will be a new life on this earth.

And all of this while, at the same time, I was deeply jealous of my friend, his quick way of getting on a footing with many people.

And something else. John spoke often of his determination to make and to have money.

"Someday we will both grow old.

"It is dreadful to be old and poor.

"I am afraid of poverty. It frightens me horribly."

Something hardened in the man when he said these things. You knew that he could be ruthless, determined. We would be walking in one of the poorer sections of Chicago's West Side. Broken-down bums were drifting past. City panhandlers stopped us, begging for nickels.

"To get a cup of coffee," they muttered.

"If you don't get money you end by becoming like that.

"I hate them. I hate all poor people, all failures in life."

He spoke with a sort of intense bitterness, the more strange to me because as a young boy he had had so many of what are called "advantages." He had had music lessons, gone to college, had always, since I could remember, been well dressed. His father was a man much respected and looked up to in the community, as I remembered him: a rather witty, lovable man always being elected to some office of responsibility, while, as everyone in our town knew, my own father was a well-known no-account, his family always shifting from house to house in the poorer sections of the town because he couldn't or wouldn't pay the rent.

As I have said there was this obsession, always in him, about making and having money.

Was it necessary to have money, to spend a life trying to grow rich?

What was to be gained?

Did a man not stand a chance of losing more than he gained? Often at night, in bed, in the little tenement apartment in which I was living with my sister and the two younger brothers, both as yet children, I lay awake for hours thinking of the conversations with John.

"Yes, he will get rich while I will not."

A hunger for things I was terribly afraid I could never get swept over me. Oh, how I wanted fine clothes, a warm, comfortable house in which to live.

So much to be accomplished. John was right. Occasionally, on Sunday afternoons, I went to walk on Michigan Boulevard in Chicago, then as now a noble and beautiful street, and there saw beautifully dressed women going along with faultlessly dressed men, myself perhaps clad in a cheap and half-worn-out suit bought on the installment plan.

When I walked along behind some young and richly dressed woman it was not for the flesh of her I longed. I hungered instead to touch her gown, feel the beautiful cloth with my fingers. I wanted to go with her into some expensive restaurant, buy champagne, myself elegantly dressed, expensive rings on my fingers, able to be careless about money, throw it about.

I would, in imagination, be living in one of the big hotels overlooking the lake, or in a great airy apartment.

"A man is a fool who does not get money.

"We who stay poor, always on the edge, deserve what life does to us.

"Or if not exactly poor, one of the so-called middle-class, always grubbing along, counting pennies.

"Saving, saving.

"God knows for what."

Money becoming too important to us.

"Money. Money. God damn money," I cried.

Such thoughts racing through my head, the result partly of my talks with John. Why did I know that he would so surely accomplish what I would not? I did know. There was a way in which I wanted passionately to be as he was, contemptuous of ordinary people.

"Why," I asked myself, "should I be sympathetic with such people?"

"I have a good brain."

You must think of me on these occasions as sitting up in my narrow bed in our little Chicago apartment. In the winter the place was heated by small coal-burning stoves. There was a stove pipe, a long one, fastened to the ceiling with wire that went across over my bed to its hole in a wall beyond my bed.

The joints of the pipe were always coming loose. Coal soot fell down on my bed and sometimes blackened my face. There were two beds in an adjoining room, my sister in one, the two children in the other.

"And why should I be saddled with them?"

A man wants freedom to go forth, to conquer.

If, in later life, I was sometimes to be called a "red," even a communist, which of course I never was, it was because every working woman I saw reminded me of my mother coming into our little frame house on a winter day, after hanging a wash out on the line, her clothes frozen to her body, the look of patient suffering on her face. I knew now that she had really died from poverty.

"I will be like John, determined, contemptuous.

"Nothing shall stand in my way."

These determinations came to me, and then doubt.

Did I have already, while so young, a sense of something that was later to grow in me?

"Get rich, get possessions, and at the same time lose.

"Lose what?"

Just the thing that sometimes happened between me and the most ordinary people met in the street, as for example between that tired waitress in the restaurant and myself.

The thing that I knew did not happen between John and others, could not happen.

Penetration into other people's lives.

Understanding.

Could a man have the determination, the faculty for using others, making them serve his own purpose, and this other faculty, understanding?

Doubt. Doubt.
Money. Money.
Eternal confusion.

4. The Capture of Caratura

The Spanish-American War had begun. Our local newspaper spoke of me as one who "had left a lucrative position in Chicago to rush to his country's defense." And I saw the girl I had left behind me.

She was a young girl, not on our street in the Ohio town, but on one in which lived people far above us in the social scale, and she had smiled on me. On the night before definitely leaving for Chicago I had gone to her. It was a summer evening and I had found her sitting on the front porch of her father's house.

It is strange that now, after all these years, I have in my mind no picture of her. Was she blonde or brunette? I do not know.

I went to sit with her. I had written out the speech I wanted to make to her.

It was a declaration of love, a proposal of marriage.

"I am going out, now, into the big world. I love you. I shall carry your dear image in my heart.

"It will be a fearful struggle but I shall win. I'll come back.

"Wait for me. Be faithful to me."

I think she must have been impressed. I have this memory of sitting with her on the steps before her house, of handing her what I had written, of her going indoors to read, of her coming back to me. I sat and held her hand. We kissed. The street before the house was lined with shade trees. I thought the night, the girl, my own thoughts and feelings all beautiful.

Later when I had got some work in the city, when I had there a little room of my own in a hall bedroom, in John's sister's rooming house, I spent evening after evening writing to her. I did not tell her of my fright, or of my creeping fear of the city, of what seemed to me the hopelessness of any effort to get ahead in such a vast place filled with so many people.

Now the Spanish War had come and I had become a hero. I had heard the call of my country—and coming home to enlist I found she had become engaged to marry another. He was, I think, a clerk in a jewelry store. He had not enlisted for the war. The sufferings of the people on the island of Cuba had not touched his heart! He had no soldier's uniform to put on and I had my moment of revenge. There came the day when we of the local military company were marching through our main street to the railroad station.

There was a great crowd of people. Country people had come into town, and all of the town people were out. The two or three small factories of the town had closed for the day. The schools had closed.

Old men, Civil War veterans, were standing, I remember, on the sidewalks along Main Street. They were talking of their own war and their own youth. I remember in particular an old man, one Jim Lane. He had been in Andersonville Prison. He had seen his brother die of hunger there. He was a tall old man and his lean face stood up above the heads of the weeping women. He also wept. I saw the tears running down his gaunt old cheeks.

A woman who had been my schoolteacher—a short heavily built woman of forty—ran out of the crowd. She embraced me.

"Oh my dear boy!" she cried.

I remember also that I tried to appear stern, to maintain an air of indifference. We, in our little company of local braves, were for the most part boys. We kept whispering to each other as we marched.

"Well, what the hell.

"I wish they'd quit it.

"I wish they'd let us alone, don't you?"

I think we were all relieved when we had got aboard our train.

And there in the crowd, seeing us off, as we marched through the main street . . . she was with a party of other young girls . . .

Tears were running down her cheeks. I remember that, as I marched past, she left the others and started toward me.

"Oh, oh," she cried. Perhaps she had intended to embrace me—to cry.

"Forgive me! Forgive me!"

I have no notion what she intended to say. She ran toward me and I turned from her.

I laughed the laugh of scorn.

"As for you—ha!

"Go to your jewelry clerk.

"You have been unfaithful to me.

"Now I go to die for my country.

"I scorn you."

To be sure I said nothing of the sort to her. What I should have said I thought of, later, in the train. I did, however, turn my face away from her, pretending that I had not seen her.

I had my revenge.

Our company went to the city of Toledo. We stayed overnight in a great armory there. There was a man of our company, the son of a saloon keeper of the town, who went up into a balcony and sang a song.

> Oh, we'll come back,
> Yes, we'll come back
> From the isle of the sea.
> For the time will come
> When the victory is won,
> And the island of Cuba is free.

I remember how my heart leaped as the saloon keeper's son stood up there. We all arose and cheered. How I envied him.

We were boys of a Middle-Western country town, farmers' sons, merchants' sons, young town roughs, gentle, quiet boys. Our hearts did not ache for the people of the island of Cuba. Our hearts ached for adventure. We wanted most of all to go to see the world, go into new strange places. As the saloon keeper's son sang, I did not see in my imagination suffering people, released from bondage by our bravery. I saw myself standing up there on a little balcony above the men and singing to them.

My heart leaped—but it was filled also with envy.

We were taken to Columbus, Ohio, to the state capitol and there we were relieved from the service of the state and became instead soldiers of the nation. Something had been learned from the Civil War. There were to be no three-month men, no hundred-day men. We enlisted for the duration of the war.

I think we were all a little frightened. I was. My father had been a soldier. I had heard many tales of courage, of battles. I had wanted to get a uniform, to parade on summer evenings in village streets, all the girls out looking on. Now there were no bands playing, no women to embrace us and call us heroes.

It was the evening of the day before we were to re-enlist and we boys were gathered in the company streets. We had not been drafted. If we did not choose to go to the war, there was nothing to compel us.

We were camped in a large field. It may have been a park. We kept gathering in little groups, talking to each other in low tones. I remember walking out, away from our camp, into an open place, under the stars.

At home my father had spoken to me.

"You don't have to do it. Why do you?"

My sister had also pointed out that there were many young men anxious to go. There were more men clamoring to go than could be taken.

"And why you?

"You have got a job. Why give it up?

"There are so many others anxious to go. Why you?

"You know we need the little money you were making."

I did not answer her.

"How can a woman know?" I said to myself.

I had got on a train and had come home, on a sudden impulse.

That job I had in the city—the one the local newspaper had spoken of as a "lucrative" position—the job in a big apple warehouse. The work was too heavy for me. I had struggles all day and every day against fatigue. Even after I had been in the place for months my muscles constantly ached. I had kept going out of pride.

"I'm a man now and must do a man's work. I can't cave in."

At night I went home to my little room. I had walked miles to save railroad fare. I was sick with loneliness.

"What I need is education," I told myself. In the neighborhood where I worked there were a few night schools and I went to one of them. I saw clerks, white collar workers, sitting in the warehouse office and I wanted to be like them.

I had tried to study book-keeping and accounting but it was no go. When I came home from my warehouse at night I put on my one suit of "Sunday clothes" brought from home, and went to school.

It was warm there and I had been in the cold warehouse all day. I sat down at a desk and, at once, my head fell forward and I slept. The teacher, a kind enough young man, came and awakened me.

"You'd better go home to bed. Try again on another evening," he said. I stumbled out of the room, went to my rooming house, fell into bed. I lay in the bed and wept.

And now I was in the army, was a soldier. I felt I had not played quite square with my sister. I was perplexed, uncertain. On the one side there was the dreadful risk of war, of being perhaps wounded, crippled or killed. I was very young. I did not want that. I wanted to live a long rich full life.

On the other hand the warehouse in Chicago. They had said, as employers do at such times, "We will keep your job for you."

The hopelessness of going back to that job, to the long days of toil, the aching muscles, the feeling that I was caught, imprisoned.

"I shall have to spend my life at this, being a mere brute laborer.

"I can never educate myself, rise out of this, be one of the well-dressed successful men I see all about me as I walk in the city streets."

I was in a dark place, there at the edge of the company street and I came to a resolution. I went back into the street.

A cry arose in the street.

"Well, I'll not be a coward, a quitter."

"Nor me."

"Nor me."

I joined in the cry.

There were three or four men of our company who were not going to re-enlist. They said so. Two of them, I remember, said little.

"I'm not going to do it," they said.

The others, I remember, made excuses.

"I've got a job at home. My folks need the money I earn."

I remember the sick feeling of guilt that swept over me when he said that.

The other was a farmer's son. He said his father was sick. He had been hurt, had been kicked by a horse.

"I got to go home and keep things going," he said.

We others formed ourselves into a mob.

Voices arose.

"Let's get 'em. The skunks."

We ran at them. We dragged them out of the side street into the company street.

Part of us grabbed one of the smaller of the men and ran him away to a place of trees. We took each man an arm or a leg. He didn't resist. We beat his buttocks against the tree. He screamed with pain.

It went on for a long time and then it stopped. None of the men who were going home, resisted much. Their clothes were torn and their bodies bruised. None of the officers interfered with us. We gave it up after a time and formed again our little groups.

"I'd never be such a skunk, such a quitter," we said. We felt that we had, each of us, asserted his manhood, and on the next day all marched up and re-enlisted for the war. It was the first time I knew how cruel men in the mass could be.

Yet it happened my re-enlistment turned out all right. Youth forgets quickly and I quickly forgot the rather unfair trick I had done to my brothers and sister by becoming a "hero." And then too perhaps, at home, my sister, in going about, would continually be hearing comments on my heroism.

How were the people of the town to know how sick I was of the job? They would keep telling my sister what a splendid thing I had done. She might become convinced. At any rate she was a good sport. She didn't complain to me.

I was a soldier and I had picked the right war. We of the local military companies of the states were taken into the national service just as we were. Our local companies had been built up on a democratic basis. I had got what I wanted. After my experience as a laborer the drilling seemed to me play. We were well fed. We had warm clothes.

As for myself I did very well as a soldier. We got our monthly pay but it was small, and presently, after a few weeks as a soldier, I started a bank with another man whose name was Burt. We did it on Burt's capital. The idea was to buy up the time of the other soldiers. We were heartless usurers. We loaned a man three dollars and when pay day came, made him return us five. We did it on capital Burt had from his father.

"It is our chance," Burt said. "We will make this man pay.

"We will use it as a starting point to our success."

Burt was a farmer's son who wanted to be an engineer. He wanted to go to college and so did I.

There were always stud poker games going on in some of the company tents.

"They might as well contribute to our education. They will lose it anyway," Burt said.

If they did not lose it at stud poker it would go to some woman of the streets. Burt always contended that we were a moral force and, in any event, we did fairly well. I remember that there was a plot hatched. It was at the end of the war.

This after we had been in Cuba for a year, after we had brought peace, joy and universal happiness to a grateful people! The plot was that all our clients, from our own company and from other companies of our regiment would, during our last month of service, borrow up to the hilt. They would get all our money and then would thumb their noses at us. We fooled them. We hung a sign up over our tent.

"The bank is closed. It has gone out of business."

At the beginning of our war we went south from Cincinnati, through a glorious mountain country—small town boys, farmers' sons seeing the great world. To the railroad stations women and girls came in flocks. They brought big baskets of food. They threw us kisses. There was one little dark-haired girl at one of the towns who gave me a great basket of food. She had put a note in it. The note gave her name and address. She wanted me to write to her and I did. We carried on a correspondence for a year or two. We exchanged photographs. We made to each other vows of love. I sent her picture post cards. I wrote her long letters. I bought a little leather case and put her picture in it. I had heard stories of soldiers in the Civil War whose lives had been saved by a Bible, carried in an inside coat pocket next to the heart. I thought something of this sort might happen to me. I thought that if I did get into a battle and a bullet came singing at me, I would be, of course, in the front rank, charging the enemy. I would be hit. I would be knocked down by the blow, but would quickly arise. I would charge with my comrades over the ramparts. (I don't believe I knew what a rampart was, but I had read of them.)

I remember a certain morning in a tub I shared with Burt and several others. I was in the tub alone and was in a good mood. I had been thinking some of the thoughts set down above. I imagined myself severely wounded in battle.

I was lying on my cot. I breathed with difficulty. I had taken her picture from my pocket and held it in my hand. I imagined a doctor, a grave quiet man leaning over me. He was explaining that her picture in my pocket had saved my life.

"But for it your heart would have been pierced."

He went out and I was alone. I was desperately wounded but I would live.

"Oh, my dear one, my dear one . . . But for you," I cried.

Another soldier had come into the tent and I had been so absorbed that I had not seen him enter. He had heard the cry out of my heart.

"Well, in the name of God, what's this?" he said.

He made a dive at me, trying to get her picture, but I fought him off. I fled but I had presently to come back. It was a long time before I heard the last of it.

Often afterward, perhaps late at night when I was asleep, one of my companions in the tent had been to town, had been drinking freely.

He punched me in the face and I sat up on my cot.

"Oh, my dear one, my dear one," he said.

There is something fascinating in this business of being a soldier—something to be learned here. There is something in men living together, using their bodies day after day in the same way. It explains, I think, why the man who, in his own person, uninspired by the feeling of being a part of a mass of other men, would flee in terror, but given this feeling he will walk calmly up to death.

Hold it and you have an army of so-called heroes. Lose it, let it slip, and you have a disorganized fleeing mob.

There were fellows in our company who knew they were going to death. The officers pinned identification cards on their coats as they went in. This so that later their bodies could be identified. Yet they went in.

In this little understood impulse that is in all men to lose self in the mass, there is a kind of relief from the pain of living. . . .

There is in it something strangely noble, strangely mean.

It can send men to the committing of unbelievably cruel acts they could never do as individuals. It can make common men act like heroes. It explains lynching. It is the strength of fascism. It is labor's greatest weapon. Some day it may be understood, and used.

I remember that before we got to Cuba we were marching along a road, down a hill, across a great valley . . . it might have been two or three miles across the valley . . . we ascended another low hill. My own company must have been somewhere up near the head of the long procession. There was a little cluster of trees at the top of the hill.

With the permission of one of our lieutenants I had dropped out of the ranks. I had a stone in my shoe. The lieutenant was the one who had been a night policeman.

"Duck into the woods. Get out of sight," he said and I ducked. I dare say he did not want other officers to see one of his men leave the ranks.

I was in the wood. I went in far enough not to be seen. I took the stone out of my shoe. I sat down under a tree. We had been marching for hours. I was not weary. It seemed to me that into my legs had come the strength of the legs of thirty thousand men. I had become a giant. I was, in myself, something huge, terrible, and at the same time noble. I remember that I sat, for a long time, while the army passed, opening and closing my eyes. Tears were running down my cheeks.

"I am myself and I am something else too," I whispered to myself.

I remember that later when I got back to camp I did not want to speak to others. I went into my tent and threw myself down on my cot. I did not want to eat. I was a man in love. I was in love with the thought of the possibilities of myself combined with others.

Then came a night in Chickamauga Park when suddenly at perhaps two o'clock . . . we were in our tents . . . games going on. The drums began to beat.

Or rather, I should say, bugles began to sound off.

There was a cry of officers,

"Fall in. Fall in."

We were to strike camp at once.

"Hurry! Hurry!"

There was alarm among the men.

"What's wrong?"

"What's up?"

We rolled up our tents, loaded them on army wagons, packed our knapsacks. We fell into line.

There was a tense silence. Nearly all of us were sons of Civil War men. What stories we had heard of night marches, sudden attacks.

"Stonewall Jackson, at Chancellorsville."

The grim all day fight in the very fields, clumps of woodland along the very road in which we marched.

We marched in darkness.

As in all armies rumors went from lip to lip . . . we spoke in whispers.

"They say. They say."

"They say that our troops are fighting desperately at Santiago in Cuba."

"The Spaniards have cut them all to pieces."

"We are being rushed there."

There was this sudden feeling of dread. It kept on raining. We were marched through the darkness to a little railroad station. There was a long line of cars, some passenger cars, others freight cars. We got aboard.

Such a night. There were men praying. Others wrote letters, to wives, mothers or sweethearts. I was one of the scribblers.

"It may be I am going to my death. I do not know.

"They say."

There were two or three men reading Bibles and one man . . . he at least had his kind of courage . . . he knelt and prayed. I think it likely that most of us would have been all right if it had come to actual fighting. The man who was praying . . . he had been a clerk in a store at home . . . had remembered a sentence.

"O God, let this cup pass from me," he prayed.

There had been, as it was later explained, a protest from politicians. There were a great many thousand men in training at Chickamauga Park near the city of Chattanooga. The soldiers were spending money in Chattanooga. Knoxville wanted some of it. Our regiment, and I believe another regiment, were moved down there. We arrived at Knoxville in the early morning. The trains stopped by a great field and the field was covered with tables. The women of the city of Knoxville had hurried out in force to receive us. The sun was shining. The tables, standing in the field, were loaded with food. I got me a girl there. She waited on one of the tables. I thought she was very beautiful. She was the daughter of a prominent citizen of the town. She was someone I could later write to telling of my adventures. She sent me later a photograph which I afterwards concealed in my pocket, next to my breast. I put her picture with the one I had got from the other young woman seen at a railroad station. I have no doubt that in my letters I declared my undying love for both of them.

We landed on the island of Cuba. We disembarked in a beautiful bay and were marched through the streets of a fine Cuban city. After the battle of Santiago there had been a truce signed. As we soldiers understood it, a part of the agreement with Spain was that the Spanish soldiers, in Cuba, were to be sent back to Spain at America's expense. Many thousands of them, unarmed, had already been marched into the city of Cienfuegos.

Place of a hundred fires.

They were in barracks there.

We were to watch them, guard them.

The men marched straight through the city, the streets thronged.

There were Spanish soldiers standing with hands in pockets. Our bands played. It is to be remembered that we were all Middle-Western boys. Already we had seen mountains, we had been in a ship at sea, we had been in several American cities, in the South we had seen cotton growing, we had jumped off slow-moving trains at the edge of fields, and had plucked cotton bolls to send home . . .

Thousands, perhaps nearer millions of picture post cards went.

Negro life seen.

Before leaving home some of us had never seen a Negro.

And now we were in this strange semi-tropical place. How strange the buildings of the city.

There were little balconies on which stood dark, and to me very beautiful, women.

"I wonder if I can get me a sweetheart here.

"That would be something wonderful."

There were thousands of the Spanish soldiers along the street. At that time apparently the Cuban people all believed that we were saviors.

They cheered us madly.

The Spanish soldiers all about us everywhere now seemed to us harmless enough.

They were for the most part rather small dark men.

Their uniforms looked shabby. As we found out, later that night, they were glad enough to see us come.

I am sure that we looked very strong and valiant.

"Well, you see, after all, we do not need to fight.

"We do not need to kill and be killed."

There was gladness in us.

We were marched out some few miles beyond the city limit . . . it was by this time late evening.

Tents had already been erected.

Some rich American woman had provided the soldiers who were to see service in Cuba with a special kind of tent.

They were set up, well off the ground. We were not to contract malaria.

They were provided with floors. There were rows of comfortable cots.

So we were in camp at the edge of the Cuban city, and were marched up before our colonel. He got on his horse. There was a grim look on his face. He made a speech. We had been sent, some several thousands of us, to the Cuban city, but it had transpired that there was no ammunition for the guns. It was true there were so and so many thousands of us but, in the Cuban city there were three times as many Spanish soldiers. There was a very solemn look on our colonel's face. The responsibility resting upon his shoulders was great. It was a terrible load to bear. There was a tense silence in the camp.

"I have brought you safely here.

"Now I command you, every man of you, to stay in this camp.

"On the man who leaves this camp I will have no mercy. He will be court-martialed at once."

It was early evening and we were in our tents. I went outside. I made a motion with my hand to my comrade Burt.

"Burt," I said, "what do you say? Shall we try it?"

"Yes," he said.

When I had called him out there was no one else in our tent. All the other men, some six or eight of them, quartered in our tent had mysteriously disappeared.

I thought I was being very brave.

We were risking something, disgrace, being court-martialed. I do not believe we knew what it meant, but it sounded bad.

We crept on our bellies along the ground. There was a little path coming down from our camp up to the city and it was black with men.

The whole regiment, all except those unfortunate enough to be on guard, were on the path.

There was another regiment, made up of men from the West Virginia coal mines. Their colonel had also spoken to them.

They were there.

There was another regiment from another state. The men of that regiment were there.

We tramped down into the city.

The citizens were waiting for us.

The Spanish soldiers were waiting.

It was a wild night, a memorable night. It was like the first armistice day in American cities at the end of the World War.

The Spanish soldiers were going home.

Some of them had been in service in Cuba for ten years.

They were half drunk with joy.

There had been the long struggle, the hatred between the army and the citizens.

Now all of that was at an end.

They embraced us.

They bought us drinks.

And many drinks.

And more and more.

We marched arm in arm with them through the streets.

We sang. We shouted. It must have been well on toward morning when Burt and I helped each other along the railroad to our camp.

There were no officers about. Whether or not any of them had gone into the city I don't know.

We fell on our cots. We lay and laughed. We were not afraid.

After all, Burt said, you can't court-martial the whole army.

"Now you look at it.

"You see," he said, "it can't be done."

We had come to free the Cuban people. We were invited to go about, dine in houses. Some of our men had got Cuban sweethearts.

We remained to the end what we had been. Each company was a unit made up of men from one small town and from the farming country about the town.

Our officers were also men of the town. They expected to go back there to live. In the later World War all of this was changed. There were seldom men of the same town in the same company. The men did not know their officers personally, had not gone to school with them, played ball with them.

I have seen a private of our company in a quarrel with our captain. The quarrel went into a fight and the private knocked the captain down, this in our company tent.

The private was not brought to trial.

By the regulations I believe he would have been sent to prison.

Our captain did not want to do that.

Like the rest of us he expected to go back and live his life in our town. He might want to run for office there.

And in any event he wanted to live there. He did not want to have the name of having sent one of our town boys to prison.

I remember later, a long time later, the telling of all this to an English army man I met in London.

He was amused.

"You Americans," he said. He declared that no army could be so loose.

"But ours was," I said.

There was talk of what would have happened had there been a real struggle, a real war. I was of the opinion that, in such a test, we would have stood up to it as well as any army . . . I was of the opinion that had our captain been a man who had won the real support of his men the incident in the company tent could never have happened. The angry private would have been rushed away by his comrades.

It is true that in our army there was all of this looseness. We had got to Cuba.

Well, the war was already won.

Just why we were kept there I do not know.

We were supposed to see that certain Spanish soldiers embarked for Spain.

They were certainly glad enough to go.

We were to quell certain disturbances, were sent out on an expedition.

I was on one such expedition. We went out to hunt bandits. We took a cow along.

There was, at the head of our detachment, a certain major. He was, I was told, the son of a rich man.

He had brought his wife to Cuba. He had brought his baby. He had brought the cow to furnish the baby's milk. We took it with us.

We marched slowly. We went with long strides through a beautiful country. On some days we marched for two hours.

If we saw no bandits they probably saw us. We were very peaceful, a very bucolic enemy. Sometimes we were in a new camp at ten in the morning and we boys had the afternoons to ourselves.

We went for long walks through the country. Some of us had picked up a little Spanish. We went into houses. We talked to people. We hired little native ponies and rode through the country and into the hills.

I was for a time very ill.

There was inadequate medical service, and I was near death.

However I recovered. I got up from my bed and marched again with my comrades. Once, with two coal miners of a West Virginia regiment, I went on an expedition. I met the two miners on the streets of a certain town, near the coast. They had, they said, borrowed a boat.

They had got a file and had filed away a chain.

"We do not intend to steal the boat," they said. "We'll put it back."

"Do you know anything of sailing a boat?" they asked.

I did not know, but I had a theory.

"I think we can work it," I said. We took the boat and sailed away. We went for many miles down the coast. The boat was rather heavy and very easy to upset and gradually we did learn a little how to handle the sails.

Fortunately the wind was fine and the sea was calm. We had put provisions in the boat. In as much as we had borrowed the boat we had set out at night.

We decided to capture a town.

We did capture a town.

"Why not?" we said.

Others had captured towns and besides we had sighted a town.

It was on the coast. It was a small place. It was inhabited by blacks. It had formerly been a plantation town, a working village. It had stood at the edge of a great sugar plantation.

The plantation house had been destroyed.

The Cuban army had done that and the enemy had fled.

They hadn't yet come back.

We went uphill and one of the coal-mining men, who knew a little Spanish, made a speech, a speech answered with many gestures by what we took to be the head man of the town. He was a gigantic black.

He stood before us, there was a little dock in a tiny bay at the foot of the town. He gesticulated. He smiled at us, he embraced us.

"Americanos," he cried.

There was a general cry of voices from men and women. There was a kind of universal embracing.

It became later a dance.

We ordered that to be held.

We ordered wine brought.

It may be that the natives of the town, in the absence of their masters, had formed a soviet.

There was a street of thatched huts and our dance was held in the single village street. It lasted most of an afternoon and night.

There were bonfires built. A woman, bent with age, a kind of leader among the women, was helped up on a table brought into the street. The table had perhaps been salvaged when the plantation house had been burned. I got up on the table with her. I put my arm about her. We danced. Glasses of wine were handed to us. We held them aloft. We rent the air with voices.

For America.

For Cuba.

For freedom.

For joy.

I tell you it was a real surrender. They had given us the town and the plantation and we gave it back.

"Take it. Keep it," we said.

We declared that we were the messengers of a new day. If but our country had done for the island of Cuba what we promised the town of Caratura when it surrendered to us!

5. I Court a Rich Girl

Yes, I had been a farm hand, a laborer, a factory hand, a soldier. I managed now to get a winter at college. This was in Springfield, Ohio. The college was a small Lutheran one called Wittenberg.

(Later they called me back. They gave me a degree.)

The end of the college year was close at hand and I had to go to work. The little money I had saved was all gone. I had been chosen as the class orator. I delivered a speech on the Jews.

I got it all out of books. I spent days in the library, cramming for it. Like John I walked up and down in a room practicing, making gestures. I declaimed. I made quite a speech. We story tellers are also, almost without exception, actors. I have always envied actors. Oh, how I would like to strut the boards.

There was a man who came to hear me speak. He was my brother's friend. He was the advertising manager of the *Woman's Home Companion*. At that time the editorial and business offices of the magazine were still in Springfield, Ohio. My brother Karl at that time was working for the magazine.

It may be that the advertising man had had a few drinks. He had a warm and impulsive nature. I remember that he was a great admirer of Napoleon.

He heard my speech and there was a good deal of applause. It came largely from my friends among the students but the advertising man rushed up to me. He embraced me.

"It was grand, magnificent," he cried. On the spot he offered me a job. He said there was a vacancy in the Chicago office of the magazine.

"I will send you there," he said. There was something Napoleonic about it all. Now I would be a business man. I would have a desk in an office building in a city. I would ride about in trains, travel up and down. I would go into manufacturers' offices. I would wear good clothes. I would become a rising young man.

Of advertising I knew nothing and at once, when I had got to Chicago and had presented myself to the man who was Western advertising manager for the magazine, I could see and feel that I was not very welcome.

I had been employed offhand. It was a gesture. The man who was to be my new boss had not been consulted. Later, he told me frankly that he had had in mind another man for the job.

He was a man from a big Eastern college and he was enthusiastic about his college. He wanted a man who had graduated from his college. Perhaps he wanted to offer the job to some football hero. He had himself been a football player.

I was in an uncomfortable position.

But a thing happened—it was amusing. I was sent to the office of a certain manufacturer. He advertised in magazines, it seemed, sold by what was called the "agate" line. I knew very little of that.

I was afraid. I went by train to the town. The man had written saying that he wanted two hundred lines of space in the magazine, and a mistake had been made by his stenographer. He wanted two thousand lines.

I was afraid and did not dare go into the office. I approached and went away. I came back and again went away.

I walked about. "Of what are you afraid?" I asked myself.

Formerly I had been employed, as workman, in just such a factory. But I was in overalls then. I went in at the factory gate.

At last I did get up courage to enter. I walked timidly in. I can't remember what happened. I stood trembling before the man who had dictated the letter. He must have realized my fright, my confusion.

He was very kind, very good-natured. He corrected the stenographic mistake. I did not have to talk. I had a rate card in my pocket and laid it, with trembling hand, on his desk.

He wrote the order and I went away. I breathed again. I went into a bar and bought myself a drink. Perhaps later I put it on my expense account. I had got an idea. I sent a wire, not to the company's Western manager in Chicago, but to the man, his superior, in the Ohio town who was an admirer of Napoleon, who had hired me.

"I have called on my first man," I said in the wire. "The order was raised from two hundred lines to two thousand lines." I said nothing of the eloquence used in getting the order raised—as suggested I had used none—I knew little enough of advertising but already, perhaps, my experience, in knocking about, had taught me something of men. I expected and what I expected came true. I returned to Chicago. There was a wire on my new boss's desk. I had got a sharp raise.

Naturally, I did not tell my boss, in the Western office, how it had happened. He knew nothing of the wire I had sent. He stood before me with a blank puzzled air. He was temporarily my boss but the man who had sent the wire to him, was his superior.

"I think he has gone a little crazy," he said, but I only smiled. I thought, that, after all, I might manage to make my way, even among the shrewd men of business.

And so, of a sudden, I am lifted up into a new world of well-dressed young men. As it turns out I couldn't sell advertising but I could write advertisements.

I now advance rapidly. I have twenty-five dollars a week, then thirty-five, forty, fifty, seventy-five. I buy new clothes, hats, shoes, socks, shirts. I walk freely on Michigan Boulevard in Chicago, go to drinking parties, meet bigger and bigger business men.

I create nothing. I boost, boost. Words of glowing praise for this or that product of some factory flow from under my pen.

I am a new man. Now, in the advertising agency the word is out that I am something of a genius. I play up to it. I strut, carry a cane. I let my hair grow long, aim to be a bit original in my dress. I do not wear neckties. I get brightly colored strips of cloth, from remnant counters in department stores, shove the two ends through an antique finger ring I have bought. I begin to wear spats. I even buy a dinner coat.

What a boy.

What a boy.

I am called into what is called a conference in the advertising agency. These conferences are always being held. They go on indefinitely. Some client of the house has become dissatisfied.

When my turn comes to speak, if the client is present, I insult him. Sometimes I walk up and down, run my hand through my long hair.

"You are talking like a fool," I say to the client.

Often it works. He begins to respect me. Every story teller worth his salt, as I have said, is also an actor and, although I do not yet know it, I am essentially just that, a story teller.

✦

It is always possible, if you have at all a subtle mind, to get around others. The man who wrote the book, *How to Make Friends and Influence People,* a book recently so popular, had something on the ball.

It was in me, this faculty. I wanted, for example, to put over some idea to a client, some rich manufacturer.

I did not put it forward as my own idea.

"Do you remember a conversation we had some weeks ago?

"You said so and so."

He had said nothing of the sort.

"What you said gave me an idea. Here it is."

For a moment a puzzled look in his eyes and then, usually, he swallowed the bait.

"Oh yes, I do remember."

It had been in me always, a rather nasty trait. Even when I was a small boy I used to practice it on my sister and on some of my brothers.

My sister had made a certain declaration.

I smiled.

"Now you wait," I said to myself. "Within a week I'll make you say the opposite of that. You have this belief, or think you have. I'll destroy it."

I went to work on her, never attacking directly. It was a game. I made flattering little remarks, dropped suggestive hints. When I got her where I wanted her, I had a nasty feeling of triumph.

"See what I have done, eh? How smart I am."

A man grows slick, foxy, smooth. In business it often pays good dividends. The world is full of it. It is one of the faculties men and women develop that most separate us, one from another. Real friendships are not made in that way.

For a time it wasn't so bad. They sent me to towns and cities where there were factories. I went to a Kentucky town. There was a man who made a machine for digging ditches, for making terraces on hillside land.

I had his catalogue and there was a series of twelve or fifteen advertisements to be written. They were to go into papers read by farmers.

I was in the train going to that town and, as I sat in the train, I wrote the advertisements.

However I did not show them to the man in the Kentucky town.

It was, I thought, a nice place to be. When I got to the town I went at once to the factory.

"Look here," I said to the man who made the machine to dig ditches and make terraces. "I cannot do this job offhand."

"This is a serious matter," I said.

He had shown me through his factory.

"A man needs time to think."

I suggested to him that the people in the Chicago office who had sent me to him might want to hurry me.

"You write them a letter. You tell them you want to keep me here for a week."

It was cheating. I was fighting something. I wanted a little leisure. I wanted to walk about the streets of the Kentucky town, look at people, talk to people. I wanted to sit in the hotel room trying to put down my impressions.

"It is a war. I am fighting for a little time, to mature a little."

Every day I went to the factory, spending an hour there. I went into the office.

"I'm thinking. I want to get this thing just right," I said.

I had gained days and nights, away from the clatter, the eternal nervous rush of the Chicago advertising office. At the end of the week I showed the man the advertisements I had written on the train.

"They're wonderful," he said. He said it showed what could be done if you took your time for it.

"You're the man for me. You don't just come here, spend an hour or two, rush away on the next train."

Oh, the precious days and nights gained, a chance to walk about at night in the streets of an Ohio River town, go and stand on the river banks, talk to men met there.

But I was on the up-and-up. The advertisements I had written for the Kentucky manufacturer were very successful. I bought a long black morning coat, such as congressmen wore, got striped trousers, patent leather shoes, a silk hat.

I had a leather case for the silk hat. I bought long evening clothes. I had one of the sort of tall hats that fold up flat.

You snap it and there you are. You can go to the theater. People will think you are rich, a rich young blade.

On Sunday morning I went to church, to a fashionable preacher who preached in a Loop theater. The preacher spoke of a settlement, on the West Side, in a poor district. It was a settlement maintained by the fashionable congregation. The preacher said they wanted workers, volunteers, who would go at night to the settlement. There were classes for tough young boys. They wanted teachers, he said.

"All right," I said to myself. "I'll go there, I'll volunteer."

I don't know now just what I had in mind. I wanted to be free. I did not want to work any more in the advertising place. It may be that I thought, "I'll get me a rich girl over there. I'm pretty good-looking," I may have thought. "And now I've got all of these good clothes."

Anyway I did volunteer. I went there for a time, at night, when I was in the city. I went two or three times a week.

And sure enough there the rich girl was.

They had a library and she sat at a desk and gave out books. "She's a pretty good-looker," I thought.

She was small and dark. She had black hair and small black eyes. I might have been twenty-two or -three and she would have been at least twenty-eight.

However her body still seemed young to me and I began to court her.

I had the class of boys and I was teaching American history. It was all right. I had read a lot. I read to them.

However they were restless. They kept coming in and going out of the room where I sat talking and reading aloud.

"What's the matter, kids? Why do you keep coming in and going out?"

The kids explained. They wanted to smoke and so did I.

The kids liked me all right. They liked my clothes.

"Gee, you wear swell clothes," one of them said to me.

"I'll bet you're rich," he said.

We could not smoke in the room in the settlement house so I took them outside. This was in the summer and we went along the street, past dark factory buildings, to where there was a high footbridge over some railroad tracks.

There was a street light up above and we stood on the footbridge under the light.

I told them about Grant at Vicksburg. I told them about Lee and Stonewall Jackson. I told them about the Mexican War and how we gypped the Mexicans out of the whole Southwest. I told them about how we got Texas and how big it was.

And then I got fired. There was an older woman, who ran the settlement house, and she told me I couldn't take the kids out of the house.

"You are encouraging the children in smoking," she said. She said it wasn't allowed.

"Oh, tell her to go to hell," the kids said, but I didn't do that. I quit.

I had, however, got in with my rich girl; had begun to court her hard. At night when the settlement closed I waited for her.

"I'll escort you home," I said.

"But I'm not afraid. I only go to the street car."

She said something that shocked me a little. She said that her father had wanted to send a car to the settlement house for her but that she wouldn't let him.

"It would seem too much like setting myself up above the people down there," she said. I didn't know why her saying that shocked me but it did. For a minute I thought, "Oh, the hell with you," but I didn't say it.

I thought, "If I was rich I'd be rich and not pretend I wasn't."

"All right, I'll take you to the street car," I said. I rode home with her in the car. I held her hand. After a time, after a few nights, when we had got to the North Side where she lived, we began to get off the car before we got to her house.

It was a big house, with an iron fence. It was right where all of the richest people in Chicago lived at that time. It was near the lake.

So we walked along.

"Let's go over by the lake," I said.

"No, I must get home," she said, but after I had said it a few times she went with me. We were there by the lake and the park on the hot summer nights. We were walking there. We were sitting on benches. We kissed. After a time we kissed a lot. She was one who when you made her any kind of proposal always said no.

She said no but she didn't mean it. We were on a bench in the dark and there were other couples on other benches in the dark. We did as they did.

"It's common. They are just common people," she said.

"Yes, they're common," I said.

"Rich or poor," I said to her, "there are certain common things they do and we do.

"They kiss and we kiss," I said. I kissed her some more.

I decided we should become engaged. When I was with her it was all right, but when I had left her I began to question myself.

"Do you want her or do you just think she's rich?" I asked myself.

I didn't know which it was. Her father was the head of a big wholesale house in the city so I looked him up. There was a Dun and Bradstreet book in the office where I worked and I went to that. He was rich all right.

She had already told me that there were only two children in her family, herself and a sister. "I'm twenty-three," she said, "and sister is eighteen."

"When you see my sister you won't want me," she said. I thought she had clipped about five years off of her age. Her sister's name, she said, was Grace.

I kept at her. I had got started and didn't stop, and for a long time she kept saying no and then, one night she said she would.

"All right. I guess maybe I'll marry you, I'm not sure," she said. She had her head on my shoulder as we sat on a park bench and when she said it, in a kind of low frightened voice, she began to cry.

I thought, "I do love her. I do. I do."

She said she'd have to take me to her house. I'd have to come and live there. I'd have to meet her father and her sister. Her mother, she said, was dead.

"You'll have to get acquainted and then you'll have to ask father. It'll be up to him," she said.

So I dressed up in my evening clothes and I went to that house. I had a close shave. I had my hair cut. I was pretty near an hour picking out a necktie to wear.

I had bought a Tuxedo.

"Shall I wear it?" I asked myself. First I decided I would and then that I wouldn't. I did wear it at last.

She had told me to get there at seven but I got there at six, so I took a walk. It had got to be late fall and it was already nearly dark.

I walked about, up and down. I looked at houses. I thought, "Maybe, some day, we'll live in one of these houses."

I remembered the little yellow house by the swamp where I had spent so much of my boyhood, the gravelly back yard where nothing would grow. I remembered my mother, grown so thin at the washtub, and the carriage and big house I had planned some day to buy her. And then I remembered myself, working as a day laborer down by the river on that same Chicago North Side. And now here I was, in evening clothes, all shaved and perfumed and I was going to dine in a millionaire's house. I was going to ask him for his daughter's hand. I'd have servants to wait on me. I'd ride about in a big car with a chauffeur.

And then it was seven o'clock. I went to the door of the house and rang the bell.

A butler in a uniform let me in and I had to wait for quite a long time and then the rich man came. He was a little man and kept tipping up on his toes. He was trying to make himself feel taller than he was. He had a little red face, a small nose and he had a bald path over the top of his head. There were a few hairs growing above his ears and they had been carefully brushed over the bald place but they didn't cover it much.

He came and sat with me.

"Well, well, young man?" he said.

"Let's see, did you come here to see Mary or is it Grace?

"Are you going to stay to dinner?"

He kept talking. He took a gold watch from his pocket.

"What's your prospects, young man. What's your prospects?" he asked but he didn't wait for an answer.

He held the gold watch in his hand and got up and came to me. He stood before me.

"It strikes," he said. He had moved the hands around to eight o'clock and a sharp little sound came from the watch. It struck eight times.

"It cost a lot of money," he said. "Do you want to hear it strike again?"

Mary came into the room, dressed pretty swell, in a low-necked dress and then Grace came and right away I began to have a hard time keeping my eyes from staring at her.

She wasn't specially dressed up as Mary was. She was tall, strong-looking and a blonde. She had bluish gray eyes. I thought the moment she came into the room that she wasn't any more like Mary than I was like her father.

"Mary's been telling her about us," I thought and I had a feeling of resentment and fear. The moment I saw Grace I knew she was the kind of woman I'd like a lot.

I'd been sitting there thinking about the father. He was a rich man, a millionaire.

"He must sure have inherited the business he's in," I had been thinking. I wondered who ran it for him. I was pretty young then but I had noticed something. I was working in that advertising place.

So there was this man, in his rich man's house, with his trick watch. He was like an old child.

There were all kinds of expensive furniture in the room and there were oil paintings on the wall.

The little millionaire didn't pay any attention to his daughters. He concentrated on me. He began leading me around the room, explaining the oil paintings to me. He told me how much each one cost.

There was a big one of a nude woman. He winked at me when we came to that. "It cost thirty thousand dollars. Think of that, thirty thousand," he said.

I didn't know what to say. I looked at the two daughters. I could see that Mary was annoyed but that Grace was amused. There was laughter in her eyes.

"It's all right to have a nude like that in your house if it's by some famous painter," the millionaire was assuring me.

"Oh, father, do come and sit," Mary said.

"Quit talking," she said.

I could see that she was sore at him.

"She's got a temper," I thought. I liked Grace for being amused. "I'll bet she wouldn't go to any settlement house or try to do good to people like Mary's been doing," I thought. Once when I had been on my way home from the settlement house with Mary she had begun talking about what a noble impulse it was in me that I had come to the settlement house to help teach the kids and I had wanted to laugh.

"Oh, I guess I just did it for an adventure, to see what it would be like," I had said to her.

And then I had said something—a kind of half-truth—about having gone over there hoping to find some woman like her.

"Maybe I'm just after a rich one like you," I said and that had started her off.

She had got very serious about it. She scolded me. She said she didn't think I should deny my own noblest impulses. She said something about devoting her own life to the working classes.

"But if I was rich I'd just be rich," I said. I said that if what she called the working classes ever got anywhere they'd have to do it themselves. I was going on like that and then, when I saw she was really getting sore, I let up on her.

This was on a street car when I was riding home from the settlement with Mary, and it was on a street car that I lost her and lost the chance to be the son-in-law of the millionaire.

Over at the house that night, during the dinner and afterwards, as we sat about and tried to talk, the little millionaire kept cutting up his capers. He kept making the watch strike for me. All evening he kept the watch in his hand and when the talk died down . . . Mary was doing most of the talking . . . she was acting nervous . . . she was ashamed of her father . . . Grace said hardly a word but her eyes kept laughing . . . when the talk died down the father explained about the watch.

"They gave it to me. My employees gave it to me," he said. "It cost a lot of money, hundreds of dollars," he added. He kept saying it, but afterwards I found out that he had little or nothing to do with the running of the business with which his name was connected. He had inherited the business from his father and it was run for him by other men. The man who told me said the others flattered the little millionaire, that they pretended to consult him.

I was there that night to ask the man if I could marry his daughter Mary and I didn't do it. She may have said something to him, as I was sure she had to Grace. Every once in a while, that evening, he would come over to me.

"What's your prospects, young man? What's your prospects?" he kept asking but I didn't answer him. I couldn't. Every time he asked it I could see that Grace was getting more and more amused and Mary getting more annoyed and angry.

And so, after a time, I left. I was at the door and the little man was standing with the watch in his hand and there were Grace and Mary. I could feel that Mary wanted to hit her father and that Grace wanted to laugh at all of us.

I left. I was outside in the street. I began laughing at myself.

"Great God," I thought. I tried to imagine myself married to Mary and living in that big house with her father.

"If it was Grace now," I thought. I thought that if I had got a start with Grace before I met Mary and if I had the luck to have her take a fancy to me we could have had a lot of fun. "She's one of that sort that can be onto herself and others," I thought. Grace, I figured, was stuck with Mary and her father. She could, I was sure, be kind to them, but at the same time, I thought, she would be one who could get some fun out of it all.

I had asked Mary to marry me so I thought I'd better see her again and I had her downtown to dine with me and it was a most uncomfortable dinner. "Shall I tell her it's all off?" I kept asking myself, but I put it off and then, when it came time for her to go home, she wouldn't take a cab.

It was some kind of an idea she had got into her head. She wanted to be one of the common people. She said something like that.

"No," she said, "you mustn't be spending your money on me." You see I had told her, on other evenings, of how, when I had first come to the city, I had to work as a laboring man. I had even pointed out places where I had worked.

"I had to live and try to keep my sister and two younger brothers on two dollars a day," I had said to her. I had rather spread it on, made it as thick as I could and now I think that she, in allowing me to kiss her, in agreeing to the engagement between us had thought that, by marrying me, she would herself become what she thought she longed to be—one of the people.

I may have got that thought that night when I was at her father's house or I may have got it later, on the night when she was dining with me. At any rate I had the thought and when I had it I began to think of Grace.

"She would have known," I thought. In fancy I could hear Mary telling her of our engagement and explaining why she wanted to marry me. It had been the reason Grace was so amused when I came to the house.

I was in the street with Mary and we were waiting for her street car and when it came, bound for the North Side, it was crowded with men. It had been raining while we dined but the rain had stopped. There was a crowd of men, working men, I thought, on the platform at the rear of the car and we were being jostled about.

There was a man stepped on the toe of Mary's shoe. It may be that I had made her angry. She wanted me and she didn't want me. In the restaurant, when we were dining, she had said something about Grace and me.

"You liked her?" she asked, and "Yes, a lot," I had answered.

It had set me off. I had been thinking that I ought to tell her then that, after all, perhaps we had better not marry, but I couldn't get up the courage.

So I had talked of Grace.

"There is something about her that reminds me of my mother," I said. I had said that and had launched off, describing a kind of woman I thought Grace might be, one, I said, who even if she had to lead a life of hardship, instead of being a millionaire's daughter, would be bound to have some fun out of life.

"You know," I had said, "the kind that knows something of what is going on among the people around her, the kind that is onto you but you don't care if she is."

I had got going like that and, as it gave me something to talk about, I had kept it up. I had been at it in the restaurant and I was still at it as we stood in the wet street waiting for the car.

It had been all about Grace, all about what I thought Grace's kind of woman to be, and she had grown more and more angry but I hadn't noticed. I was too absorbed with what I was saying.

And then we were on the rear platform of that car and there were a lot of working men, who have to wear the same clothes day after day, and they smelled pretty rank after the rain.

They stank. They were pushing and shoving.

"There you are, gal. Now you are one of the people. How do you like it?" I was thinking. I may even have given her a shove or two myself. And then the big man stepped on her foot.

He was big all right. He was in greasy overalls and he was standing on her foot and she grew suddenly furious. There was something in her that came out with a rush.

"You big brute," she cried. She began to swear. "She sure has become one of the people now," I thought. "God damn you, get off of my feet," she screamed. She kept on screaming and all the men on the platform began to laugh at her.

The big man who was standing on her foot was laughing and it made her so angry that she began to strike at him with her fists.

"God damn you. God damn you," she was screaming. "She must have learned to swear like that over at the settlement house," I thought. I had got into a kind of joyous ironic mood. I wished her sister Grace was there.

"But Grace wouldn't be enjoying this as I am doing. She'd be too decent," I thought.

What else I thought I don't know. It was the end of my chance to be the rich man's son-in-law. While she was standing there on the crowded platform of the car, striking with her little white fists at the big man, a worker, who was laughing at her, I had dropped off of the car. I never saw her again.

6. The Golf Ball

As a boy in my Ohio town I had been half the young hustler and half the dreamer who wanted to sit forever looking at people, listening, wondering about people. In the town it was the dreamer that was remembered. Only last year I saw and talked with a man who had been my boyhood companion.

"What was I like then? What was your impression?" I asked and he told me that he remembered me only as a lazy fellow, sitting on the curb on the main street or before the little frame hotel at evening, listening to the tales told by traveling men. Or I sat with my back against a barn wall listening to men talking within a barn or to women gossiping in the kitchen of a nearby house.

"But whose barn? We had no barn back of our house."

"No. It was our barn. You would be listening to my sisters and to mother talking in our kitchen."

"Ah! And so I was at it even then?"

"I would come out of the house. I wanted you to go play ball with me or to go with me to bring home the cows.

"I remember your sitting there, your eyes glassy, and that I walked over and stood before you. I shouted but you did not hear. I had to lean over and hit you before I could get your attention.

"With a book in your hand you were ten times worse."

"But," I protested, "I was called Jobby."

"You were both a hustler and bone lazy," he said. "I do, now that you speak of it, remember periods of intense activity, when you worked feverishly at any job you could get. You used to go about at such times declaring your determination to be a rich man, the most powerful man in the state, and when we others laughed you wanted to fight."

If the two things had been in me at the beginning, it is certain that, in the period I am about to record, the hustler had won. About this time I visited my home town and people spoke of a change in me. There was an old carriage builder who stopped me on the street. I was about to hurry past. "Stop," he cried. "There isn't any fire." I stopped and we talked, I speaking of my fine prospects in life and he said to me, stepping a little away and looking, "Why, you have changed," he said. "When you were here, living here, a kid here, you used to pull your words and now you speak crisply. And you look so like a hustler. When you were here you were always sitting lost in your dreams."

I had grown to hate advertising and returned to Ohio, to a town neighboring the one where my youth had been spent. I have spoken of myself as having become a manufacturer but really I wasn't a manufacturer. I was in house paint—as a salesman who had got control of a factory. Most of the factories were already being run and controlled not by the mechanically-minded men who had invented the things being made but by financiers, and I was one of the slick ones. I dare say I never did make any first-rate house paint. There were always traveling men coming to my office to show me some substitute for the more expensive ingredients I had been using and usually I bought. All the time I had a kind of pride in my ability as a word slinger and most people who buy house paint are, like the people who are sold anything else, at bottom probably yaps. I was plausible, thought faster than most people, was always putting others in the wrong.

You readers must know what this means in America, this being plausible—a ready salesman. In America no one buys anything. In America everything, even art, is sold to people.

And as I had picked up ideas about selling goods by mail by my earlier experience as an advertising writer, presently money came rolling in. I do not mean to say that I was rich or even on the borderline of anything like great riches but I had learned how men get rich. There is something you do. You strike upon an idea.

Or there is some man you have stumbled across quite accidentally—it may not be an accident. The hunger for money begets schemes for getting money. Some mechanic has invented some mechanical contrivance, or another man has invented a process for refining oil. There are always men working in the mechanical world making inventions, discovering secrets they do not know how to sell. You hop aboard. O individualism! O survival of the fittest! O rugged individualist! And here your word-fellow comes in. This new thing you have got your hands on must be rammed down people's throats. Up and at 'em, boy!

I will admit that to the clever man there is a kind of temporary excitement in all this. You get money and money brings possessions. Now for the fine house on the principal street of your town. You have become a solid middle-class citizen of your town.

But where do we go from there?

Wait. There are places to go. You have got a talent now, the talent for getting money. Cultivate it. Go on. You have found a method. Expand it. You may well land among the great ones.

But are these great ones of America's past, that is to say the "heroes" that a man in middle-life may look back upon, are they really great?

There is that annoying question.

I had gotten into the position described, the money beginning to roll in, my house on a good enough street. I was married and already had children. If I went on, doing over and over the tricks I had learned, I told myself, there was no special reason why I should not establish a family of my own. We Andersons had been down long enough. If my father had stayed in the Southern state from which he said he came, we would have sunk into the hopeless class of poor whites. But I, Sherwood Anderson, was going to be something different. I was going to be a rich man, establish my family. We were in this respectable house now, the biggest and best that, at least up to that time, I had ever lived in; but I told myself that it was nothing. "Wait and see," I often said to myself as I walked along the street toward my house at evening. "Next year a bigger house; and after that presently, a country estate." I had no idea that we would stay in the town we were then in. The stopping in that town, perhaps for a few years, was but an incident. I had to find out how things were done in the American business world. "Talk a good deal about honesty but keep your eyes open and when the chance comes slip it over on them," I often at that time said to myself, laughing as I said it. Of course this may all be somewhat twisted, but I am trying to put down what went on in me at that time. I think I did realize that I had a good mind and I remember that often, even then, I said to myself that it wasn't the stealing, robbing others, cheating others, that ruined a man, but that what did ruin him was getting to the place where he did not know he was stealing.—You see what I mean, a man trying to make himself a success in the American business world of that day and at the same time keeping an honest mind. An impossibility, to be sure.

As for the family—when the time came, I'd send my children off to some fashionable Eastern university. None of this Middle-Western stuff for my sons and daughters—Yale or Harvard at least for my sons and some place like Smith or Bryn Mawr for my daughter. Oh gorgeous future. My wife in swell gowns all day long with a cloud of servants about to wait on her.—You see that it was all to be in the end a kind of decoration of self, the woman who happened to be my wife not at all considered, my children never considered.

Still, as I have tried to suggest, there was something else in the air. In trying to make a kind of background for the story I would like to tell, I am representing myself here as a young American business man, as a good deal of a Babbitt, but I was never very completely that. No man really is. Look at President Harding. Poor old dear. It is the most natural thing in the world for men of this kind to lie to themselves. It is so easy to do—I know I must have done it constantly.

To play the game was the thing, and men who did play the game were looked up to with respect. Well, we all wanted that, the respect of others. I know I did.

I did at any rate when I was at the office of my factory, in the bank, where I was arranging for the extension of a loan, at some public meeting, or even when walking alone in the streets. In the street I looked about to see if I was observed.

My point is . . . the picture I am trying to give here is of a man not easy flowing, in fact terribly self-conscious. I was that and hated it in myself.

I was doing the thing millions of Americans do, trying to make my life and my work at that time, which was of no importance, seem important. Having been a slow-moving dreamy boy I had made myself into this crisp thing that hurried to an office, sat at a big desk, rang bells, got suddenly and sometimes nastily executive. Do this and that, I cried to others. . . .

Someone had organized a golf club in the town. And I had begun going there in the afternoon. A business man needs exercise. No man likes to get fat.

"I tell you what—I sit too many hours a day at my desk."

"We men who have responsibilities—"

So I played golf, to ease my tired brain that wasn't really tired. It is an old story. After all, the amount of real energy put into work by the average man of business generally is small. This was known to me already as a Chicago advertising writer. I knew about the men who got the most money from advertising, the solicitors, salesmen, contact men. These men going to the Chicago Athletic Club, going off to play golf with clients. Coming back to hurry into the office. "I am so busy."

Busy, hell!

It may have been the golf playing, chasing the little white ball over the Ohio fields, just such fields as I had once worked in—planting cabbage in fields—cutting and husking corn in fields—that finally started me. A good stiff drink at the nineteenth hole. "I tell you what—let's you and me skip off to Cleveland some night next week. My wife is out of town. I know a pair of little blondes." I had already been unfaithful to my wife. Most of the bright young business men I knew were. Why not? There was so apparently a hole somewhere in our own lives, and our wives—I dare say most of them were thinking of their children, not of us. I must have begun looking with open eyes at the other men.

There was evidence enough in these my companions in the new sport of what my friend Paul Rosenfeld afterwards called "the American mouth." There was a queer tired droop to all their mouths. What was wrong?

What indeed was wrong with all of us?

Later I told myself that at the time when I was a boy there had been a great and glowing faith in Americans. It has weakened since. That is the obvious reason for the puzzled uncertainty about life in America as I write, but at that time no man much doubted our great destiny. We Americans had got into that great empire, the Middle West, the real body of America, the great fat land stretching from the Appalachian Mountains to the Rockies, and had built our towns and cities. The land had opened slowly at first . . . then had come what we now call the industrial revolution. The pace of life that had been set by the horse, the ox, and the plow, was being set in my time by the locomotive. Great trains roaring through the Ohio towns. On to the West! New towns and cities still to be made to the west. Thomas Jefferson had died thinking it would take two thousand years to settle America and he had hardly been dead a hundred years. Look at us go, boy!

In my own family there had been something which made us "go."

It may have been my mother's influence. On her deathbed she told us frightened youngsters, gathered in, that we were made of a special clay. "I do not fear to leave you. You are of the stuff of which kings are made."—What nonsense! The poor woman could not have said that but she did say something that fixed a certain impression on our minds. Of that I am quite sure. We had all been stung by something and knew in our hearts that we were not to remain as we were, really of the very poor laboring class.

But what was wrong with labor? Obviously there *was* something wrong with labor in the forests and fields of early America. Probably the heavy brutality of it. I myself had been rather a slight boy and had been compelled to work the long twelve-hour day of that time, in the corn-cutting, the cabbage-planting, at the digging of ditches and the shoveling of coal and earth until my bones ached, and in the morning, in some cheap rooming house or in a farmhouse at dawn, I had been compelled to fairly pry myself out of bed and walk about the room naked, slowly lifting one aching leg after the other to get the stiffened joints to working again.

That must have been the tone of life in early America, say in my father's youth. The South had escaped it by bringing in slave labor, but in New England and the East . . . Well, I have always thought, since I saw the play one night in New York, that the figures of the two sons who went off to California in Mr. Eugene O'Neill's play, *Desire Under the Elms,* those dumb creatures, tied to the soil and brow-beaten by the arrogant old father—that grim hard European peasant life transferred to America—I have always thought that was the true note of early New England.

Then had come the machine, and oh the faith in it! It must be true that a nation, the tone of a nation, is made by the necessity of the land, and that America was so big, the Middle West so wide-spread, that the mechanical flair that came into its people and became a part of its people was inevitable.

The machines had come with a rush. Everyone was inventing, but my own impulses did not run to mechanical invention.

What then?

Why not be a salesman? If you cannot *make* the new age, try to help *sell* it. There is the place for you word fellows in such a time.

But, whoa! Something has struck me. Do you suppose, dear American readers—if I write this book as I should I am quite sure no one but an American will ever quite understand it—do you suppose that we—Americans—human beings dropped down as we were in such a glorious continent, have always been rather buffaloed by the land itself? That is at least an idea. We do not feel so damn superior to any other people, even the English whom we beat. Do you suppose the land has got us that way?

It is such a goddamn grand land.

Perhaps God, when he let Christopher Columbus discover us, should have been considerate enough to invent a new people to occupy the glorious land he let Columbus stumble onto. It's an idea, as we old advertising men love to say.

Return with me now to my manufacturing time in Ohio. I had gotten into it and there was something wrong. I was on the road to prosperity, and if I kept on, to riches—I was on the way to being at least one of the smaller American kings and why not the American house-paint king—and I was sick. There was a queer kind of stoppage of something at the center of myself.

Was the sickness in me general among men of my sort? Do not think me egotistical. It is to be borne in mind that all of this attempt to think out my own situation at that time has this meaning—that I believe myself and have always thought of myself as a very typical American. That is the only justification for this book, for all this word slinging.

I will not attempt to answer the question.—There I was playing golf in the afternoon, and something happened. There are these moments that come in all lives. There are in any life certain moments intensely remembered ever afterwards. Here again comes something that has always puzzled me. Does a man's life, then, consist of hundreds of little revolutions?

I was playing with three other bright young business men of the town and suddenly at the fourth or fifth hole I deliberately sliced my ball and drove it far off its course into a neighboring corn field. I went after it, remember very vividly climbing over a barbed wire fence and into that corn field and one of my companions shouting at me.

"Aw, let it go, Anderson," he called, and suddenly something cracked in me.

I stood there in that corn field, having walked perhaps a hundred paces from the fence. The corn was already knee-high. Another plowing and it would be ready to lay by. There was a wood beyond the corn field and I walked toward it muttering. I found myself muttering, "You go to hell, you bastard," to myself.

At whom were the words addressed? The man who had called to me was a young Jew. He was one of the bright young business men of the town and I think owned a department store there. He had walked down to the fence that separated the golf course from the corn field and stood looking over. "You go to hell," I muttered, being careful that he did not hear and pretending to look on the ground under the corn for my ball, putting the corn aside with the golf club held in my hand and then, gaining temporary control of myself, I spoke, telling him to go on. I said, "I've got a splitting headache. I hate to break up our foursome but I've got to go back to the club house." I walked obliquely across the field pretending I was going toward the club house but in reality making toward the woods, and, after a moment's hesitation, he went back to join the others.

It had begun. What?

I went on my way that day, walking across the corn field, looking back at the others, at the men of that foursome, men who were my friends in that town. One or two of them were in deals with me. They had money in ventures of mine.

I kept watching them furtively. There was talk among them, a foursome spoiled. "Hell, what do you suppose is the matter with him?" "If he had a headache, why the hell didn't he say so before we got up this foursome?"

There must have been something, perhaps a kind of warm male comradeship in life sought. I had already read Whitman. The night was my reading time—after all, the town where I had my factory was not yet a city. The night life was, to say the least, meager. The wife I had got—I never knew her. She was, I dare say, absorbed in her children—our children—American children. Was there ever such a people as the Americans for always looking to the children, vaguely hoping they may live, may get something out of life we actual Americans do not quite dare let ourselves take? "Why not to bed and a book?" I said to myself. I had fixed up a room in my house to which I fled, and there was a cot in the room, a table and books. I had got a passion for history and spent long evenings reading the story of man's efforts. "Why was I not a soldier?" I asked myself.

That night I went home in a silent sullen mood, and after eating, looking at my children, fled upstairs to my room.

"But what's the matter, dear?" This from my wife.

Matter? How was I to know? I went upstairs to the room, and shutting the door, locked it. "I have to work," I called down to her.

"But I too have a life to live. All day I stay here attending to these children and then in the evening you go off by yourself."

I have put down the words as the probable thoughts of the woman. In reality I do not know what she thought. I had got a certain feeling about my house and my room and I think I had better try to speak of that here.

"There must be a place, some place," I had said to myself. I had selected this room in a wing of the house, upstairs, a room to which the noises of the house did not penetrate often, and had furnished it myself, after my own fashion, keeping it very plain, a plain flat-topped desk, unpainted, and two chairs, the cot to sleep on, my books. I had got a special lock put on the door and kept the key in my pocket.

"But how will it be cleaned?" my wife asked and "Never mind. I'll clean it myself," I had answered. I did. Well, there was no use unnecessarily hurting her feelings. I had become canny. "Wait until she has taken the children out for a walk," I used to say to myself and when she had left the house I would run down into the kitchen and get a pail and a cloth. There was a huge Negro woman in the kitchen and it was from her and her attitude toward me that I got the impulse for the book written long afterwards, a book called *Dark Laughter*. The laughter of the Negro woman in that book, house servants in another house, in a town down on the Ohio River, was the same laughter I had heard coming from the lips of the Negro woman servant in my own house. I ran down the stairs and spoke to her. "Quick, Kate, a pail of warm water, and some cloths." She stood looking at me, the laugh beginning to form about her lips.

"And some soap, please."

The laughter came and she went to get me what I wanted. She was hired to do certain work in our house but if I wanted to do it what did she care? I took the pail of water, the soap and cloths and ran up the stairs and she came to the foot of the stairs to see me go. She put her hands on her hips. How huge, how black she was! A little game had begun between us. Sometimes I stopped at the head of the stairs and stood looking down at her. The wife and the children had gone out of the house. There was just this big black woman and myself. She was laughing at me, her laughter ringing through the house and, as I stood looking down at her, I also laughed.

"O you worried, neurotic whites, always trying to solve things. So you think it important that you do something with your lives?"

I stood looking down at her. Were those her thoughts?

Certainly not.

She wasn't thinking at all. She was amused.

"But oh," I thought, "if some white woman who might conceivably love me, who would be willing to live with me, would but be willing to take the attitude toward me this Negro woman now takes.

"There's a thought. There's an idea to play with," I told myself, going on up into my room and closing the door.

In the room I could be what I pleased. I had already read *Sartor Resartus,* and at home, when I was a lad, my father in his rare gay moments had often sung a ballad . . .

> Fair words can make fair songs, me lad,
> But it's the clothes that make the man.

That might be it. The room into which I had got was then but another suit of clothes to cover my nakedness. "Uncover not thy father's nakedness." There was my own nakedness, the naked fact of myself, my own figure in the little world of men and women about me, a subtle kind of cheating I was always practicing. I couldn't face it yet. "I will not be myself. I will not admit to myself that what I am I am," I cried in my closed room.

I escaped out of myself. I had enough of my father in me to be often quite silly. I had been reading, let us say, a life of Napoleon—he being the hero of more than one young American business man—and I had got, in a store in Cleveland, some little lead toys which I had brought home and carried to my room. I had told myself, when I bought the toys, that I had got them as playthings for my children but the children never saw them. You will understand I had got, at the moment of the purchase, the nice feeling of being thoughtful to others in remembering my children, had absorbed that nice feeling, had wrung it dry like a sponge, and then, when I had got home I had taken the toys to my room, to which the children were never allowed to come.

They were on a shelf in my room, little red soldiers in red coats, some on black prancing horses and others in blue coats and mounted on white horses. There were foot soldiers in red coats and with tiny guns on their shoulders and all of these I arranged in rows . . . an absurd picture, all this, I realize, but a quite true one. I got a walking stick out of a closet and walked up and down. "What the hell, after all, this Napoleon!" I cried. I stood before the little lead soldiers and shouted at them, imagining myself at the moment some great figure . . . little Corsican corporal . . . little Ohio paint maker too.

Outbreaks of this sort couldn't last long, although the tendency in me to pretend, to be always trying to make myself out something I wasn't, went on and on.

There would be these times of such pretense, not always so obviously absurd as the little game with the lead soldiers but also not often so harmless, and then came the reaction. Let us say that I was naked, strutting up and down in my room so . . . there was a kind of sickening fear also that someone would catch me at one of these absurd moments . . . my being naked and in particular bare-footed was not without reason . . . I was no admirer of the beauty of my own body . . . the being bare-footed prevented my being heard about the house as I tramped restlessly, often at this time in my life for hours, up and down the room.

I got my clothes and put them on and going to my desk sat down. The desk was by a window and I looked out into the back yards of neighboring houses.

It must have been that winter that the thing began in me, eternal questioning of self, effort to lose myself in books, the lamp burning in my room often until three or four in the morning. Often I walked about the room talking to myself, arguing with myself. Did my wife conclude I was a bit insane? Perhaps I was. But here let me explain what the artist is. Why not add my own explanation to the thousands of others that have been given? It will be as good as any of them.—The artist, any man born artist, has this hunger always to remake, to re-create. There is this shapeless thing all about him everywhere and the fingers ache to reshape it.

"What—a whole civilization?"

"No, leave that to the statesmen."

"This thing—your own life?"

"Well now, go easy on that too."

"You are a tangle of God knows what influences coming down into you out of the past and now, at the present moment, playing over you."

The foregoing was put down as though there had been a conversation going on in a room, say as between two men, and perhaps there was. However I am only trying here, as anyone who has gone this far with me will readily see, to make a picture of what must go on constantly in a million rooms of houses when men and women are alone.. There is this restless questioning spirit in all of us and I have probably been a bit too pretentious in thinking of myself, at this stage of my life, as a more or less thwarted artist and thus a little set aside from the others.

I have an idea that my wife spent a good deal of time crying that winter. I seem to remember her, for a long period, as a person whose eyes always looked as though she had just wiped tears away. "Well, never mind her now," I said to myself, "never mind anyone." It must be that I am a genius as it is only the genius who can be as cruel as I was then. You see I take the genius to be no more than a man who has something to settle with himself, and I presume that I did at that time feel that there was something in me trying to arm itself against the enemy, society, and I remember often thinking thoughts like these . . . "Hell," I thought, "there is this woman I have happened to take as wife. It must be an accident that I have taken her rather than some other woman. It is quite sure I do not love. How can such a man as myself love?"

"There must be," I did at other times think, "such a thing as love." Men in the books I read were always speaking of it, and I think that faintly I did begin, perhaps during that winter when all of this began in me, to conceive of love as a kind of flow, the sort of thing that D. H. Lawrence was always afterwards speaking about . . . consciousness of others, self, lost. Well, I can't yet define it. What's the use trying?

Cruelty then. The woman I had got as wife and the children I had got by her simply did not exist for me. "Why, as for these people . . . my wife and children, brothers and sister, some of whom I might have been helping and wasn't helping . . ." I at that time never wrote to my brothers and sister, already scattered about America . . . "to hell with them. They are after all but people and in what way do a few people more or less matter?" By some accident of life, I told myself, I had got married. It was a thing men did. Perhaps like old Ben Franklin I had thought it would be more economical. "If you have to be eternally chasing after some woman it takes a lot of time and costs too much money." "What the hell, I am making them a living," I told myself.

7. The Italian's Garden

Meanwhile, I had an Italian neighbor. His house stood alongside ours and was one of those pretentious huge frame affairs, great square boxes, often with a kind of chicken coop stuck on top, the chicken coop having little windows, a place to which you could climb to view your enemies, that is to say, your neighbors. The front of the house, that I saw daily as I walked to my factory office, was always closed and the blinds were drawn.

The Italian, a short heavy-set fellow, with just such great hips as my own Italian grandmother and with a black shiny mustache, did not live his life at home at the front of his house, or on the porch built on in the front as did we Americans, his neighbors, but lived in the back yard and in his garden.

From a window in my room I could not see the house he had bought but I could see his garden. It was the garden that first attracted me—and now that I think of it I am positive that this period of questioning everything in my own life must have begun in the winter. There were a good many sleepless nights but at that time I was very strong and did not feel the want of sleep.

The Italian had come to Elyria and he had prospered. Like myself he was in business in town—he had opened a restaurant there and I had been in his place, a great long shining room, filled with cheap shiny American furniture, scenes painted on the walls, a place of soapy-looking red, pink and yellow soft drinks, young blades coming with their girls to eat and drink—American girls in pink and blue uniforms to wait on them—on the walls, scenes painted, towering snow-clad mountains overlooking dark little lakes. On one of the lakes, in the far distance, a solitary man in a row boat. A bird mounting into the distant sky. No Ohioan of that town had ever painted such scenes. It must have been done by some visiting Italian.

The Italian, who was my neighbor in my so respectable part of the town, had built up a chain of such places, and had selected our town and our neighborhood to live in.

There had been comments among the neighbors. "Such a fellow as that coming in. This part of town is going down." There was the resentment. "This damn Dago, pushing into our neighborhood. Buying a house here."

These words from my own lips, talking to some neighbor, we walking together, under trees, along our respectable street, going each to his own scramble.

I think however, always, even then, another kind of reaction in me. I left my neighbor at some corner and was alone. "Whoa!" I cried to myself, "don't be damned biggity."

Often, after such a talk regarding our new neighbor the Italian restaurant keeper, I came home later to my house. Let us say that my wife had someone in to dinner. It would be some quite respectable person of the town, perhaps the local superintendent of schools . . . or some of the professors from a nearby college town. My wife was a college woman and had a degree while I . . . I remember now that the college in the nearby town had a rule against smoking and that the men and women who came to us liked to smoke so that, after dining, we would draw all of the house curtains and have cigarettes, with beer.

Oh choice wickedness. Damn. I got habitually nasty. There were stories I had begun to pick up. I had begun going furtively, through back alleyways, to the town saloons, spending secret hours there when I should have been attending to the building up of my paint dynasty . . . none of this sort of waste of time and energy in the Rockefeller . . . I was already sure of that. . . .

I had got stories that would curl the guts of college professors in for an evening with their wives and other men's wives, and I wanted to tell them and sometimes did. Painful moments of silence. Quick talk of other things, literature preferably. Oh Literature! Hast thou got respectable too? Names mentioned, Thomas Hardy with held breath . . . *Tess of the D'Urbervilles* . . . *Jude the Obscure* . . .

". . . such vulgarity creeping into books . . ."

"Now there is W. D. Howells, an Ohioan." I got him and read him.

All of this was, at that time, a comparatively new world to me. If I had always been rather an omnivorous reader, my reading had been largely confined to men's lives, histories of people, etc. . . . It still is. I, however, got Howells and went through him and found him flat.

"What the hell's he so afraid of? He is like me in his fear," I thought.

I think, am quite sure, that it was on some such evening that I first heard the name of a later friend, Theodore Dreiser. There would have been a college professor at the house, from the English department of the college, and he would already have written a book on English literature. For a college professor in any field to get anywhere at all it is almost necessary for him to have written a book. I didn't know that then but found it out later.

The women and men, gathered at our house, listening to the college professor. I remember now that Arnold Bennett had just come to America and, as he got off the ship, had been asked by some reporter what, in America, he was most interested in and, "Why, Theodore Dreiser," he had replied, shocking, I dare say, innumerable college professors in America as he had shocked the one who came to us.

"Why, Bennett . . . Bennett says . . . I can't understand it. Yes. I got the book. His *Sister Carrie*. It is so crude."

But this Bennett. He had already written his marvelous first books, *The Old Wives' Tale, Clayhanger,* and others—was being proclaimed in London and, as usual, with a reverberating echo in New York.

A real writer that Bennett, laughing in his sleeve at our Howells and others of his type dear to the professorial mind at that time, long chain of respectables. . . .

In painting, in America, the Chases and Alexanders on top of the heap . . . forgotten kings now.

At any rate a certain reverberation through me. The name Dreiser. Although at that time I had read nothing of Dreiser and oddly did not until much later, after I had myself begun to write and publish books and stories and the critics had begun to say that I had got my stuff from him . . . as later more than one young American writer was to be accused of getting his stuff from me . . . myself in vainglorious moments also often saying it . . . although I knew nothing of Dreiser, when I first heard his name so mentioned, in a rather stuffy room, during what must have been an exceedingly stuffy conversation, I can say, I think truly, that the name of the man did, at that moment, reverberate through me like a bell hit by a hammer and also that something else happened. I wonder if I am now romanticizing. It seems to me now that, at that moment, when I first heard Dreiser's name mentioned, I saw the man standing in that room, behind the closed curtains . . . the curtains closed so that none of the neighbors could see certain college professors drink beer and smoke cigarettes . . . and that I hated him.

He being, if my present imagining of the incident is at all correct, just the Dreiser physically I later knew . . .

My hatred of him at that moment was not, however, personal, and not at all the hatred which the college professor discussing him at that moment felt, but a deeper and more pregnant hatred.

Was there in the very name, heard thus, in that company, a challenge? That I do not know now, and it may well be that what I think happened immediately after is but a myth too, for it seems to me that having heard the name, I jumped up crying . . . "that Dreiser, the heavy Germanic son-of-a-bitch!" shocking everyone in the room; and, having cried out so, I stamped out of the room where the others were sitting and going up to my own room above, slammed and locked the door, and then, going to my desk, sat down with my head in my hands and became for the rest of the night sleepless and utterly miserable.

Myth or no myth, let it stand and let us now return to my Italian neighbor. It was he that got me, and I think now that he got me just because he was in no way close to me. If there was something wrong with me and with my whole attitude toward life he was in no way to blame. By no stretch of the imagination could I blame him as I was inclined, at that time, to blame the woman who chanced to be my wife, the children whose coming had, I thought, cramped my life, throwing on my shoulders obligations I didn't want to take, and the society in which I lived, that had set up certain moral codes, laws, axioms, etc., that also, I thought, cramped me and held me bound.

In the early spring of that year my next-door neighbor, whom I had never made a neighbor, began working in the garden back of his house and I sat often in the window of my room above and watched.

There was something stirring back there, in that Italian man's back yard. Spring was coming.

But there . . . I will not try to describe here the wonders of the coming of a Middle-Western American spring, ice beginning to break up in little creeks, water running along the gutters in Main Streets, flurries of snow coming, to melt quickly, little ugly heaps of ashes in yards back of houses, the appearance of the first robin, men bragging,

"I saw a robin today," and the answering brag, "Ah, I saw one. There was one in my yard more'n a week ago."

That and something new in people, even in us business men. I presume that, at that time, I was a great egotist and thought that what I felt then . . . the same sense always of struggle in me, feverish times of activity in business followed by times of depression . . . I must conceal from the other young business men I knew as something peculiar to myself.

At any rate there was that Italian man, my neighbor, beginning his work in his garden. "What's the use?" I said to people, telling them about him. "You fuss with a garden endlessly, get your hands dirty, fight bugs, and raise a few tomatoes, and then along comes a man in a wagon who will sell you a whole basket of better tomatoes than you can ever raise for twenty-five cents."

And so that pronouncement from me, wiping earth away, man's relations with earth quite gone. It didn't pay such a one as myself. Yet with the first faint coming of spring that year the Italian had appeared at the back door of his house. He had a paper in his hand and came out followed by his wife. The wife was round and growing fat and had dark skin and large dark eyes and the husband was the short dark squat man with big shoulders and a mustache.

As for myself I had been in Cleveland on the afternoon before, having gone there in a car with three other young business men of the town, and we had been drinking.

But never mind that. The night in the city is now mixed in my mind with a good many other such nights . . . all of us a bit ashamed . . . a big dinner and then drinks . . . "What about women?" The women had been managed. They always can be. As I remember that particular evening and night one of our party had called up some Cleveland business man . . . a long argument over the phone . . . "ah, Ed, come on down. I've got three other live ones here. We want to cut a watermelon." Something of that sort. Young business men in the pagan mood. Wives safely at home. There might have been a meeting of the wives on that evening, say a literary evening, some American or English writer got in for a lecture . . . or it might well have been a musical evening . . . God save us all!

Then Ed's appearance. Oh, how many Eds have I not known! He would have been a big heavy-set fellow with big hands . . . red hairs sticking up from the back of his hands, a big cigar. He sold something to someone in our crowd and had felt it expedient to come to our call.

"Sure, boys. Let's have a shot or two. I can see that you boys are several shots to the good." God, why did we always have to call each other boys?

More phoning now, to certain Lillians, Kates, Sues, and then into our car, Ed at the wheel, and off to some apartment where there would be an older woman . . . she making her living out of just such fellows as we were . . . keeping a place where gentlemen could meet the "ladies."

Lillian, Kate, Sue . . . Jesus Mariar! I was to meet them again, over and over, with advertising men in Chicago and New York, in Denver, Rochester, Des Moines, in the apartments of publishers, out with successful writers too. They hang queerly in my memory, at the edge of consciousness, the Kates, Lillians, and Sues.

May, Mabel, Agnes.

Tall ones, blonde ones, little things with black hair and eyes, big red-haired ones . . . loud ones, too obviously shy ones.

Give 'em the works, Kate, Lillian, May.

Mabel, Agnes, Sue!

Little lusts awakened, not really awakened. Who was it that said that our American movie lovers were the worst any stage has ever known? The same thing in the Cleveland apartment, the women already showing wear, although they would have been young. The woman of that place getting them on the phone. Ed had told her . . . "Now we want live ones," and she telling the Mabels and Sues that we were men of importance. "Put on your best. Show 'em a good time. They'll pay for it."

I presume Ed paid, and my most vivid memory of that evening now is of Ed, getting rather gayly rough with some Mabel, grabbing her, his big hand with the red hairs upstanding, hands on her bare shoulders, a look in her eyes she thought no one saw . . . intense hatred.

"You boys come on. We'll have a hot time tonight."

But why were we boys? Too many oldish boys in America, and I must suppose I was tired of them, tired of myself, filled also with hatred of myself, as I was of my companions, and, now that I speak of it, I must say that I have hated every method by which I have ever been able to get money in America and, although I was an advertising writer for years and, as an advertising writer was compelled to attend many of the meetings called "conferences," sitting often in them for hours . . . individuals remembered as I now remember the eyes of that Mabel in a Cleveland apartment, Ed's hand hurting her shoulder . . . he would have pulled her down onto his lap and she would have smilingly let him kiss her . . . doing her poor job of the moment the best she could, as later I was to try to do my job . . . throwing words onto paper, to try to help sell some damn soap or toothpaste, some man who had already too much money . . . sitting in conference . . . men in such conferences afterwards to be remembered, say as one might remember seeing a dog tear at the flesh of a long dead horse beside a desert road . . .

. . . words. Words . . . Words, I apologize to you . . .

. . . words. Dear little lovers . . .

. . . A man in an advertising conference who had a bald head. There was a queer furrow straight across the middle of it. He was one of these fellows who pick up words. "Psychology." "What is the psychology of this situation we confront . . . ?"

. . . myself sitting there, near a big inkwell, fingering it. Hatred, as in the eyes of that Mabel later pawed by the Ed. Hello, little sister whore! We are all whores, sunk in our whoredom. Don't you worry, little Mabel . . .

. . . to have bounced that inkwell on the head of that bald man. Ah, freedom.

. . . that sort of thing not for us, Mabel, little sister whore . . .

Just the same there must have been something of the same sort of hatred in all of us bright young men that night in the Cleveland apartment, for I remember now quite clearly the ride homeward afterwards. We might have arrived in our own town at three in the morning. Automobile tires were still uncertain experiments. Read Dreiser's delightful *Hoosier Holiday*. On the way home a fight broke out between two of the men of the party. . . . God knows what it was all about . . . and I sat in the car, a fourth man trying to quiet the two . . . profane names roared in an empty road, blows struck . . .

Then afterwards the two in tears in each other's arms. "I'm sorry, Joe." "Fred, you know I love you."

The next day the men meeting. "Jesus, Joe, what'd you say to your wife? Mine was sore as a boil."

At least I said nothing to my wife. "Well, I went to Cleveland. What the hell of it?" So that was that.

And then myself in the window at dawn the next morning and that Italian man coming out of his house. He held a piece of paper in his hand and walked down a little path to where the garden was to be, stopped, stood a moment and then ran back to the door of his house to call his wife.

The two people had come out of their house into the dawn and I was at the window of my room, behind a curtain, watching. I was absorbed. There was this shame in me, memory of a hot over-furnished city apartment . . . shall I say smell of the Mabels, Lillians and Sues still on me. I have always had a passion for dancing and there was one Mabel with whom I had danced up and down the rooms, her body held close to mine, a phonograph playing jazz . . .

. . . an incident. I bit her on the shoulder. Why? God knows there was nothing inviting to me in the flesh on her bones. It was a vicious bite. "Goddamn you and myself and all men and all women." Something like that.

. . . anyway she turned and struck me a vicious blow on the cheek. "All right, now we're even. We have expressed what we feel for each other," I said to her and she laughed a little and we were a bit closer to each other after that.

Oh vice! What a sellout you are!

Staleness of all this on me in a dawn as I watched the two people preparing to make a garden. The paper the man held in his hand was evidently a plan. He held it before the woman and the two talked in Italian. The man went to the house and got a ball of string and when he came out again several children followed.

And now the whole family was in the garden, the people in all the other houses of the neighborhood still sleeping . . . the curious dawn quiet that lies over cities and towns . . . little sounds heard . . . the chattering of the Italian's children. They began running about the little bit of ground back of his house like birds. They were pulling old weeds and carrying them to a place the father had designated. The father, having got the string, was busy, with his wife at the other end of the string. Stakes were put into the ground and strings run from stake to stake. One of the children, a boy of nine or ten, suddenly began to dance. He threw his arms up and began whirling about the pile of dead weeds and vegetable stalks left from another year, the other children, some three or four of them . . . one a babe that could just totter about . . . the boy the oldest of the children . . . the others all laughing as he danced there in the dawn . . . the father and mother also stopping the work of laying out plots, to laugh with the children . . .

. . . myself above, in that room I had set aside for myself in my house . . . myself stale and dry-mouthed from my night of so-called fun, American business men's fun . . .

. . . myself and my own attitude toward my children at that time . . . self-absorption . . . ambition . . . self. Self. Self.

Dance on, life, but no use my going on about that particular Italian family in America, the other dawns of watching that followed during that particular spring of my life, sense caught in both the man and woman of earth love, their fingers seen putting out plants, the man making rows and the wife or one of the children dropping seeds . . . the children later taking turns in driving early birds away, the father and mother coming out of their house often to greet each particular plant as it emerged from the ground . . . cries of greeting . . . the children coming running . . . the broad hips of the woman and the man, working side by side, bending over to pull weeds . . . something horse-like in that man, cow-like in the woman . . .

I had got in me a great curiosity, and although the man and I never became friends . . . I was still too stuffy to go toward him as I should have done . . . I went sometimes during that spring into his restaurant to note the change in him away from his garden and in his so gaudy place of business. He was so polite there, so withdrawn. Was he, when he was in that place, full of the American notion . . . get every year a bigger and bigger restaurant . . . a chain of restaurants? Already he had a chain . . . four restaurants, all alike, in four Ohio towns . . . I had asked my banker and he had told me . . . "a good shrewd fellow," the banker had said . . . had he got an idea fixed as I had . . . pretty soon I'll be rich . . . my kids will be Americans . . . maybe go to Harvard, Yale or Princeton, play football maybe . . . big American me? . . . Ah!

I used to go into his place and sit, drinking a cup of coffee I didn't want and wanting to shout at him.

"Come here. You tell me. Is the whole swindle worth a damn? What the hell do you think you are up to? Hello, brother! What the hell do you suppose I am up to?"

. . . memory in me suddenly as I sit writing of a night long after my morning when I sat in the window of an Ohio house and saw the Italian-American making his garden, a Paris night, walking in Paris streets, as ugly as any in America . . . streets of workingmen's houses —in that old French city—as ugly as any in an American city . . . profit-taking going on there too . . .

There was on that night an American man, Ralph Church, then a student at Oxford, who had come over to Paris to meet me and we walked and talked of all this, of my own American experiences in business, of Ralph's father and the money he had made . . . profit-taking . . . money, money . . . business . . . business . . .

Ralph and I, on that later night, must have used the word "business" a good deal, the influence of the business world on American education, American thinking, American politics, words running, we walking absorbed in our talk through street after street, stopping now and then to look about . . . "God, I didn't know there were streets like this in Paris," . . . wandering into little bistros to drink . . . dark little holes, very like the pubs in Eastside London, ghastly enough specimens of humanity all about . . . we nevertheless absorbed in our talk . . . coming out of some such hole to walk again in more dark ugly little streets!

. . . all of this old in its ugliness, the festering going on a long time . . .

. . . America rapidly coming to it . . .

. . . just the same, between us two, at the moment, one of those rare fine moments of comradeship that come occasionally to men . . . if Ralph ever reads this he will remember the night . . .

. . . the talk jumping about as such talk will . . . first American business, the American universities . . . from that to Synge in Ireland and George Moore in London . . . then back again to American business . . .

As I have already suggested, the word "business" must have floated up time and time again out of our conversation for suddenly, in a dark little Paris street, we found ourselves surrounded by a mob of French people. There they were, a street full of them, they having surrounded us in our absorbed conversation, thinking no doubt that we were a pair of American business men, in Paris on a bust . . .

. . . saying in an America of an older generation that when he died the good American went to Heaven while the rich American went to Paris . . .

. . . hatred of America and its success at money accumulation having begun to grow before the World War . . . intensified during the war . . . more and more intense later . . . that very America that was once the hope of Europe . . . one of humanity's greatest dreams betrayed . . . "land of the free and home of the brave . . ."

. . . plenty of misunderstanding too . . .

. . . how?

. . . Why?

. . . damn little realization in Europe of the nameless masses down below in America, as in all European countries . . . real quality of the nameless masses down below in America as yet unknown . . .

. . . the masses in America as yet being shaped, educated only by advertising billboards, newspapers run for profits, educational institutions as yet all being controlled from up above, by business . . .

Presto, Sherwood! Don't preach like a soap-box orator! Tell your story!

But don't you see, man . . . this is also a story of thoughts . . .

That night in Paris, Ralph Church and I surrounded suddenly by that strange mob. How vivid the scene yet, the dark street with the tip of an old moon just looking over the corner of an old building, little passages running out of the street we were in, ragged men and boys . . . a few women and girls . . . gaunt faces . . . vice-touched faces . . . these confronting America as represented at the moment by us two, there, in that place, on that night . . . they all suddenly dancing, throwing gaunt arms upward, dancing, jeering . . . derisive laughter. They had got a little refrain out of some Frenchman's meager knowledge of our language and suddenly they all took it up, dancing about us as they sang, I remember two French working men . . . they might well have been bums, criminals . . . how do I know? . . . they suddenly separating from the others and walking up and down before us, imitating the earnest mood we had been in . . . looking at each other, making gestures to each other . . . each saying over to the other with profound earnestness . . .

. . . "business is business . . ." "business is business. . . ."

. . . the crowd surrounding them and us taking up the refrain . . . more dancing . . . more and more derisive laughter . . . the cry running through streets, echoing through streets . . .

. . . "business is business" . . . "business is business . . ."

Then Ralph Church and I . . . two stout-enough American figures . . . hurrying through street after street, followed by that dancing, singing, laughing mob . . . we wanting both to laugh and cry . . .

. . . afraid too. At any moment stones might be hurled . . .

. . . "business is business" . . .

. . . "business is business" . . .

. . . "business is business." . . .

. . . thus Europe to America. Who now dares say there is not everything, all history, all thought, in such illuminating moments in life?

8. The Man of Ideas

Now see how things click.

I got in with a certain man of the town. He had a small business in the town, a little print shop on a side street and occasionally he did printing of form letters and circulars for me.

The fellow used to come into the office of my factory.

"Well, Anderson," he said, coming into my private office and closing the door. He did not come more than two or three times before he began calling me Sherwood.

He would come into the office with one of my paint circulars in his hand, having brought it for me to read proof, and would stand at the door looking about. One of the girl stenographers sat by my desk. "Could I see you alone?" he said mysteriously and when the girl had gone out of the room and had closed the door he drew a chair up close to my desk and whispered. He was a small man of perhaps thirty with a dry leathery skin and unmarried.

"Sherwood," he said, when the girl had gone out of the room. He looked at me with curiously weary eyes. "Do you mind," he said, "if I talk personally and intimately to you?"

"Of what?" I said, and he began to explain.

"I have got this circular here," he said, holding up the sheaf of proofs.

"Well," I said.

"Well, it's like this. You see me sitting here at your desk. I am a man in a small business. It is my business, as a commercial printer, to print what is given me to print."

I remembered the first time he said something of this sort to me because I had been angry. Afterward I was always amused by him but the first time I really grew angry.

"Well, what's wrong with it?" I said, taking the circular from his hand, and he laughed and winked at me.

"It is so eloquent, and so full of bunk," he said and got up from his chair and walked about the room.

At first, when he tried to tell me what was on his mind, he was somewhat hesitant. "You are sure you will not get angry with me?" he kept asking, and when I reassured him, he began trying to tell me that I wrote well. And I remember now that this little Ohio printer, with his shop on a side street, told me something that was afterwards told me by Gertrude Stein in Paris. "You sometimes write what is the most important thing of all to be able to write, passionate and innocent sentences," Gertrude Stein said, and the little printer in trying to tell me what was on his mind, said something of the same sort.

At any rate the man interested me and I am not sure but that he became the first friend I ever had in this town. We began going about together. The man did not dress well, going about the streets in shabby clothes during the week, but on special days, or when we were going off somewhere together, dressing always in a loud, half-vulgar way.

We began going about in the evening, walking sometimes on dark streets of the town, going into little saloons and drinking together. The man always drank sloe gin, saying that he thought the drink increased his vitality. "It puts me on edge," he said, "makes me want women. And women," he said, "are among the few things in life it is worth a man's while to desire."

It was this man, whose name was Luther Pawsey . . . he is dead now so I may write of him with ease . . . and besides Luther Pawsey was not his name . . . with whom I began spending a good many hours and going off with on secret trips. "We will go to Cleveland tomorrow," he would suggest suddenly, coming into my office and closing the door, or perhaps it would be a visit to the Ohio town of Ashtabula or Sandusky that had taken his fancy. "Come on now. You must go home and get your bag. We will stay three or four days."

"But what will we do there?"

He said frankly that he did not know. "It is another place. It is not this place," he said. In a fresh town, where we were unknown, there would be more chance for adventure. "Who can tell what will happen? We will go there, not to a big central hotel but to some little hotel where there is small chance of seeing someone we know."

"And then?" I asked. At first, when he first made these proposals to me I was puzzled.

"There is the matter of time wasted," I said, and he smiled. "Time? And what are you doing that makes time so important?" At that time, like most Americans, I was always being in rather a hurry, often about nothing.

"Well, and then," he added, "you see . . ." He was himself puzzled. "A town is like a suit of clothes," he said once, in trying to explain.

He had difficulty in making an explanation, stuttering and walking about in my office. "Well, you see, I am not exactly like you. I am a small man in a small business. Unlike you I have not married. That is because I cannot make up my mind about one woman.

"Oh, I do not mean to be immodest," he said quickly. "I have never asked any woman to marry me and so the matter of my attractiveness to a particular woman for a prolonged period, as in marriage . . . you see it has never been put to the test but as for women in general . . ."

He laughed. Always when he got upon the subject of women a curious change came over the person of my friend. There would be a sudden glistening of the eyes, a new aliveness in his body. "Look at her," he would cry suddenly, when we had gone off together to some town and were walking in the streets. There was a woman walking on a sidewalk before us. With him curiously it was not often the sort of woman who usually attracts men. "Such women do not attract us," he would say, pointing out some quite richly dressed woman we had passed, some woman with what is called a good form, such a woman as most men turn the head to look at. "As for that one," he would say, "I have nothing she needs. Such a woman is like one walking in an orchard where there is plenty of ripe fruit. Every tree is loaded with it. She has but to put out her hand to pluck and eat the apple.

"But this other one," he would cry, pointing out another woman we had passed or were, at the moment, following . . . The women so pointed out were always of a particular sort and, after I had gone with the man on several such trips, I myself began to see a good many of the type.

They were always women not too obviously attractive but, when you looked at them sharply, always with a kind of sweetness. "You see, they are starved ones," Luther explained to me; and on this subject he would go on for a long time, talking in little rushes, a bit I must say like the figure of the man Joe Welling in the story called "The Man of Ideas," in my book . . . It may well be that I got the figure of Joe from Luther.

He would go on talking thus for hours, sometimes coming to the office of my factory in the evening or sometimes I would go to his print shop where we would sit talking or we would go for a walk on the back streets of the town at night or off on one of our seemingly meaningless trips. Sometimes, on such occasions, he would get on to the subject of women and again on the subject of words.

"As to the matter of words," he said . . . we would be sitting in his shop in the evening . . . it was a dark messy little place and he would run and get one of my paint circulars . . . as we grew to be better friends I gave him more and more of my printing to do, not asking him to bid. "Now, you see, here is a sentence you have written," he began, reading aloud a sentence from the circular. When he began in this manner he always looked at me a bit doubtfully. "You are sure you will not be angry because of what I may say?" I reassured him, filled with curiosity, and he read one of my sentences aloud. "Of what were you thinking when you wrote that?" he asked.

He did not wait for me to answer. "Ah," he cried, "I will tell you. You see it is a sentence purporting to describe a certain paint you are making and that you want to sell but when you wrote it you were not thinking of your paint.

"As to your paint that you make down there in that factory of yours, well, as to that I say nothing, and when it comes to that you yourself do not make it. Your hands never touch it.

"When it comes to that you are not interested in the making of paint. In what are you interested?"

When he was talking in this vein Luther always jumped out of his chair. Let us say that the two of us were in his little Ohio print shop. It might be a night of the early fall and raining outside. The street on which Luther had his shop was just off the main street and it was dark. There were several wholesale houses down that way and at night they were all dark.

So Luther had jumped out of his chair and was walking up and down in his shop. There was a gas light burning. The office of the place was not partitioned off from the shop. There were two desks, two typewriter stands and three or four chairs. When Luther walked thus, expounding his views on the subject of words, man's curious obligation to words, there was a curious effect.

The shop had a cement floor and there were printing cases and flat-topped tables, each with its printers' stone, these making shapeless masses in the darkness at the back. All of this is rather queer, as so much of life is queer, if we but dare feel its queerness. There was Luther, with his rather small and dried-up-looking face and his slender short body. He walked quickly but there was a peculiar dragging of the feet. There were always papers lying about on the floor of the shop . . . "we do not sweep until morning . . . a boy does it . . . he is a stupid boy and never sweeps clean but I only pay him two dollars a week . . . he cheats me by not sweeping clean and I cheat him by paying him such a small sum," he had explained to me several times . . . there were these papers on the floor and as Luther walked and talked, going sometimes into the darkness at the back of the shop so that his figure was lost among the type cases back there and then suddenly emerging . . . as he did that his feet made a queer shuffling noise among the papers. It was like a man walking in a wood in the fall among dead dry leaves.

"And so there you are, a man sitting and writing," cried Luther, holding one of my paint circulars in his hand and walking up and down in his shop. He had a peculiar gleam in his eyes now as he sometimes had when he saw a woman on the street. "You sit and write and the ostensible purpose of your writing is to sell paint.

"But what has happened. You do not know but I do. I myself am not a writer. I can talk but I cannot write. When I sit down and get a pen or pencil in my hand I become paralyzed. But for that fact I might have become one of the great writers of the ages.

"But never mind that. Let us talk of you," Luther said. "You sit and write. I know well enough what happens to you. Someone told me that, before you came here, to our town, to set up as a manufacturer here, you were an advertising man in Chicago. Is that a fact?"

I told him it was. I was curious as to what he was trying to say and besides I was flattered by his interest in me and in my paint circular.

He began to scold me about my writing. "Suppose you were a woman with some beauty of person and went and threw yourself away, going into any kind of dive, lying with any kind of man. How long would you be thought of as any kind of woman at all? Why, you'd be a slut, a whore, wouldn't you?"

He began then to talk of words as no one had ever spoken of them to me before.

"The truth is," he went on, "that, as you wrote, you were thinking of someone else. I know how it was. You imagined some man getting the paint circular in the mail. He is a man you never saw and never will see. Now you tell me this. At bottom you are not so proud of this business you are in. You are a word man. I can tell from reading these circulars you give me to print that you are not interested really in making paint.

"And you are not interested in getting rich. If you were, you would not be wasting your time with me. Suppose you should begin to respect words and ideas," he said. "You can't continue to use them really to deceive people, as you are doing here." He pointed again to my paint circular. There was something he was trying to say and that I was trying hard to understand.

I was confused, he thought, and did not know what I wanted. In reality, according to this fellow, as I sat writing, I thought nothing at all of my paint or of my money-getting but rather thought of some mysterious man, away off somewhere in the distance, to whom I wanted to get close.

"I was attracted to you," said Luther, "because one day in setting up one of your circulars I suddenly realized the truth about you."

I laughed, but was at the same time embarrassed, and I remember going homeward one night, after one of our first talks of this sort, and that there came one of those odd moments that I contend are of such infinite importance in a life. There was the going away from Luther, after a lot more of the same sort of talk with him. I never went to a psychoanalyst but I have often thought of what must happen, at least at the first . . . some other man attempting to thrust in and in, to search out your very soul . . . resentment, all kinds of resistance. "Whatever I am you let me alone." The psychologist Trigant Burrow will remember an experience he once had with me, at Lake Chateaugay, in northern New York, he trying to get at me, my resistance, the half comic situation that developed between us.

I would have walked away from Luther's print shop on a fall

night, thinking, trying to understand what he was driving at with me.

I dare say what I had thought of the art of writing, when I had thought of it at all, was that at bottom it was very much like paint making, or like running an advertising agency. You did it to make money.

To be sure, to do it at all you had to have, born in you, perhaps a certain kind of talent.

For example to be a real story teller. I rather think I always was one. You see this experience with the man Luther must be thought of also as a growing thing, my being more and more with the man, sensing things in him. Let us think of it as a kind of love making on his part. And I do not mean a physical love making.

But he had got hold of something in me. When we were together we did not always talk seriously. Sometimes he spoke of nothing but the art of printing. He had a passion for certain fine papers and for certain fonts of type, and would sometimes run clear across town to my office to show me a page. "Look. Isn't it beautiful?"

It may have been. I did not know. This matter of the surface of things in life, the shape of an apple or a pear hanging on a tree, the tree, the bed you sleep in, the chair you sit in.

The effect of a room on an inner thing in yourself. All of this was, I think, at that time, rather Greek to me . . .

And here let me say something to those who are beginners in the arts. It is a slow painful process, this training the senses toward the more subtle things of life, toward something of getting, or at least beginning to get, some sense of the real beauty of life in its physical aspects. Why I, who now have rather trained faculties in this direction, when I began . . . I thought many things beautiful that I now think ugly. I think it must have been under Luther's influence that I began . . . in the matter of pictures for example. I got a scrap book and kept it in my room. "This man has something I am going to get," I said with determination and so I kept the scrap book and began cutting drawings out of magazines. I pasted the drawings in the book and sat thumbing it. Occasionally I took it to Luther.

He was polite. I can see his eyes yet, looking at my book, and I can hear his polite words. "Very nice. Some of them are quite nice." It was like a man speaking to a child.

"What the hell is it?" I asked. It was the old cry, "What is art? What is beauty?"

"Oh, beauty, truth, where are you?"

The slow painful effort of a man to arise out of something. It is quite true that, at that time, I had no connection at all with the world of art or letters. Is it any wonder that all of my reactions to those immediately about me at that time, my own family for example, were often so brutal?

I was walking home from Luther's shop on a night in the fall. I remember several such walks. "It is curious," I said to myself, "but this man is doing something to me." There were moments of doubt. I have never been a man to whom homosexual men are attracted . . . the sort of thing that happens to men . . . leg grabbing, sudden caresses bestowed . . . the sort of thing that other men are always telling me of having had to go through . . . but already I knew of such things.

"Is it something of that sort he is after?" I asked myself. The idea that love could grow as between man and man, a thing outside sex, a feeling perhaps founded upon brotherhood . . . realization of self in another man . . . your own curious loneliness in life in him too . . . understanding of self a little got at perhaps through understanding of another . . . all of this was, at the time of which I am now speaking, new to me. "Bunk," I would have said had anyone suggested such an idea to me and would have gone on defending my scorn of any such notion by pointing out that life was but a game. "You are cast down here," I would have said. "Well, you came out of something . . . out of a woman of course. The chances are that you really know little enough of the woman who gave you birth . . .

. . . a seed from some man starting all of that in her . . .

. . . back of it all, to be sure, some sort of mystery . . .

. . . what have you to do with all of that? . . .

. . . you can't fathom it so you do what you can."

Men talking, in the churches and in other places of love, as between man and man, but all the time you knew or thought you knew, from your own experience, that what you got, in the way of joy, pleasure in life, you got really by watching your chance and then grabbing as other men all about you were grabbing.

"Well, what do you get?"

I had begun asking myself that question. I must assume Luther had rather started all this in me too.

The question asked and then thoughts coming, and I remember sharply a night, going homeward to my own house from Luther. There was no doubt that something he had said to me about my paint circular was true enough. Already for several years I had been doing what I was doing when I wrote the circular.

And what was that?

I had been using the words of our human speech, really to deceive men. I was making and selling paint and there was no doubt that houses needed painting; and if all of this reasoning of a quite ordinary man as he walks along the streets of an Ohio town alone, say on a moonlit night, having just come from the shop of his friend, an obscure little printer, seems somewhat primitive and simple it at least should be of interest as revealing what must go on in many such men.

The questions asked, defenses made. The real implications of what Luther was at that time saying to me were that I was sinning in some odd way in writing my paint circulars rather well. A great deal of the business that at that time came to me was done by mail, and to create confidence in the breast of some man at a distance, who had never seen you, knew nothing of you personally, it was of course necessary to write well.

It was quite true that in writing anything . . . for example a paint circular . . . the object sought was some sort of entrance into the confidence of the other man and so, even in such a crude approach to the art of writing, you thought, not of the thing about which you were presumed to be talking, but of the man addressed. "Now how can I win his confidence?" you thought and this led inevitably to the secret of watching men.

So you went about in life, always a bit on the alert, listening, watching. In modern society you were like a little animal in a jungle. It was a question of survival. Some men were strong. They fought and bullied others.

Others were shrewd and sharp. They could think faster than other men, take advantage quicker.

And you?

Perhaps you had none of these qualities so you developed another. You had found out that words could throw men off their guard and so you began, more and more, to use words to serve your own private ends . . .

. . . and all the time also using them to keep up the illusion in others that you were really naïve, quite innocent, had nothing but their good, rather than your own good in mind . . .

. . . this never however done too obviously. You watched yourself always to grow more and more skillful.

It is to be borne in mind that I had been at this thing . . . this advertising writing, for several years. An accident had led me into being an advertising man.

But was it an accident?

. . . you must think of me now as going along a street in an Ohio town and arguing with myself, much as I am doing here . . .

Walking at night through the night streets of an Ohio town, after one of my talks with Luther, he having put his finger on something in me . . . love of words . . . "you have a kind of talent in the use of simple words" . . . "occasionally, when you try, you can make a sentence" . . . "it's rather a shame, really, Sherwood, for you to be in the bunko game you are in."

These little knives stuck into me by Luther, left sticking in me. I walked uncomfortably, coming from his shop. Sometimes, even though it was raining and my clothes were wet, I didn't go home. I think I must have made over and over to myself the kind of protest most men make.

I think it not unlikely that had I been able to go into my house and sit down, call my wife and children to me, and say to them . . . "here, you. Listen to me. I am a man born with a certain sort of talent and I have just discovered it in myself. I have been dreaming a dream, a childish sort of dream but I am beginning to awaken. As for you, my wife and children, if you have got off on the wrong track in life, it is not your fault, but now we must right about face" . . . had I been able to explain to them all might have been well.

I felt myself unable to explain. Oh land of the free, what is freedom? I think that my notion of the life of the writer, a possibility a little opened up to me by Luther's words . . . "I might be able to do it," I found myself saying to myself . . . afterwards when I did become a writer and began telling tales it was said of me by critics that all of my tales were of one sort . . . they were stories of escape . . .

. . . it must have seemed to me then, as for that matter it does yet, that the real tale of American lives is as yet just that.

. . . eternal fleeing from something.

. . . "I will. I won't. I will. I won't." . . .

. . . "it is the fault of this woman. I will flee from her" . . .

. . . "I can do nothing in this town" . . .

. . . "city life may save me" . . .

. . . "no. It is not that. I will flee from the city to the town, from the town to the country . . ."

It must have been that upon me, as upon all men, rested a responsibility. How loath we are to take it. Upon me, an obscure and scheming little paint maker, dreaming my dream of riches to be acquired, great houses to be lived in, myself clambering up to all of this over the shoulders of others, dragging after me my wife and children, a penny lifted out of the pocket of this man, a dime out of the pocket of that man, slow accumulation at first, then faster. Now you have more elbow room. Now you may begin to play with thousands, not hundreds.

Really big men playing with railroads, whole railroad systems, chains of newspapers, great oil companies, steel companies, chains of retail stores . . .

. . . bigger and bigger you grow. Now there are gigantic children playing with gigantic toys and you are one of them . . .

All this, as I have suggested, after starting home fom Luther's shop. . . . How much of the starting of this in me he intended I'll never know,—but having, as suggested, started homeward, I did not go home. And wandering in the streets at night, schemes began coming into my head. It was at this time, and under the influence of Luther, who never spoke of politics, that I became a socialist.

9. Brother Earl

Still running the factory I wrote a long book called *Why I Am a Socialist,* afterward fortunately destroyed. It must have been very naïve. At the time it seemed to me that I was the first man in the world to have discovered the idea of socialism. I had for a time a wild dream of socializing my own business. How wonderful it would be, I thought, if all the people of the town could repaint their houses. What bright glowing tones. I imagined all the houses freshly painted with my paint—to accomplish this result I was willing to give up all idea of profit to be made of paint making. I myself would work and manage the factory for a bare living, bread and butter, no more. As advertising writer and company promoter I had made some money, most of which had been spent on clothes. My wardrobe was full of gaudy suits—I dare say there was always something of the sensualist in me. I had a natural liking for fine fabrics, for all sorts of delicately woven clothes. I wanted to array myself in these expensive and finely woven garments and I remember a picture of myself as a small boy, rather thin and poorly clad, standing beside a frozen pond in my native Ohio town. There was skating going on on the pond and among the skaters a rich young man from the city of Cleveland. He came skating along the pond's edge and called to me, taking off his overcoat and putting it into my arms. "Here, kid, hold this coat for me. I'll give you a nickel." He skated away and I remember standing there at the pond's edge under the great winter skies, my hand caressing that coat. It must have been an expensive one. What beautiful fabric. How rich the lining. Was there any possibility that I would ever own and wear such a coat? My best boy friend in the town was the son of a grocer and we used to walk together at night telling each other our dreams of the future. "The time will come when I will make my twelve hundred dollars a year," I declared passionately but my friend laughed at me. He was a conservative and a moralist. "Don't put your hopes too high. You'll never make it, Sherwood," he said.

The gaudy suits I owned should last me for at least ten years, I thought. I began publishing a magazine called *Commercial Democracy,* writing the entire magazine myself; I spent money circulating it by thousands of copies. I went from town to town preaching my idea of altruism in manufacturing and retailing to retail merchants. I have no doubt they thought me a little insane. All writers are perhaps hopelessly naïve. I decided to hold a great convention of retail paint dealers and hired a hall in the town. I went to an undertaker and rented several hundred chairs, got out a special edition of my magazine: I pictured hundreds of dealers coming to listen to me as I talked to them—they also were to join with me in my plan of making business altruistic. I would prove to them that I wanted nothing for my own work and they in turn would be satisfied with a small profit. We would make the purest, the best and the most wonderful paint in the world. How prices would be slashed! All the town would become suddenly beautiful in shining new coats of paint. The great day came and one man got off the train to come to my convention. I shall remember him as long as I live. He was a tall, awkward, bald, and sad-faced man who owned a little general store in a town of fifty people. His little business failed the year after he came to me. He had brought with him to my convention his son, a sickly child of seven, and I remember that he had a bag of bananas in his hand. I took the man to a hotel of the town and he stayed with me for three or four days. Just why he came I shall never know, as he had read none of my literature and understood nothing of my purpose. Evidently he just wanted to go somewhere. I think that until the day I die I shall remember his long sad face and the smell of the bananas in the paper bag he carried in his hand.

It must have been that now I wanted more than anything in the world to draw close to someone. Even at this late hour there were furtive and often half desperate efforts of myself and my wife to draw close to each other. But the efforts to draw close never succeeded. If I did during that dreadful period of my life have moments when I saw my wife and children, the visions were as from a great distance. There was such a moment. Being strong and often sleepless—if I had not been made physically for physical labor I am sure that I was in my own way quite strong—I was never bothered much by the matter of heat and cold and I never did need much sleep, even during the time I am now describing, when I worked rather long hours in a factory office, surrounded constantly by a cloud of young women stenographers, dictating letters for hours at a stretch, getting up very plausible-sounding form letters that went out in thousands, going to the golf club to play golf, running to the bank to arrange about a note coming due that I did not want to pay—well, being sleepless and tiring of the eternal sitting alone in my room, I had begun to creep out at night. I waited until the house was, as I thought, soundly asleep, and then, with my shoes in my hand, crept down a flight of stairs and got into the back yard. This might have been at two or three in the morning. I got out into the street and, putting on my shoes, walked, often for hours, in the silent empty streets of that town, and sometimes into the country—and little revealing moments did come. There was a night when I came back to my house just before dawn and was about to creep back to my room but as I came about the corner of the house I saw the figure of my wife doing the same thing I was doing. Why I did not go to her and try to establish some sort of real human relationship with her at that moment I do not know. It must be that I confused her with something I had begun to hate. She had come out of a middleclass family and I credited her with having impulses she may never have had. I thought that she also wanted me to go on in the individualistic business world into which I had got, that she believed in it and that, if she were unhappy, it was because she felt the resistance to it arising in me and wanted to put it down.

At any rate there she was, in the back yard of our house that night, there in the darkness, walking nervously up and down. There was a lawn and a hedge at the back and across the side of the yard, and getting to my hands and knees I crept to the hedge at the side and got under. I stayed under there watching her and she walked from the house to the hedge at the back, back and forth, making little movements with her hands. Occasionally there was something very like a little cry from her lips, but I was unmoved. "No you don't," I said to myself. This must have been in one of the periods when the abhorrence of the thing I was in was strongest in me and I must have thought that her unhappiness was all predicated on the thought that I might break loose at any time. It is hard to get a clear sequence of events in such a history as this I am trying to write and even now it seems to me that this incident happened after I had begun trying to be a writer. You see the woman I had married was educated. She had traveled in Europe while I . . . to tell the truth I could at that time just spell the simplest words—I was a man just out of the laboring class and to the American middleclass that was then, and is perhaps yet, a disgrace.

I do not believe the woman felt that, and in fact I am now sure she did not. But she did perhaps think, quite naturally, that a man as ignorant of the world of words as I was could never be a writer and she had already spoken to me of the matter. Her speaking to me on the subject must surely have happened before the night I saw her walking in the yard. She had said to me, intending only, I am very sure, to be kind, that I was not at all the sort of man that could ever become a man of letters . . . trying, as I thought unfairly, to shut a door that might be a way out for me and perhaps, just because I may have been more than half afraid she was quite right in her pronouncement, I hated her for making it.

But no. I did not hate her personally. I must rather have hated something I had the illusion she represented and so I could lie under the hedge watching her quite coldly that night. "No you don't, god damn you. You don't get at me in that way," I must have said to myself that night and I remember that I did lie quite indifferently under the cries from her until she returned into the house.

I remember also that I did not on that night return to my house at all but going down into the town ate breakfast at a downtown restaurant and went from there to my office and to work, getting up new form letters that I hoped would sell more and more of my particular brand of paint to the American people.

Did I say there was no one I loved? There is a possible exception. There was a younger brother named Earl who came to live with me. In our family there had been from the beginning a kind of instinctive feeling for the arts.

And there was this younger brother, Earl, who came to live with me at that time.

He was a tall gaunt boy, with narrow hips, broad shoulders, and large rather strange eyes, and was markedly unsuccessful. Having, like all of us, his living to make, he could not do it. Since he was a lad of fifteen he had been drifting from place to place. He got jobs and immediately lost them. He was absent-minded and likely to do strange things. Once he arose in the morning and came down to my factory clad in a bathrobe, having walked thus through the streets of the Ohio city. It was a cold day and he had put on the bathrobe thinking it was his overcoat. I gave him a job as shipping clerk in my factory and he sent every other shipment to the wrong destination. It cost more to employ him than it would have cost to keep him in luxury unemployed but he was sensitive and the situation was embarrassing. He did not want to be dependent upon his brothers— He was the youngest of all the sons in our family and when he was born the family was passing through one of its worst periods of poverty. He had got the idea that he was an unwanted child—a fixed idea that always stayed with him. Among my other enterprises I had taken a contract for painting a whole group of buildings belonging to a steel company in southern Ohio, having taken the contract to do the work in order to sell the paint and my brother asked to be allowed to go there and work on the job.

He did go and one day absent-mindedly walked off the roof of a building, falling some forty feet and injuring his head so that he was for a time insane—a blood clot formed on his brain which was afterward absorbed although in the end it killed him.

Earl had come to me from the city of Chicago where he had a position as cashier in a cheap restaurant in South State Street. The restaurant did its big business at night and was patronized chiefly by women of the town and their pimps. He had come to know these people intimately and afterward when he came to me and when he walked about with me at night, myself at that time still a good deal the bright young business man, the young American go-getter, he talked to me at length of these people. He had left the place and come to me at my invitation because the terrible food he had been eating had brought on an illness.

I think now that it was this brother, as well as my friend Luther, who had a great deal to do with my becoming a writer and understanding a little the impulses and purposes of the artist man. I think I must have clung to him a good deal—this was before the day of the automobile but I got a horse and buggy and we drove into the country on summer nights. Tying the horse to a tree beside the road we went walking over moonlit fields. My brother Earl was ordinarily no talker but on these nights walking across fields or standing by a fence, at some wood's edge, trees casting long shadows over fields washed by moonlight, he began to talk.

Why, here was talk such as I had never heard before. It was always of people. Of things in people felt and of the wonders and glories of nature. Sometimes he talked thus passionately for hours. He knew that he would never become the painter he dreamed of being—"I cannot finish things," he said. And I understood that there was a kind of passionate eagerness in him that constantly defeated him. He wanted too much—I cannot finish one thing because I am always driven to begin another—I cannot get into life, steady myself.

I remember his telling me on one of these nights of his experience with women. The story was a little terrible. He saw some woman and fell in love with her beauty but could not talk to her, could not approach her. "I have to run away," he said. "If I stayed near I would assault her. I would have to do it. It would be the only way I knew of trying to get some of her beauty for myself."

My brother left me one day going to another brother, a manufacturer in New Orleans, staying with him a short time and then disappearing entirely. When he disappeared he wrote a letter to the family addressed to the wife of one of my brothers with whom he must have set up some sort of accord—he said in the letter that he would have to disappear, could not go on being dependent upon his brothers. "I have to learn to stand alone on my own feet first," he said. For thirteen years he disappeared entirely and one day when I was returning from Europe and was stepping off the boat a telegram was handed to me. My brother had been picked up suffering from a stroke on the streets of Brooklyn. He had fought in the World War and had taken a position as a laborer working at night in a big bakery in Brooklyn and had lived alone all these years in a Brooklyn rooming house, painting during the day. Under his bed in the room there was found a great pile of unfinished paintings. What he had said of himself was true—he could not finish anything—never became a complete workman. It may be that his inner nature was too rich. He lived for a few months unable to talk and just able to scribble an occasional sentence but told me once by this method that he had once followed me for several blocks along Fifth Avenue in New York. He had walked so close to me that he could have put out his hand and touched me. "I didn't," he said. "I couldn't. I had first to learn to stand on my own feet.

"I had not learned to do it yet," he said.

I think it must have been after my brother left me in the Ohio city and after our walks and talks together that I began to write fiction and I am trying to think now what impulse led me to it.

About this time a woman came to the Ohio city from the East. She was a guest in a house near the one in which I lived and I made her acquaintance. She was a delicate, not very strong woman somewhat older than myself and liked to walk in the woods and fields. We began walking together.

She was an intellectual, a woman of a type I had never seen before. She knew the literature of many countries, told me many little stories of the lives of writers. She knew nature—the names of trees, flowers and grasses. She knew the world of birds and of insects. Being with her was a kind of wonder to me, and I walked with her every afternoon and often at night. There was a scandal in the town about us although our relationship was always quite innocent and I think she knew of the talk going around but did not mind. I found myself able to talk to her as I had been unable to talk to my brother and she it was who suggested that I actually begin writing. "Do not do it as a career," she said. "Do not think of publication or of making money by it. Do it as you would play a game for its own sake."

I began and during the next two or three years wrote three or four long novels. Words began to flow from me. On some days I worked several hours in the office and then going to my room wrote all night. I wrote what must have been imitations of novels I had read, trying a little always to bring them a little closer to the reality of life about me.

But I did not know the reality of life, had been for too long absorbed in the effort to succeed in life, to raise myself up out of poverty and into some sort of affluence.

All of my relationships with others had been corrupted. "Can I make anything out of this fellow?" "How can I use him to my own ends?"

I threw my pen down on the table in my room and went again to walk. I began more and more stopping along the way to talk to people. I was trying to learn to approach other people without any personal motive, to be quiet, to look and listen. Formerly when I was a young advertising man in Chicago and afterward during my first year or two as a young company promoter and manufacturer in an Ohio city I had continually hurried from place to place—walked rapidly, even I think set my jaw in a certain way. There must have been in my head some notion of a part I was to play in life as a successful young man. Perhaps it had been built up in me by my reading of popular literature. I talked rapidly, rushed through the streets to my office, slammed doors, gave orders to my subordinates in sharp tones. I was merely trying to enact the part of the pushing, bright successful young American business man.

It was all absurd and I began to realize it. The realization must have come partly from my brother and partly from the woman with whom I walked and talked. Both of them spoke slowly with soft voices—there were long times of quiet, of silence as we walked. Dimly I began to realize that in quiet and in silence there is also a growth of relationships. So I began trying for a quiet of my own, forced myself to stroll rather than rush through streets. I practiced talking slowly and even developed a drawl which I still have.

It was very difficult. It was like a child learning to walk—the blind rush of so much of American life had got into my bones. I had to begin over and over. I was on a country road and spotted a tree in the distance—I will walk slowly, will stroll, rather than rush from here to that tree, I told myself. In the same way I had to check my rush of words—I stopped at some farmhouse in the country or to talk to some farmer plowing in the field. "Be quiet. Do not try to impress him with your own personality. Let him talk. See if you cannot be quiet, lead him to tell you something of himself," I whispered to myself.

It worked. All people want to tell you their story. Innumerable people are being hurt and thwarted by life—they want to talk—they want affection.

More and more I found I could return to my desk and lose myself in the writing of others. I tried to put down little sketches of things seen—little glimpses out of life given me by others—my writing began to have a little form. I felt it. If I could not think clearly of what seemed to me the false position in life into which I had got I could take some imaginary figure, a tall man with red hair, let us say, and put him in the same position in life in which I found myself.

It was not myself. It was another. The imaginary figure perhaps created in my fancy began a little to live. He had adventures. Life beat in upon him. He became more and more real to me and in his growing reality I more and more lost self. I became happier, went less often on sprees with other men, began to be more and more absorbed in the life about me.

But it was all disastrous to my business. There was a note due at the bank and I forgot to go and get it renewed. I spent less and less time at my office and turned the work there more and more over to subordinates. "Here, answer these letters yourself," I said, throwing a pile of business letters on the desk of one of my stenographers.

But now there came a new sense of guilt. I had induced other men to put money into my business—there had been a company formed. Other men, some of whom could ill afford it, had invested money. There were professional men, doctors and others who, because of their faith in me, the bright young business man, had invested their money.

What was I to do? It seemed to me impossible to explain to others what was going on within me. It was all too unformed in my own mind. I had had very little schooling. After all I thought of writers as educated men and I had no education. It is true perhaps that I had been acquiring education very rapidly during the last two or three years in that place but it did not seem to me the kind of education I could explain to others. I wanted to leave, get away from the business, turn it over to someone else but did not know how to go about it.

Again I resorted to slickness, to craftiness. Already I had got a reputation for a kind of queerness among my acquaintances. Men had seen me walking somewhere in the outskirts of the town and suddenly beginning to run. Men saw and noted these things. Some of them spoke to me. "What is the matter with you?" they asked. The impression got abroad. I perhaps encouraged it—that I was overworking, was on the point of a nervous breakdown and I encouraged the notion. I have told something of all this in a book of mine called *A Story Teller's Story*. The thought occurred to me that if men thought me a little insane they would forgive me if I lit out, left the business in which they had invested their money on their hands. I did it one day—walked into my office and called the stenographer— It was a bright warm day in summer. I closed the door in my office and spoke to her. A startled look came into her eyes. "My feet are cold and wet," I said. "I have been walking too long on the bed of a river." Saying these words I walked out of the door leaving her staring after me with frightened eyes. I walked eastward along a railroad track, toward the city of Cleveland. There were five or six dollars in my pocket.

BOOK III

A ROBIN'S EGG RENAISSANCE

1. The Nest

It was in Chicago that I first knew other writers and men deeply interested in literature. I had come back to my big town to try again. I was living about in cheap rooming houses trying to get some ground under my feet, to give my own life some decent purpose and meaning, growing often discouraged and going off with others to carouse in so-called low saloons. And here in Chicago I wrote many of my best-known stories. It was in Chicago that the newspapers first both damned and praised my work. . . .

Something was stirring at that time in the world of arts in America. I think everyone felt it. Little magazines with several of which I was to have connections broke out like measles in that period. There was the *Little Review* in Chicago. The *New Republic,* the *Seven Arts* and also what is now known as the *Old Masses* got under way in New York. In Chicago the old *Dial* changed hands—later on moving to New York. The impulse reached out over the country. There was a Mid-Western magazine called the *Midland.* In New Orleans another called the *Double Dealer.*

It was the time of the struggle for woman's suffrage, women parading, picketing the White House, going to jail. It was the time of the Little Theatre Movement, represented in Chicago by Maurice Browne. In writing there was what is now called "the Middle-Western movement." George Ade, the Chicago newspaper man, had attracted wide attention with his fables in slang. He had gone to New York, grown rich writing plays. Edgar Lee Masters, who had been a law partner of Clarence Darrow, was at work on his *Spoon River Anthology.* Carl Sandburg was at work on his Chicago poems. He was, I believe, a reporter on a socialist daily which afterwards failed, when he went on to the *Chicago News.* In the *Chicago Tribune,* Burt Leston Taylor was conducting his famous column and I believe Ring Lardner was writing baseball.

To Chicago from New York came the famous exhibit of modernist paintings known as the Armory Show. For the first time we saw the gorgeous work of Van Gogh, Gauguin, Cézanne and the rest of the French moderns. Thousands of citizens stood waiting at the door of the Art Institute in Chicago when the show opened. One of the paintings which roused a great clamor in the newspapers—it was called "Nude Descending a Staircase,"—one of the first of the abstract cubist paintings—was bought I believe by Mr. Sherwood Eddy.

It was a kind of outburst of energy and penetrated even to the copy department of the advertising agency where I was employed.

And how many remarkable men known, thoughtful friends made in those Chicago days. Henry Justin Smith, Ferdinand Schevill, Robert Morss Lovett, Burton Rascoe, Lloyd Lewis, Ben Hecht, Floyd Dell, Arthur Davidson Ficke, Harry Hansen, Carl Sandburg, Lewis Galantière, Ernest Hemingway.

With these men and others I sat about in restaurants, talked of books, had the works of old writers brought to my attention, discussed new writers.

With Ben Hecht in particular I often went while he covered news stories. We quarreled and fought, made up, remained friends.

Other men not to become literary figures made lifelong friends. The big Irishman George Daugherty, one of the sweetest natures in any man I have ever known, and Marco Morrow, an ex-newspaper man and the closest thing to a genius I knew. Both were engaged in advertising writing. They were both from Springfield, Ohio, where for some six or seven months I had attended the Lutheran college known as Wittenberg, and I had known Morrow when I was in school there and for a time he and I had lived in the same house, a large boarding and rooming house filled with college professors, lawyers and writers, run by Mrs. Folger, of whom I shall have a charming story to tell. Then there was Roger Sergel, now at the head of the Dramatic Publishing Company. Talking with all these men of books and writers, drinking with them, sometimes spending most of the night walking and talking.

And there was the fascinating figure, Margaret Anderson. I knew her when she burst forth with her *Little Review,* wrote for her first number, wrote for the old *Dial* when it was published in Chicago. I became a part of what was for a time called "The Chicago School" of writers.

How many men known, women known, during the years there. They come flocking into my mind, men of the advertising office where

I was for long years employed as copy writer, men infinitely patient with me and my idiosyncrasies.

And there was that rather volcanic fellow, the Italian poet, Carnivali, who came from the East to help Harriet Monroe on *Poetry: a Magazine of Verse*. He sometimes raged about my rooms at night.

And Bodenheim, with his corncob pipe and the broken arm he carried in a sling, although it was but an imagined break.

It was the time of a kind of renaissance in the arts, in literature, a Robin's Egg Renaissance I have called it in my mind since. It had perhaps a pale blue tinge. It fell out of the nest. It may be that we should all have stayed in Chicago.

So many of us began there, got our early impressions of life there, made friends there. Had we stayed in the home nest, in Chicago, where it all began for so many of us, the Robin's Egg might have hatched.

There we would all have been chirping away and pecking at worms up and down Michigan Boulevard until this very day.

2. Bayard Barton

I had come back all but broke. I found a room in an old building on the South Side. It was near the end of a street car line, and street car conductors and motormen lived in the building.

They had little apartments there and one of them rented me a room at two dollars a week.

I was on the street car conductor's car, and as I stood with him on the back platform had asked him about a room.

"I am looking for a cheap room. I am promised a job soon but may have to wait for a time.

"I have a little money but must make it go as far as I can."

This was in the early fall and the street car conductor asked me to meet him at the street car barn that night.

I went there and he took me with him to his apartment.

"I'll have to explain," he said. He said his wife had tuberculosis.

"She is going to die, one of these days.

"We are up against it for money," he said.

I remember that as we walked along a street from the end of the street car line to the apartment building he was embarrassed.

"It may seem a little queer to you that I am willing to let a young man come to live in my apartment," he said. He explained that he had no children.

"I will be going away, every day, and leaving you alone there with her.

"But it does not matter," he said. "She is a sick woman. Nothing can happen."

I was there for some three or four weeks in a small room in that place and there was the sick wife, lying in the bed in which she slept with her husband or sitting in a rocking chair by a window.

While I was there the street car conductor and I did the housework. We made the beds, we swept, we cooked our own breakfast. I had found a place where I could get a great stack of wheat cakes and a cup of coffee for fifteen cents. When the street car conductor came home from his work at night I cooked his dinner.

"No, I do not want to eat. I have had my dinner," I said.

I went to the advertising agency perhaps twice a week to inquire for my mail but did not again speak of a job.

"If I seem anxious they will not want me again," I thought.

"There will come an emergency," I thought. Emergencies are always arising in advertising agencies. Some big advertiser is playing golf with a friend. He is advertising in magazines, in newspapers and on billboards. His account is very important to the advertising agency. They are making a lot of money on it.

So there he is with his friend, playing golf, and the friend has missed a putt.

"Say, what do you think of my advertising?"

The man who is spending all the money through the advertising agency has holed his putt. He has won the golf match.

"I think your advertising is damn bad. It's commonplace," the friend remarks.

And so an emergency has arisen in the agency. The advertiser has come roaring in.

"You are doing bad work on my account. All of my advertisements are too commonplace," he cries.

"You must do something and do it quick or you will lose my account."

What an uproar now arises. Men are running up and down. Conferences are being held.

"Where is Smith? Where is Jones? Where is Albright?

"We must have something absolutely original now.

"Where is that Anderson? Where is he?"

So they called me to come to work.

For three or four weeks I had been sitting through long fall afternoons with a sick woman far out on Chicago's South Side. In the evening I had been cooking her husband's dinner.

She was a woman who had been a girl in an Illinois small town as once I had been a boy in an Ohio small town. We spoke of that.

"It seems so queer to have a strange man like vou in the house," she says.

"Yes, it is strange as all of life is strange.

"It is strange that we did not live, as boy and girl, in the same town."

I tried to describe to her the Main Street of my own town. She coughed violently. Once she had a hemorrhage and I had to hold a bowl for her.

"You would not think, to look at me now, that I was a fat little girl.

"If I had been a girl in the town where you were a boy you would not have looked at me. I was too fat," she said.

One day the conductor told me that he would have to give up the apartment.

"I will have to send her home to her mother."

The street car conductor and his dying wife never spoke of each other by their names. She did not say "Frank thinks" or "Frank says." She said "he thinks" or "he says."

It is odd to think that I never knew that woman's name.

"I cannot keep the apartment. The doctor bills are eating me up. I will have to send her home to her mother."

But by that time I had begun to strut again. I was back at my place in the advertising agency.

When I had left my factory, walking down the railroad track that day in 1910, I had kept on walking until I got to the city of Cleveland. It was summer and I slept for two nights out of doors. One night in a lumber yard and another night in an open field. In Cleveland I had borrowed a little money from a friend, Mr. Edwin Baxter, now I believe an official in one of Cleveland's larger banks, and had returned to Chicago. The days and nights of walking and of lying out under the sky had been a time of soul wrestling. I had come to a certain conclusion. "I cannot change American life," I told myself. "It is not in me to be a leader of men leading them into new paths." I already knew that when I returned to Chicago there would be but one fate open to me. I could again become an advertising writer. Essentially as an advertising writer I would continue indulging in lies. I had a gift for words, a gift of statement. Deep within me somewhere there was a respect for words. I would be compelled, as advertising writer, to corrupt these words. They were the instruments by which possibly men might find each other in the confusion of life. "Very well," I said to myself, "I will stick to those dependent upon me. I will be corrupt but, God give me this grace," I cried, "let me in some way keep an honest mind. When I am being corrupt, perverting the speech of men, let me remain aware of what I am doing." I dare say that many times later I either lost this impulse or became confused about it but I always returned to it. It seemed to me then, as it does now, that hypocrisy in this matter, this believing your own bunk, was the real sin against the Holy Ghost. As writer I believe it yet. I have nothing, for example, to say against the American writer who flies off to Hollywood and gets his thousand a week for what must be done to get the thousand a week in Hollywood, except when I hear such a one talking, as they are always doing, about the wonderful possibilities of the movies and trying to convince themselves that they are not being corrupt. With a few exceptions, the movies, as I have seen them, have done nothing to improve the relationship between man and man in America or to make our common lives more understandable.

It was the advertising agency which formerly had employed me that, after some hesitation, had taken me back.

"I do hope you'll go straight now."

This would have been Bayard Barton, who had now become president of the agency, talking to me. Bayard was too gentle a man to be really gruff.

"And what do you mean by going straight?"

The conversation would have taken place in his office.

"Well, Bayard, you have certainly risen in the world." He had been a copy writer as I had been. We had sat together in the same little hall of a room, writing of cough cures, fertilizers for farms, rouge for women's cheeks.

I had something on Bayard. Did he not formerly show me verses he had written?

And now he was lecturing me. It was an old story. From my own wife I had got just such lectures.

"It is about this scribbling of yours. You cannot have such divided interests. Either you are an advertising man or you are a writer."

"Yes, I know," I said. "You are about to speak now of my lack of education. Such men as myself, who are not college men, whose minds have not been disciplined, cannot become real writers.

"I have heard all of that, have heard it to weariness, but I do not see that what I do after hours, when I am not employed here in this office, can matter to you."

Bayard would have called my attention to my failure as a manufacturer.

"It was because your real interest was not in the business.

"And then besides I know well that in coming back here you are only coming because you are broke.

"You have no interest in advertising writing. In a month you will be swaggering before us, your tongue in your cheek."

"And writing down good copy for you," I said, laughing at him. For well I knew he would not turn me down. There was something between us, a kind of affection.

And had he not also once said to me that, when he had made his pile . . . that an old dream.—No man or woman among us doing what he wanted to do. We were writing, dreaming, hoping.

"When I make my pile."

Among us writers the dream of writing for the popular magazines or the so-called "pulps," or, if more lucky, getting a script job in Hollywood. Big money to be made and put aside. Then some real work done.

It didn't seem to work out.

I sat looking at Bayard who was looking at me. There was a silence between us. We were both thinking of former days, when we had both been copy writers together, walks taken in the evening, talks we had.

"There is so much whoredom. I wonder if it is possible to escape it. All of this spending our lives struggling to get a little ahead of the other fellow, make more money. It is a disease of our civilization."

Bayard, as a copy writer like myself, had been sent to Akron, Ohio, to write copy for the Firestone Rubber Company. Something had happened that often did happen among us advertising writers— Mr. Harvey Firestone had taken a fancy to Barton. It led later to his also getting the Ford account. Mr. Firestone had perhaps grown impatient with the type of man often found in the position of salesman or contact man in advertising agencies. These fellows were often without subtlety in human relations. They were of the well-known go-getter type. Often they were physically the type of man you used to see pictured in advertisements of Arrow Collars, answering quite perfectly the popular conception of the type of young American bound to succeed. You can still find plenty of men of this type pictured in the advertising pages of our popular magazines. Let us say that the man is young and rather handsome. He is iron-jawed and big-fisted—and when in college was a football hero. I should say that Mr. Hamilton, who managed the campaign of Mr. Landon in one of our last presidential campaigns, was of this type, these men who were always intent upon increasing the size of advertising appropriations. They were eternally salesmen. Such a man was often successful in inducing some large advertiser to bring his account to our agency. He rushed the man, overwhelming him with talk, but he never knew when to let up and it was then that the advertising copy writer who had to be called in to do the actual work on the account got his chance.

And so Mr. Firestone, being, I dare say, bored with some such go-getter, had designated the man Barton to take charge of his advertising.

Barton was a quiet gentle one. He had a mind and I can imagine a conversation between him and Mr. Firestone, who was also of the quiet type—"Look here, Barton," I can fancy him saying, "you take charge of my advertising. I have decided that I am going to depend upon you and for all I care you may, if you choose, leave the advertising agency with which you are now connected and start one of your own. At any rate I don't want to see any more of your salesmen. I am forced to employ men of that sort but I do not like them. You take charge. I haven't time. I will depend upon you and hold you responsible."

As you the reader can well understand, this was an opportunity for Barton.

It is possible for a humble copy writer having got control of a large account to walk into the agency employing him with a mighty club in his hand. "Do you want me to set up my own agency or are you willing to talk business?" So Bayard, controlling in this way for a time both the Firestone and the Ford accounts, had been lifted up to his new position of power.

He could force his way up.

"Give me what I want or I will take the account somewhere else."

He had been made president of the company. Well, he was on his way to making his pile now. Poor man, he did not live long to enjoy it. You get into some such position, in the world of business, and where are you?

It is true some men can stand it. They go on and on accumulating and accumulating. To them at times the seemingly insane struggle is a kind of game at which they play.

But my friend Barton had other dreams—to rake in shekels for a few years and then to live in the country somewhere in the hills. I saw the tired look in his eyes.

We were both remembering vows we had taken to each other.

"Oh, what the hell! You have chucked the attempt to be a manufacturer. You're broke and don't know where to turn.

"All right. Go to work. I'll give you a job for old time's sake."

He arose from his desk. "Look here," he said, "you know how I got to where I am. I stole an account, a big one. I was proud and glad when I did it.

"And now I have a hold of something and I can't let go. I don't know why but I can't. My pride is in some way involved.

"So let me tell you something. If you ever have a chance to steal an account, take it away from me as I have taken the Firestone account from the others here, but do not do as I did. Steal a little account, steal two or three little accounts. Do not get into the big time. Stay under the guns."

He laughed and turned away and oddly enough I did later steal two or three small accounts from him and when I did it he laughed again.

There wasn't, however, on each occasion, much joy in his laughter. He was no longer the old Bayard Barton with whom, when we were both younger, I had walked and talked on many a summer evening while we told each other of our dreams.

So I had begun again where I had left off when, with a good deal of beating of drums, I had gone off to Ohio to become a rich man. I was on a comparatively small salary, as it was a time of depression in advertising. In re-employing me, Barton had told me frankly that he did not need me. I had been compelled to accept the salary he offered. I began something that was to go on for the next ten years while I gave as little as I could to my job, continually saving myself for my writing, faking a good deal, being frank at least with my employer as to what I was doing, living as I continued to live for the next ten years in cheap rooming houses about the city. I lived on the North Side, the West Side and the South Side. I moved restlessly from room to room.

I think it must have been at about this time that I wrote a book of verses I called *Mid-American Chants* and there was in this book a good deal to be said about laughter. For I would have my readers to know that while the tale as set forth by myself here may sound rather solemn I was not solemn myself. Could it be that by acceptance of the fact of a rather unscrupulous and dishonorable quality in myself I had got a new freedom? I think I had. There was continual laughter on my lips. In the agency there was a woman of sixty with a reputation of being perpetually sour. It was her job to pass the traveling expense account of those of us who were always being sent out over the country to advertisers and there were always bitter words said when the day came for a reckoning. She had a little cage in the front part of the office and was known to us advertising writers as "Mrs. Sourguts." Once, after I had come back to the office, she was still there, still in the little office, with the same sour look in her face. I stopped and spoke to her.

She leaned out of her little office and a glad smile spread over her face. "Oh, Sherwood, Sherwood," she said, "how glad I am to see you back. No one has really laughed in this office since you went away."

In his office with the door closed Bayard often pled with me.

"Quit doing as you do, Sherwood."

"But what is it I do?"

"It is the way you come into the office, the way you walk. It is a certain expression on your face. It is as though you were always laughing at yourself and us."

"But I am laughing. It is the only thing I can do to save myself. I am like you. I am caught in a trap. If I could not laugh I would be often on the point of suicide."

(During the years when I worked always for one American advertising agency there were five suicides in the agency, all by people working in the copy department.)

"But, can't you help me out? You know my own position. I should fire you because of your impertinence but you know I won't—"

"But I do not yet understand just what it is I do that so offends you."

"I think it is for the most part the way you walk. I sit here at my desk with my door open. I look down a long hallway. You, Sherwood, are presumed to be at your desk at eight-thirty in the morning. Often you do not arrive until ten. You do not hurry in. You stroll. It is as though you were saying, 'I don't give a damn for this place.'"

"But that is true. I do not give a damn."

"You are taking advantage of my friendship for you."

"Do not insist too much upon our friendship," I said, "if you do not want me here."

Such conversations with my boss often ended by our both sitting and facing each other, both of us near the point of tears.

The truth was that as I got deeper and deeper into writing I had become more and more aware of other people. There were certain days when a kind of super-sensitivity took hold of me. Walking in Chicago streets it seemed to me at such times that a single glance into the face of another told me a whole life story. There were too many stories, too many people to try to understand. In such a mood I sometimes left my rooms in the morning in plenty of time to arrive on time, but I could not go there. I did not dare keep on looking at faces seen in the streets. There was a kind of temporary insanity. I found myself rushing along streets with bowed head, staring at the sidewalk. I bumped into people. I had begun talking aloud to myself. "You must be quiet," I said to myself. "Wait. Be patient. Go slowly," I muttered to myself. For a year I had been trying to train myself to stroll rather than rush through the streets. I had no intention of insulting my fellows in the advertising agency when I strolled in late and went to my desk. For the half insanity that sometimes took hold of me at this time I had found but one remedy. It was to quit talking rapidly, repeating over and over the jargon of success. It was to stroll. It was to laugh. As a lad and as a laborer, before I had become a business man, I had talked always with a slow drawl. The drawl was returning to me.

I sat in the office explaining all this to my boss, who sat in silence staring at me. He had gone a little white about the lips. "For God's sake do not talk any more. Get out of here. I will stand for you, will not fire you as long as I am in control here, but I'll tell you this: I will never stand for another working for me who has your attitude toward his job.

"Now get out of here," he said as I got up and made for the door. However, I knew that such talk always drew us closer together.

As for the trick I eventually pulled on him—

I had got into a certain position. I had become a little known as a writer. There had been a story of mine in *Harper's*. Word had been whispered about.

I had begun to let my hair grow a little long. Upon such a trifle as the necktie you wear a reputation may a little be built, and I did not wear such neckties as other men wore. I resumed wearing the strips of brightly colored cloth, passed through the ring. I was a little noticed. We, of the American business world, were . . . it was at least true at that time . . . in our dress, all of a pattern. Any little variation in any of our garb was, at once, noticed. I began, a little, to attract attention. When I was engaged, on these occasions, in one of these grim wrestling matches with advertising ideas, I continually passed my hand through my hair.

I had begun to get a little ahead. After all, the solicitors, the salesmen, had to depend upon us. We were the writers. They were compelled to send us to the factories where the goods we were to advertise were made. Sometimes we stayed at such a factory, in some town, for days.

Acquaintances and sometimes something like friendships were made.

There were two men in a Kentucky town, another in an Ohio town, a fourth and fifth in Illinois towns, on whose accounts I had worked. I had selected these men from among all those whose accounts I was sent to write. I made it my business to cultivate them. All of them were men who had a certain flair. They or perhaps their wives or daughters were after culture. It is an American passion. I got invited to their houses. I spoke of books. Some of my stories had begun to appear, for the most part, it is true, in the smaller literary magazines, of which they had never heard, but I saw to it that they did hear of them.

And then there was my older brother, a painter. I spoke of him. There was an exhibition of his work in one of the Chicago galleries and I saw that they got a catalogue. All of the men thus worked upon were manufacturers of goods sold to farmers. None were big advertisers. In the aggregate the commissions, from all of the accounts, if I captured them, might be five thousand a year.

I worked steadily on all of them for a year or two, went to see them as often as possible and then, when I thought my position quite comfortably safe, I made my move to "steal" the accounts.

I succeeded. I made a bluff. I went to each man with my story.

"I am dissatisfied," I said. "It may be that I shall resign from my job and go instead with another outfit." I put it upon grounds they could not fail to understand. "I was not getting enough pay for what I did." As for the morality of what I was doing I do not believe that I thought much of that.

"It is a matter of survival," I told myself. "Can I escape from this trap in which I am caught before my nerves are gone?" If I was to do anything of account, in the field in which I wanted to work, it would be a long pull. If I could capture thus some accounts of my own there would be no more time clocks for me.

I could come and go, wander about in streets, sit in little bars, spend days and even weeks consorting with all sorts of men.

I would be picking up stories. I would be finding out more and more about the lives of other men.

"If I do go to another place, may I depend upon you?"

One by one I got them, and when I thought all was secure I made my plan. "Was it plain stealing?" I am sure I do not know.

"I am going to resign, quit," I said.

"But what is wrong?" Bayard asked and I explained.

I did not like being compelled to ring a clock. There were certain accounts on which I was willing to work. On others I was not.

"Now I have got some accounts of my own," I said.

I frankly explained what I had done and there was talk.

I had been disloyal, in fact a scamp.

"It is to laugh," I said. Did I not know by what road he had got to where he was? I remember that for an hour we sat in talk. It was understood that, first of all, he would make an effort to shake the accounts loose from my grip.

"And, if you do not succeed?"

"Yes. In that case we will deal," he said, and, "I should have watched you more closely," he added.

So our deal was made and I got a certain freedom. All the detail work, the getting out of cuts to newspapers and magazines, the checking of these to see that advertisements appeared, all such work was to be done by him and there were to be no more time clocks for me. I now think he envied me a little.

I remember that he spoke of it. Formerly he had been one of us and formerly also he had been a scribbler of verses.

"It is a theft you have committed here," he said, "but it may be you have been wise.

"You have not tried to steal too big a chunk.

"It may be that you will get away with it."

There was the dream of retiring he had. Now he spoke of it to me. I can remember the hour, late in the afternoon of a Chicago winter day, when I stood with him in his office.

It was a large office, occupying a whole upper floor of a Chicago skyscraper. When he talked to me, on that particular occasion, he was very tired.

I remember that I spoke of it.

"You are very tired," I said and, "Yes," he answered. He was a tall and a thin man and formerly, before he made his own strike, we had been rather intimate friends.

And now he was about to realize the American dream. And he was being harried and hunted. On the evening, when we were together, in his expensively furnished office, it was growing dark outside, and, stepping across the room, he snapped out the light.

He came over to where I stood, near a window that looked out upon a sea of city lights, the roar, from the street below, coming faintly up to us, and stood beside me.

We did not look at each other and there was a time of silence. Now he was the man I had formerly known and he was something else. Together I remember we had gone through our Browning period. Sitting together, on some train or in a Chicago barroom late at night, we had fished out, from our portfolio of advertising papers, our copies of Browning.

Or it might be my little leather-bound copy of Shakespeare's sonnets.

We had read aloud to each other.

And then he had got what we in business called "his chance."

He was like a man who has suddenly uncovered a gold mine. He would, with any luck, in a few years, be comfortably rich.

"Even if I could have written verses that were worth printing, how could I have lived by that?" he suddenly said.

This as we stood together by the window of a Chicago skyscraper on a winter evening, the room in which we stood in half darkness. He was like a man suddenly put to his own defense.

"It may be you will get away with it.

"It may even be that you have some talent.

"You may be wise enough to stay small, not to want too much.

"Not to grab at any bigger hunk than you have stolen from us."

He was forcing himself to be severe. A certain huskiness came into his voice.

"You may be able to do what I wanted to do but I hope you don't," he said, and turning from me went out of the room.

3. In Jackson Park

My first story had been written and published. It had appeared in *Harper's Magazine* and was called "The Rabbit Pen." I had not taken the writing of the story very seriously. In fact it had been done in answer to a kind of challenge.

I had gone into the suburbs to spend the week end at a certain house. An old friend, Miss Trilena White, a schoolteacher with whom I had become acquainted when I was at Wittenberg College, had come to visit there. Miss White was a woman who read a great many books, and during the afternoon while we were walking in the garden back of the house we sat down and discussed the art of writing. Near the bench we sat on was a pen of rabbits belonging to some of the children.

My friend, the schoolteacher, was a great admirer of Mr. Howells, then editing what was called "The Easy Chair" section of *Harper's,* and had once called on him at his home. We had been in correspondence for a number of years and she had induced me to read Howells. A statement of his in particular had offended me. It was something to the effect that a writer should present to the public only what he called "the more cheerful aspects of our common existence." Howells had seemed to me a good deal of what Van Wyck Brooks later called "one of the dry sisters of Philistia"; and I got into a half quarrel with the older woman with whom I was sitting. "There is no real flesh in him," I declared. "There is no feeling of blood and bone in his people."

"They are all of them, Howells, Twain, Hawthorne, too much afraid," I declared. "In all their writing there is too much of life left out."

There was, for example, the matter of sex. My own experience in living had already taught me that sex was a tremendous force in life. It twisted people, beat upon them, often distracted and destroyed their lives.

"It must be that these men know what an influence it is on lives, but they are afraid of it."

But what about conversations in everyday American life, in saloons, in the backs of stores, in factories, workshops and streets?

"And I dare say often enough among American women, too? Why hesitate to put down whatever is in men's and women's lives, making the picture whole? I tell you that some day, soon now, men will come—"

As we sat arguing thus, myself being rather high, a birth took place in the nearby rabbit pen and immediately something startling happened. A buck rabbit was in the pen and as the baby rabbits were born of the female he killed them; did it, as I remember the incident now, with blows from his powerful hind legs. "Why, there is something of life," I said to the schoolteacher who sat watching, fascinated and shocked. "There's something of the pleasanter aspects of our common existence. I'll tell you what I will do," I declared. "I shall write a story of this incident that *Harper's Magazine* will buy and publish. I can catch the tone."

The woman laughed at me for my presumption but I did write the story and the magazine did buy it. I received for it seventy-five dollars, and although I had written the story rather with my tongue in my cheek, when I did see it in print, in such a respected magazine and with my name to it, I was proud. I became to my fellow advertising men that man of mark, a literary man. . . . Once I remember I was dining with several advertising men in a fashionable restaurant in Chicago when a man, a stranger to me, walked through the room. A look of awe and respect came to the faces of my dinner companions. "That is the man who wrote 'Eventually, Why Not Now?'" one of them whispered to me while another began boasting of the fact that he knew personally the man who had written the sentence "It never rains but it pours." . . . It referred, I believe, to a certain brand of salt at that time widely advertised.

As it was with these men who had thus by a sentence touched the skirts of fame, so it was with me after my story appeared in *Harper's*. The story itself I never republished in any of my books and have completely forgotten what it was like. But my stock was up among advertising men and my fellow advertising writers working in the same office must have boasted widely of my achievement. Occasionally a business man, one of the clients of our house, spoke to me. "There, you are a writer," he said. "Well, I tell you what you do. Some day you come to my office. You bring a pad and pencil. I will tell you the story of my life.

"Ah, what a life it has been, what a story it will make!" he cried—

Because of what I have said here and elsewhere I'm a little afraid that my readers will gather that I have a kind of contempt for business men. The contrary is true. Almost every business man with whom I have been associated in life has been extraordinarily kind to me, but it does seem to me that the life of a business man, this continual absorption in making profits, in buying and selling, makes for a kind of immaturity and often I have thought that even some of our great business men, masters of huge fortunes, have remained at bottom children. These great skyscrapers they build, the railroads they control, the industries they control are, after all, but toys; they remain children playing with toys.

I recall a conversation had with a certain manufacturer in a Mid-Western town. He had been a vice-president of a large carriage factory but the automobile had come and was destroying his business. He had a great deal of stock in the company and it was decreasing in value. He was a middle-aged man and was facing ruin and failure.

A lucky opportunity came to him. In the city there was a poor workman who had invented a new agricultural tool. The tool had great possibilities but the workman did not know how to exploit it. He did not know how to borrow money from the banks, how to promote the sale of his invention. He went to see the middle-aged business man, thinking him rich.

"I thought I saw my chance but I was not sure," the business man later said to me. He was in a desperate situation and took a chance. The workman having no money and being in debt and desperate, the business man bought all rights in the invention for ten thousand dollars.

It was then that I was called in. I wrote a series of advertisements setting forth the story and the wonder of the new tool. The business man had organized a company which he capitalized at three hundred and fifty thousand dollars and within two years the stock of the company was paying ten per cent in dividends. With this business man I was once walking in the streets of his city on a summer evening. "I am getting a good deal of credit in this town," he said. "Men are calling me shrewd and able." He began telling me as I have set it down here of his buying of the rights to the agricultural tool. "I am being given credit for being shrewd and able but deserve no credit," he said. I looked at him with surprise. "Why, you deserve a great deal of credit for shrewdness," I said.

"But, no," he said. "I deserve no credit. I did not do it," he declared.

"But who did then?" I asked.

"It was God," he said.

Fortunately I controlled my impulse to laugh and he told me a story of how when the working man had come to him with his invention and he saw that he could get control of it for ten thousand dollars, he had been uncertain and frightened. "I was down to my last twenty-five thousand," he said. "If I went into the venture and failed I would be sunk. I went home and shut myself in my room. I knelt down beside my bed. I prayed until three o'clock in the morning and then the voice of God spoke to me. It was God who told me to buy the man out. It is God who is responsible for my success." I wanted to shout with laughter. I excused myself and got away.

Not all business men with whom I was associated were like this one. There was another one who had also been a manufacturer of carriages, and the day of carriages was at an end. This man fell into my hands and together we worked out a scheme. There was in Chicago a manufacturer of cheap phonographs and the phonograph was new. The bigger companies were getting, as I remember, from seventy-five to a hundred dollars for these instruments and I had found a manufacturer who would turn them out and deliver to my carriage manufacturer at fourteen dollars each. They were undoubtedly cheaply made of unseasoned lumber but they had a temporary outward look of quality. Our scheme was a unique one. We shipped several carloads of these machines to some city, took a two-page spread in the daily newspaper. For two days we rented a store building. For two days we were to sell a hundred dollar phonograph for twenty-nine-fifty. People came in crowds. In every city we cleaned up magnificently.

But I had been crooked with my client. My Chicago manufacturer delivered machines to him at fifteen but privately gave me a bonus of one dollar on every machine sold. I of course made the usual commission on the advertising in newspapers. For a time money rolled in to me. I grew embarrassed and ashamed. I had not spent any of this money but kept it at a separate account in a bank and I do not know now whether I was really ashamed or afraid. I could not sleep at night and finally in desperation went to my client and confessed. I showed him my bank book. "Here is the amount of my graft," I said. "It is really yours," and he laughed and slapped me on the back. "Do you not know that the whole transaction stinks?" he said. "Keep the money, you are a young fool. If it had been me I would have managed to shave off at least three dollars each on the machines."

There were many odd experiences of this sort. In one of the companies I had got the confidence of a certain politician, a client of Mark Hanna's. He had put money into one of my schemes and this particular scheme had turned out successfully.

But he was also treasurer of the little company we had organized and had invested rather largely in some of my other promotions. When I left the Ohio city he had lost some thousands of dollars.

I did not hear from him for several years and then one day he called me from a room in a Chicago hotel. He counted out some fifteen hundred dollars in cash and laid it on a desk. "It is yours," he said. "It is your half of the profits from our little scheme."

"But," I exclaimed. "This is not fair. You were in several of my schemes. You must have lost through me several thousands of dollars—"

He laughed. He explained to me that to him life was a game of poker. You sat in a game at one time and lost and at another sitting you gained. "I always knew you were a crazy anarchist, Sherwood," he said. "But I thought you were brighter than you are—you take life too seriously. If some of these other schemes of yours had turned out profitably, if you had not discovered you had a soul, if you had laid off your damn scribbling, you might have made all your schemes work and in that case I would have pocketed my profits with no special thanks to you. Take this money and get out of here and do not waste your breath thanking me," he said. But when I was at the door he called to me. "But wait," he said. "We might at least have a drink together, my boy."—We did drink together and in fact went on a carouse that lasted some two or three days. In these latter two men there was certainly a quality that I was after. They did not fake themselves. There was none of the eternal talk of "service," etc., that so annoyed me in the more conventional business men.

But I must get on. I had taken rooms in Fifty-seventh Street— I can see the rooms clearly as I write, the cheap rugs on the floor, the pictures on the wall. There would have been two or three Maxfield Parrishes. A calendar got at a drug store or hardware store and showing a pretty girl with just a suggestion of nudity. The furniture in the room was horribly ugly, but when I was in my writing mood I did not mind. Beside my bed I had a cot and could have a guest for the night; there was what in modern cities is called a kitchenette, and I had gone to a second-hand store and bought myself a big old table at which I could write. The table had formerly been used I believe in a clothing store to display men's clothing, and had had to be taken apart and put together again in order to pass through the door. It occupied one whole side of the room—it was almost large enough to be used as a stage in a small theater—and from end to end it was piled with huge stacks of manuscript, most of it written in longhand. I had begun again at my stories, and had before me the manuscripts written in the room at the top of the house in the Ohio town where for five years I had struggled to be what nature never intended me to be—a man of business. There were four or five long novels, any number of attempts at verse, articles on every conceivable subject and I do not know how many short and long-short stories. I have always had bales and bales of such manuscripts about me, great boxes filled with them, often left some place, forgotten.

What peace and quiet in the room. Though I was back in the old grind, I had my evenings and there were the week ends. How much I thought then of the matter of publication, of becoming a real author, I do not know. It seems to me now that I did not take that into consideration. I was hoping through writing to clear up the tangled mess of impulses within myself. For years I had been going about, observing, making notes in my mind. There was a notion that by transferring everything into an imaginary world I could get things straighter.

In Cleveland, for instance, there had been one tall, rather handsome prostitute who had taken a fancy to me.

"You be my man," she said.

I had been sitting about in the parlor of such a house, with companions picked up. Men were drinking with the women of the place and now and then one of them disappeared up a stairway with one of the women.

So it had come to that, the relationship between men and women of which I had dreamed such dreams in my boyhood.

"And why am I here?"

I kept asking myself that question. I kept drinking. I became drunk and fell off the chair in which I had been sitting.

I had spent the night in that place. The tall woman had taken care of me. I awoke there in the morning.

I was on a couch, in a little alcove off what was called the parlor of the house, and presently there was that tall woman sitting beside me and we began to talk.

It was a strange conversation. When I had become drunk on the night before some of the other women of the place along with the men with whom I had come there had wanted to undress me. The idea had been to expose me to the view of all who came into the place. They had planned to paint my body, decorate certain very private parts of my body, make a kind of vulgar spectacle of me, but the tall woman had stopped it. She told me of that. She had, she said, a brother at home who was much like me.

"Did you come here to get a woman?" she asked and I told her that I had not come with that in mind.

I had come to that place in an effort to escape from myself.

"There is something about myself I do not like."

There is, I realize, a danger of sentimentalizing all this. Men are always doing that in regard to prostitutes. All I can be sure of is that on the morning I left that place filled with shame, my eyes taking in the street as I emerged from the door and hurried away, the same shame that came when on a nearby street I passed some children playing on the sidewalk. But later, on two or three occasions, I did see the tall prostitute again. In a kind of spirit of defiance I phoned to her. I invited her to dine with me at one of the big Cleveland hotels, took her to the trotting meeting, walked in streets with her, was seen in her presence by men from my town where I was a respectable manufacturer.

And all of this out of a spirit of defiance, wanting in some way to defy the respectable, money-making, scheming, money-grasping life of which I had been a part.

"And do you want to be my man?" The tall woman was puzzled.

"It would be a little like sleeping with my own brother. You and he look so alike."

There was of course her own story told to me. Whether it was a true story or not I cannot say. It was all connected with the brother, who it seemed I resembled. He did not know what she was doing. He was, she declared, a student in a college in the West, was at the University of Wisconsin.

"We are Italians," she said. She was going to get her brother started in life. He had no idea of what she was doing. When she had seen him through college, had got him established, she would no longer be a prostitute.

"More than one woman who has been a whore has afterward turned out to be a good wife to some man," she said.

"Do you want to be my man, my special man?"

"Well, I do not want you to be. It would be too much like being with my own brother—"

Such happenings in my life. Obviously that tall woman wanting something outside the life she was living, kind of grasping at a friendship. Or so it seemed to me.

It was all very puzzling, very strange to me. Could I get at the puzzle a little by writing? So I wrote, rapidly, in my rather large hand that is so difficult, my friends tell me, to decipher. When I sat down at my table a great surge of energy seemed to come over me. Sometimes it has seemed to me that I only lived during these periods of writing. At times, often, I wrote for six or eight hours, wrote with furious energy, using large cheap tablets, tearing off the sheets and dropping them on the floor when they were full. They accumulated in great piles about my chair. Package after package of cigarettes was consumed. It seemed to me that I must be creating world-shaking masterpieces, and I was careful enough to number the sheets as I tore them off.

I kept writing at odd moments—I had trained myself to write in off places and at odd moments. There was a railroad station in Fifth Avenue (now Wells Street) near Twelfth. It was called Grand Central but was not *grand*. The Pere Marquette and two or three other rather minor railroads unloaded their passengers there. The station had a dining room upstairs above the train shed. It was somewhat difficult to find and little patronized. A few business men of the neighborhood used to come into the place for lunch. Most of them ate hurriedly and went away. I could sit undisturbed in this restaurant for hours and it became one of my haunts. I never took my advertising friends there. I sat in the place with pads of paper before me. There was a seat in a corner that more or less became my property.

A rather handsome tall woman waited on my table. I thought she must have been some five or six years older than myself. Her figure was like that of the poet Eunice Tietjens, who later married the poet and playwright Cloyd Head. At the office I would say, "I can do a better job on this assignment by myself. I cannot work in this clatter." Gathering up my papers I would go out of the office. "I'll be back in a few hours." I did not tell anyone where I was going. Sometimes I would bring books, three or four of them, carrying them in my portfolio, to the quiet restaurant in the Grand Central Station. Was it quiet? At any rate there were new sounds. Occasionally trains came in and unloaded their passengers. I could hear the sound of the scurrying feet of the newcomers in the city. Not many years before I had been such a newcomer, full of ambitions that now were gone. I had been intent on being a big man in the city, getting rich there. Now I had these new, more puzzling problems—

Still as fast as I wrote, I threw away. On other occasions a kind of sickness overcame me. For a week or two I would do no work. I would destroy bales of my writing, walk restlessly about at night, get myself drunk. It seemed to me that these hundreds of thousands of words put down amounted to nothing, that I was merely aping the writings of other men I had read, that I had no clear and honest outlook on life and was utterly incapable of getting one. I must say that in all the writing I had done up to this time there was little or no originality. I was "the sedulous ape," continually reading novels—but not, as was afterwards said, the Russians, whom I read only long after I was accused of imitating them. I was under the spell of the earlier novels of H. G. Wells, and those of Thomas Hardy, Arnold Bennett and George Moore. Of George Borrow I had long been a devotee, and like most young men who have a leaning toward literature I read and reread George Moore's *Confessions of a Young Man*. How I longed to be such another, to live in some city like Paris, the center of the art expression of a nation, to have beautiful mistresses, to have an estate in Ireland as Moore had, from which I would get sufficient money to sustain me in the life I loved. I would not of course have objected if the money had come from an estate in Iowa or Kansas.

But beautiful mistresses did not flock to me. . . . During these periods all the ugliness of my quarters came more and more into my consciousness. At such times I did not want to return to my rooms to sleep and sometimes went the length of going to some hotel for two or three nights. I was not quite clear whether it was my surroundings, the physical texture of the life about me, that I so hated, or myself for the reason that all the writing I had done with such fervor and hopefulness had suddenly seemed false. But the very sight of my pile of manuscripts made me ill. I avoided people, ceased going about in the evening with the comrades I had found in business. When I drank, I was inclined to get into fights. Some innocent enough statement, made by one of my comrades, would arouse my ire. I threw a glass of beer into a man's face and got a black eye. I wanted to fight but was not a fighter. I wished I were one and this led to absurd dreams. I dreamed of becoming a champion prize fighter or a baseball player famous because he always hit home runs. Sometimes as I walked along the street I began sparring with some imaginary opponent and came out of the dream realizing I was being laughed at by a passer-by.

In the afternoons I hurried home from the office. I was constantly cheating my employer. I would call up some client for whom I was writing advertisements telling him I wanted to see him, then telling my copy chief I had been called out by the advertiser, and go to see my man, spend a few minutes with him and then go home. "What does it matter if I am caught? They can go to hell," I said. I didn't mean it. I wanted the money I was getting. I wanted the luxuries it could buy—I was craving luxuries. Evenings, walking across Jackson Park to the lake—the building in which I had rooms lay only half a dozen blocks from the Park—I had other absurd dreams of becoming some kind of crook, perhaps a bank robber. I went to bed at night and dreamed of having become a bold and skillful robber. I crept into some bank, blew a safe, walked away with thousands.

I had any number of other absurd dreams. Some other man had robbed a bank. He was fleeing along the street with a hand bag filled with hundred dollar bills. I met him on a corner, in a dark street, and he thrust the bag into my hands. He had arranged to have a confederate stand on that corner but the confederate had not appeared. Luckily I had appeared instead and in the darkness he took me for his confederate. He thrust the bag into my hands and I stepping into a store emerged into another street. I got into a cab and went to my room. I was suddenly rich, did not have to write any more advertisements. All of these absurdities were often very real to me. I planned to go to London, to Paris, to Vienna to meet other artists, to talk to them of what I wanted to do. These dreams, often vividly real, seem absurd now but at the time of which I am speaking they were, at least while the dream lasted, real enough. It is a wonder I did not become a writer of detective stories or stories of crime. "I must quit this kind of absurdity," I told myself. It was a kind of mental masturbation.

I would return to my rooms and sit at my desk and write. My life had become an absurdity. But perhaps I could bury myself in other, imagined lives. Words poured out of me. Often it did not work. The pencil dropped from my fingers and I sat at my desk, staring out at the window. I seemed to myself altogether alone in the world.

I turned to look at the pile of manuscript on my desk. "Why am I doing this?" I asked myself. "I have so and so many hundreds of thousands of words, but why?" Nothing I had written seemed to have any life. Could I make my stories live? Would I ever achieve that wonder? "If I could do that I would not be so lonely," I kept telling myself. I could surround myself with imagined figures so real that they would be like companions to me.

There was something I constantly sought. What was it? It seemed to me that most of all I wanted to lose self. There was a constant feeling of dirt within. "I have made myself filthy," I told myself. I think it was this feeling of dirt in life, in myself, that had destroyed my relations with my family. I had children but did not live with my family. I kept trying to think my way through my own muddle. It was at about this time that the woman suffrage movement reached its peak. Some of the women in the office where I worked were in the movement.

I did not believe in it. They would get the vote, but what of it? Basically men and women were not alike. I tried to think my way through this problem. "A woman can exist fully in a physical world. She can create in a physical world. Children come out of her body." Often at this time I half wished I was myself a woman. I would go get a lover, would have many children.

But I, a male, was striving to have children in another world and they would not emerge. I threw my pencil down, walked out of my room into the street. Often I went along muttering to myself. "The male world is the world of the spirit," I told myself. All of my pronouncements were, to be sure, constantly being refuted by women artists but they were very dear to me. I had wanted in myself a kind of great tenderness toward all life but the dirt within kept making me more and more disagreeable with others.

"I cannot go on in this way," I kept telling myself. The mood I was in at this time led to a sort of nervous breakdown. I was still strong, could at times work in the office all day and coming home write all night, without a sense of weariness, but I had a disease. It was the disease of self. I knew that. Perhaps I could escape out of myself into the life of some woman. I began creating a new dream, that of becoming a great lover, the lover of any number of beautiful women.

It was early summer and I left my room. I was unable to work, and went along Fifty-seventh Street to the park. I walked restlessly about. "I will go get myself a woman, will lose myself in her." The dreams of having women were as absurd as the other dreams I was having. What did I expect? I half expected some beautiful woman to stop me on the paths. "I want you. You are very beautiful to me. Come with me. Come into my arms." Did I expect something of this kind to happen? Really, I didn't in a real world, but in the world of the dream it could happen. I constantly passed couples walking together. There was a very beautiful young woman, elegantly dressed, who walked with a very dignified, gray-haired man. He was, I had no doubt, her father. I began to follow them. They strolled through the Park and went to walk by the lake and I was at their heels. It was a wonder I was not arrested. They went to sit on the stone steps of the Field Museum. They were on the side of the building that looked out over a small lagoon and were engaged in low-voiced conversation. There was no one else near and I went to sit near them. I kept looking at the woman. How beautiful she was. Why did she not speak to me? Why did she not leave the older man, her father, and come to me? "I am not physically unattractive. I have a mind. I have an imagination. I am a poet." These sentences I whispered to myself. I grew suddenly ashamed and getting up crept away. There had been a pause in the conversation of the man and the woman. The man had noticed me hanging about. "Who is that fellow? He has been following us. Do you know the fellow?" I did not hear his words but in some inner way knew they had been spoken. I crept away like a thief.

A strange sort of fear took possession of me. Sometimes I wandered about half the night in the streets. There was an outbreak of holdups in Chicago at the time and twice I became a victim, once losing my watch and some small change and at another time a roll of bills containing $20 or $30. In the state I was in, the holdups did not frighten me. I tried to laugh and joke with one of the holdup men, but he cut me short. He gave me to understand that business with him was business.

"Shut your trap or I'll plug you," was what he said.

The depression continued for months. I could not come out of it. Occasionally I picked up some woman of the streets, tried to get comfort from association with her. It did not work, and after such experiences I fell into deeper gloom. I went about alone and into the lower class of saloons. Tried to get into some sort of relation with men and women picked up in such places. There must have been at the time in me some notion that if I could find people sufficiently low in the social scale, I would find comrades. Myself I felt to be an utterly defeated man and wanted others who were defeated. I drank a good deal and went muttering through the streets. I carried a little note-book in my pocket and sitting at some beer-stained table in a low saloon, wrote sentences.

"It is only when you are defeated and drift like a rudderless ship that I can come close to you," I wrote.

During this deep depression, a mood that everyone working in the arts, particularly in America, must know, I had a rather strange experience. It may be that I was for the time slightly insane. I had left the advertising office at noon, had gone out to lunch and found myself unable to return. I took a street car and went south to my old quarters, but could not stay there. I went to walk in Jackson Park.

There was in the Park a small island that during the Chicago World's Fair had been known as the Japanese Village. It was approached by beautiful little bridges built by the Japanese, and I went there to sit. I had brought from my room a thick tablet of paper. At that time I had always the feeling that at any moment I might begin to really write. There would be some response out of my very self to the life about me.

"Somewhere within me there must be sleeping a true man," I kept saying to myself.

I was sitting on a bench beside a path on the island in the park and people kept passing up and down before me. There were young men and old men, young women and old women. A pair of lovers came and sat on a nearby bench, but were soon embarrassed by my presence. They went away. At the moment none of them seemed real to me. The tree under which I sat, the grass in the Park, the water in the nearby lagoon, the beautiful little Japanese bridges, none of these things seemed real. I remember that I leaned forward on the bench and touched the gravel path with my fingers.

"It is real. This is the earth. These are little stones I hold here in my hand," I muttered to myself.

There were a young man and woman passing and I began suddenly to laugh.

"I have gone a little crazy," I told myself, but I did not care. "How do I know these are little stones I hold in my hand? They may be rare and precious jewels," I said aloud.

The young man and woman paused and stared at me. A look of fear came into the eyes of the woman. The man and woman were whispering together.

"You do not need to be afraid. You are quite beautiful. No woman who is beautiful needs to be afraid," I said.

Turning occasionally to stare back at me, the young man and woman hurried away.

Left alone on the bench beside the path on the little island in the Park, I suddenly began to write. I wrote rapidly, with a kind of insane abandon. Hours passed and I continued writing. It seemed to me that I wrote a thousand, ten thousand, a hundred thousand words. At last I wrote a long and completely beautiful story. Oh, with what precision the words were laid against each other. The words had become like beautiful jewels to me. How tender I was with them, how skillful my fingers, how superlatively skillful my brain.

The truth is, of course, that I was exhausted when I went there and what had really happened was that I had sat down on the bench and gone to sleep. All of the things that I have put down here as having happened, my feeling the earth with my fingers, my speaking to the young woman accompanied by the man, all of this took place in a dream.

But the strange part of the experience was that the dream seemed to continue when I awoke. I did not look at the tablet I held in my hand, so convinced was I that I had written a beautiful story. I walked home to my room and laid the tablet on the table, went out to a restaurant and dined and returning to my room, undressed and went to bed. I was happy and relaxed and fell at once into a long and dreamless sleep. I did not awaken until morning and my awakening brought a strange shock to me. For a time I lay in the bed, still convinced that I had at last written a beautiful story and then, getting out of bed, I went, filled with both hope and fear, to the table where I had laid the tablet. The tablet, of course, was blank.

4. We Little Children of the Arts

The big German man came along the river bank to where I was lying on the brown grass at the river's edge. The book I had been reading was on the grass beside me. I had been gazing across the sluggish little river at the distant horizon.

I had hoped to spend the day working. There was a story I wanted to write. This was in a low flat country southwest of the city of Chicago. I had come there that morning by train with the others, Joe and George and Jerry, the big German.

They all wanted to be painters. They were striving. The Sundays were very precious to the others and to me. We were all working during the week and looking forward to the week ends. There were certain canvases the others wanted to paint. If one of them could get a painting hung in the Chicago Art Institute it might be a beginning.

We used to speak of it at the lunch hours during the week.

There was a certain story that had been in my mind for weeks, even months. We were all living about in little rooming houses. We were clerks. Jerry, the big German, had been a truck driver. Now he had a job as a shipping clerk in a cold storage warehouse.

I had tried time and again to write the particular story that was in my mind. I told the others about it. I didn't tell them the story. That would bring bad luck. I spoke instead of how I wanted the words and sentences to march.

"Like soldiers marching across a field," I said.

"Like a plow turning up its ribbon of earth across a field."

Fine phrases about work not done. There had been too much of that. You can kill any job so. Just keep talking about the great thing you are to do some time in the future. That will kill it.

"Yes, and it is so also that paint should go on a canvas."

This would be one of the others, one of the painters speaking.

There was this big talk, plenty of that, words, too many words. Sometimes, after the day's work, in the hot Chicago summers, we all got together to dine in some cheap place. There was a chop suey joint to which we went often, soft-footed, soft-voiced Chinamen trotting up and down. Chop suey and then a couple of bottles of beer each. We lingered long over that. Then a walk together along the lake front on the near North Side. There was a little strip of park up there facing the lake, a bathing beach, working men with wives and children came there to escape the heat, newspapers spread on the grass, whole families huddled together in the heat, even the moon, looking down, seeming to give forth heat.

We would be full of literary phrases, culled out of books.

Only Jerry, the big German, was a little different. He had a wife and children.

"What's it all about? Why do I want to paint? Why can't I be satisfied driving a truck and working in my warehouse?

"Going home at night to the wife and kids?

"What is it keeps stirring in a man, making him want to do something out of just himself?"

He grew profane. He would be describing a scene. He had come to the Chinese place from his warehouse across the Chicago River, this before the river was beautified, in the days of the old wooden bridges over the river.

He had stood for a time on one of the bridges, seeing a lake boat pass, lake sailors standing on the deck of the boat and looking up at him standing there above on the moving bridge, the curiously lovely chrysoprase color of the river, the gulls floating over the river.

He would begin speaking of all that, the beauty of the smoky sky over buildings off to the west. Sometimes he pounded with his fists on the table in the chop suey joint. A string of oaths flowed from his lips. Sometimes tears came into his eyes.

He was, to be sure, ridiculous. There was in him something I knew so well later in another friend, Tom Wolfe—a determination, half-physical, all his big body in it, like a man striving to push his way through a stone wall.

Out into what?

He couldn't have said what any more than I could of my own hopes, my own passionate desires, of which I was always half ashamed.

To get it in some way down, something felt.

A man was too much in a cage—in some way trapped.

A man got himself trapped. All of this business of making a living. There were Jerry and Joe, both married. They both had children.

Joe had been a farmer boy, on his father's farm, somewhere in Iowa. He had come to Chicago filled with hope.

He was like Jerry, the German. He wanted to paint.

"That's what I want.

"I want something."

And why the hell did a man get married? They spoke of that. They weren't complaining of the particular women they had married. You knew they were both fond of their children.

A man got stuck on some dame. A man was made that way. When it got him, when it gripped him, he thought, he convinced himself, that in her, in that particular one, was the thing he sought.

Then the kids coming.

They trap you that way.

Joe speaking up. He wasn't as intense as Jerry. He said we couldn't blame them, the women, his own or any other man's woman.

How'd we know they weren't trapped too? They were wanting to be beautiful in some man's eyes, that was it. They had, Joe declared, as much right to want their thing as we had to want ours.

But what was it we were all wanting, the little group of us, there in that vast Chicago, who had in some way found each other?

Comradeship in hungers we couldn't express.

Anyway it wasn't really success. We knew that. We had got that far.

George said we ought to be skunks. "A man should be a skunk," he said. George wasn't married but had an old mother and father he was supporting. He was laying down a law he couldn't obey.

"So I'm a clerk, eh?

"And whose fault is it?

"Mine, I tell you.

"I ought to walk out on them, on everyone, let 'em go to hell.

"What I want is to wander up and down for a long time. Look and look.

"People think of it as a virtue, a man like me, sticking to a clerk's job, supporting my old father and mother, when it's just cowardice, that's all.

"If I had the courage to walk out on them, be a skunk."

It was something he couldn't do. We all knew that.

✦

By the river bank, on the Sunday afternoon, after a morning trying to write the story I had for weeks been trying to write, I had torn up what I had written. There were the pages of meaningless words, that refused to march, thrown into the sluggish river, floating slowly away.

White patches on a background of yellow sluggish river.

"Patience, patience."

White clouds floating in a hot sky, over a distant corn field.

"Oh, to hell with patience."

How many men like me, over the world, everywhere, all over America, in big towns like Chicago and New York, small towns or farms.

Trying for it.

For what?

There was something beyond money to be made, fame got, a big name. I was already past thirty. There were the others, Joe, Jerry and George, none of them any longer young.

The World War had not yet come. It was to scatter us, shatter us.

The big German Jerry came down to where I lay on my back on the dry grass by the sluggish stream. He had with him the canvas on which he had been working all day. Now it was growing late. At noon, when we had together eaten our lunches, he had been hopeful.

"I think I'll get something. By the gods, I think I will."

Now he sat beside me on the grass at the stream's edge. He had thrown his wet canvas aside. Across the stream from us we could see stretched away the vast corn fields.

The corn was ripening now. The stalks grew high, the long ears hanging down. Soon it would be corn-cutting time.

It was a fat rich land—the Middle West. At noon Jerry, the German, —son of a German immigrant—who had been a city man all his life, had suddenly begun talking.

He had been trying to paint the corn field. For the time he had forgotten to be profane. We others had all come from farms or from country towns of the Middle West. He had said that he wanted to paint a corn field in such a way that everyone looking at his painting would begin to think of the fatness and richness of all Middle-Western America.

It would be something to give men new confidence in life. He had grown serious. He was the son of a German immigrant who had fled to America to escape military service. Germany believed in the army, in the brute power of arms, but he, Jerry, wanted by his painting to make people believe in the land.

I remembered that, in his earnestness, he had shaken a big finger under our noses. "You fellows, your fathers and grandfathers were born on the land. You can't see how rich it all is, how gloriously men might live here." He had spoken of his father, the immigrant, now an old man. We others couldn't understand how hard and meager life had become for the peasants in all the European lands. We didn't know our own richness, what a foundation the land, on which to build.

But he would show them through the richness of the fields. The skyscrapers in the cities, money piled in banks, men owning great factories, they were not the significant things.

The real significance was in the tall corn growing. There was the real American poetry.

He'd show them.

He sat beside me on the grass, by the stream. We sat a long time in silence. There was a grim look on his face and I knew that he had failed as, earlier in the day, I had. I did not want to embarrass him by speaking. I stayed silent, occasionally looking up at him.

He sat staring at the sluggish stream and looking across the stream to where the corn fields began and I thought I saw tears in his eyes.

He didn't want me to see.

Suddenly he jumped up. Profane words flew from his lips. He began to dance up and down on the canvas lying on the grass. I remember that the sun was going down over the tops of the tall corn stalks and he shook his fists at it. He cursed the sun, the corn, himself. What was the use? He had wanted to say something he'd never be able to say. "I'm a shipping clerk in a lousy warehouse and I'll always be just that, nothing else." It was a child's rage in a grown man. He picked up the canvas on which he had been at work all day and threw it far out into the stream.

We were on our way to the suburban station where we would get our train into the city. All the others, Joe, George and Jerry, had their painting traps, their easels, boxes of color, palettes. They had little canvas stools on which they sat while painting and Joe and George carried the wet canvases they had done during the day.

We went along in silence, Joe and George ahead while I walked with Jerry. Did he want me to carry some of his traps?

"Oh, to hell with them, and you too."

He was in this grim mood. Fighting back something in himself. We went along a dusty road beside a wood and cut across a field in which tall weeds grew. We were getting near the station where we were to take the train.

Back to the city.

To our clerkships.

To his being a shipping clerk in his warehouse.

To little hot and cold Chicago flats where some of us had wives and children waiting.

To be fed, clothed, housed.

"A man can't just live in his children. He can't, I tell you."

Something rebellious in all of us.

What is it a man wants, to be of some account in the world, in himself, in his own manhood?

The attempts to write, to paint, these efforts only a part of something we wanted.

All of us half knowing all our efforts would end in futility.

I am very sure the same thoughts were in all our minds that evening, in the field of tall weeds, in the half darkness, as we drew near the little prairie railroad station, the lights of the train already seen far off, across the flat prairies.

And then the final explosion from Jerry. He had suddenly put his painting traps down. He began to throw his tubes of paint about, hurling them into the tall weeds in the field.

"You get out of here, damn you. Go on about your business."

He had thrown his easel, his stool, his paint brushes. He stood there dancing among the tall weeds.

"Go on. Go away. I'll kill you if you don't."

I moved away from him and joined the others on the platform by the station. It was still light enough to see the man out there in the field where the tall weeds grew waist high. He was still dancing with rage, his hands raised, no doubt still cursing his fate.

He was expressing something for us all. He was going through something we had all been through and before we died would all go through again and again.

And then the train came and we got silently aboard but already we could see happening what I think we all knew would happen. We saw Jerry, that brusque, profane German already down on his knees among the weeds in the field.

We knew what he was doing, but, when our train arrived in the city and we separated at the station, Joe and George still clinging to the canvases they both knew were no good—when the others had gone I hung about the station.

I had been a farm boy, an American small town boy like Joe and George. I was curious. Jerry, the big German, had spoken of the land. We had, all of us, been thinking of ourselves as rather special human beings, men with a right to that curious happiness that comes sometimes, fleetingly enough, with accomplishment.

Forgetting the millions like us on farms, holding minor jobs in cities.

What old Abe Lincoln meant when he spoke of "the people."

I was remembering bad years when I was a small town boy, working about on farms, farmers working all through the year, from daylight until dark.

Big Jerry wanted to express something out of the American land.

Droughts coming, hail storms destroying crops, disease among the cattle, often a long year's work come to nothing.

Something else remembered out of my own boyhood.

Springs coming, after such disastrous years, and the farmers near my own Middle-Western town out again in their fields, again plowing the land.

A kind of deep patient heroism in millions of men, on the land, in cities, too.

The government pensioning men who went out to kill other men but no pensions for men who spent long lives raising food to feed men.

Killers become heroes, the millions of others never thinking of themselves as heroes.

There would be another train in an hour and I wanted to see what I did see, keeping myself unseen, the arrival of Jerry, most of his painting traps again collected.

Knowing, as I did know, that on another week end he would be trying again.

5. Margy Currie

Margery Currie (called Margy) was the first person with whom I came into relation in the rather wonderful new world I managed to enter about this time. It must have been a year or two before the American intervention in the World War. The relation was brought about by my brother Karl.

He was holding an exhibition of his paintings in Chicago. The period was an altogether exciting one in the city. The so-called Armory Show had been brought from New York. Something about the show went deep into us. Karl and myself who went to see it every day both felt there a new approach to nature in art. Color was speaking in its own tongue. We walked about in the streets at night talking, Karl telling me of what had happened among the painters in New York through the exhibition. The older and established painters were deeply disturbed, trying to explain it away. "It's just a trick of the Jews," an older painter mirthlessly told him. "The Paris art dealers are doing it. They are all Jews." My brother laughed.

One evening Karl, who was staying with me in my rooms, brought home a little yellow book called *Tender Buttons* by someone named Gertrude Stein. We read it aloud. It was a wonderful medley of words. Words seemed to glance in a new light, to stand away from one another, play games together, roll and tumble about, laugh at me from the page.

"But what is this? So you are writing now." He had picked up one of the novels I had written. He took it away with him one morning. He was taking me into the new world. It began with his visit.

He had taken one of my novels, the one later published under the title of *Windy McPherson's Son,* to Floyd Dell. Miss Currie who at the time was a reporter on one of the Chicago dailies had been sent to my brother's show to write a piece about it. She and he immediately had become friends, and he had told her about the manuscripts, short stories, novels, attempts at poetry piled on my table. At this time Miss Currie and Floyd Dell had separated, each living in his own quarters, but they still were friendly, and she had asked my brother to bring her one of my novels, saying she would take it to Floyd Dell. Floyd was then editor of what was called in Chicago *The Friday Review of Literature,* the widely read supplement of the *Evening Post.* It was a position that had been held by Mr. Francis Hackett and Dell had been his assistant, but Hackett had gone off to New York, to become one of the editors of the newly established *New Republic,* and Dell had become the literary editor of the *Post* with Lucian Cary as his assistant.

So there was Dell reading my novel, and presently, in the columns of the Friday *Post,* writing of me.

I was, it seemed, the great unknown.

Why, how exciting. There I was, as Dell was saying in print in a newspaper read as I presumed by thousands, an unknown man (I do not now remember whether or not he mentioned my name) doing, in obscurity, this wonderful thing.

And with what eagerness I read. If he had not printed my name at least he had given an outline of my novel. There could be no mistake.

"It's me. It's me."

I pranced excitedly up and down in my room.

"I must know this man."

It seemed to me that I had, of a sudden, been chosen, elected as it were, given a kind of passport into some strange new and exclusive world.

It was true that I had already published a story, but I had not taken the story very seriously. So it was quite another thing to have Dell writing in a newspaper of an unpublished novel of mine. Shortly after I got a letter from Margy Currie asking me to her home.

I went, filled with excitement. Now I was to go into a new world, men and women whose interests would be my interest, the curious feeling of loneliness and uncertainty broken up. I thought of the nights when I could not work, the hours spent walking the city streets, great projects forming in my mind, coming to nothing.

I went to the address, at the corner of Fifty-seventh and Stony Island Avenue and found there a row of low one story buildings. The buildings had been, I was later told, hurriedly thrown up at the time of the Chicago World's Fair. There had been stores there but now they had become the homes of men and women of Chicago's intellectual and artistic set. On that first night I walked back and forth alone before the fronts. Curtains had been put up which were now drawn and behind the curtains in the rooms I could hear voices. Shouts of laughter went up and a voice began to sing.

There was a party going on in Margy Currie's quarters—indeed they were a single large room that had once been a retail store, in which a partition had been thrown up to provide a kitchenette. As it was a warm spring evening, the door leading into the street was open. There were a dozen young men and as many women sitting in the place.

They were seated on the floor, on couches, on chairs. Drinks were being passed about. A man I later knew to be Floyd Dell, was holding forth. I stopped near the door, stood against the front of the building, out of sight, and listened. What gaiety within. A discussion was in progress. "Here," I began to tell myself, "is the kind of talk for which I have been hungry." I began to idealize the life within the room. Occasionally a street car passed and the talk in the room was lost in the rattle of the wheels of the car, but when it had passed I could pick it up again, and it seemed to me very wonderful. Here was a world of men and women, of my own age, absorbed in the thing in which I wanted to absorb myself. Could I ever enter that world?

I saw Margy Currie running about the room. She was serving drinks to the others. She had a shrill and laughing voice. In some way I sensed the fact that she was carrying the tone of the party, making it go. She was a small woman with a big mouth. I could not see her eyes. "She will have merry eyes," I told myself. What a contrast to the beauty I had been following. Now I did not want that beauty. I wanted this other beauty of relationship with people who I had begun whispering to myself were my own kind.

But I lost courage, went into the Park. "They will find me out," I thought. "They will sense the fakiness in me." I had been faking for so long a time both as a manufacturer and as an advertising writer, working so long with my tongue in my cheek, that I had begun to fear that everything in my nature was poisoned by fakiness. True, I had tried to make a philosophy for myself. I had clung to the idea that I could preserve an honest mind. "I am not responsible for the society into which I have been born," I had told myself. It might be necessary to be a pretender. But you must not lie to yourself. At moments I had had visions of a life I might lead. There was the real world in which I was immersed, and there was this other world, the world of fancy. I had come to think that it also could have a reality. People could exist also in it. I had felt my struggle in the lives of many of the old writers. I presumed it had also existed in the lives of the painters. I had talked over the matter with my brother. But if in the world of my physical existence I had become a slick one, at bottom a crook, would this not affect my life in the world of fancy? I asked my brother this question. "There are these figures in the world of the book, the story. They are constantly being sold out." At that time as now, our magazines were filled with so-called plot stories. A kind of violence was being done in the imaginative world. People were being sold out there, and the plot story to my mind was the result of the domination of the writers by business, which was ruling more and more in America—the result of the influences which made slickness and trickery inevitably a part of business. "To sell out a character in a story or novel for the sake of arriving at some slick tricky ending to the story is the same thing as selling out your friend or your lover in life," I told my brother.

But wasn't my own work as a writer being touched by the same slickness? (I think all of my earlier work was. Like most young writers I had copied many of the tricks of successful American writers.) In seeking to divide my life I was fighting a losing battle. How indeed could I spend my days often being clever, being an actor, doing work in which I did not believe, and then come home and make a straight and honest approach to this other work? How could I be half a crook and half a straight and honest individual? "A man's life shows up in himself," I thought. "My novel may have impressed them but they will immediately be on to me myself." So I hid myself that evening in the bushes.

But there was a movement in the room and presently all emerged into the street. They crossed the street, seeming to me a gloriously happy group, and went into the Park. They were going to walk by the lake. For a time I followed, muttering to myself, "I will never be a part of such a group. How can I? What am I but an advertising writer?" Afterward, when I got to know him, Floyd Dell once hurt me bitterly by saying to me the very words I was saying to myself that night. We had got into a quarrel. "You are only an advertising man who would like to be an artist," he said.

I said the words to myself that night. "You are nothing but a pimp for business men."

I gave up following the group of people and went to walk by myself. I was bitterly lonely. I went to sit on a park bench under a light.

There was another bench nearby and on it sat a woman. She was, as I found out a little later when I talked with her, a working woman. She was employed in some factory.

On that night she sat there on the park bench, lonely as I was. I think I was attracted to her because like the woman I had seen among the artists she was small and had a big mouth. As I soon found out, she had also a crippled foot.

She was rather poorly and shabbily dressed.

We sat thus, the woman and myself, on the two park benches near each other. The light overhead shone on her face. It was a sad, hurt little face. Something stirred within me. I was already keen enough to know that the dress she wore was a cheap one. She had left her own place and had come into the Park, perhaps like myself wanting companionship. She might even want a lover. I grew suddenly bold and turning smiled at her and she returned the smile.

I went to her. "You are alone here and so am I. Come and walk with me."

She hesitated. There was a curious half frightened, half hopeful look in her eyes. "I will walk a little way. I can't stay long. I must soon go home," she said. She got up from the bench and walked with me and it was then I discovered that she had a crippled foot.

I felt suddenly very close to her. "You are crippled and so am I," I thought. We walked along in silence, and when we had got into a dark place, I put my arm around her, and pressing her body to mine, kissed her on the lips. "No, no! You mustn't!" she said, but I knew she did not mean it.

There was something fighting within me. There was pity for myself and for her, this fighting within me with lust. I continued holding her, pressing her body to mine. "I mustn't. I mustn't. Please. Please. I must go home. I mustn't. I mustn't."

I released her and walked with her along the street. We went out of the Park and westward and got presently into a street of rather small and shabby frame houses. We stopped before one of them.

The street was silent and dark and again I held her in my arms, pity had gone out of me and I wanted only her little crippled body.

She was frightened but she was also warm and excited by the excitement in me. I could feel the quivering of her body. I asked her the question bluntly. Would she let me be her lover? Could I come for her on another evening? I wanted to know. Would she go all the way with me?

She protested, saying she could not do what I wanted but presently weakened. "Yes," she said. "Come." She spoke of the park bench where I had found her. "You come there. At eight o'clock. I will be there waiting for you." She turned and ran, with a curious little limp, in at the door of the house and for hours I walked alone in the street. I was bitterly ashamed. It was because of her loneliness, so like my own, that she had agreed to my proposal. She was a cripple and it would be difficult for her to find a lover. She had consented to my proposal only because she was afraid she would lose me. After I had walked for hours through streets and by the lake I returned to Margy Currie's house. It was dark and silent. I returned to my own rooms. I did not again see the crippled girl until three or four years had passed. On a summer Sunday afternoon I was walking with a woman friend in the Park. The woman was a painter, and was speaking to me of her work, and there on a park bench alone sat my little crippled woman. For just a moment she looked into my eyes and I could see that I had only deepened the hurt of one already wounded by life.

Then on a day, perhaps a week after my hesitation, I went along a path and emerged in Stony Island Avenue. I stood until after I saw little Margy Currie enter alone. Again I was about to turn away when the door opened and she came out. In a stumbling, apologetic way I told her who I was.

A new life began for me. Like other women time and time again in my existence, Margy Currie was infinitely kind to me. At once she put me at my ease. "I am going for a walk in the Park. Come with me," she said. We walked about along the paths under the trees, myself silent while she talked. She had read the manuscript my brother had taken to her to give to Dell and had also been impressed by it. As we walked and talked, myself frightened, feeling that at any moment she might turn upon me, she continued talking. Her words were like wine to me.

She was one who had an extraordinarily sharp and sensitive feeling for people and perhaps even at the beginning of our acquaintance she felt something of the struggle going on in me and wanted to help build belief in myself. She spoke of the world of the arts, the world that had seemed such a shadowy, dim, faraway place to me, as having a real existence. I could find comrades there. I could find friends. The whole American world was not involved in the world of business. It may be that my brother had talked to her and had told her something of the struggle going on in me. While she talked thus, we walked for an hour. Then I left her at her door. She had given me a kind of new hope. For the first time I had got a new and to me a strange kind of feeling. It was not concerned with sex and all my approach to women had been dominated by sex. If I could find two, three, a half dozen such friends, I felt, I had not failed, I could go on. I did not need to make the great surrender.

I could not sleep and spent the rest of the night walking through the streets and in the Park and building a new life for myself.

All that summer a little refrain from a popular song I had picked up kept humming in my head. I remember but a few words:

> Life went gaily, gaily
> In the house of Maggie Grady.

I fancy that by the house of Maggie Grady I meant that of Margy Currie. I was no nearer an escape from the advertising trap in which I was caught than I had been, but my deep depression had blown away.

Figures of men and women again are marching through my mind, apparently marching in and out of my room as I sit writing at my desk. All are young. All are part of that Chicago summer. Through meeting Margy Currie I had got ten new friends.

It was through her that I met Ben Hecht, that fellow so rich in words, Arthur Davison Ficke, Floyd Dell who for a time became a kind of literary father to me. Her marriage to him had broken up as my own had broken up, and this fact may have drawn me closer to Margy. In her company I saw the tall poetess Eunice Tietjens, beautiful in her tall slenderness. Lucian Cary came to Margy's house. I went with her and Ben Hecht to a town down state where Ben, then a star reporter on the *Daily News,* was covering a murder trial and a hanging. Warm weather came and we went off, often a great crowd of us, to some little town on the lake.

It was during that summer that I met Carl Sandburg. I was introduced to him by Ben Hecht and we went for a long afternoon's walk through the factory district on Chicago's West Side. At the office I had been given what was called an important assignment but I forgot it. Michael Carmichael Carr, that infinitely charming man known to us as Mike, with the red beard and the endless flow of talk, came from the University of Missouri where he had been teaching art, glad to escape into the city; Alexander Kaun, a Russian Jew, short and squat of frame, came to tell us stories of life in Russia, of the persecution of the Jews there, of life in little Russian villages. Ernestine Evans, that strange world traveler, was there, later always turning up in some unexpected place, in Europe or the Far East. I was to see her later in several European cities but was to have occasional notes from her from all over the world. She was then newly graduated from the University of Chicago and had taken, for living quarters, one of the vacant store rooms near Margy. She brought Robert Lovett to her rooms. Llewellyn Jones came. Through Ben Hecht I also met Henry Justin Smith of the *News,* Burton Rascoe, then doing books for the *Tribune,* and Lewis Galantière, who was to become a lifelong friend. We were all from the Middle West. We were all full of hope.

It was the time in which something blossomed in Chicago and the Middle West. Dreiser from Terre Haute in Indiana had written and published *Sister Carrie* and Norris who already had written *McTeague* was fighting for Dreiser as Dreiser later was to fight for me, and had been joined in his fight by Francis Hackett, Floyd Dell, Henry Mencken and others. Edgar Lee Masters had written his *Spoon River Anthology;* down the state Vachel Lindsay was shouting forth his stirring verses; Sandburg was writing his magical *Chicago Poems;* and Margaret Anderson, still working as editor on some church paper, was soon to break loose and start her *Little Review.*

All over the country indeed there was an outbreak of new poets. Something which had been very hard in American life was beginning to crack, and in our group we often spoke of it hopefully. And how exciting it was. Something seemingly new and fresh was in the very air we breathed— So there I was, a little under the wing of Margy, who knew so well all of these to me so wonderful people. She was untiring, working all day as a reporter and ready every evening for any kind of adventure with the rest of us. She would run out to arrange for gin and sandwiches and then seat herself on a low bed at the side of the room. She would put flowers in her hair and we others would gather about, Mike Carmichael of the flowing red beard serving the drinks, some woman of the party, Eunice Tietjens or Mrs. Lucian Cary, seeing that we were supplied with sandwiches, the rest of us—and we were often as many as twenty—sitting about on the floor.

What ho! for the new world. And what cannot such a woman do for such a man as I was then. I had wanted comradeship and she had provided it. And there was something else. . . . I have spoken a good deal here of my fears but I do not believe that my fears were based on lack of faith in my own talent. I was then as I have always been, not a proud but an infinitely vain man. At bottom I was an egotist, as Ben Hecht once said of me, so much the egotist that nothing ever really touched the central core of my egotism.

"Why, I can write as well as any man alive. I have not come to it yet but I will come to it," I was always secretly saying to myself. Among the men I had known who were interested in books and writing, O. Henry had been time and time again pointed out to me as the great American Story Teller. But I did not think he was great. "He has learned too many tricks," I thought. I thought that Mark Twain, in his *Huckleberry Finn,* and Melville, in his *Moby Dick,* had been our great tale tellers. I was myself a man outside the schools. At the time I had not come to Chekhov or to Turgenev in his *Annals of a Sportsman,* but I had found the delightful and swaggering George Borrow. I was, I knew, in a curious position. Although I had been a passionate reader, my reading had never had any fixed direction. There were whole continents of literature that I had never visited. My own vocabulary was small. I had no Latin and no Greek, no French. When I wanted to arrive at anything like delicate shades of meaning in my writing I had to do it with my own very limited vocabulary.

And even my reading had not much increased my vocabulary. Oh, how many words I knew in books that I could not pronounce.

But should I use in my writing words that were not a part of my own everyday speech, of my own everyday thought?

I did not think so.

"No," I had long been telling myself, "you will have to stay where you have put yourself." There was the language of the streets, of

American towns and cities, the language of the factories and warehouses where I had worked, of laborers' rooming houses, the saloons, the farms.

"It is my own language, limited as it is. I will have to learn to work with it. There was a kind of poetry I was seeking in my prose, word to be laid against word in just a certain way, a kind of word color, a march of words and sentences, the color to be squeezed out of simple words, simple sentence construction." Just how much of all of this had been thought out, as I have spoken of it here, I do not now know. What I do know is the fact of my awareness of the limitations I had to face; my feeling that the writing, the telling of tales had got too far away from the manner in which we men of the time were living our lives. And what was wonderful to me in the new associates I had found was a certain boldness of speech.

We men in fact were wallowing in boldness. Freud had been discovered at the time and all the young intellectuals were busy analyzing each other and everyone they met. Floyd Dell was hot at it. We had gathered in the evening in somebody's rooms. Well, I hadn't read Freud (in fact, I never did read him) and was rather ashamed of my ignorance. Floyd walked up and down before us. At the time he was wearing a stock and looked I thought like pictures I had seen of Poe. When he was on the subject of literature he talked, I thought, brilliantly. I had never before heard such talk. How it flowed from him. What vast fields of literature he covered. He became excited. He shouted. The intense little figure became more and more erect.

And now he had begun psyching us. Not Floyd alone but others in the group did it. They psyched me. They psyched men passing in the street. It was a time when it was well for a man to be somewhat guarded in the remarks he made, what he did with his hands. On a certain evening when there were several of us gathered together, in an unfortunate moment I brought up the subject of homosexuality. I was puzzled. Some years before, when I was newly come to Chicago, when I was employed as a laborer in a North Side warehouse, I had for the first time seen homosexuality that was unashamed.

It had happened that in that place I worked a part of the time on an unloading platform at the warehouse door. The warehouse was on a street on the near North Side and in a house further down the street several men lived together. They came by our platform sometimes in groups, they had painted cheeks and lips, the others, the workmen and truckmen on the platform with me, shouted at them.

"Oh, you Mabel!"

"Why, if there isn't sweet little Susan."

The men passing, who were so much like women, giggled at us. There was a tall German who worked beside me. He began to swear.

"If one of them made a pass at me I'd knock his goddamn block off," he declared. Once when I was alone on the platform (it was late fall and darkness had come) one of them stopped and spoke to me. He approached and whispered to me.

"Don't you want to come and see me some night?"

I didn't answer, was a little shocked and even frightened.

"I have had my eye on you. You do not shout insults at us as the others do. You know where I live. Do come some night. There is so much I could teach you."

He went off along the street, turning to throw a kiss at me and I stood dumbly staring at him.

What did it all mean? I felt a strange unhealth within myself. I was not angry, and am quite sure that, when this happened, I felt even a kind of pity. There was a kind of door opened, as though I looked through the door into a dark pit, a place of monstrous shapes.

It is difficult now, as I write after the years, to remember just all I did feel on that occasion when first I came face to face with a fact in many other human lives, but in the years since, several such men have come to me and have talked to me of their terrible problem; some few stories of my own, the story "Hands" in the volume *Winesburg,* and the story I called "The Man Who Became a Woman" in the other volume, *Horses and Men,* have led them to think I could sympathize with them in their fight. But at the time, during the summer when I first found comrades in the little places in Fifty-seventh Street in Chicago I was, on the whole, only puzzled.

So I asked the question.

"What makes men like that?"

I went further. Perhaps I expressed a kind of fear of something in life I couldn't understand and the fear in me was pounced upon.

Why, I was myself, unconsciously one of them. The thing was in me too and the fear I had expressed was a sure sign of its presence. On another occasion when I had been walking in the Park on a Sunday afternoon with one of my new acquaintances we sat on a bench, and as we talked of books and life, I leaned over and picked up a twig from the path before us and began to break it between my fingers. "Oh!" he exclaimed.

It seemed he had found me out. I was breaking the twig between my fingers, and obviously, he explained to me, the twig was a phallic symbol. I was wanting to destroy the phallic in myself. I had secretly a desire to be a woman.

But it was not all like that. What nights we did have, what excursions at the week ends! There was in us, I am sure, something of the fervor that must have taken hold of those earlier Americans who had attempted to found communistic communities. We were, in our own minds, a little band of soldiers who were going to free life (first of all, to be sure, our own lives) from certain bonds.

No, it wasn't exactly free love we wanted. I doubt that there was with us any more giving way to the simple urge of sex than among the advertising and business men among whom I worked for certain hours each day. Indeed sex was to be given a new dignity and, as for marriage, well, it was obvious that on all sides of us there were men and women living the lives of married men and women without love, without tenderness.

I think we wanted to reveal something, bring something back. Later my own observation of life in small Middle-Western towns as boy and young man was to lead to the writing of my *Winesburg*.

We had been brought up on English literature, sifted down to us through New England; on walls of houses all over America, pictures of Longfellow, Whittier, Emerson. The New Englanders had lived in a cold stony land. Their fields were the little fields, surrounded by stone walls. Save during the sudden warm flush in nature in the summer months, through a large part of the year the skies overhead were cold and forbidding.

Puritans, eh? Well, I dare say they were no more pure than we of the Middle West. They were to be found in Ohio, Indiana, Illinois, Michigan, Iowa. Their blood had been mixed with that of those pushing up from the South, with those who had pushed down through Pennsylvania into the valley of Virginia and over the mountains, and through Cumberland Gap into Kentucky, and on into the Middle-Western states bordering on the Ohio River.

These joined also by men of North Carolina, Scotch-Irish, many of them. They would have come also seeking the warm deep soil of the Middle-Western states.

There was an empire there, Chicago its capital, to become the bread basket of the nation. My own father would have come up that way, from the North Carolina country.

And, I dare say, the North Carolina soil was rather thin and sandy too, a place of small farms, a few slaves, more poverty. My friend Paul Green, one of the great story tellers I have known, has told me many rare, often Rabelaisian, tales of the North Carolinians.

Anyway there we were, intellectually dominated by New England. Their portraits hanging in the parlors, above the mantel; the room usually dark, the shades drawn, and a large crayon portrait of grandpa sitting on an easel in the corner. We wanted to escape from it. We all were in revolt. Our land was not the New England land. The soil in our fields was black and rich. It went deep. The corn in our fields grew like forest trees. Could the New Englanders, who having no rich warm land underfoot, had gone off into transcendentalism, leaving the good earth to dwell in what to us seemed thin upper air—could they express us? I think we all felt it. I know that it was during that summer that I worked out my own *Mid-American Chants* in an attempt to sing smoke-laden city streets, great corn fields, the barnyards of our farmers, their great horses, the mud-banks of our rivers flowing sluggishly under their bridges.

And a new race was being made. If European literature had not come into our Middle West the Europeans had come. We had got the Irish, the Germans, the Swedes, Danes and Norwegians. Great swarms of Italians and other men from the warm Mediterranean shores had come. But their sons did not speak their strange language. Besides we had in our towns and villages of the Middle West seen a kind of life going on that had been reflected by our story tellers. We had read our *Huckleberry Finn,* that amazingly beautiful book—something of the whole vast valley of the Mississippi in it, though it was, after all, a tale of childhood.

But what about the real life on the Mississippi, on the river boats, in Natchez under the hill, in the red-light districts of St. Louis and New Orleans. What stories really told in the pilot houses of river boats. Abe Lincoln, telling his stories in little taverns in Illinois; stories told in the back rooms of saloons in the towns in which we had lived; our own experience of thwarted lives; twisted lives in New England, so many of the men striking out into the richer Middle West, leaving their women behind.

Howells at the same time shushing Twain, so many of the stronger words of our everyday speech absolutely barred in our writing.

I remembered an experience of my own. I had for a time, when I was newly come to the city—this when I was still working as a laborer—been at a certain house. They were people to whom I had been given a note of introduction and I went to call.

There were a great many books in that house and I was hungry for books, and seeing there a volume of Walt Whitman I borrowed it, but when I got it home to my own room, in a workingman's rooming house, I found certain pages torn from the book.

I was curious. I managed to get hold of an unmutilated volume and discovered the reason. Old Walt had simply expressed, in certain verses, his healthy animalism and they couldn't take it. The idea being that it would be terribly corrupting to read, in the printed pages of a book, what was so much in all our minds.

And another experience, this out of my own life in a country town, before I came to the city. I had gone to the house of a certain girl at night, on a Sunday night. I had, in fact, met her as she emerged from church.

We had walked about. It was a summer evening and we were both young. We began to kiss.

We went to her house and sat on a porch at the back of the house. It was dark there.

And now she was lying on the floor of the porch.

"I am sleepy," she said. She pretended to go to sleep.

"Take me if you please. Do take me. Do it while I sleep."

"I must pretend to you that I do not know what is going on."

It ended so and later she could pretend to me, and even perhaps to herself, that she did not know what had happened, that it had happened in her sleep.

No, I do not think that any of us at the time wanted to over-play sex. But we wanted in our stories and novels to bring it back into real relation to the life we lived and saw others living. We wanted the flesh back in our literature, wanted directly in our literature the fact of men and women in bed together, babies being born. We wanted the terrible importance of the flesh in human relations also revealed again. No doubt Emerson had been a great writer. But while he could sing "Give

All to Love," we were sure he could not express love in the way we of the Middle West were coming to feel desirable.

All this desire of revelation I found among the new acquaintances in the little converted retail storeroom at Fifty-seventh and Stoney Island Avenue in Chicago—Floyd Dell, Arthur Davidson Ficke, Lawrence Langner, a patent lawyer interested in the theater, coming now and then from New York to give us a feast with drinks, to speak to us of the new figures, Eugene O'Neill, Jigg Cook and others coming to the front in the East, Ben Hecht, Alexander Kaun, occasional young professors from the University, talk and more talk.

A kind of healthy new frankness in the talk between men and women, at least an admission that we were all at times torn and harried by the same lusts.

Our own lusts faced a little. It meant everything to me. And then excursions on the week end to the country, often to the lake country, the dunes south of Chicago.

Ben Hecht, having just read Flaubert, walking up and down declaiming. Ben then, as he remained, full of strange oaths, adjectives falling over adjectives, Mike Carr with his little red beard and light red bathing trunks flirting with every woman he met, "it is my purpose to be sincerely insincere," and reciting Swinburne by the hour. Alexander Kaun, telling again his tales of life in Russian villages, myself, hearing more and more of Russian writers, Tolstoy, Dostoievsky, Chekhov, Turgenev, a new world of writers to be opened up to me later.

Was I not later to be called, by one of our American critics, "The Phallic Chekhov"?

I am trying to give here an impression of what was to me a gay happy time, the gayest and happiest I have ever known, a feeling of brotherhood and sisterhood with men and women whose interests were my own. As yet I had not begun to face what every practitioner of any art must face, the terrible times of bitter dissatisfaction with the work done, often the difficulty of making a living at your chosen work, the facing of the petty jealousies that pop up among fellow craftsmen, the temptation, always present, to try to get into the big money by attempting to give them what you think they want, the times when the ink will not flow, when you have worked, perhaps for weeks and months, on some project only to have to face the fact on some sad morning that it is all no good, that what you have attempted hasn't come off and must be thrown away.

All of this still ahead of me during that summer with my newly found fellows.

And then the women. How we do need them. There were two Marjories, Margy Currie, who had been Floyd Dell's wife, and Marjory Jones, a very attractive black-haired woman of twenty-five, and a photographer. It is to such women that a man takes his first work.

"Now you tell me frankly what you think."

To be sure a man doesn't mean that. What he wants is praise, to be reassured, and it is this that women understand.

For often enough for the young worker it is only praise that helps.

"Yes. You have real talent. Do not be afraid."

Such a woman will often remember for years some sentence you have written, and how it stirs and flatters a man to have such a sentence remembered and repeated. It is a special gift some women have, due perhaps to a lack of the competitive feeling in them, they wanting to make you happy and being not too scrupulous about it, thank Heaven for that.

So there was that summer, to be always remembered, the days got through in the advertising place and then the summer evenings, the walks in the Park, the gatherings in one of the little rooms. Arthur Davison Ficke, already itching to throw all of that over and to devote himself to poetry, coming to town to give us a blowout. Wine, whiskey, and beer brought in. Some singing. Ben Hecht trying out a play in a tiny theater arranged in one of the rooms.

The week ends at some little town on the lake shore, six or eight of us men and women sleeping perhaps, or at least trying to sleep, under one blanket by a low fire built on the shore of the lake, even perhaps going off in the darkness to some secluded spot to bathe, all of us in the nude, it all quite innocent enough, but such a wonderful feeling in us of leading a new, free, bold life, defying what seemed to us the terribly stodgy life out of which we had all come. And then perhaps a walk during the evening alone with one of the women. For me it would have been with little Margy Currie, her hand on my arm.

I would have given her an attempt at a story to read.

"Do not be afraid, Sherwood. You have real talent.

"You will do it. You will do it."

Oh wonderful words.

Songs being sung by a fire on the beach at night.

"Have you read Stephen Crane's *Maggie: a Girl of the Streets?"* Men and women, far more widely read than I was, talking and talking. Poems recited. Myself taking notes.

"I'll read that. I'll get it tomorrow."

It was all, I dare say, in the great dreams we had, the vows of comradeship taken, a little childish, an interlude, for most of us the difficulty of what we wanted to do, dreamed of doing, not yet faced, some of us to fail dismally enough, all of us to have to go through years of disappointment to accomplish little enough. But, for that summer, a gay time, for me at least a happy time.

6. Ben and Burton

In Chicago, Ben Hecht, Burton Rascoe, Justin Smith, Carl Sandburg, Harry Hansen and I, and half a dozen others, used to dine often at a place called Schlogl's on Fifth Avenue. Later I believe the name of the street was changed. It became Wells Street. The *Daily News* was in a ramshackle old building over there under the elevated railroad.

We all dined around a big table and indulged in literary talk. At that time Henry Mencken was our great hero. We all read the old *Smart Set,* and later Mencken and Nathan's *Mercury*. Many of us had got letters from Mencken. He was the great letter writer. At that time he must have been in correspondence with all of the young writers in the country. It must have paid the *Mercury* well. A man was in great luck who got more than twenty-five dollars from a story from that point.

Still we got the letters and the letters made us proud.

"Well, I had a letter from Henry Mencken today."

You said it offhand, but in your heart you felt that it was like being knighted by a king.

You knew damn well the others felt the same. Henry made a great mistake. He should, at just that time, have made a grand tour, as Gertrude Stein did later, picking, as Gertrude did, just the right moment. In Chicago we would have delivered the town over to him.

A few years before, Francis Hackett and Floyd Dell had been the literary band masters in Chicago but they had both departed for New York, Hackett to the *New Republic* and Floyd to the old *Masses.* Floyd published a novel that Hackett reviewed and the review was a masterpiece. He took Floyd's skin off inch by inch. It was the best job of literary skinning I ever read.

They were both however now gone from Chicago and Burton Rascoe on the *Tribune* and Ben Hecht on the *Daily News* were doing books for the town.

We were all at lunch and an agreement was made. I think it must have been Ben Hecht who proposed it.

"Look here, Burton. We'll take up some writer. You go big for him and I'll go against him. We'll keep it up. You blow your horn and I'll put on the Bronx Cheer."

I think something of that sort must have been said. At any rate the agreement was made and, as usual, Ben had got himself into an advantageous position.

Abuse was meat and drink to him. He loved it. He was a genius at it. Later, I am told, he used the talent with wonderful effect on the movie magnates of Hollywood. I am told that the more he abused them the more they paid him. He could do it with a smile on his face.

The point is that it was all fun to Ben, in reality a very sweet man, full of kindnesses, but it was temporarily poison to Burton.

For Burton was then, as he always was, a highly nervous, sensitive man. He was easily hurt.

The two men decided upon James Branch Cabell as the man to be praised and abused. They began, and I have no doubt that Burton, although Ben had proposed the plan, had proposed the man. He was sincere in his admiration for Cabell while Ben was out to be vehemently insincere.

It began; it was carried on for weeks. Columns in the newspapers were filled with it and the Chicago book stores were, for the time, loaded up with Cabell's books.

For the book dealers it didn't, I was told, turn out so well. Too many people, induced to buy by all the clamor being raised, brought the books back.

They said they didn't understand the books.

They were too sophisticated, they said.

At that time among us in Chicago who were literarily inclined, there was a great passion to be sophisticated but our rank was small in numbers. Ben and Burton were overselling the possible Cabell market.

It had all begun by the praise and abuse of Cabell but presently it became more personal. Ben began to call his opponent the sophomoric Rascoe and Rascoe attempted to meet Ben halfway in the matter of personal abuse.

It was for him a hopeless struggle, although, naturally, he had made of Cabell a lifelong friend and you can understand that. Cabell later dedicated a book to Burton. Under the circumstances I would have done the same.

It had all been begun as a stunt but it had grown serious. Now Ben and Burton, when they met, did not speak. Ben grinned and Burton frowned. Two men who had been, and later were to become again, real friends were for the time bitter enemies.

I decided to give a dinner and invited ten or twelve men. I invited Ben without telling Burton and when I invited Burton did not tell him that Ben was coming.

The dinner came off and we all sat at a long table, Burton and Ben opposite each other, and Ben was in fine feather. He talked. He made insidious remarks, for the most part directed at Cabell. He did not look at Burton but kept addressing his remarks to the others at the table and Burton kept hopping up and down on his chair.

He could not eat. He kept opening and closing his mouth. He stuttered. There was a bottle of whiskey on the table and he kept filling a glass and drinking it off. I am quite sure that, at the moment, he was so excited that he did not realize that he was not drinking water.

And then at last he spoke. Burton, as all his friends know, always was, to the last inch, a literary man. He pointed a trembling finger at Ben.

"You talk," he shouted.

"You think you know something about life, about literature.

"But what do you know of life? You tell me. You answer me. What do you know of life?"

Burton turned from Ben to the rest of us. He spoke of Ben with infinite scorn.

"You look at him. What does he know of life?"

Then the really tremendous statement that set the table roaring and in the end patched up the broken friendship came from Burton's lips.

"This Ben Hecht," he said. "He knows nothing of real life. Why, the man has never had but one mistress and she was a charwoman."

It was the final literary thrust. It broke something. It was all of England's literature come to our modest dinner table. When he had said it even Burton had to laugh. It patched everything up, made Burton and Ben what they had been before the great Cabell controversy was begun, again warm and intimate friends.

7. All Will Be Free

I was always a little sore at Ben Hecht that he first told the story. When last I saw him in New York he was at work making it into a movie.

However, I cannot resist the temptation to tell my impression of the man. He was so cheerful, seemingly so full of life.

We had gone, Ben and I, with some four or five others to lunch at the German restaurant. It was a cold rainy day in the late fall, let us say in November, and we were all in a cheerless mood.

For one thing it was during the time of prohibition and, on such a Chicago day, in the mood we were in, we all wanted drinks. But drinks were expensive.

Yes, they could be had in the place, at say fifty cents a drink, for second-rate stuff.

So we sat there growling at each other. Except for myself, all the others were newspaper men. Although at bottom Ben Hecht is one of the kindest men I have ever known, he has always had a talent for insult.

We had begun insulting each other, insults thrown back and forth, each man trying to get some other fellow's dander up.

We were interrupted by the waiter.

"That man over there, that little dark man sitting in the corner, wants to buy you all a drink."

"Listen, man, don't attempt to torture us."

"Is this some crude and cruel attempt at a joke?"

We were all staring at the little foreign-looking man who smiled blandly at us.

"No, he means it. What will you have?" the waiter was asking us. There was no one else in the place except ourselves and the man at the table in a corner at the back of the room.

"Sure. Sure. Hell, yes."

"He wants you to have the best stuff."

Ben half arose from his chair.

"I've a notion to go and kiss him," he said.

The drinks were brought and we raised our glasses to the man and in a few minutes, there the waiter was again.

"He wants you to have another drink."

It was too much. We were all so filled with gratitude that we were struggling to keep the tears from running down our cheeks.

"What a man. What a man. Bring him over here."

Two of us arose to escort him to our table. This wasn't a fellow to miss. Why, the drinks we had been having were costing seventy-five cents each.

The man came. It is something shameful in me that I have forgotten his name.

He was so cheerful, so generous, so happy seeming.

We began to question him and he talked. More drinks flowed. Ben later told the story in a book he called *A Thousand and One Afternoons*. At this point in the story he made me begin singing a song. Ben couldn't remember the words of the song he put into his story. He invented words. He made me responsible for his misquoting of the words of the song I didn't sing. He was, I dare say, too lazy to look them up. Or he was just taking a good-natured shot at me.

"This is the song as Sherwood sang it." He said something of that sort.

Anyway there we were at the table in that place and a gloomy cheerless day had become bright and shining. More and more drinks kept coming.

The man we had thus found was a little dark Russian Jew. He was in a mood for talk. He told us his history.

He had been born a poor Russian Jewish boy in a ghetto. He was drafted into the Russian army. He went to serve in the Caucasus.

He spoke at length of that, describing his life in the army under the Czar, the mountain villages seen, the herds of cattle on the green hills, the rushing rivers, the beautiful village girls.

"They were Tartar maidens," he said.

"Oh, they were so strong, so straight, so full-bosomed." He went into a kind of ecstasy as he described the mountain maidens seen while he was a Russian soldier.

And then he was in America, had escaped from the army life and had come here. He was in New York, working there, having hard enough times.

"But, oh, the beautiful country, America. Life so free here. Here, in America, and here only, on all the earth's surface, such a poor Russian Jew as I has my chance."

Words kept flowing from the man's lips and the liquor, at seventy-five cents the drink, also kept flowing.

"You are all newspaper men, are you not?"

Except for myself, all were. The others put me in among themselves.

"Yes, yes. We are all newspaper men."

"I knew it. I could tell by looking at you. You all have such intelligent faces."

"You must have been looking at me," Ben Hecht said.

He had, he said, come to Chicago and had become a manufacturer.

"I make boxes in which other manufacturers ship their goods. It is a box factory."

He explained that his factory was in the northwest section of the city. He had begun in a small way but his business had grown large. There had come the necessity of building a larger factory and he had done that. The factory was almost completed.

"It is now November but by Christmas time it will be completed. Or let us say, by the first of the year, on New Year's Day.

"Here is the point," he cried. He had become more and more excited. His eyes were shining.

On that very morning he had gone to have a look at his new factory.

"Oh, it is so beautiful. It is such a beautiful factory."

He had walked about on the floor of the new factory. There was, he said, a great room, as large as a hall. He had been standing in the great room there and looking about.

And then a thought had come. It had come upon him suddenly. He had gone pale. It was, he said, as he stood in the new factory (this he explained was in the very early morning before the workmen who were building the factory had come) as though there were voices coming out of the walls and calling to him.

"It is like this," he said. "I cannot manufacture boxes in that factory. It is too beautiful. I can't do it. I can't. I can't."

He explained that he had suddenly realized what America had meant to him. He had come here so poor. He was a Russian Jew but America had opened her arms to him.

"I can go on with my old factory. What do I care? I have money enough. I am prosperous enough."

He had decided that he would make of the new factory, when it was completed, a place of joy. That was it. It would be a place for dances and plays. Everyone could come. It would cost the people nothing. He would build a stage, would hire musicians to play music.

"It is to be free, free, like America itself, a place of joy.

"There is more joy wanted, more places of joy!"

The little man got up from the table at which we had all been sitting, listening and drinking his drinks. At that time in Chicago there was an intense struggle for control of the streets going on between the Yellow and the Checker taxicabs. Battles between them were being fought in the streets.

He was proposing that we all write of his plan in our newspapers. We were to invite the whole city to come. Everything would be free. He kept saying the word over and over.

"Everything is to be free. A place of joy. It will all be free."

He had taken a little notebook from his pocket. He took each of our names and addresses. We were to bring our friends. All would be refined. It was to be a place of refined joy. As he wrote our names and addresses, saying that the great opening would be on the day of the beginning of the New Year and that he would send a taxicab for each of us, he asked us each a question.

"Do you prefer a Yellow or a Checker taxicab?" he asked.

He had got up to leave. It was growing dark outside in the street. It was still raining a cold drizzle of rain. At the bar he stopped and bought for us another expensive bottle of whiskey.

He bought a quart. He bought us a box of expensive cigars. He stood at the door smiling his joyous smile.

Would we all come? Would we write it all up? Would we promise him?

"Yes, yes," we cried.

"By the gods we'll give you a send-off.

"We'll be there.

"We'll be there."

The man had gone and we sat stunned. The men with me were all so-called "hard-boiled" newspaper men but they had believed. There had been something so very convincing about the man.

"He means it."

"Yes, he does."

"Sure, he means it. What are you talking about?"

We separated, each going his way, all convinced. It may be that the impulse in the man was something we all secretly wanted in ourselves.

We also wanted freedom. We wanted more places of joy in our city.

It wasn't until the next morning that I found out the truth. Ben phoned me and he was excited.

"You come over here and at once," he said.

It was true that the little man we had met in the restaurant was a box manufacturer. He had been.

He had owned a little box factory over on the northwest side of the city but it had failed.

On the morning of the day when we had met him he had found himself on the edge of bankruptcy. He had gone to his bank and there was a little money left, perhaps a hundred dollars, and he had drawn it out.

He had come down into the city and to the German restaurant and he had found us there. He had had the afternoon with us, had built for us his new factory, that was to be his place of joy.

The place where all would be free.

He had left us and had walked alone in the cold rain-washed streets. He had come to a bridge over the Chicago River and had thrown himself in.

Ben told me that when they hauled out his body they found ten cents in his pocket.

How could I help hoping that he had found his place of joy, the place where all is free?

It is Ben's story but it is also mine. I was there. I was a part of it. Such a story will bear telling over and over, from many angles. It should become—by someone's telling, one of the classic stories of American life.

8. The Death of Mrs. Folger

I went up the stairs in the little suburban house, her son staying below. It was very cold outside, a stinging wind and drifting snow. It had been a long cold ride out from the city after the phone call came from the son.

He said, "Mother's dying. She keeps asking for you. Will you come?"

I had had to wait for a long time for a street car. I had no money for a taxi. It was one of my hard-up times.

The son was a short, rather fat man with a mustache. He had red cheeks and watery eyes.

As I climbed the stairs I tried to remember what he did.

"Let's see, does he run a store?

"He may be a doctor or a dentist."

I had him connected in my mind with rubber stamps.

"That's it," I told myself. "He makes rubber stamps."

I remembered her speaking of him.

"He's religious," she had said.

"My husband was like that too."

I had never seen her husband, had never until that night, when she died, seen her son.

I had a sharp feeling of guilt climbing the stairs.

Why had I so lost touch with her? She had been a sort of second mother, something wonderful for me.

I was remembering her little sharp eyes, so like the eyes of some little wild animal seen at evening at the edge of a wood, her small gray head, alert, alive little body.

I had gone there, to that Middle-Western town, wanting an education. There was a college in the town and she had taken me in.

It was beyond the college, just at the edge of town, a huge old brick house, a great stretch of lawn, trees, a big barn. Some of the professors from the college lived there. There were two lawyers, both unmarried, a newspaper editor, a dentist. There must have been ten or twelve men and there were three or four women, all schoolteachers, one of them to become my life-long friend. She was a big-legged, big-breasted German woman. She discussed books with me. She brought me books to read.

The little woman with the eyes and the gray hair said, "Look out, boy."

When my work was done in the evening she saw me going off for long walks with the German woman. She was afraid I might fall in love. She said she had seen it happen once, there in her own house, a boy like me had been taken in. He had married a woman much older than himself, some twenty years older, who was also a school-teacher.

"Look out, boy."

I was in a room with the little gray one. It was my job at that place to take care of the yard. I kept the grass mowed. I got my meals and a place to sleep and there were two others, students, one to take care of her cows and another to wait on table.

They were both trying to work their way through the college. They planned to be preachers.

She had taken me into her own room. I had been living there for a month. She stood before me, such a small alert young old figure.

"Are you also planning to be a preacher?

"Do you believe in God?"

I had begun trying to explain. I neither believed nor disbelieved. I said I just went along, didn't try thinking of such things.

"And heaven. Do you believe that, if you are what is called good, you will go to a place called heaven when you die?"

She was very serious. Her little sharp eyes were peering at me.

"I don't believe," I said, hesitating, "that I will ever be anything of enough importance to be preserved through what they call 'eternity.'

"It's such a long time," I said. An idea that had got into my boy's head began to find words.

"It's such an egotistical idea. I can't believe that most people are worth keeping alive in any form through eternity.

"No, I'm afraid I don't believe."

She came toward me, put up her little old face.

"Kiss me, boy," she said.

We became friends. What talks we had. In the evening we went often into her own room and closed the door. She had helped many boys through college but she had had bad luck. They had all turned out to be preachers or they were religious.

It had been so with her husband who had long been dead. It was so with her son.

"I have always had religious people about me.

"It isn't that I don't like them," she said. "I try to forget what they are."

When she was a child at home, before her marriage, all her people had been pious, but very early in her own life, she declared she had decided not to believe. It wasn't that she had ever had much impulse to sin. She just didn't want to believe.

"I want to be just the same as a flower or a tree and a house or a dog. I am getting old. Already, a little, I am dying.

"You see my hair is gray. When I awake in my bed in the morning I don't want to get up.

"I can feel death coming. Little bites it takes of me. Now soon it will take me, all of me."

There had been but a few people to whom she had confided her secret. She had never told her husband. When her son, as a young boy, got religion and joined the church she had told him she was glad.

"I don't want to disturb anyone at all by my unbelief," she said.

It was something to which she clung. It was a secret between her and me. In the presence of all the others who lived in her house and when we were all at table and grace was being said . . .

It was said by one of the young boys she had taken in, one who planned to become a minister.

. . . when it was going on she sometimes lifted her head. She sat at the head of the long table and I was far down toward the other end. She winked at me.

She was very ill. She was near death. Because of growing weakness she had long since given up her house.

She had come in to the city to live her last days with her son and her son's children. For a time we had exchanged letters but for several years I had heard nothing of her.

I was at the head of the stairs, near the door of the room where she was lying when a nurse came out. She came and whispered to me.

"She wants you but you mustn't go in. She is very low. She will try to talk.

"The doctor says she must not talk."

The whispering of the nurse was interrupted by a voice. It was her voice, very small.

It was like the voice of a child.

"It is you," it said. "They will tell you not to come in to me but pay no attention to them." The nurse made a gesture with her hand and followed me into the room.

She was very small. Her body was like that of a very small child.

How small her face, her voice, her little, shrunken hand.

With her hand she made a motion to the nurse.

"Go out."

The nurse went and I was alone with her. I took her little shrunken hand in mine. Only her little sharp eyes seemed alive.

Her little voice seemed coming from far off.

"I wanted you for a moment," she said.

"I did not want them to be hurt.

"They believe and I do not believe. I wanted someone to know that, at the very last, at the edge of the grave, I did not believe."

The effort to speak had seemed to have exhausted her. Her eyes closed, the nurse came into the room and I went softly down the stairs.

The son was there.

"Mother was very fond of you," he said.

"Yes," I said. "She only wanted to say good-by."

I stood with him there in the little hallway of the house, when the nurse came down the stairs.

She said my friend had died. At the very last she had thrust up her little banner.

It was against those who thought they were fit to live through all eternity. She hadn't wanted to hurt them so she had waved the little defiant banner only for me.

9. A Chance Missed

Whenever a new writer begins to come a little into prominence in the literary world the critics do strange things to him.

First of all they overpraise him. It is understandable enough. It is a boring job, this sitting at a desk, day after day, reading and passing judgment on other men's work.

Think, for example, of the man who becomes the literary critic for a daily newspaper. Some of them actually write of a new book every day.

To be sure it doesn't take long to pass on most books. You pick the book up, read a page, five pages, ten pages. It doesn't take much reading to find out whether or not a writer can write. A bit of originality, a flair for words—you are not asking too much. That curious inexplainable thing, the hidden music in prose, the overtone, the quality in real writing that sets your imagination flying off on a journey of its own, you'll not find that appearing very often.

The critic is fed up on commonplace books. A book comes that is a little alive. It is good story telling.

You cannot blame the critic if he throws his hat into the air, begins to shout.

Very likely he overdoes it. When my own first novel was published I was compared in the *New York Times* to Dostoievsky.

"An American Dostoievsky," something of that sort.

To be sure I liked it but, at the same time, it made me secretly ashamed. The book, I felt, didn't come off. I felt that the book was largely a result of my reading of other novelists. I hadn't as yet turned directly to the life about me. It was an immature book, not completely felt, full of holes and bad spots. In a later edition of the same book I rewrote the whole later part of it.

There was an upward and onward note in all the early pages of the book, a boy, coming out of an Iowa corn-shipping town to rise in the business world, that fitted into the American mood of the day. I had not got the slant on business I got later.

The book sold well. It was praised by many critics. They did not like the ending but neither did I.

I had made my man, who had risen a little in the world of affairs, come to a place where he had begun to feel sharply the futility of his life.

I didn't know what to do with him.

A man from the Curtis Publishing Company came out to Chicago to see me.

Once, several years earlier, I had been visited by Mr. Curtis himself.

It was an exciting adventure. Mr. Curtis, with his *Saturday Evening Post, Ladies' Home Journal* and the newly founded *Country Gentleman,* was a gigantic figure in our Chicago world of advertising.

The advertising agency that was then employing me as a copy writer published a little house organ of its own and I had written a piece praising the life of the business man. It was quite sincere.

I wore good clothes, dined in expensive restaurants, had begun to learn to drink wine and have women.

It seemed to me that business had done all this for me and I was grateful.

So I wrote, in our little company magazine, praising the business life, speaking highly of business men, and one day Mr. Curtis himself, in person, appeared at the door of our agency.

There was great excitement. Messages flew back and forth.

"It's Mr. Curtis himself."

Mr. Curtis, as I now remember him, was a rather small, clean-looking, alert man coming with rapid steps down the long hallway from the reception room of the agency to the president's office. We used to speak of the hallway as Main Street. Along it were the offices of the more prominent men of the firm. We copy writers sat crowded into a long narrow room off to one side. We were packed in there, our elbows almost touching, as we scribbled away, praising in words the virtue of some tooth paste, some automobile tire, corn cure or toilet soap.

There was Mr. Curtis himself, holding in his hand a copy of our little house organ. As he passed along the hallway, heads popped out of offices.

"Hush. Be silent. It is Mr. Curtis."

The general opinion, later reported, was that he was angry. Someone had written something in our magazine that had offended him.

He darted into our president's office and laid the magazine on the table before our president. It was open to the little article I had written.

"Who wrote that?" he demanded to know, pointing to the article. It was unsigned.

Our president, at that time a Mr. Long, did not know. He was a little frightened. It would not do for our agency to incur the wrath of the great Curtis Publishing Company.

"Why, Mr. Curtis, I do not know. I'll find out. What is wrong with it, Mr. Curtis?"

"Why, nothing is wrong with it. It's all right. It's fine. What I want is for you to find out who wrote it and send the man to me.

"I want that man."

Mr. Curtis had left our agency. He was gone but my own stock had gone up. For a time it soared. It all resulted in my taking a trip to Philadelphia, where I had a talk with Mr. Curtis and was offered a position as an editorial writer for the *Saturday Evening Post,* a position I did not accept.

Just why I did not accept I did not at that time know. The Curtis Publishing Company was so big. It may have a little terrified me.

Or perhaps already I had begun to be a little afraid of all bigness, didn't want to be a big shot.

I had that chance and lost it and then came another. I had published my first novel, the one spoken of above, and a man from the Curtis office came to see me.

It was a Sunday morning and I went to meet the man at the Blackstone Hotel. We were in a room in the hotel.

"We want novels, such as you started to write when you wrote *Windy McPherson's Son.*

"We can pay well for what we want.

"We felt that the last part of the novel wasn't what we wanted.

"In all the first part of your novel there is a fresh note. As for the later part, the ending—

"In such novels that can of course be corrected.

"We feel you stumbled there."

"Yes," I said, "I guess I did."

It was what interested me, that stumbling.

I was trying to think and feel my way through a man's life. I wanted it to come to some satisfactory end for him as I would like my own life to come to some satisfactory end.

I think that, on that morning, in the hotel room, I tried to explain. Now that I think of it, there were, I'm sure, two men present from the Curtis house. I had got into the writing of novels and stories in a curious way. I had not begun by thinking of myself as a writer. I do not yet think of myself so. There is something of the eternal amateur in me. I wanted if I could to clear up certain traits in myself.

I had discovered something. I had discovered that I could, in writing, throw an imagined figure against a background of some of my own experiences—a thing all writers must do—and through the imagined figure get sometimes a kind of slant on some of my own questionable actions.

I doubt that it ever reformed me. It did give me a certain satisfaction.

I was there in the room with the two men from the house of Curtis. I tried to explain. No doubt I made a mess of it. I do not think I made them understand what I was driving at.

"But we can pay well. We pay for what we want."

It was true, and how I wanted money.

"Do you play golf?"

The two men both said they did.

"You enjoy doing it just for the sake of doing it, not for money."

You see how confusing this is. I am always crabbing at my publishers because they do not make more money for me.

10. The Conquering Male

It was winter in Chicago and I wanted the South. There was the dreary round of advertisements to write, day after day.

"I will have to quit this. I am using here the words that are the tools of my real trade. I am soiling my tools."

Having saved a little money I went to Mobile, in Alabama. I had never been there. I had just put my finger on the map.

Perhaps I remembered how Grant, after he had taken Vicksburg, kept wanting to go to Mobile.

They wouldn't let him. They called him East to meet Lee, made him the head of all the armies.

But there was no danger of anyone's making me head of anything. I was glad of that.

I was in Mobile, on a winter day, had found a room in an old house, not far from the bay. It was a rooming house in which dock workers lived.

It was night and I went to walk. It was one of my memorable nights.

I thought the city very beautiful. It had begun to rain, a soft slow rain and I walked through a little park, in the heart of the city. Something happened to me.

I had come out of the park, where, even on the winter night, there was a scent of flowers and had got into a dirty, poorly lighted street when my foot struck something on the pavement.

It was a pocketbook and I picked it up. It was filled with bills. I hurried back to my room.

There was a billfold and in it was a hundred and forty dollars.

What luck. I sat in my room counting the money over and over. I do not think it occurred to me that night that the money belonged to someone else. It seemed sent to me by God.

A hundred and forty dollars. Why, it meant to me two or even three months more of freedom. There was a novel I wanted to write, the novel I did begin and carry along all that winter.

It was the novel *Poor White*. I wanted to tell the story of a town, what happened to it when the factories came, how life in the town changed, old patterns of life broken up, how the lives of people of the town were all affected by the coming of the factories. The book has since become a sort of historic criticism of that change. It is used nowadays by a good many historians to give present-day students a sense of the so-called industrial revolution brought down into a single American town.

I was in the Southern city and had suddenly grown rich. Although I did look in the newspapers for the next several days I never saw any demand for the return of the money. I wondered what I would do if there came any such a demand.

I went again out of my room, into the rain of night, having hidden the money in my room. I walked. I was so excited I couldn't sleep. I was free. Now, for weeks, perhaps for several months I would not have to write advertisements. I had got into a Negro section of the city. It was late, after midnight, and the streets in which I walked were unpaved. There were long rows of little shacks and although it was so late I could hear voices in the houses. There was something found, a new adventure for me. It was in the voices I heard in the night, in the dark muddy little streets. There was something, not tense, not full of the false excitement and nerve-tension of the advertising place and, for that matter, of all Chicago. I heard soft voices. I heard laughter. There was a Negro woman's voice, perhaps speaking to her man.

"Now, honey, you be quiet. We got to sleep now."

It wasn't what the woman in the house said. It was the timbre of her voice, something I felt that night in the Negro street, something I wanted. It seemed to break something in me.

There was that money found in the street and hidden now in my room. There was the soft black southern night, the gentle rain, the voices of Negroes in the darkness, something in me released. I had been thinking—"Now I have these few free weeks and months. I must work hard, constantly. If I am ever to do this novel, I so want to do, I must be at it at once. I must work on it day and night."

The feeling of tenseness was still in me, the rushing, pushing Chicago streets still in me, Illinois Central trains to be caught, to be at the office at just a certain hour, a time clock to be rung.

Or, when I had moved to the North Side and came down into the Chicago Loop afoot in the morning, no time to lean over the rails of the old wooden bridges then spanning the Chicago River, to watch the gulls floating so beautifully over the lathery, green water of the river.

Freedom. Soft voices. Laughter.

"Be quiet, honey. We got to sleep now."

I found myself, on that night, my first night of freedom in the far South, going along in the Negro streets saying over and over the words of the Negro woman to her lover.

"Be quiet now.

"No hurry.

"Let your book come as it will."

A great sense of relief, of tension taken off, something I have always got in the South. It made me very happy that night. I must have walked for hours in the rain. I talked to myself, reassuring myself, an old fear that had long been growing in me, that I would never succeed in escaping the advertising place, that I would never get to the work I wanted, quite gone.

"Why I could sleep here in the street. A few cents a day would buy me food here."

Earlier in my walking that night I had gone down to the docks and there was a banana boat being unloaded. Ripe bananas were lying about and I had picked up and eaten two or three.

"I could feed thus, as a bird or a beast feeds."

It was all absurd enough, I dare say, the feeling the Southern night, the Negro voices gave me, but it was all wonderful to me and I remember that later, as I walked in the rain that night, I doubled my fist into a hard knot.

"The North, from which I have come, is like this," I said, speaking along to myself.

"And the South, I have found, like this."

I opened my fist, let it lie open and relaxed before me.

I had crossed the bay in a little steamboat. Jack Jones, who at that time was running a place called "The Dill Pickle," in Chicago, had written me, asking me to go to the little town of Fairhope across the bay. There was a woman named Ann Mitchell who had come down there.

"She wants to talk with you. You go see her. She has something on her mind."

The town of Fairhope had been established by the followers of

Henry George. There was some scheme in regard to the ownership of land—I never did understand that.

As for Jack Jones and Ann Mitchell, I shall have to tell their story against two backgrounds. For Ann it is a tragic story but the tragic part of it comes later. It belongs to another place and another setting.

There was a rumor that, earlier in his life, Jack Jones had been one of a band of safe robbers. He had been, it was said, "a soap maker," meaning that it was his job to handle the nitroglycerine used in blowing safes. He had several fingers missing.

He had reformed. Once he talked to me of his impulse in establishing his Dill Pickle.

"I had cut it out but they were always bothering me," he said. "Whenever there was a job done in Chicago they raked me in. I had to explain my every movement to the police."

Jack had decided to organize a club.

"If you have some sort of a club, with an enrolled membership, they think you control votes. They let you alone. They think you can swing some votes for them."

If it were true that Jack had been where he pretended he had been always, in the wrong pew, he was a born showman. He had let his hair grow long and wore a black flowing tie.

He had gone in heavy for the arts. Having got an old building on Chicago's North Side, he established a little theater. Poets came there to read their verses. There were plays given and lectures delivered.

It had all worked out quite splendidly for Jack. There was a touch of the bizarre, the strange. You went there in the evening and there was Maxwell Bodenheim, or some other poet, reading his verses. Many of the respectables of the rather well-to-do neighborhood had come. They whispered to each other, pointing to Jack.

"They say he's been a safe blower." It was a little like being in the actual presence of, say, Jesse James. Whether or not Jack had ever been the desperate character he represented himself as having been, I have no way of knowing.

"I give them the high-brow stuff until the crowd begins to grow thin and then I turn on the sex faucet," he once said to me. I had gone there to hear a woman speak. "Men Who Have Made Love to Me" was the subject of her talk. Jack knew his public. He was raking in money.

He was a new kind of man to me, very vain, shrewd with something brutal under a sensitive exterior. I was very curious. I went about with him. We took walks together. He seemed very proud of his past, had got, because of his past, a certain standing among us intellectuals.

"He is a man of action," we thought. He made great claims to being an expert mechanic.

"You see," he said, "I have been what you know.

"And now . . . here I am.

"I am providing a place for poets to recite their verses. I shall presently open a theater. We will do fine things.

"The plays of Synge and Chekhov."

We, of the Chicago intelligentsia, had already some of the passion that was later to sweep over and well-nigh engulf our world—the passion for the proletariat. Jack spoke with biting contempt of the bourgeoisie. He called them "bourjoices."

"I want you to talk with Ann Mitchell," Jack wrote. "You tell her just what you think."

There had been a lot more to Jack's letter. Ann had come one day to the Dill Pickle and had, at once, fallen in love with Jack. She was a small woman and a painter. She had, I gathered from Jack's letter, had a hard rough life but she was, he declared, a woman of talent. "She is the real thing. She's got it," his letter declared.

Jack had proposed marriage to her but she was undecided.

"Well, you go away. You go off down South. You think it over."

It was evident that Jack was really touched. He had given her money. He was also in love.

"I don't want her to do anything that isn't the right thing for her. I want her to have her chance as a painter," he declared.

This was not the Jack Jones I had known. I had seen him on the street just before I had left Chicago and had told him of my proposed trip to Mobile and he had, through the office in which I had worked, got his letter through to me.

I had gone across the bay to Fairhope and had found Ann. She was small. She was far from a beauty. She had about her something you couldn't mistake.

She was an aristocrat, that was it. There was evident, from the moment you first saw her, a quality, a fineness of spirit that could not be mistaken. It was that that had got Jack. It had cut through to him and, as for Ann, I knew, after the first hour with her, that she had also found in Jack something none of us others who knew him had ever seen.

She was troubled however. Was a marriage with her the best thing for Jack? "I'll never be much of a housekeeper," she said. Jack, she said, had a new plan in his head. He was planning to turn his Dill Pickle into a real playhouse, do only high class plays. I gathered that what he had in mind was something the sort of thing Jasper Deeter was later to do with his Hedgerow Theater in the little town at Media near Philadelphia.

It was Ann's notion that he needed a wife, a woman skilled in the theater. She was afraid, she said, that she would only be in the way, and I wanted to protest to her.

"He is what he is. He will always be the same. He will always be making these grand plans but they will come to nothing," I wanted to say, but I kept silence. It was so evident that Ann was in love with Jack.

"It is none of my business," I told myself.

I had a day with Ann at the little town of Fairhope on Mobile Bay and decided to go there to live. I could get a little house, facing the bay, at a low price. I would do my own cooking. The bay was full of fish. I could get clams and crabs. I talked it over with Ann, who helped me find a house. There was a table, a kitchen stove, chairs and a few dishes. There was a small iron cot and Ann thought that the getting of enough bedding to keep me warm would not cost me much.

So there I was, with a house of my own, a view of the bay, with steamers going up and down. The bay was fed by three great rivers coming down from the north. All the country above was a red clay country, the red washed down into the bay after the heavy winter rains, and when the sun went down over the city on clear evenings, its lights shining at night, the bay became a warm blood red.

It was blue. It was green. It was pale green and there were miles of open beach on which to walk. Living there would cost me little or nothing. There were people with whom I could play about. There were the piny woods stretching away behind the town, the bay with its changing colors and the long stretches of deserted beach. Storms of the past had cast up strange fantastically shaped tree stumps swept down into the bay from the rivers. Some of them had been lying for years in the southern sun. They had been washed by waves and rain.

In the night, on moonlight nights, as a man walked on the beach their shapes constantly changed.

It was a fantastic world. There was Wharton Esherick who at once became my friend, and Ann, both painters; there was Wharton's wife Letty, very dark, very beautiful and presently another, Florence King (we called her the Kinglet), the wife of Carl Zigrosser, who would do my typing for me.

It was all something wonderful. It was the out of doors in a strange and beautiful land. It was good companionship and freedom.

And so a new life began, a winter not to be forgotten. I wrote and wrote, I swam in the bay, my little hoard of money made me seem to myself suddenly rich. I loafed with Wharton, quarreled with him, as one does with a friend.

I even did some painting and a curious thing happened. When I returned to Chicago, after the free winter, broke again, again in the advertising place, there was an exhibition of my paintings.

They were crude enough. I had merely been experimenting with color, its effect on the forms of things I saw. When it was suggested that I show the paintings, I had an exciting evening.

How does a man put a price on painting? I was in a room with my own crude attempts. "All right, I'll put prices on them. Two hundred, three hundred, two hundred and fifty," I thought.

It was all, to be sure, quite meaningless. I had my stories I could not sell. I was no painter. I put the prices on my canvases thinking, as I wrote down the figures, of stories I would like to sell and then, at the showing of my paintings, a strange woman, from Denver, appeared. I never saw her. She sent me a check for seven hundred dollars and walked off with two of my paintings. There was a note from her.

"They make me feel as I would like to feel," she said; and I danced about in the little coop where I sat with the other advertising writers and waved the check under their noses. I was a slave suddenly freed.

It meant freedom again, more freedom for me.

As for the story of little Ann Mitchell, unlike myself a real painter, she married Jack Jones. She was in love with him and he believed in her talent, but he believed even more in himself. It was that belief that led to her death.

She had been living with Jack for perhaps two years when I saw her again. It was summer and I had been lent a house on Lake Michigan, up near the town of Ephraim on Green Bay, and was at work again. The house had been given me for the summer by my friend Doctor Charles Millspaugh, curator of the department of botany at the Field Museum, and I was very happy there. The house was built of logs, a replica of one the Doctor had seen in Norway; there was a large stone fireplace and there were rooms for guests.

The guests kept coming. Waldo Frank came with his wife, my friend George Daugherty came from Chicago, and others followed.

And then Jack Jones came with Ann.

It was a summer night and there was a storm. The wind blew, a half hurricane, and the rain beat against the walls of the house.

It was a night to be indoors, to sit with friends before a fire, to drink, to talk, to tell stories. A little party of friends, men and women, had come from Chicago.

The house was in a wood and on the shore of the bay. It was a mile or more from the town of Ephraim.

There was a knock on the door and I went and threw it open and there they were. They had come up, the whole length of Lake Michigan, in a little open boat with an outboard motor and had just got into the bay before the coming of the storm. They were wet to the skin and Ann was pale. When I had got them into the house I saw the terror in her eyes. There was no terror in Jack's eyes and at once he began to boast. He had beat the storm. The boat was one he had built with his own hands. People had warned him of the dangers of the lake in such a boat but he had laughed at them.

"It is my boat. I built it with my own hands. I wasn't afraid of the storm. I would have ridden it out," he boasted. He went with me into the kitchen of the house.

"It is all right," he said.

He took a marriage certificate from an inside pocket and water dripped from it to the floor.

"Take a look at it," he said. "It is all right. We are legally married," he said, thrusting it into my hands. Jack and Ann stayed with me for several days. The weather cleared and we fished and Ann got out her equipment and painted. It was then she painted the charming little watercolor I have here now on the wall of the room in which I sit writing of her.

"But, Ann, you will not venture back with him, not in that boat?"

The question was being put to her.

"Yes, if he says so, I will.

"He is my man. I will do what he says."

There was a little fishing village along the shore and Ann was painting there. The fishermen, who knew the lake, took me aside.

"That woman," they said, "she will not get back with him in that boat."

They talked to me and they talked to Jack.

"It is my boat. I built it with my own hands. It will ride out any storm that can come."

As the fishermen talked, Ann stood a little aside. She grew a little pale. I could feel the terror in her.

"He is my man. What he says I will do."

There was something she had always wanted. There was her Jack. He made a living for her. She was free. She could paint.

"I'll do what he says. Anything he wants me to do I will do."

I pled with her and the fishermen pled. They grew angry with Jack.

"It is by sheer luck the man has got here in that boat.

"If he had arrived here an hour later that other night when he came, the boat would have been swamped."

The fishermen went about swearing at Jack.

"Let the damn fool go in his boat he has built with his own hands, but do not let the woman go with him," they raged.

However he did set off and he insisted upon taking Ann. The sun was shining as I stood on a little dock before the house pleading with Jack, but he only laughed at me.

"What? It is my boat. I built it. You have been listening to the fool fishermen's talk. I tell you, I myself built the boat."

Ann was smiling. I could see the terror in her eyes but they set off and I watched until the boat disappeared down the bay into the lake. It was the last of her.

It was off Racine that the storm struck the boat and they were there floating on the upturned boat for thirty-six hours before they were found, and Jack was still alive but Ann was dead. When the boat had overturned he had managed to tie himself and Ann to the upturned boat with a rope, but the waves kept washing over them, and Ann had drowned.

"He is my man. I'll do what he says." She had gone to her death for him. I have always thought it gave him pride.

There was a curious end to the story. The Art Institute of Chicago had offered a prize for young painters and Ann had won the prize. It would have meant much to her. She who had never won any recognition as a painter would have got thus the recognition for which she had hungered so long. The prize, however, was for living artists and she was dead, so they did not announce her name as the winner. The prize was given to some other painter.

"It is for him to say. He is my man. I will do what he says."

It was the final word for her. The artist in her had surrendered to the egotism of the male. I never want to see him again.

II. The Finding

(Taking Eleanor to the room where I wrote *Winesburg*)

It is the most difficult moment of all to write of. You are in a room. The particular room in which I sat was in an old house, old as Chicago houses go. Once it had been the house of some fashionable family.

The family had moved into some other, some newly fashionable section of the city. There had been one of those sudden shifts of the rich and fashionable from one section of the city to another, so characteristic of our American cities. There had been a bathroom on the third floor of the house but now, that whole section of the city having fallen into a place of cheap rooming houses, thin partitions had been put up.

There were many little rooms separated by thin partitions and they were all occupied.

The occupants were all young. They were young musicians, painters, young women who aspired to be actresses. I have always wanted to write of the people of that house. They were, for the time, so close to me.

I was no longer young. I was the oldest in that house. At the time the room in which I lived seemed large, and later, in my thoughts, it kept growing larger.

I had often described it to my wife.

"There was a great desk as long as this room in which we now stand," I had said. I described for her my bed, the shelves built into the wall. I have always, when at work, loved to walk up and down. I am sure I gave her the impression of myself striding up and down a long room, grown in my imagination into something like a great hall. The council room of a king, something of that sort.

And then once, years after I had lived there, I made the mistake of taking her to the house.

It was still a cheap rooming house. We drove up in a cab.

Why, how shabby it had grown. There were dirty torn lace curtains at the windows, and, as we went into the little hallway, on the ground floor, the street door being open, we came upon a young couple engaged in a quarrel.

They stood facing us, paying no attention to our entrance. The woman was young. Her hair was in disorder and a cigarette burned between her fingers.

The quarrel was over money. He was accusing her of taking money from his pockets.

"Liar! Liar!" she screamed at him.

She ran suddenly up a flight of stairs, the man following, and we heard a door slam.

The landlady appeared. She was a short, fat woman of fifty clad in a torn dirty dress.

I wanted to run away. I didn't.

"We are looking for a room," I said and followed her silently up first one and then another flight of stairs. In a room on the second floor, behind a closed door there was the sound of a woman crying.

"That would be the woman we just saw, quarreling with her man down below," I thought.

We had got to the door of the room. How heavy I felt. My feet were heavy.

"This room is unoccupied," the landlady said. Her hand was on the door knob.

"Don't," I wanted to scream. "Don't open that door.

"Leave me my dream of the room, what it was."

The door opened.

Why, what a shabby little hole. It was all tawdry, the room so small, the wallpaper so dirty.

"We will go there. If the room is unoccupied we will spend a day, a week there." I had dreamed of sitting with her at the window that looked down toward the Chicago Loop in the evening, as the day faded, as the lights flashed on in the great buildings of the Loop.

People passing along the street below the window, passing under the street light at a nearby corner—shabbily dressed old men, smartly dressed young women. The house had stood just at the edge of the once fashionable section of the city and then to the west began the streets where the poor lived.

"It was in this room it happened."

What dreams, hopes, ambitions. Sometimes it had seemed to me, when as a young man I sat at the window of that room, that each person who passed along the street below, under the light, shouted his secret up to me.

I was myself and still I fled out of myself. It seemed to me that I went into the others.

What dreams. What egotism. I had thought then, on such evenings, that I could tell all of the stories of all the people of America. I would get them all, understand them, get their stories told.

And then came the night when it happened.

But what happened? It is the thing so hard to explain. It is, however, the thing every young man and woman in the world will understand.

I had been working so long, so long. Oh, how many thousand, hundreds of thousands of words put down.

Trying for something.

To escape out of old minds, old thoughts put into my head by others, into my own thoughts, my own feelings.

Out of the others, the many, many others, who had worked in words, to have got so much I wanted but to be freed from them.

To at last go out of myself, truly into others, the others I met constantly in the streets of the city, in the office where I then worked, and still others, remembered out of my childhood in an American small town.

To be myself, and yet at the same time the others.

And then, on a day, late in the afternoon of a day, I had come home to that room. I sat at a table in a corner of the room. I wrote.

There was a story of another human, quite outside myself, truly told.

The story was one called "Hands." It was about a poor little man, beaten, pounded, frightened by the world in which he lived into something oddly beautiful.

The story was written that night in one sitting. No word of it ever changed. I wrote the story and got up. I walked up and down in that little narrow room. Tears flowed from my eyes.

"It is solid," I said to myself. "It is like a rock. It is there. It is put down."

There was, I'm sure, an upsurge of pride.

"See, at last I have done it.

"It is true. There it is."

In those words, scrawled on the sheets of paper, it is accomplished.

I am quite sure that on that night, when it happened in that room, when for the first time I dared whisper to myself, perhaps sobbing, that I had found it, my vocation, I knelt in the darkness and muttered words of gratitude to God.

That I had been on the right track, that I dared hope.

Pride, exaltation, all mixed with a new and great humbleness.

"It happened in that room.

"There I found my vocation.

"It is what we all want.

"All of this frantic search for wealth, for fame, position in life—it is all nothing.

"What we want, every one of us, is our own vocation.

"It is the world hunger."

Those words going through my mind as I stood at the door of a shabby room in a shabby rooming house years later with my wife.

Remembering all my failures since that night when I, alone there in that room, found for the first time my own vocation.

Getting for the first time belief in self.

I must have muttered words to the landlady, taken my wife's arm, hurried out of that house, feeling deeply the shame of my many failures since that, the greatest moment of my life.

When I found what every man and woman in the world wants.

A vocation.

BOOK IV

THE LITERARY LIFE

1. Waiting for Ben Huebsch

Theodore Dreiser had got my first book published. At that time the house of John Lane, an English house, sported a New York branch in charge of a man named Jeff Jones. Dreiser had spoken to him of me, and Jones dropped me a letter. I sent him my novel and went to see him at his office. I think that at this period I had an illusion regarding publishers. It was to the effect that they might be interested in writing.

I found the man Jones a very pleasant fellow. He reminded me of a good many business men. That was what he was, I thought. When we had been together for a half hour, he began speaking of the manuscript of *Windy McPherson's Son.*

"I've read it," he said. There was the implication that the reading was rather a remarkable performance. In reaching the decision to publish the book, he confessed, he had been largely influenced by Dreiser's opinion.

"I wondered what kind of a guy you were," he added. "I thought you might be some kind of a long-haired highbrow." I spent some moments trying to figure out how he had gotten such an idea from *Windy McPherson.*

We went to lunch together. He continued to show his relief. "Why, I can talk with you as with any other guy," he said.

Windy McPherson had a good enough sale. It was the story of a young boy who became a sort of minor captain of industry and sickened of it. More or less it was my own story. I had the man in a state of revolt and hadn't known how to get him out of it. "Where do we go from here?"—that was the question; and I couldn't really solve the problem, which was to set my man on a new and satisfactory way of life. Later, I rewrote the last section of the novel for a new edition of it. But at the time the book sold some ten, perhaps even fifteen thousand copies—and I gave Jeff Jones another book. It was the novel *Marching Men,* a piece put into the form of a novel, that should have been put into the form of an epic poem.

From my army experience I had got an idea that men's minds are influenced far more by their physical activity than they can ever be by reasoning. And one afternoon coming from my office I had stood on a platform of the elevated railroad. Near the station there must have been some loft buildings. Day was closing and the workers poured out of the buildings. There they were, men and women, clothing workers, stenographers from office buildings, shipping clerks, a great shapeless mass, and for a long while I stood on the "L" platform watching them.—Besides, it had long been obvious to me that in a mechanical, industrial age the individualistic and capitalistic idea was outworn. Working in factories I had seen and felt there a curious diminution in men, the result of this separateness, this isolation, this "individualism"—seen and felt it in the men as they came to the factories in the morning and left them for their homes at night. There was a certain power in us that could not get itself expressed. As individuals we were what the owners thought we were, or what they thought themselves to be—cowards, brave men, fools, some of us intelligent, some good craftsmen, others bad. But there was something else, this power that could not get itself expressed.—And standing watching the disorganized mass of workers, I remembered my army experience. I remembered the thing called "discipline." We men marched. Thousands of us learned to do things together. Going into the army as a boy, I had at first thought the long hours of drill, the continual co-operation, a bit absurd. You were in the army to kill, weren't you? Someone was shooting at you and you shot at him. Then this other experience, the realization of what the drilling, the marching, the continual co-operation without words, in silence, hour after hour, day after day, did to us, had come to me. I had seen that a feeling of the whole had been given each individual, and that it was this feeling, finally absorbed into our very blood, that made it possible for men like ourselves to subject ourselves to anything, even death.

In the gloaming I began to see the workers in the place of the soldiers. What had we in the army been but a gang, a group of boys and men, snatched quite suddenly out of civil life? A few of us might have been naturally brave men, but as a whole were probably not at all so. Armies of labor! What the newspapers were always speaking of, and what didn't exist! Suddenly, the feeling of a new kind of labor leader came to me. What rose in my mind was the gesture of a labor leader with an instinctive understanding of massed men. Through an influence on their physical activity he was to release their latent power.

Of course he was entirely noble. He only wanted to help humanity, teach the workers to march shoulder to shoulder as soldiers in armies march. In the morning all the men and women of a certain industry were to meet at a prearranged place and march to their work. At night they were again to form into companies and march away from the factory doors. Men who employed labor were thus to be made to feel its terrible power, but labor itself was also to feel what man is capable of doing.

It was Hitler who eventually worked out what was in my head! The Brown Shirts took the place of my labor-armies—which is to say that Hitler did work out my idea and didn't. There was a danger which I did not see, the one that inheres in all ideals. It is that their beneficence or harmfulness depends on the sort of man who puts them into practice. All depends upon his spirit. Besides, God alone knows what can happen, almost of itself, when you release the power latent in massed men!

Later, when I became a bit more sophisticated, perhaps knew mankind a bit better, I came to feel that if by some odd chance the power to upset the social structure, let us say by the simple turning over of my hand, were given me, nothing on earth could induce me to turn the hand. I could not assume the responsibility. Other men I knew might do so. I knew simply that I myself never was to be a leader, a director of men's actions. If there was a place for me, and I thought there was, it was as observer and historian.

But Hitler and my sophistication were in the far thin future. I put my conception into novel form, and *Marching Men* didn't come off, and didn't sell. Thereupon I gave John Lane, who was no doubt rather discouraged with me, the little book of verse called *Mid-American Chants*. How many copies of that little book were sold I do not know. But if I learned it sold two hundred I would be surprised.

It cooked me with that house all right. So when I offered their American representative *Winesburg, Ohio,* he turned it down. There had come the moment which comes to any man who is a writer. It is a moment a good deal after all like another one in every young man's life. I refer to the moment when, perhaps after a long campaign —let us say that we are referring here to a young man in a village, when for weeks he has been courting—and she has been, time and again, on the point of surrender and then, at last, the moment comes—he has got her. It is a little like that, the moment when, to the man who has been struggling with words, courting them, they at last begin to march.

You are sitting at your desk. Oh, how many hours you have sat there! What stories, novels, songs, begun! Some of them have even been finished, after a fashion.

But you are dissatisfied.

"No. That is not it. I have not yet found it."

You have been getting too many ideas from the work of other men, from books read. We all begin in that way. A man has, in this way, gone to school to George Borrow, to Balzac, to Flaubert, to Turgenev, to George Moore, all of whom I, for example, had been reading assiduously.

"No. That is not it. Chuck it."

There is this life, in the streets through which you walk daily, life in men in shops and factories where you have worked. You were a boy in an American small town. You ran about the streets there. You worked for a time as a delivery boy for a grocer. You were for a time a newsboy, you delivered papers, went to kitchen doors. Because you were a seller of newspapers you, unlike other boys, could go into saloons. You saw men getting drunk, heard their talk. There would be these thousands of impressions in your mind. The journalist in doing his daily job must, at once, on the spot, use these impressions, but with the imaginative writer it is somewhat different. He must wait. He is like a woman who has become pregnant. Often I have found that an impression got for a story must stay in me for years. It comes into my mind, stays for a time. Perhaps I try to write it but it is not there. I must throw it aside. [I think for example of a story called *Death in the Woods*. It is a story I must have tried to write at least a dozen times over as many years. I am not one who can peck away at a story. It writes itself, as though it used me merely as a medium, or it is n.g.]

I had been published. Books, with my name on their backs standing on a shelf over my desk. And yet, something eating at me.

"No. I have not yet written." These words whispered to myself in the night.

"It is not my own clear reaction to life. I have been following paths made by other men. I must find my own path."

I would not, however, upon the particular occasion I am speaking of here, have gone to my desk with any such thought in my mind. What happened was that I came home late, after a particularly trying day. It was perhaps ten o'clock at night and I undressed and got into bed. . . . And here I must ask the reader's indulgence for again trying to describe here a particularly gorgeous, glowing moment in my own life. It happens that I am writing this part of my story on a March day in the city of Acapulco in Mexico. I am here in a room overlooking the Pacific, in the far south, far, far from the room in the Chicago rooming house, in which the adventure I am trying to set down here took place. I am here with a friend, a Detroit newspaper man, Sam Marshall, and he is at this moment slamming his typewriter in an adjoining room.

He has just come in here, to get matches for his pipe, and as he went out the door, he delivered himself of an epigram. "We newspaper men do not write for the public," he said, "we write for other newspaper men."

And so it must be that I am writing here for other writers, recalling to them a certain moment in their own lives. It may be that many writers do not get to the moment. . . .

I had got into bed in that rooming house. I was very tired. It was a late fall night and raining and I had not bothered to put on my pajamas.

I was there naked in the bed and I sprang up. I went to my typewriter and began to write. It was there, under those circumstances, myself sitting near an open window, the rain occasionally blowing in and wetting my bare back, that I did my first writing.

I wrote the first of the stories, afterwards to be known as the Winesburg stories. I wrote it, as I wrote them all, complete in the one sitting. I do not think I afterwards changed a word of it. I wrote it off so, sitting at my desk, in that room, the rain blowing in on me and wetting my back and when I had written it I got up from my desk.

The rest of the stories in the book came out of me on succeeding evenings, and sometimes during the day while I worked in the advertising office. At intervals there would be a blank space of a week, and then there would be two or three written during a week. I was like a woman having my babies, one after another but without pain.

To get the stories published was a harder matter. In New York *The Seven Arts* and the old *Masses,* in Chicago *The Little Review* had begun printing them and in one or two instances I got as much as ten dollars for one of them. Once later I counted up—it must have been in a base moment, when I was thinking of money. For the whole series, printed in this way, I figured I had got eighty-five dollars. I mention the matter because I am always getting letters from young writers and they seem, most of them, to be up against what I was up against.

They want freedom to write. "How am I to make a living?" they ask, but unfortunately while our manufacturers, as for example our automobile manufacturers, seem to have been able to make the public pay for their experiments, we who experiment in prose and in verse cannot do it.

Often the new writer, addressing me thus, seems to feel that I, being somewhat established, have got hold of some secret. There is, they seem to think, a key, a golden key that one finds and with which one at once begins to open doors. They want to borrow the key. They have read, perhaps, romantic stories of writers. There is a man of rare but unrecognized talent who has been living in a garret. He is down to his last crust of bread. He eats the crust and, with the strength thus got, writes a story or a poem. He sends it off to a publisher but as he has been unable to pay his rent he is kicked out of his room.

So there he is. It is a dark rainy night and he spends it on a park bench and, in the morning he awakens, very hungry and also stiff and sore, but, at that moment, blown by the wind, a part of one of the city's morning newspapers . . . it would be the front page . . . lands at his feet. He looks down and there is his name, in big type, staring at him. He has got fame. A new genius is born and some editor, or publisher, filled with excitement, has been announcing him to the world.

The above, to be sure, exaggerated, but having in it the nub of the matter. There is something that the young writer believes if I but would, I could do; some secret I could let him in on.

I had got some of my stories printed in some of the little magazines but wanted them published in book form. It was the first work of mine about which I had felt such anxiety. Perhaps I thought that in it I had had something to say to other writers.

And there was something else. The stories belonged together. I felt that, taken together, they made something like a novel, a complete story. There was all of this starved side of American small town life. Perhaps I was even vain enough to think that these stories told would, in the end, have the effect of breaking down a little the curious separateness of so much of life, these walls we build up about us. I thought of our puritanism. It seemed to lead so inevitably to hypocrisy.

The publishing house of John Lane did not want them. Naturally I thought Lane all wrong. I considered then, as I now consider, that my earlier stories, both *Windy McPherson* and at least in the writing, *Marching Men,* had been the result not so much of my own feeling about life as of reading the novels of others. There had been too much H. G. Wells, that sort of thing. I was being too heroic. I came down off my perch. I have even sometimes thought that the novel form does not fit an American writer, that it is a form which had been brought in. What is wanted is a new looseness; and in *Winesburg* I had made my own form. There were individual tales but all about lives in some way connected. By this method I did succeed, I think, in giving the feeling of the life of a boy growing into young manhood in a town. Life is a loose flowing thing. There are no plot stories in life. I had begun writing of the little lives I knew, the people I had lived, walked and talked with, perhaps even slept with.

There is still another sense in which I believe that the little stories are as revolutionary as anything I shall ever be able to write.

You do not need to go far back into the history of writing to come to the place where the life of a common man or woman, the worker, was not thought interesting. Such lives were not thought of as material for the story teller. In the old fiction, old poetry, old plays, the workers and peasants were invariably introduced as comic figures. Go to Shakespeare and you will see what I mean. It is so in all the older fiction. The notion that the worker in the factory, in the sweatshop, in the mine, or any one of the obscure figures, in any American town, might be as sensitive and as easily hurt as the well-to-do man or woman, and that the strange thing in life we call beauty might be as alive in such a one—man or woman—as in the rich and successful, is still new.

If our present capitalist system did in fact produce, even for the few, the kind of glowing lives some of our romancers pretend, I would myself hesitate about deserting capitalism. It doesn't.

And I believe that those who call themselves revolutionists will get the most help out of such men as myself by not trying to utilize such talents as we have directly for propaganda but in leaving us as free as possible to strike with our stories of American life into a deeper soil.

I mean that the lives of those who now succeed in getting money and power in our present individualistic capitalistic society are neither happy nor successful lives. That illusion needs to be destroyed.

When it comes to the others, the workers, the real producers, the downtrodden people, theirs are the stories that need to be told.

I think I have always wanted to tell their stories and still want to tell them. It is my one great passion. If *Winesburg, Ohio* tried to tell the story of the defeated figures of an old American individualistic small town life, then my later books have been but an attempt to carry these same people forward into the new American life, into the whirl and roar of modern machines. I do not believe my own impulses have changed.

The book came back not only from John Lane. It came back from several other publishers. One of them, on whom I called, handed me a copy of a novel by an Anglo-American author he was then promoting. "Read this and learn how to write," said he.

Then on a Sunday, a cold wintry day, I waited at the corner of Fifty-ninth Street and the Park in New York. I had gotten a letter from Ben Huebsch, now editor-in-chief of the Viking Press, but then doing business under his own name. He wrote asking me to see him when I next came to New York, and, within a few weeks, being in New York, I phoned him. He told me where to meet him, as I understood at the Central Park corner. We were to go to a certain restaurant.

"I will meet you there at the corner at four," he had said over the phone and I think I must have been, at what I understood to be the appointed place, at three.

I stood and waited and he did not come. The hours passed. It was four o'clock, then five, then six. I am sure it will be difficult for me to make the reader understand how I felt.

It is to be borne in mind that, by this time, my stories had been rather kicked around for three or four years. I had been tender about these people of my stories, had wanted understanding and tenderness for them; and it had happened already with men on whom I had counted, that when I had shown them the stories they had rejected them.

I was there, in the city, on the Sunday afternoon, waiting on the street corner and it was cold and my heart was cold. I had got the notion that Mr. Huebsch, like so many other publishers, did not want my stories.

What a shabby trick he had played me! "Why," I asked myself, "did he need to encourage me?" As regards the particular stories there had been so much rejection, so much head shaking among my friends, that, unfairly enough, it did not occur to me that a simple mistake as regards a place of meeting had been made. I do not think that at any time later I ever told Mr. Huebsch but, on that afternoon, I certainly cursed him. I became a Nazi. "He is a Jew," I said to myself and standing there, in the city street corner on the wintry afternoon, I raised my hands to Heaven and cursed the Jews. Under the same circumstances, feeling as I did at the moment, I am sure I would have done the same for the English, the Germans, the Irish. I would have thought them a deceitful and a tricky race.

"But why did he ask me to meet him? Is he a sadist? Did he want to torture me?" At least other publishers, to whom my book had been submitted, had been frankly cold. They had not aroused my hopes. I went back to my hotel and threw myself on the bed. It all seems very silly now but on the evening in the hotel room, with the tears flowing from my eyes . . . Occasionally I stopped weeping to curse, consigning all publishers to hell and reserving a special place in hell for poor Ben Huebsch . . . on that evening I was really more desperate than I had ever been before in my life.

And then, at last . . . it must have been at about nine . . . my telephone rang and there was Mr. Huebsch and I managed to control myself while he told me that, while I had been on one corner waiting for him he had been on another waiting for me. There had been a simple misunderstanding and, as for the book, he said that he would make no bones about that.

"Yes," he said, over the phone, "I want the book. I only wanted to meet you to talk over details," he said.

"And you do not want to tinker, to change my stories, to tell me how you think they should be written?"

I am quite sure that my voice must have trembled as I asked the question.

"You do not want to tell me that they are not stories?"

"No, of course not," he said.

2. I Write Too Much of Queer People

The fear expressed in my phone talk with Ben Huebsch had its origins. Curious things had happened to me in connection with that book from the very start. When I wrote the stories I was in Chicago and took them to Floyd Dell. Up to that time Floyd had been more or less my literary father. He had been very kind. He had written about my work in the *Chicago Evening Post* and gone to no end of trouble to get my first novel published. I believe it must have been Floyd who got Theodore Dreiser interested when Dreiser said the word that got my scribbling into print.

But when Floyd saw my Winesburg stories he condemned them.

"They are not stories," he said.

"They are no good."

I am afraid I was rude to Floyd. A man gets arrogant at times. He boasts.

"Listen, man." I said, "If a passenger train comes in at a railroad station, stops for passengers and then after a time, goes on its way and you are not there to get aboard the train, do not blame the engineer."

It was a necessary statement on my part. I felt I had to make it.

Mr. Henry Mencken saw some of the stories and his reactions at that time were much the same as Dell's.

"The stories won't do. They are not stories."

Perhaps fifteen years later I saw an article by Henry telling how he had at once recognized the merits of the stories and of how he had given me words of encouragement.

Well, it was all right with me. Our minds work like that. We can't help it.

Presently the book was there between its boards, clad in its light yellow dress. I well remember my getting the book in Chicago, my going into my room and locking the door. "Don't be silly," I told myself. "You have already had three books published." But as I tore the wrapping from the package and at last had the book in my hand, I am sure that my hands trembled.

Something I had long wanted had come to me. I had got a book that was my own. I felt it was my first real reaction to life uninfluenced by reading. And what had I not put into the book! I thought it had my life, my feeling for life, my love of life in it.

Well, it was published. And immediately there was a strange reaction, a strange reception. In justice I ought to speak of the fact that criticism had been poured over all my Chicago contemporaries from the start. We had the notion that sex had something to do with people's lives, and it had barely been mentioned in American writing before our time. No one it seemed ever used a profane word. And bringing sex back to take what seemed to us its normal place in the picture of life, we were called sex-obsessed.

Still the reception of *Winesburg* amazed and confounded me. The book was widely condemned, called nasty and dirty by most of its critics. It was more than two years selling its first five thousand. The book had been so personal to me that, when the reviews began to appear and I found that, for the most part, it was being taken as the work of a perverted mind . . . in review after review it was called "a sewer" and the man who had written it taken as a strangely sex-obsessed man . . . a kind of sickness came over me, a sickness that lasted for months.

It is very strange to think, as I sit writing, that this book, now used in many of our colleges as a textbook of the short story, should have been so misinterpreted when published twenty years ago. I had felt peculiarly clean and healthy while I was at work on it.

"What can be the matter with me?" I began asking myself. It is true that nowadays I am constantly meeting men who tell me of the effect had upon them by the book when it first came into their hands and every now and then a man declares that, when the book was published he praised it, but if there was any such praise, at the time, it escaped my notice.

That the book did not sell did not at all bother me. The abuse did. There was the public abuse, condemnation, ugly words used and there was also, at once, a curious kind of private abuse.

My mail became filled with letters, many of them very strange. It went on and on for weeks and months. In many of the letters there were dirty words used. It was as though by these simple tales I had, as one might say, jerked open doors to many obscure and often twisted lives. They did not like it. They wrote me the letters and, often, in the letters there was a spewing forth of something like poison.

And for a time it poisoned me.

Item . . . A letter from a woman, the wife of an acquaintance. Her husband was a banker. I had once sat at her table and she wrote to tell me that, having sat next to me at the table and, having read my book, she felt that she could never, while she lived, be clean again.

Item . . . There was a man friend who was spending some weeks in a New England town. He was leaving the town one morning on an early train and, as he walked to the railroad station, he passed a small park.

In the park, in the early morning, there was a little group of people, two men, he said, and three women, and they were bending over a small bonfire. He said that his curiosity was aroused and that he approached.

"There were three copies of your book," he said. The little group of New Englanders, men and women . . . he thought they must all have been past fifty . . . he spoke of the thin sharp Calvin Coolidge faces . . . "they were the town library board."

They had bought the three copies of my book and were burning them. My friend who saw all of this, thought there must have been complaints made. He said he spoke to the group gathered in the little town square before the town library building . . . and that a woman of their group answered his question.

He said she made a sour mouth.

"Ugh!" she said. "The filthy things, the filthy things."

Item . . . A well-known woman writer of New Orleans. She spoke to a friend of mine who asked her if she had seen the book.

"I got fire tongs," she said. "I read one of the stories and, after that, I would not touch it with my hands. With the tongs I carried it down into the cellar. I put it in the furnace. I knew that I should feel unclean while it was in my house."

There are these remembered items and there were others, hundreds of others. Some of them were quite humorous. Winesburg of course was no particular town. It was a mythical town. It was people. I had got the characters of the book everywhere about me, in towns in which I had lived, in the army, in factories and offices. When I gave the book its title I had no idea there really was an Ohio town by that name. I even consulted a list of towns but it must have been a list giving only towns that were situated on railroads. And the people of the actual Winesburg protested. They declared the book immoral and that the actual inhabitants of the real Winesburg were a highly moral people. Once later, when the book began to make its way, the *Cleveland Plain Dealer,* as a Sunday newspaper stunt, sent a representative to the real Winesburg.

The reporter, a woman, wrote me about it. It must have been an amusing experience. She had interviewed a local preacher.

"Did you ever stand so, on a bitter cold night, in the belfry of your church, waiting to see a naked woman lying in her bed in a nearby house and smoking a cigarette?"

Perhaps she was not so bold. At any rate she wrote me that the people of the town declared that they had not read the book but that they had heard it was dreadfully immoral.

Later they softened a little. There was to be a town homecoming day and they wrote and asked me to come. A preacher living in the real Winesburg wrote and printed a little pamphlet on the town. He mentioned my book and the people of my book. He suggested that if I ever came to the real Winesburg I would find quite different people there. At least he must have read the book. The suggestion was that the people of the real town were not bothered by secret lusts, walked always in the straight line, lived what is called clean lives, and I remember that, when I read the little pamphlet, I was myself indignant.

For certainly the people of my book, who had lived their little fragments of lives in my imagination, were not specially immoral. They were just people, and when I answered the preacher's letter I told him that if the people of his real Winesburg were as all around decent as those of my imagined town then the real Winesburg might be indeed a very decent town to live in.

And here is something very curious. The book has become a kind of American classic, and has been said by many critics to have started a kind of revolution in American short-story writing. And the stories themselves which in 1919 were almost universally condemned as immoral, might today almost be published in the *Ladies' Home Journal,* so innocent they seem. All of that new frankness about life while a new born babe is growing to voting age. But many other writers are responsible for the change. We have all got a new freedom, a new license to look more directly at life.

At the time however I was half ill for months. "I will write no more," I told myself, and sometimes when I had received in the morning mail perhaps a half dozen abusive letters I went and got drunk. "If I am so filthy I shall be filthy," I told myself.

I was at a little town in Indiana, had been sent there to write advertisements for some manufacturer. Let us say it was a manufacturer who made a medicine for gaps in chickens. Or for blackleg or abortion in cows.

Anyway I was at a railroad station and bought a magazine and there was Mr. Waldo Frank writing in the magazine of my Winesburg stories.

He did not say they were not stories. He praised them. He said they were clear stories, a new and healthy note in American writing.

I was at that railroad station waiting to take a train when I began reading Waldo's article. I did not take the train. Evening was coming on and I went to walk in the streets of the town and out along a country road.

It had seemed to me, for a long time, that everyone who had bought my little book had immediately written me a letter telling me how vile I was.

But there was Waldo Frank saying publicly, in the pages of a magazine, that I was not dirty or filthy-minded.

It had grown dark when I got out of the Indiana town in which I had bought the magazine. I sat on a grassy bank beside a country road. It was one of the happiest evenings of my life. Someone was speaking with respect of my book I had felt so happy and clean while writing.

In the end a story summed up the entire episode for me.

I had a little place in the country and went there for week ends. On Sunday afternoons friends from the city, men and women, occasionally drove out to see me. A certain young man, a friend, liking the country, took a place near me. He was the son of a college professor. As a young man he was threatened with tuberculosis and had gone to Saranac, in upper New York, to take the cure.

He met a woman there. It seems that this woman had been through an unfortunate experience. She had been a stenographer in New York

City and had fallen in love with her employer. She became his mistress. Something happened and she had been compelled to have an operation. She was ill after that and her employer sent her to Saranac to be cured.

She and my friend met there. They became friends and presently found themselves in love. They talked it over. They decided that, because he was threatened with tuberculosis and she had been through a very sad experience, they would marry but they would live in continence. They did that.

It went on so for a year, for two years, and then she fell in love with another man, my friend's friend. The three talked it over. Having lived with my friend for the three years in continence she wanted to continue living so with him. She could not think of him in a more intimate position with herself. She told him so.

They decided to go on living together. He was in love with her. He felt that he was himself responsible for the situation. He decided to take his friend into his house, to live there. The friend became his wife's lover. Later I had all this from the lover.

Now I think you can all see what a "healthy" situation this created! It was this man who, with the wife and her lover, took the house near me in the country. At first I knew nothing of the story but, as anyone must have done who was at all sensitive to other people, I felt something was wrong. I think they must have been three of about the most unhappy people I have ever known.

But they were trying to keep up an air of cheerfulness. They came in the evening to see me. We talked. We told stories. When a story was told we laughed together.

But there was something hysterical, a bit unhealthy about the laughter. I wondered. I kept wondering.

It went on so for a time and then the husband no longer came out to the country place. Only the wife and lover came. I used to meet them on summer nights walking in country roads. They no longer came to see me.

And then came the tragedy. I presume to console himself the husband, although still married to his wife, took up with another woman. She was, I believe, a Russian girl. I dare say he told her his story and, as a woman will, when she is in love with a man, she put all the blame for the quite terrible situation on the wife.

She decided to kill her. She got a gun and came out to the country place. The wife had employed a gardener and was working with him in her flower garden.

The Russian woman came there. She saw the two people working in the garden, fired at the wife, missed her and killed the gardener.

She fled. She managed to get back into the city. She took a train to another city. She went to a hotel and engaged a room. She went up into the room and shot and killed herself.

Two or three years passed and one day I was walking with my friend, the husband. I had begun to publish stories and he was a man much interested in literature. He began to scold me. He said, "Anderson, I have no doubt that, as a story teller, you have some ability but there is something wrong." He said that I wrote too much of queer people. He said he thought it was unhealthy. It gave the wrong understanding of life, of people. "Most of us, after all," he said, "lead quite uneventful lives. Nothing unusual," he said, "ever really happens to us."

3. Be Little

Jacques Copeau, then in America with his players of the Vieux Colombier Theatre of Paris, had come to me in Chicago. He wanted to dramatize *Winesburg* and did me the honor to say that the stories were the first full rich expression of something he, a Frenchman, after living among us, had come to feel about American life.

The dramatization didn't come off. There was a little tragedy at my house, or rather at my apartment in Chicago. The apartment was a small one and was on the ground floor of a three story brick building on Division Street on the North Side in Chicago, and Copeau, while he stayed with me, slept in a small bedroom at the back. Like the office of Dr. Reefy in the play, the bedroom looked out on an alleyway and, like the alleyway in my mythical *Winesburg,* the Chicago alleyway was filled with stray cats.

Really to make the situation between myself and my guest in Chicago more clear I should go into a few details. Clemenceau was Copeau's friend and Clemenceau knew also our Mr. Otto Kahn.

He had got our Otto to finance the bringing of Copeau's company to New York. Otto put up the cash. I dare say the idea was to draw Americans closer to the French, to help bring us, as in the end we were brought, into the war. The company was I think to have a year in New York.

The company did play its year in New York and then, as I understood it, Mr. Kahn's financial assistance was withdrawn. Perhaps he had already got his red ribbon. I do not know but I do know that Copeau kept the company going another year. I saw his performance of Molière's *Doctor in Spite of Himself* and thought it beautiful. (What gorgeous players he had with him. I remember a certain portly Russian actress with whom I once dined. What life, what vitality . . . But never mind.)

Copeau must have spent all his money keeping the company going. I know that he was broke when he came to me. He was smoking a corncob pipe and I also remember how he insisted on smoking it in Chicago street cars. The conductors always protested but Copeau pretended not to understand English. He winked at me and I tried to explain to the conductors. "He is a distinguished foreigner," I said. "He does not understand our ways.

"In Rome, in Paris, in London, in Moscow," I explained, "even the ladies smoke corncob pipes in street cars."

And so Copeau, being an artist to the bone and having little or no money left after the breakup of his company, was clinging desperately to certain American luxuries he had acquired. There was, I remember, a soft yellow astrakhan overcoat. There were luxurious neckties, a certain gorgeous pair of striped trousers, a dozen of the finest of shirts. There were pigskin bags and several pairs of expensive shoes.

"See," cried Copeau. "Look, Sherwoodio. I am being an American. I am being rich." There was, I am sure, a certain picture in his mind . . . the return to Paris, walks, in all this newly acquired finery, on the boulevards.

There was no closet in the little bedroom at the back of my apartment so I got hooks and Copeau's luxurious clothes were hung in full sight from a window that looked into the alleyway. It was a mistake.

Together we were going to write our play. We never did. Like all thorough artists, Copeau was intensely interested in life, and just at that time in American life. In New York he had been terribly busy. Now he had leisure. He wanted to go about, ride in the street cars, walk through the streets of Chicago at night, go into all sections of the city. He wanted to see life in Chicago not from the Boulevard Michigan but over the back fences. "Let us go into a saloon," he kept saying. We went to Hinky Dink's. We walked on many streets. We went on the North Side, the West Side, the South Side. We spent long evenings in Halsted Street. We visited Greek bars and little Italian bars under railroad embankments. We drank together. We talked of the making of our play.

"There is the one story, 'Paper Pills.' Oh, that story! It has in it the wisdom of the gods." You, the reader, can imagine how I felt, the ecstasy I was in. Just at that time my stories were being abused. No magazine that could pay anything would buy a story of mine. The words filth and sewage were being slung at them.

So there was this man Copeau, distinguished, fine of spirit and sensitive. What happiness he was giving me. There were these days, spent thus, talking of the play we might write. Such a man, actually, to love my work. I was sleeping on a sofa in the dining room of my little apartment. At night I did not sleep, did not want to. I lay awake and tears of joy were on my cheeks.

And then . . . there was an evening and I had got the poet Carl Sandburg out to the apartment to sing for Copeau. He sang "Frankie and Johnnie" but not the version he sang for literary ladies when on a lecture tour. We had some drinks. It was a charming evening. Sandburg left us.

We walked, Copeau and I together, to the door of the little bedroom in which he had been sleeping. We had begun again talking of the making of our play. "Oh, Sherwoodio, we will make this play. You will come to me in Paris. We will produce it there.

"We will make the French feel and understand your America in a new way. Then we will bring it here. We will make it a triumph of life over art.

"Art is after all a woman of the town. Art is a whore."

We got to his bedroom door and I threw it open. What a shock. The room had been stripped. Everything was gone. Oh, the striped trousers, the astrakhan coat, the ties, hats, shoes, pigskin bags! Oh, the gray suits, the brown suits, the black suits!

All gone, quite gone. The window that looked into the alleyway was open. As we stood together at the door, struck as by the hand of God, someone threw a milk bottle at a cat in the alleyway. The bottle crashed against the brick wall of the building.

A kind of despair settled down over the little Chicago apartment and I remember only two huge Chicago policemen who came later that night. I had my typewriter going and was making a list. Copeau was walking up and down in the room. I wonder if the man has ever played Hamlet. He should. One of the policemen spoke. He went to raise a window and spat tobacco juice into the street outside. Copeau was calling off his list of stolen treasures and I was typing. "Oh, Sherwoodio . . . never in my life again will I acquire such another pair of striped trousers. And oh, Sherwoodio, the pigskin bags." The policeman spoke. "Was either of youse guys," he asked, "was youse hanging around any saloons and bragging about all of this stuff youse had?"

It may be we had been. Who can tell? The precious stuff was never found. The play we were to write together never got written.

There was a long period when there was no more thought of the stage. In respect to the commercial stage there is always this difficulty . . . that it costs a lot of money to produce a play; and whenever money is involved, there is inevitably caution. I do not know what it costs to print a novel or a book of short stories but surely not much, let us say a few hundred dollars. The characters that run through the pages of your novel do not demand a salary. There is no union of stage hands, no Actors' Equity. Horrors . . . imagine the situation, the characters of our stories organizing a union, demanding justice.

Still in my imagination I was with Copeau in a Chicago saloon. It would be somewhere on Chicago's West Side, near a factory. There were in the city any number of ladies' literary societies, associations for the cementing of the friendship between France and America, etc., who had been eager to have Copeau speak to them, but he had refused. "No, no. This is what I want." We would be standing inside or outside some such West Side saloon. It is the noon hour and the workmen are sitting along a factory wall in the sun. "Oh, that I could go sit with them, be for an hour one of them." It will not work. There is something that marks the man as a stranger, a man of distinction. When we go into a saloon or approach a group of workers they become silent.

All of this before the robbery. Copeau wearing none of his carefully hoarded finery. Often we walk sadly, Copeau stopping in some street in Chicago's vast dreary West Side. He makes one of his broad gestures. "Oh, the theater, theater! It should bring all of this in. Life should come pulsating into the theater from the very streets.

"Try, Sherwoodio. You must try." He puts a thought in my head. "Who knows. There is a great new drama here, in America.

"You may be the American dramatist. You may be it without knowing what you are."

A sweet thought. I held it for a time. Once a man wrote me a letter calling me "The eagle of American authordom." I had it framed, hung it over my bed. I began going to the theater. There I met my boyhood friend again, Mr. John Emerson.

I think it must have been at about this time that John secured a sinecure for me in New York. He did not say that there was no need to work at the job he got for me . . . that of being a publicity man for one of the big movie companies at some seventy-five dollars a week . . . but I am quite sure he knew well enough how it would turn out. It was, you see, during the first flush days of the movies. Money was being flung about. Why not cut in on it a little? I did. I never did write any publicity, or at least none worth printing, but it must have been several months before some clerk found a name, that of a stranger who never did any work, on the pay roll and cut it off.

It was O.K. with me. By that time I had finished my novel.

I got a cheap room, somewhere over on the West Side in the Twenties between Ninth and Tenth Avenues, and there I worked.

The World War had lately ended and I had been opposed to the War and had narrowly escaped arrest. Some of the political radicals, Jim Lawson, the English labor leader, and John Reed had been my friends. It was a relief to be in New York where I was comparatively unknown.

It was a good room. There was the hoarse cry of steamers in the river at night. I was at the back of the house, upstairs, and looked across little city back yards at people making love, dining, quarreling. I saw a good deal of the inside lives of young married couples, old married pairs, bachelors and old maids, all, I dare say, of the working class.

"Perhaps it would be well for you to at least be seen, now and then, at the studio." It must have been some man met about the theater who gave me that tip. I did go, for a time quite often, in the afternoon. The studio was at a place called Fort Lee.

Why, how very like the factories to which I had been going as advertising writer! There was immediately something sensed. "It is not the actors or the makers of plays, those who write for the theater, who are in command here," I told myself. There was immediate disillusionment. It was as it was in the factories, the workers every year less and less having anything at all to say about the work they did . . . so here also, in this new art of the theater, the movies, there was a force certainly up above all writers, all actors.

"Business is business."

"It's money makes the mare go."

The movies were relatively new then. The disillusionment that came did not come at once. When I first began going to the studios I was for a time excited. There was this great new field for actors and for play makers opening out. For a long time I had held to the notion that every real story teller was in part at least also an actor. At that time I knew few actors, was just beginning to know them, but I felt close. "There is a great door opening here," I told myself, a door through which the actor and the play maker may go out into a new wide world.

"What is stopping it, what is closing the door just opened?"

Was it money again . . . business? It is true that while I was hanging about the movie studios I did not try to write any movies. For a time the whole thing seemed too wonderful to me. I went about in a kind of daze. "Now," I said to myself, "if the impulse to write for the theater comes I will not need to confine my imaginations within the proscenium arch. I can let my fancy roam over the wide world. Short stories may be done in pictures. It is even possible to do novels in pictures.

"Some man's life, here in America, can be taken, put on the screen. It will be possible to show in pictures that everyone can understand how accidental life is, how men are blown about like dry leaves before a wind, some called 'good,' others 'bad.' It will be possible to tear down, before everyone's eyes, some of the little lies by which we all live."

A time of inner excitement. It didn't last. Business is business.

There was a place for me, I told myself, but not in the theater or in the movies. Finally I got this notion fixed in my head.

"You can make it all right if you will only be satisfied to remain small," I told myself. I had to keep saying it over and over to myself. "Be little. Don't try to be big. Work under the guns. Be a little worm in the fair apple of life." I got all of these sayings at my tongue's end, used to go through the streets of Chicago muttering them to myself.

4. Old Mary, the Dogs, and Theda Bara

There were two of them, sisters, Mary and Kate, but I did not know Kate well. When I got the little house, at Palos Park (it had been Kate's house) she came to see me once.

She was, as I remember her, a tall woman, and at fifty-five still handsome while Old Mary was growing fat.

I had been strolling about, taking trains out of Chicago to nearby towns. I was looking for just such a little house as the one I found when I found Old Mary. It was Sunday and I had taken a Wabash train.

Palos Park.

I remembered some verses Mike Carr had once recited to me.

"When out of Palos came the gold."

I thought of Columbus's ships sailing out of the little Spanish port.

"Perhaps I will find my own gold here."

The little town (I hear it has grown since, that there are paved roads leading to it) was perhaps a mile from the station.

It was a strange little place at the edge of a state forest, a little town occupied for the most part by old people. They had come out there. They had little money. Many of them were widow women. They raised chickens, tended little gardens.

I was walking in a dirt road at the edge of town where the forest began when I first saw Old Mary. She was sitting on the front steps of her house and there was a cigar box beside her and in the cigar box was tobacco.

She was fat. She might have been sixty. She was rolling a cigarette. At that time women did not smoke cigarettes.

"She is one of my own sort, a rebel. I'll bet she is a grand old girl," I thought. Her dress was clean and the yard before her little frame house had been neatly trimmed. The porch on the steps of which she sat was banked with flowers.

There was a plot of ground, surrounded by a low fence and on it stood two small frame houses. I opened a gate and went in.

So there I was, having my first talk with Old Mary.

"I am a writer. I am looking for a small house. I would like it if the house were furnished.

"I cannot live much in the house. I want a place to which I can come, be alone. Perhaps occasionally a friend, man or woman, will come to spend the day with me."

"Or a night," Old Mary said and laughed.

"No, that is not my object," I explained. "I am employed in the city. Although I am a writer I cannot live by my writing. Occasionally however I have a week end or even, now and then, a whole week free. I want the house as a place in which to work, where I won't be interrupted."

There were the two sisters, Kate and Old Mary. They had been in burlesque, the vaudeville circuits. They had done a song and dance act. They were in the Far West, in the little boom mining towns, had been in Goldfield, Rawhide, Virginia City.

"Out there," Old Mary told me, "we made our best money getting a cut in on the drinks. We'd do our act; then we'd go sit at the table with the miners. The waiters would serve us tea in a whiskey glass. We worked 'em. We kept them buying. 'My God, woman, but you can sure store it away,' they would say to me and Kate. We got a good cut on every drink they bought."

I had got Kate's house. The two women had retired. They had saved some money and planned to live together in the country but, as Old Mary explained, Kate couldn't stand it.

"She isn't like me," Old Mary explained. Old Mary liked to dig in the ground. She didn't mind the loneliness. It was true that most of the others in Palos Park had little to do with her.

It was her past, she said. It was because she smoked and swore. She said she couldn't help swearing.

"I always did swear like I do now. Goddamit I can't say ten words without swearing."

It was because of the people with whom she had always associated. She had got used to it. It meant nothing to her.

Kate was different, she always had been. Kate could swear too when she wanted to turn it on. There was that time when Kate and Old Mary were doing their act in New Orleans. There was another team, two women who were also doing a song and dance act on the same bill.

"They were jealous of us. You see we wore tights in our act.

"So one night we came to the theater to do our act and what do you think the two goddamn bitches had done. They had thrown our tights down in the privy hole, that's what they had done.

"And you should have heard Kate then. Goddamn, I was proud of her. The way she cut the ground out from under those two goddamn bitches with her tongue was something to hear."

The cellar of Old Mary's house was a museum. It was filled with the sort of apparatus vaudeville actors use for their acts. It all belonged, Old Mary explained, to old-timers like herself and Kate.

She explained how it was with them. They had got too old to do their acts but wouldn't or couldn't believe they were through.

"They bring their junk to me. 'Keep it for me, Mary,' they say. They are always looking to get good billing again but they don't get it.

"So their junk stays here in my cellar and now and then they come to see me. Jesus, they are all through, washed up, but they can't admit it to themselves so I just keep their junk for them."

She told me how, sometimes, when such an old actor came to see her, he went down into her cellar and got his equipment out. He might be an old trapeze performer. His equipment for his act was silver plated and he got it out and polished it.

"Christ, it makes me want to cry to see him but I don't let on," Old Mary said.

I was there in Old Mary's house for the first time on a Saturday morning in the spring. There was a little sitting room, a kitchen, a bedroom. It was neatly enough furnished.

But where and how was I to eat?

"I'll consult Old Mary," I thought. I went to her. It was a mistake.

"Could you, Mary?"

I was wondering if she might be persuaded to cook my dinners; my breakfasts when I stayed overnight, I thought I could manage.

"Well, I'll be goddamned. Of all the goddamn nerve. What the hell do you think I am? I'll have you to understand, young man, that I'm no servant to any goddamn man."

It may have been on that occasion that she explained to me, her explanation richly larded with profanity, how she had always differed from her sister Kate.

They had had their troubles and it had always been because of men.

Old Mary had always liked men all right. Occasionally she had been, she said, stuck on some man.

"So I gave him what he wanted—what the hell—but I would not marry one of them."

And then Kate had gone and got married and Old Mary had been furiously angry. She said that she and Kate had fought with their fists. They had torn each other's clothes, scratched each other's faces. She laughed telling of it. For over two years, she said, she and Kate had stayed at the same hotels or boarding houses, had traveled on the same trains, done their act, sometimes twice nightly, had even often occupied the same room; but during the two years they had not spoken to each other.

Old Mary would make no arrangement to cook my dinner. She had rented me Kate's house. Kate, unable to stand living in the country, had moved into Chicago. She had bought a movie house there and was doing all right. She was still in the show business and the show business was meat and drink to Kate. She had rented me Kate's house but wanted me to understand that she had not rented me herself.

And that evening she brought my dinner to me on a tray, a wonderful dinner, beautifully cooked. She brought it to the front door of my little house, set it on the step by the door, knocked and went away, and later, as long as I stayed in the house, she did the same nightly. She simply wanted me to understand that she was not to be my servant.

Yes, I could bring her presents from town. I could not buy food for her but I could buy her hats or dresses. I could buy her a dressing gown to keep her warm on cold mornings when she got out of bed, could buy her bedroom slippers or, in the winter, flowers to put in a vase in her bedroom. My gifts showed my admiration for her and we became devoted friends.

While I was there in my little house there was an occasional visit from Kate, who came in a big car with a chauffeur. Old Mary, she said, was an old stick-in-the-mud. She liked it, grubbing in the ground.

"But I don't," said Kate. Kate was even a little on the literary side. I had brought out books from the city and had arranged them on a shelf by my typewriter desk and she went to look at them. There was even a novel of my own, my first published one, *Windy McPherson's Son.*

"And did you really write it yourself." She seemed full of admiration for the feat. She was very sorry, she said, that, because of a busy life, she had never had time to do much reading.

"I suppose Mary has told you what we did for years, ever since we were young girls?"

Yes, Mary had told me.

"She would," Kate said and smiled. She was very handsome standing in the room in the little house and fingering my books. She borrowed *Windy McPherson's Son* and read it but was a little shocked because of the way I had treated my father.

"I guess it was your father?"

"Yes," I said.

She thought I was a shade too rough on him. She did not remember her own father.

"But I always terribly wanted a father," she said.

It was winter and I was walking in the forest. All summer and through the fall I had been coming to the little house, working there, and a curious thing had happened. I came to the house, I worked there, I ate Mary's dinners and in the evening, often, sat on the steps before my house talking with her and hearing always new tales of her adventures.

The town was full of dogs, belonging for the most part to old women, and Mary had one. It was a great shepherd dog and in the afternoon and often in the evening when I went for a walk in the forest, her dog accompanied me.

I left her house for my afternoon's stroll usually at three o'clock and when I opened the door to go out there the dog was lying by the steps at my front door and waiting for me. It made Old Mary a little jealous.

"He is growing fonder of you than of me," she said with a laugh of regret in her voice. She swore about it.

There was Mary's dog waiting for me by the door and presently there were other dogs. They kept increasing in numbers until the yard was full of them. I was the only one in the village in the habit of walking thus in the forests and they wanted to go along. When they were not there, when I took my stroll at odd hours, I whistled for Mary's dog and he came barking with joy and his voice brought the others.

It was a winter night and there was snow on the ground. It had snowed all afternoon but now the sky had cleared and the moon had come out. I set out followed by the troop of dogs.

Something that seemed to me very strange happened during my walk. The dogs, big and little, ran in a troop before me. They seemed excited by the night, the moonlight, and the white world in which we walked. They ran in circles, they snapped at each other, they rolled and tumbled in snow. It was on that night I got the impulse for one of my best stories, the title story of the volume *Death in the Woods.*

I came that night to an open place in the forest. Someone had evidently intended building a house there. Trees had been cut and the ground cleared of underbrush. No doubt the building project had been stopped because the state had taken over the forest.

A large tree at the edge of the open place had been cut and in the falling had lodged against another tree so that I could walk up the trunk. I did walk up the trunk and stretched myself on the log.

I was halfway to the top of neighboring trees. The one on which I lay had been a giant among them. In the afternoon the falling snow had been soft and had clung to the limbs of trees but now it had turned cold.

There was the moon floating in the sky. White clouds drifted across its face. I looked up through the bare branches of neighboring trees and little clumps of snow, freed from the leaves, kept falling.

The little clusters of snow crystals in falling thus softly touched my upturned face. It was as though soft cold fingers were caressing me. I lay very still, something of the mystery of the night, the white world and the frost having come into me. How long I lay there that night, I'll never know. I was warmly clad. It is possible that I slept and dreamed although I do not think so.

The dogs had become silent and then suddenly there was one of them, a large German police dog, with his legs on my chest. He was standing, his hind legs on my legs, his forelegs on my chest and his face close to my face. In the moonlight I could look directly into his eyes.

I thought there was a strange light in his eyes.

Was I frightened?

Well, I can't remember. The dog stayed there, his eyes staring thus into my eyes for two or three minutes and then he turned and ran down the log.

I turned to look and there the dogs were. They were running in a circle in the open place in the forest. There may have been twelve, fifteen, even twenty of them. Each dog ran with his head at the tail of the dog before him. They ran in silence. They had made a path in the snow in the forest. At least I did not dream that. I went on the next day and saw the circular path they had made in the snow.

They kept running thus silently in their circle, and I lay still on the log. There was this strange feeling of having been transported suddenly to a primitive world. It was a feeling I once, years later, had at a place called Grande Isle on the Gulf of Mexico south of New Orleans. Once I went fishing there at night in the moonlight. I had waded out into a channel that separated an inner bay from the gulf and stood, almost shoulder deep, in the sea.

I was alone that night and suddenly again I had the feeling of being in a primitive world. That night porpoises came and played about me. They were close and I could almost reach out my hand and touch them.

In the forest on the winter night dogs kept leaving the mysterious circle in which they ran and coming to me. Other dogs ran up the log to put their forelegs on my chest and stare into my face. It seemed to me, that night, that they were caught by something. They had become a wolf pack but there I was, man, who had made of the wolf a dog. It may be all nonsense. It seemed to me that night that the dogs, in breaking thus out of the running circle to come to me, one after another, wanted to be reassured—that there was such a thing as man, that they were the servants of man, that they were really dogs, not wolves in a primitive world. That night I stood the strange performance as long as I could and then I arose and ran down the log. I shouted. I picked up a stick and ran among the dogs, hitting out at them. The running circle was broken and, as I walked home along a woodland path, the dogs again played about me. They got up a rabbit and with a glad outcry gave chase. They were village dogs again.

I kept the little house beside Old Mary's house for several years and we became fast friends. I got several stories from her. On summer nights when I was alone she came often to sit with me. She was growing old and spoke often of death.

There was a summer night of stars.

"Look," she said, "do you know what all of those stars are?

"They are each a separate heaven," she declared. She said that in her opinion God was far from the damn fool a lot of people seemed to think he was.

"Just imagine," she said, "the goddamn fool people think everyone is going to the same heaven. What a lousy mess. As though God would do us dirt like that.

"No," she said, "he is not that kind of a damn fool. He has all these heavens. You go with your own kind of people, with your own gang, with people you like to be with.

"Just imagine," she said, "having to stay in a heaven forever with a lot of goddamn swine you meet while you are here on the earth."

I had been for a summer in Europe. It was a trip I had taken with Paul Rosenfeld and I will speak of that in another place. I had kept my little house at Palos Park and for the summer had given it to two friends, both young painters. They were like me, compelled to work at jobs. They used the little house during the week ends.

I had met in London an actress who had been the wife of the English poet and dramatist John Drinkwater. During the following winter she came to Chicago and I, on several occasions, dined with her.

She was in the company of the American actress Theda Bara. Theda had been the Greta Garbo of her day. She had been the American glamor girl of the movies, America's vamp, but she had quit the movies —or the movies had quit her—and had gone on the stage.

She was in a play called *The Blue Flame* and my friend, the English actress, was in her company.

I had been dining with my friend the English actress and had told her of my little house in Palos Park and of Old Mary.

"You should come to see me out there." I wanted her to meet Old Mary and I kept urging her until she said she would come. She would drive out bringing Theda with her, and an appointment was made. They were to come for the afternoon.

I told Mary and she was excited. She hurried off to town and bought herself a new dress. To her Theda was one of the great ones of the world.

She was afraid that, in Theda's presence, she might inadvertently begin to swear. That would be awful, she thought. For days she had been busy, cooking all sorts of delicacies. What was to have been but a modest tea party had become a feast. She kept trying on her new dress and running over to me.

"Is it all right? Do I look all right?"

Although it was winter she had been at work in the ground and her hands were rough.

"Do you think I should wear gloves?"

She kept swearing.

"Now you stop me if I do it when she is here. You wink at me if you hear me beginning, you remember to do that and I'll be watching your face."

The great day came and Old Mary told me she had been unable to sleep the night before.

"Think of it," she said, "Theda Bara coming to see us."

All morning she kept running in and out of my house, interrupting me in my work. She had washed and ironed my window curtains, had brought table napkins and linen of all sorts from her own house, had brought her silver.

And then Theda arrived and she snubbed poor Old Mary. It was a brutal snubbing and we all felt it. I kept explaining that Old Mary had also been an actress and my English woman friend, sensing the situation, sought to help but it came to nothing.

I could not understand it but later I thought that perhaps Theda thought we were playing a joke on her. Later my English friend said she thought that might have happened.

"The critics have recently been rather rough on her," she said.

We kept trying and trying to take Old Mary in on the conversation that afternoon but it was no go. With a kind of pleading hopeful light in her eyes, Old Mary kept addressing remarks to Theda. She tried to tell of some of her own experiences as an actress but she got no response. Theda did not even look at her. She did not answer her questions and presently Old Mary fled.

She had been deeply hurt. She had behaved herself and hadn't indulged in any profanity. She came to see me after Theda had left. We had all been through an awkward two hours and I was furious.

And then Old Mary came and sat with me and she cried. She cried for a time and then she swore. She let loose. She did some of the most illuminating swearing I had ever heard from her and then she cried again. My little party which I had arranged thinking of the joy it would give my Old Mary had turned out to be a sad failure indeed.

5. Certain Meetings South

I was on a train in lower Arkansas. It was a slow day train. At a certain little lumber town the engine broke down. I went to walk in the wood.

It was really a cypress swamp. A road had been made through it by putting logs down. I walked along the road a long ways—had indeed forgotten my train.

I came finally to a river, a slow yellow sluggish stream. Negroes were rafting logs in the stream. I stood in the wood watching them. They had not seen me.

What great strong brown fellows there were. On the bank of the stream there was a row of Negro cabins. Evening was coming on. They had still not seen me. I sat on a log behind a tree to look and listen.

The Negroes, on the log rafts on the yellow river, began to sing.

A woman came out of one of the houses on the river bank and began singing. It went on for some time like that, song full of strangeness, sadness, race feeling.

Then, from somewhere in the wood came another voice. It was a woman's voice, very tender, high, with tremendous carrying power.

Well, alas, I am a poet. It is the nature of the poet to have something primitive in him. The poet is in some odd way akin to the savage. It cannot be denied. When he is a true poet he is tender, cruel, isolated from others, intensely a part of others in a way the generality of men will never understand.

And so there was I sitting in a cypress swamp in Arkansas listening to this Negro singing, the most real, the most tender, the most significant singing I have ever heard.

As I sat thus the Negro woman with the high tender voice came in a small skiff out of a bayou into the yellow river. She had been rowing but dropped her paddles and let the skiff float toward us.

How shall I describe this scene? There had been a constantly changing light on the river and the cypress forest. Gray patches of clouds floated across the face of the late afternoon sun and then passed and the sun shone again.

I sat watching, drunk with all this as I have seldom been drunk. Long, long I had felt something of the soil in the Negro I had wanted in myself too.

I mean a sense of earth and skies and trees and rivers, not as a thing thought about but as a thing in me. I wanted earth in me and skies and fields and rivers and people. I wanted these things to come out of me, as song, as singing prose, as poetry even.

What else have I ever cared for as I have cared to have this happen, what woman, what possessions, what promise of life after death, all that? I have wanted this unity of things, this song, this earth, this sky, this human brotherhood.

I have felt it often in Negroes as I felt it that afternoon in Arkansas. Of course my train, with my bags on a seat, went away and left me sitting there. The Negroes sang for a time and then stopped singing. All the educated Negro singing and white man's singing I have ever heard in America was as nothing to what I heard that day.

There was the woman in the boat. She was a young yellow Negress, with white blood in her. The woman on the bank was old and black, the men rafting the logs were black.

The song came first out of the red throats of the blacks and then out of her young throat. She was leaning a little forward in the skiff. The yellow of her skin was as the yellow of the river. I dare say I loved her at that moment as I have never loved any other woman.

Because of the sky in her voice, the yellow river, the cypress trees, with their strange knees protruding from the black swamp muck.

Because of something long submerged in her and the others set free in song.

Have I not myself been submerged, by need of money, possessions, women, what not?

A race for a moment singing thus out of one throat. Is it not what I also have wanted?

For that would I not give, freely and gladly, all hope of such things as a future life, duty to society, to wife, to family, to all the white man's shibboleths?

I was in Mobile absorbed in the mixed life of the South. The position of the Negroes in Southern life continued to fascinate me.

The docks were, at the time, extremely busy. Ships were being built in a nearby shipyard and on the docks and about the shipping both Negroes and whites were at work. The work was portioned off, a certain part of the work for the Negroes, another part for the whites. The one job seemed about as hard as the other.

There was a thing I felt, that the Negroes, when grouped together, no whites about, were one thing, but when a white man appeared a change took place. I wanted to prove this to myself and so, on several mornings, I went very early and concealed myself in some piles of lumber near where I knew a group of Negroes would be at work.

I felt that the thing I had anticipated did take place. When the Negroes were away from the whites at their work there was a tone of sadness. The songs they sang were in a low key. They spoke to each other quietly and it was only when laughter broke forth that there was a change. To me the laughter was a bit too hearty. It shook their bodies. It was as though they were shaking a load off their backs.

And then a white man came among them and they became, I thought, self-conscious. They seemed to be performing for the white man, being for his benefit what they thought of him as wanting them to be. The slave outlook had not gone out of these Negroes of the Southern city. In the presence of the white men the Negroes spoke of other Negroes in the group as "Niggers." They didn't do that when there were no whites present. Then each Negro was Mr. Jones, or Mr. Smith, or Mr. Gray. In the presence of the white man there was no Mistering.

"Hey, you Nigger. The boss done speak to you. Didn't you hear him, Nigger?"

A kind of human dignity gone, self-respect gone.

At that time there still were river steamers running up-river from Mobile to Selma in Alabama and I often went for the round trip. The men who loaded the river boat, the *Peerless,* on which I took the trip, employed a crowd of deck hands. They loaded and unloaded cargo on the way up and down the river but did not load or unload at Mobile. For that job another group of Negroes was hired.

So there I was on such a river boat as Mark Twain might have been on, first as a cub and then as a full-fledged pilot. I kept traveling up and down. The fare for the trip was very low. I had brought with me on each trip a basket of fruit to lighten the somewhat heavy and greasy diet.

I was walking up and down the deck of the boat. I was in the pilot house talking to the pilot. One of the pilots was a young, rather handsome, mustached fellow and a great braggart, always telling of feats of piloting he had done, vessels saved from disaster, etc., a great liar, I thought, and the other a quiet and rather small gray-haired man of fifty.

And there were the Negro deck hands. They had a reputation of being a tough lot. They sang constantly. They had no beds or bunks, but slept about on bags of fertilizer on the lower deck. When feeding time came the food was dished out to them in tin pans. They had no knives or forks. They ate with their fingers, and they were called to duty at any time of the day or night.

It was a moonlight spring night in that Southern climate and I was sitting in the darkness on an upper deck of the boat. There was flood water in the river and great logs were floating down and now and then one of them struck the boat making a heavy booming sound and seeming to shake the boat.

And then, down below in the engine room, the bells began to ring. We were to make a landing and presently there we were, the gangplank out on a high muddy bank at the edge of a deep wood.

There was a dirt road going away into the darkness of the wood and on the river bank stood a solitary white man with a lantern in his hand.

He was a small, pale, rather yellow-skinned man in shabby clothes. The floodlight from the boat was turned on him. He shouted something to the mate, a tall gaunt fellow, and the mate began to swear. He kept swearing, a string of profanity flowing from his lips.

And now the Negro deck hands were at work. They ran up and down the gangplank at a strangely rhythmic lope. It was a curiously sprawling lope, with the muscles of the body relaxed.

They were running thus, up and down the gangplank and away along the dirt road into the forest. There was perhaps some trick of the light. Their bodies, as they loped up and down, carrying cargo aboard the ship, seemed strangely huge. They were carrying roughly hewn staves, for the making of wine barrels, from the forest to the boat. They sang as they pranced thus up and down. Their bodies as well as their voices seemed to be carrying the song. The song was a dance in their bodies.

And there was that tall, sallow-faced mate standing on the deck below me. He swore. He cursed the workers. He was striving to hurry them but his swearing and shouting seemed to have no effect. The rhythm of the movement of the workers did not change, and suddenly it seemed to me that the white mate down there was like a man standing and swearing at the stars on the spring moonlight night because at his command they did not move faster across the Southern sky.

I was on the lower deck of the boat (this must have been on another trip, perhaps in another year) and there had been low water and that day as I stood on the deck looking down at the slow-moving water of the river a Negro deck hand came and also looked.

He turned to another deck hand. "I see des worken de road," he said, and another Negro came to look. Several came.

"Dey sure is worken de road," they said.

I was puzzled. What had they meant? I went to the captain. I described the scene to him, repeated the remark of the Negroes.

"What did they mean by saying someone had been working the road?"

He said he didn't know.

"Very well, I'll ask one of them."

"But you must not do that. I don't want these Niggers to think that sometimes I do not know what they are talking about."

The captain was a fat, rather jolly man and we had become friends.

"But look here. I am curious. I want to know what these men meant when, after looking at the river, they began talking of someone working some road. If you do not find out I'll go and ask one of them."

Again the captain begged me not to do it.

"I'll work it out. You give me a little time," he said. He explained to me that the Negroes sometimes did seem to have almost a language of their own. I am not able to quote his exact words but what he said was that the Negroes of the South had developed among themselves a kind of figurative language. He thought it might have come down from slavery days. The Negroes, working as they did in gangs under a white driver, often wanted to say things to each other they didn't want the slave driver to understand.

"They make up these figures of speech.

"And now I've got it about this road work," he said.

He explained that most of the Negro deck hands were country-bred Negroes. They were adventurous fellows, often what he called "bad

Niggers." They wanted to get out and see the world so they became "river Niggers."

And up in that back country, where they were bred, the roads all during the winter are horrible and, in the spring, often the planters up there cannot get their crops out until the roads are worked for them.

He explained that, during the last trip up-river, the water had at certain places been so low that the boat had got stuck on sand bars. It had made a lot of hard work for the deck hands. They had to run ropes ashore, help haul the boat over sand bars.

"You see," he said, "there has been rain up-river. The river is rising a little. That's what they were telling each other."

We were at the dock in Mobile. It was a hot day in May and we had come down-river with a heavy cargo of fertilizer in bags. When the Negro deck hands had loaded the boat at Selma there had been much low-voiced cursing and groaning, for the acids in the fertilizer, mixed with the sweat of bodies, had made festering sores on the shoulders of the men.

However, at the dock at Mobile the deck hands did not have to unload the boat. They had hired out for the trip only and their work was done. It was the custom aboard that boat to pay off at the last stop up-river above Mobile, keeping back one dollar of each man's pay.

That the captain had explained to me was what he called "tie-up money." It was held back so that the Negro deck hands would not, the moment the boat touched the dock, jump ashore without waiting to tie up the boat.

So the deck hands had been paid off. Their work was done and they had been warned by the captain and the mates to say nothing about the nature of the cargo to the Negroes who would unload the boat.

The Negro deck hands had been marched silently off the boat, watched by the captain and mate, and had disappeared up a street into the city and the cargo of fertilizer had been concealed under tarpaulins. We were ready to hire Negro stevedores to begin the unloading.

They were gathered together in a group on the dock. They had seen the deck hands march silently away. They were suspicious.

And there was the mate, shouting at them, swearing at them.

"You goddamn Niggers, are you going to come aboard and sign

up or aren't you?" He kept swearing at them, pleading with them, but no man moved.

They must have stood thus, in silence, for half an hour and then one Negro man did come aboard.

He went up into the captain's quarters and came down. No doubt he had been told by the captain to go down and get the other men to come aboard. When he had gone down a stairway and along the lower deck of the boat, heavily loaded with its concealed cargo, he had perhaps lifted a corner of one of the tarpaulins. It was a scorching hot day and he would have known what the unloading of the boat, the carrying of the heavy bags of fertilizer on shoulders in that heat, would mean in festering sores. He went ashore and stood before the silent group of Negroes. He looked up at the boat. The name *Peerless* was printed in big letters along its side.

He sighed. He shook his head. He spoke in a long voice.

"Peerless, Peerless, why, that ain't the *Peerless*. It's the *Titanic,"* he said and immediately all the Negro stevedores walked away, leaving him standing alone while the long gaunt mate poured a whole river of profanity down on his head.

I was in a rich man's house. I was a guest there and they were being very nice to me.

It was a great country house in the South and there were many Negro servants.

Everything was beautifully arranged, very formal. The people of the house did not meet at breakfast. There were several other guests and everyone breakfasted in his room.

They met later in the day. They walked, they rode horses, played games, drank together.

In the evening, often, there was music. The master of the house arranged to have some of the Negroes come in the evening to sing.

They did not come into the house. There was a wide veranda on which the whites sat while the Negro men and women stood at some distance, half hidden among trees.

The man who had bought the Southern house with some thousands of acres of land was from a distant city. He had made a fortune in the city and was spending it on the land. He was a collector of first editions of books. He bought paintings. After he had made his fortune he, with his wife, had traveled abroad, in many lands.

Their Southern house was filled with art objects from many lands. There were so many art objects that they had become meaningless. They meant nothing.

The Negro people were under trees, in the darkness. They sang Negro spirituals. They sang Negro work songs.

The singing was very beautiful. The voices seemed to run away into the dark distance, under the trees, across distant fields. The voices ran away and came back. Their voices were along the ground, in the grass. They were in the treetops.

Voices called to each other. There was one high clear Negro woman's voice that seemed to go up to the stars in the blue black Southern sky.

It did something to me. It seemed to me that, for the first time, I saw something clearly. I sat among the other guests in the rich man's house thinking what were to me new thoughts. My thoughts concerned the land on which stood the great house in which I was a guest.

The house was in the so-called Sugar Bowl in the lower delta country of the Mississippi.

There were many flat acres of sugar cane fields stretched away from the river and the door. In the distance there were forests—in a low swampy land—forests of cypress and gum trees.

It was a dark land, a strange rich land. The Negroes had been there a long time. The Negroes singing that night, standing in the darkness in a grove of live oaks hung with ghostly moss, had been born on the land.

From childhood they had worked in the fields. Their ancestors had been slaves on the land. It was under their finger nails, in the creases of their flesh, in their crinkly hair, in their eyebrows.

As I sat that night listening to the singing Negroes something came clear to me. It concerned ownership.

How could a man really own land, own trees, own grass, own flowing water of rivers? The land had been there so long.

There was a rich man who had money and what a strange thing money. The man had been shrewd. He had, no doubt, a certain talent, the talent of acquisitiveness. There had been in him an instinct that had enabled him to see certain opportunities. At a certain critical moment he had bought certain stocks.

Then, at just the right moment, he had sold them and bought other stocks.

Stocks were like money itself. They were pieces of paper with words printed upon them.

In the case of money, the picture of some man, a president.

Oh, the power of words.

"I promise to pay," etc., etc.

You could burn the pieces of paper and they were gone.

The land remained. The trees, the grass, the flowing brown water of the river remained.

Burn the trees and they would grow again.

The land was there before man came. It would be there when there were no men left.

But there were certain people, the poor whites of the South, the Negroes, slaves and free, farmers of my own native Middle West who worked their own fields, who were related to the land.

There had been a marriage, man and the land.

The land was in them as a lover is in his sweetheart in the embrace of love.

So, as far as there is ownership, it is their land as a man's wife is his wife.

The thought set down here, coming to me as it did in a certain house in the South on a certain night, was no doubt not a new thought in the world but such thoughts mean nothing to a man when set down in books, when expounded by some speaker, some political revolutionist. The thought was in the throat of the Negro singers, it was in the trees under which they stood in the Southern night. It explained so much of the South—the landed aristocrats, the predatory whites, the secret hatreds, the insistence upon white supremacy, the secret jealousy of something the Negroes had, something that had come into them from the land as it sifted through their black fingers. I was suddenly quite sure that the man sitting beside me that night, my host, the rich man, deep down within himself would have given all his wealth to have been, not as he was, the overlord, but one of the brown men, a man closer to the land, living simply as an animal lives.

He had gone about seeking something he did not have. What did all of his buying of pictures, his collecting of objects of art, of first editions mean?

It meant obviously an attempt to buy his way out of one world into another, to, at any rate, get a little closer.

He had even said something of the sort to me.

A few months earlier he had come to me. He had wanted very much to buy the manuscript of my *Winesburg*.

"Did it exist?"

"Yes. It existed."

The book had been written on pages of a cheap tablet. The manuscript existed only because a certain woman, at the moment in love with me, had collected the scrawled sheets, thrown carelessly aside and had saved them.

So the manuscript had been saved, and later, when it began to have some value, I had managed—because the woman who had saved it had died—by lying to her sister, by telling the sister that the dead woman had only been keeping it for me, by such slickness I had got it back.

So there it was in my possession, and did I value it?

I did not.

I had been told that, some day, it would bring money.

Well, I wanted money. I was no fool. Well enough I knew that without money the artist man is helpless.

So there had been this rich man who had come to me wanting to buy this manuscript, and I had been shrewd.

Was I shrewd or had a moment of honesty come to me?

I had not yet sold the rich man the manuscript.

I had laughed at the man.

"But why do you want them, these sheets of cheap paper upon which certain tales have been scrawled?"

I had told the rich man that his wanting the sheets upon which certain stories had been scribbled was like wanting an old dress discarded by a woman rather than the woman herself.

However the rich man had been patient with me. He had invited me to be his guest. This was in the winter and I was hungry for the South and the sun. I had been given a separate house, at the foot of a path lined with bushes. It was by a little quiet bayou.

I slept there and, as it was winter, there were no mosquitoes.

In the early morning an old Negro woman, very black, a huge old woman with big hips, came to me. The door and the windows of my little one-room house were open and there was a sharp tinge of frost in the air.

The old woman had brought me a pot of hot black coffee. She built a wood fire in the fireplace.

I was in bed, drinking my coffee. I began a conversation with the old woman. She had lived as a child in the West Indies. A kind of friendship sprang up between her and me. I lied to her, told her I had Negro blood in my veins. It was a trick I had got from my father.

If you are with a Catholic, become, for the time a Catholic, if with a Swede, a Swede, if with an Irishman, Irish. There was, I told the old black woman, a grandfather who having much white blood had gone North and had gone white. The old woman was not to tell my secret.

"You see I am here, a guest. You come here and wait on me. I can go up to the big house, can dine there. By law, by all the social customs of the South, I am really like you, a Negro."

There was something established between me and the Negro servants about the rich white man's house. The servants were always coming secretly to my little house. I was presumed to be at work there, creating masterpieces. The rich man and his other guests were impressed. I must not be disturbed.

I was getting many stories out of the lives of the Negroes on the place. It pleased them that I was, as they thought, cheating the whites. I was gathering up all the servants' tales.

There was one young Negro woman, very straight and strong of body, who came often secretly to my cabin. She had stolen a bottle of champagne which she brought to me. Sometimes she came late at night when I was in bed. She had brought some delicacy from the kitchen.

She came in and sat on the edge of my bed. She had heard the white guests speaking of me and my work.

She was impressed.

"So you are really one of us. They look up to you. You should be telling the story of our lives."

There was one of the guests, a young white man who had married a rich woman much older than himself. He was after the young Negro woman.

He was giving her money.

He had given her a ten dollar bill. Once when she went into his bedroom he came in there.

She had gone in the late morning to make up the bed, to arrange the room, and he had been watching for her coming.

He was somewhere about the house or he was sitting with the other guests on a terrace before the house and when she went upstairs, to arrange the rooms, she made a point of letting him see her.

She said he always sat in the late morning where he could see her going up the stairway. He was a great horseman. He had on riding breeches. There was always something he had left in his room, so he followed her up.

She said, "I let him kiss me. I let him hold me in his arms. I keep promising him I will meet him outdoors at night.

"I am not married but I tell him I am. I tell him my husband is watching me.

"I pretend I am crazy about him. When he is holding me in his arms I cry a little and when I do he always gives me money.

"He has given me several presents. He thinks he is going to get me but I am only fooling with him."

The young Negro woman was sitting on the edge of my bed. She laughed, the laugh of a Negro woman. I was smoking cigarettes and she asked for one. She sat smoking with me. She told me little human stories of the rich man, his wife, the other white guests. One night she came at two in the morning. It was her woman's time. She had become the daughter of the moon. She explained that it was always a terrible time for her.

She was in great pain. She said that the great pain lasted but a few hours, but that, at such times, she could not bear to be alone.

"I want someone to be with me and hold my hand and I do not want a woman. I want a man."

I put her into my bed and, having put on my bathrobe, sat beside her holding her hand.

She kept groaning. Tears ran down her cheeks. It was a cold clear moonlit night and the moonlight came in through the open door. I could feel with her the spasms of pain. When they came her hand gripped my hand so that the fingers ached. It was like a childbirth. When it had passed she got up and I returned to my bed. She had gone out of my little house but presently returned. She had been with me nearly three hours and soon day would come. I felt curiously close to her.

She came running into the cabin and kissed me on the cheek. I was smoking a cigarette.

"I guess it is better for you to stay white. If you took one of us in, for example, it would spoil it all.

"It is better for you to stay white. You get all the best of it by being white."

For a moment she stood thus beside my bed, in the moonlight. She was of a light brown color and the moonlight, coming through the door, made highlights on her brown skin. She stood thus, in silence, for a time, looking down at me. To her it was inconceivable that a white man, a real white, could tell a lie, claiming Negro blood. She believed my lie. She wanted me to go on fooling the whites. She went slowly out of my cabin and while I remained a guest in that place she did not return to me.

6. New York, the '20's

An ecstasy—being well-fed—having been to a Night Club.

O Mecca, O dream of youth, O Athens, Ohio, O Rome, O Springfield, Illinois.

Pitter-patter. Feet on pavements. Hundreds of miles of pavements. Subways. Busses on Fifth Avenue.

Lovers on benches in Central Park. Policemen standing on street corners. Where do they get all the big New York policemen? Sure we're a great race to produce such men. Smart girls on Fifth Avenue. Furs. Legs. Little shop girls too.

Bill said in one day he did more think-loving than ever before in his life. He was all tired out by night.

It gets hot in New York City. It gets mighty cold there.

You have to have a lot of dough to get by. Bill says, Why get by?

Jake says you can have more fun in New York with ten dollars than anywhere else. He says he bets that Paris can't get you more for your dough.

Bill says it's a lie. He says no dough—nothing doing.

Jake says Bill lies.

If you're broke landing in New York, say from Illinois now, it looks so big.

You get used to it, Jake says. Jake has been here ten years. He walks right along as though he were on some main street. He doesn't look at anything.

Bill and I looked and looked. You get an eyeful all right. Such a lot to look at.

Buildings. Men. Women. How could they get so much done in so few years? It's only three hundred years at most, Bill says. What's that?

Ah that's nothing, Jake says. You go away ten years. Then come back. You'll see what's what.

Jake told Bill and me that the life of the big skyscraper in New York was—on what he called the average—about nine years.

Great God! Speed, eh?

When Jake told us that, Bill and me went back to our hotel. We said it was enough for one day.

Of course we saw it all wrong. Most Americans—from the Middle West—save and save before they ever go to New York. We didn't. We just dumped right in on the town.

We were in a little dingy hotel far down below where the swells live. There was an elevated railroad somewhere near. Bill and I had a smoke or two and then we went to bed. There were two beds in the room.

Pitter-patter, feet on pavements. A man kept shouting somewhere out in the street. The steady roar of teams and trucks on stone pavements. The elevated trains going by. You know how trucks back-fire sometimes. Like a skyscraper coming down. Like a skyscraper going up, eh?

Bill was a tall man with red hair. He snored when he slept. Sometimes he back-fired too. I had picked him up in Syracuse, beating my way east to New York.

It was he who knew Jake. Jake had black hair and a big mustache. Bill said he was a Pole.

There in that hotel, amid the roaring noises, sleep coming to me—dreams—that first time coming to New York.

O Mecca. O dream of youth. O Rome.

City majestic—whirling dreams. The roar of elevated trains, trucks going by, teamsters shouting, became in dreams skyscrapers getting themselves torn down, skyscrapers getting themselves reared up.

Faster and faster. Faster and faster. Speed. Speed. The life of buildings in New York became not nine years but nine days, nine hours, nine minutes, nine seconds.

They tell me a whole long dream takes place in the fraction of a second. Scientists say that. How scientists know some things they do know I don't know.

Anyway that roaring dream-night gone now. Bill and Jake gone somewhere. I never saw them again after those few days in New York.

Wind-swept prairie towns, all the Middle West, the South, the Far West, the North sending its men up to New York. I dare say there are some men who were born in New York.

The life of a nation always breathes through some great city. It is the center, the heart of things.

O Chicago—why did you not grasp that thing first?

Chicago too far away yet. From what?

From Europe of course.

Chicago's turn may come yet. A few hundred years more. What's the hurry?

Fling wide your arms, O Chicago. Stretch yourself. You've got plenty of room. Prepare yourself for your own day. It will come. Fling wide over prairies the ultimate American city. Make and re-make a hundred times. That may be your job.

New York holds the cards now. Long years of New York's supremacy yet.

Until Europe as a force in American life disappears perhaps. Until great European cities become outlying places.

The center of all western things drifting west and west.

Money. Beauty. Power. The new imperialism.

The imperialistic mood has come to New York. I felt it that first time when I went there with Bill and saw Jake. Jake was imperial with Bill and me. The second time it had got into buildings, into streets, into the way people walked in the streets.

I came alone that second time, wandering in the streets at night, saw more and more clearly the vast grim imperial beauty of our great American city.

Sometimes I thought it wonderful that men could walk there thinking of their own little affairs, being in love, eating, sleeping. They seemed like tiny crawling meaningless things going along under the great towering walls. I used to walk along behind groups of men and women, pretending to look in shop windows, listening to hear what they were talking about. It seemed to me then the most lovely testimonial to men's courage that they could live in such a city at all.

And meanwhile the walls going higher and higher, buildings flinging themselves up into the sky, buildings of stone and iron.

American working men—far up there in the sky—flinging the buildings up higher and higher.

✦

You see all that, think all that, get yourself all filled up with pride, being American, and then go away to dream a while by the shore, say of some Southern river. You see blacks on boats. You see men plowing fields. In little openings in the forest you see men cutting down trees, floating them away on rivers.

You write perhaps a novel, a poem, a tale. What does it matter? "This novel-garbage" old Thomas Carlyle called it. Such books as my kind write.

Then you come back. All the new buildings gone. Other buildings gone up, higher and higher. Forms of buildings changing as dreams change.

Any possibility there—in New York—in Chicago—in America?

Beautiful cities. To me an American provincial, wandering occasionally to New York, always a mere guest there, New York is already beautiful. When I see it most clearly, I see it always after an absence—as guest—as wide-eyed countryman looking at it. Sometimes men who build cities like New York, so swift, so imperial, seem to me as gods.

What nights I have walked alone in your streets, O greatest American City—always frightened a little—seeing how streets have changed—how men have changed—how cities make the men who live in them—I mutter to myself words: "New York is imperialistic, brutal. It shall make a brutal imperialistic race." Myself cowering sometimes against stone walls at night, expecting great walls to fall down on me, expecting great buildings to embrace me, squeezing my life out between them, half expecting great buildings to swing off their moorings into the air and float.

A new art this, eh, I say to myself. A new art this of building cities, of building great American cities. I, being from outside, want its story from inside. I become annoyed with American writers. The writers of New York, I say to myself, are like me. They are outsiders. They have only come here as guests. When, I cry, will New York have its Balzac, its Victor Hugo?

It wants such men too. But wait. Their time has not come.

As yet the great American art, to be developed, glorified, that of city building. I have a kind of faith in them—the builders.

The movies, I tell myself, may be the key to the matter. A new art being born.

Something done instantaneously—like a flash of life. Brushed away like clouds of smoke. In the far future sometime each man making his own city to dwell in—as men now lay paint on canvas—write words on bits of paper.

All this a dream, coming to me every time I go to New York. New dreams, the children of that first dream.

The city itself, our greatest American city, what it is. To me, an American, something strong, imperial, often brutal, ever changing, beautiful.

Pitter-patter, feet on pavement. So many men. Where are they going? What are they doing?

Men, American men in so short a time, in these last twenty years, have made their greatest American city. It is a European city no longer. It is American. It is itself.

Imperial New York. Plenty of time yet. Men and machines. We are all so young yet.

Wait and see. Wait and see what New York will do.

Wait and see what Chicago will do.

7. Dreiser's Party

I was staying in New York City. Already I had got some literary recognition but little or no money had come in.

I had been offered the use of an apartment in St. Luke's Place in New York. It was a quiet little street, a row of three-story brick houses facing a school and playground. Whether or not I paid anything for the apartment I can't remember. It was a cellar apartment. You went down a flight of steps. It was very comfortable. This was in the summer and the place belonged to two young professors at Columbia. They had both gone away for their vacations. If I paid for the apartment I paid little enough.

It was a quiet time for me, a little money ahead. I was at work on a novel. How many novels begun by me and never finished! My friend, Paul Rosenfeld, lived then on Irving Place in the city and I went often to see him.

This must have been about the time of the new *Dial* so I must have been seeing Gilbert Seldes, Waldo Frank, Van Wyck Brooks, with whom I had always a secret quarrel that never came out into the open. My brother Karl, the painter, lived nearby in Connecticut. Otherwise I was pretty much without friends or acquaintances in the city.

Still there were occasional meetings with other writers and with painters, sitting with them at tables in little restaurants, long hours of talk, perhaps later with some one of them a long walk through the quiet after-midnight city streets.

Someone had told me that Theodore Dreiser was also living in an apartment in St. Luke's Place. The building was pointed out to me.

I had been an admirer of Dreiser's for a long time.

His books filled me with admiration for his courage. Here was a man doing something that I also wanted to do. He was actually writing about the life about him frankly and boldly as he had seen and felt it.

I think it may well be that it was the reading of Dreiser, his *Sister Carrie* and his *Jenny Gerhardt,* that started me on a new track.

The books jolted me. "Look homeward, angel," they shouted at me. They did, I felt, turn me away from books, from other writers, to the life about me, as I had myself seen and felt it.

I was profoundly grateful to Dreiser. I dedicated a book to him. I wrote to him a prose poem, using it as the foreword to a book of stories I called *Horses and Men.*

I had never seen Dreiser and did not know until years later when we became friends that it was his word, given to the publisher John Lane, that had got my first two books published.

I decided I would go and call upon him. His apartment, unlike my own, was above the street level. You went up a flight of stairs to the front door.

I went up the stairs and there was his name on a little white card and there was a bell to punch.

My fingers trembled above the bell but I did not ring it. I turned and hurried away.

"But how do I know he will want to see me?" I asked myself. To me he was and has always remained a great man, one of the few really great ones of America.

"He may be at work on a book," I said to myself. On several occasions I climbed the several steps to his door, my finger hovered over his bell but I did not ring it.

And then, one morning I did. I rang the bell and waited. I dare say I trembled a little.

"Well, you sure have a nerve. You've got a nerve bothering the man," I said to myself.

And then the door opened and there he was.

Once before I had seen him. He was walking in a street in Chicago, and I was walking with Ben Hecht. He had a woman with him. He was dressed, I remember, on that occasion, very gaudily.

There was a mauve overcoat, a mauve tie, a mauve shirt. He was all pastel colors. We, in Chicago, had all been making him our hero. This must have been after his *Sister Carrie* had been got out of hock to a puritan publisher and after Arnold Bennett had come to America to proclaim him.

I was walking that time with Ben Hecht and he pointed.

"Look. Theodore Dreiser."

There was awe in Ben's voice, a sure sign that he was tremendously impressed. It took a lot to impress Ben.

So there I was on Dreiser's doorstep facing him. I am quite sure my voice trembled.

"I am Sherwood Anderson. I thought I would come to see you."

"Oh, hello," he said. He shut the door in my face.

So there I was on Dreiser's doorstep, facing the blank door. I was shocked. Then I was furious.

"The beast," I said. I went to walk. I swore. I cursed him. In that prose poem I had written to him I had spoken of him as an old man.

But I had been careful to say that I did not mean old in years.

"He is old in spirit and does not know what to do with life, so he tells about it as he sees it, simply and honestly."

I had only been speaking of his great tenderness that had so attracted me to his books.

"The old bastard. I'll bet he's after a new girl, some young thing no doubt. He's sore because I said he was old. He's a fool. He hasn't sense enough to comprehend what I was really saying of him."

I went along a street, muttering thus against Dreiser. I went into a saloon and had drinks. I got half drunk.

And then, later in the day, I went home to my apartment and there was a note from him. The man had simply been embarrassed, as I was, when we stood facing each other. He knew that I was newly come to the city and he thought there were many interesting men in the city I should meet.

So he had arranged a party for me. It was all very characteristic of Dreiser, the awkwardness—that is also in his prose—the thoughtfulness for others, the kindness always covered by a gruff manner.

The note from him made my heart jump with gladness. There it was. He was as I had thought he would be.

I was at the party in the evening in Dreiser's apartment and there were a dozen other men present. They were all men of some note in the city. They were men of whom I had heard. I was excited and a good deal scared.

We were in a large room with pictures on the wall and at an end of the room there was a large flat top desk at which no doubt Dreiser sat every day at work on his stories. Along the walls of the room were bottles of hard liquors of various kinds and there was also beer and wine.

We sat in little groups talking. An hour, perhaps two hours, passed and at last Henry Mencken, one of the party, said what we were all thinking.

"Dreiser," he said, "I see you have got this liquor here. You have beer and wine.

"What's the idea?" he asked. "Are you keeping it? Do you plan to drink it all yourself or what the hell?"

Dreiser laughed.

"Go to hell, Mencken," he said. "If you fellows haven't sense enough to help yourselves you can go without."

There was a thing happened at Dreiser's party that I have never forgotten. Scott Fitzgerald was in New York at that time. His glowingly alive books had just begun to appear. I have no doubt that Scott, at least at that time, felt toward Dreiser as we in Chicago had been feeling. He must have felt as I had felt and as I had written in the foreword of the book dedicated to him that Dreiser, the heavy-footed, had tramped through the real wilderness of Puritan lies making a pathway for all of us.

Fitzgerald had in some way heard of the party being given at Dreiser's, and had wanted to come. He had wanted to pay his respects to the man.

So he had bought some bottles of champagne. He came to Dreiser's door as I had come. He rang the bell as I had done.

And then it happened to him as it had happened to me. He was there, standing at the door and holding the bottles of champagne, and there was Dreiser standing and facing him.

Dreiser would have stared. He would have said nothing.

"I am Scott Fitzgerald. I have brought you this champagne."

It is true that, on that night, sitting in the room with the others, I did not hear what was said at the door.

"I am Scott Fitzgerald. I have brought you this champagne."

Dreiser would have reached out and taken the bottles. He could not have failed to know of the man who stood there before him. At the moment the whole literary world was filled with the name of Fitzgerald.

"Here is this champagne."

"Hello.

"Thanks."

Dreiser had closed the door in Fitzgerald's face as he had in mine.

He came back into the room holding the bottles. Already he would have realized what he had done. He would have known how eager we all were to meet Fitzgerald.

He had simply been unable at the moment to do what he had wanted to do, invite the man in.

"Hello.

"Thanks."

He had shut the door in the man's face.

"What the hell, Dreiser?" someone said. We were all as he was, deeply embarrassed.

He sat in a chair and had put the bottles of champagne on the floor.

"Oh, you go to hell," was all, at the moment, he was able to say to the one of us who, by the tone of his voice, had rebuked him for not having Fitzgerald in to be one of the party.

I have no way of knowing whether or not Fitzgerald ever knew what happened that night when he came to pay his tribute.

Years after, I was at the house of a friend in Pennsylvania. A play I had written and for which I had at the time a good deal of hope, had been produced the night before. It had been produced at the Hedgerow Theatre, directed by Jasper Deeter.

A good many of my friends had come to see the play and, after the performance, many of us went to the house of my friend who lived but a few miles away from the theater. It was a Sunday morning in the summer. There must have been at least twenty people who had slept the night in my friend's house. Others drove there in the morning. With me, when I arrived, was a certain Southern woman of sixty, a very old and very dear friend, one of the extraordinarily keen, alive, witty and gentle women often found in the South.

We were at my friend's house, on the lawn, some fifteen or twenty of us, drinking our morning coffee out there when Dreiser appeared. He was quite naked. He had spent the night in the house, had wanted a bath when he awakened and perhaps all the bathrooms in the house were occupied. He had got a young son of our host, a mere boy, to come out on the lawn and turn the hose on him.

He stood there before us all. He quite unconsciously took his morning bath and returned to the house. There were murmurs of indignation.

"For me it doesn't matter but there is Mrs. Blank."

The Mrs. Blank would be my Southern woman of the gray hair, of the intelligent eyes. I sat beside her.

The whispers must have come to her ears for she turned to me and smiled.

"They expect me to be shocked," she said, "and indeed, had Mr. Dreiser come out thus, to take his morning bath before us all thinking to shock us, I would have been shocked.

"He didn't," she declared.

She explained, "While he was taking his bath I did not look at his body, I looked at his face. I was curious, I am too old to be concerned about men's bodies. I only wanted to be sure that he was quite unconscious that he was doing anything startling and he was.

"He is a very innocent man," she said.

He is a gruff man, fundamentally very tender. He is heavy-handed, heavy-footed. He is the most honest man I have ever known, is honest with the honesty of a fine animal. Often when I have been with him, I have in my own mind compared him with one of the race horses in a stable of race horses for which I once worked as groom.

There was a particular young stallion named Doctor Fritz, for a time in my charge, and sometimes when I entered his stall and he was feeling fit he let fly with his heels but, before doing so, always turned his head to be sure he missed me. He just felt like kicking up his heels. That was all.

There are innumerable touching stories going about concerning Dreiser. His friends call him Teddy. The poet Arthur Ficke told me one.

He said, "Teddy came to my house. There was something on his mind. He wanted me to take a walk with him.

"I was living in the country and it was winter so we walked in frozen fields. He wouldn't talk so I talked. I went chattering along. I don't know what was on my mind but all of a sudden I made a remark at which Dreiser stopped, and stood staring at me.

"We were in a frozen meadow, in a wide flat place.

"'A man must learn to forgive himself for what he does to others,' I said. 'He does something, hurts someone. If he could not forgive himself, he would go insane.'"

Ficke had made the remark. He said that Dreiser stopped walking and stood staring at him. He went a little pale. He walked away from Ficke. Tears were in his eyes.

" 'It is wonderful,' he said. 'It is what I had forgotten. It is what has been troubling me. A man is a man. He is like other men. He does someone else a wrong. He must learn to forgive himself. He must. He must.' "

It was the sort of remark that Theodore Dreiser would treasure forever, some chance remark, made by a friend, that helped him a little in the difficult business of living. He would be forever grateful to the friend. I can imagine him later speaking of Ficke. "That Ficke. He is a wonderful man. What a mind he had. It is wonderful, wonderful."

There was a woman who taught a class of children in an orphan asylum. She said, "I got Dreiser to come visit my class." She spoke of a habit he has. When Dreiser is absorbed or moved, he takes a handkerchief from his pocket, lays it on his knees, begins folding and refolding it.

She said, "My children were reciting their lessons and he sat looking at them. I'll never forget his figure, that great hulk of a man, sitting there, folding and refolding the handkerchief, the tears running down his cheeks.

"Just because—well, I don't know—because," she said.

"It was pity, not for one of the children, for all children.

"Life, what it does to people."

Dreiser will call a friend on the telephone.

"I think you had better go see Fred."

"Why?"

"Well, I saw him on the street. There was something I felt. I am quite sure he is a little low, a little discouraged. You had better go to see him. Go at once."

Dreiser is a great writer. No more awkward writer ever lived. He can write sentences that fairly jar the teeth out of your head. They flatten out. In his hands words go sick and lame. They get rheumatism. They have pernicious anemia. Many of his sentences have broken backs. They can't walk, can't even crawl.

He is a great novelist. He builds and builds, slowly, patiently. Something arises, huge, significant, real. He does not play cheap scurvy tricks on life. Many another, honest enough in what we call the "real" world, is a crook in the world of the imagination. It is the world of real significance, where men get shown up for what they are. The arts are very dangerous institutions to fool with and how casually many people go into them. Look out. They give you away. They show you up for what you are.

Theodore Dreiser is a great figure. He is something out beyond his books. He will remain a significant figure to other American men working in the arts long after men have quit reading his books.

8. Writing Stories

I have seldom written a story, long or short, that I did not have to write and rewrite. There are single short stories of mine that have taken me ten or twelve years to get written. It isn't that I have lingered over sentences, being one of the sort of writers who say . . . "Oh, to write the perfect sentence." It is true that Gertrude Stein once declared I was one of the few American writers who could write a sentence. Very well. I am always pleased with any sort of flattery. I love it. I eat it up. For years I have had my wife go over all criticisms of my work. "I can make myself miserable enough," I have said to her. "I do not want others to make me miserable about my work." I have asked her to show me only the more favorable criticisms. There are enough days of misery, of black gloom.

However this has leaked through to me. There is the general notion, among those who make a business of literary criticism and who have done me the honor to follow me more or less closely in my efforts, that I am best at the short story.

And I do not refer here to those who constantly come to me saying, "*Winesburg* contains your best work," and who, when questioned, admit they have never read anything else. I refer instead to the opinion that is no doubt sound.

The short story is the result of a sudden passion. It is an idea grasped whole as one would pick an apple in an orchard. All of my own short stories have been written at one sitting, many of them under strange enough circumstances. There are these glorious moments, these pregnant hours and I remember such hours as a man remembers the first kiss got from a woman loved.

I was in the little town of Harrodsburg in Kentucky . . . this when I was still a writer of advertisements. It was evening and I was at a railroad station—a tiny station as I remember it and all day had been writing advertisements of farm implements. A hunch had come to me and I had bought a yellow tablet of paper at a drug store as I walked to the station. I began writing on a truck on the station platform . . . I stood by the truck writing. There were men standing about and they stared at me.

It did not matter. The great passion had come upon me and the men standing about, small town men, loitering about the station, now and then walking past me . . . the train must have been late but it was a summer night and the light lasted. . . .

There were crates of live chickens at the other end of the truck on which I rested my tablet. There is this curious absorption that at the same time permits a great awareness. You are, as you are not at other times, aware of all going on about you, of the color and shapes of the clouds in the sky, of happenings along a street, of people passing, the expression of faces, clothes people wear . . . all of your senses curiously awake. . . .

At the same time an intense concentration on the matter in hand.

Oh that I could live all of my life so. Once I wrote a poem about a strange land few of us ever enter. I called it the land of the Now.

How rapidly they march. How the words and sentences flow, how they march.

It is strange, but, now that I try to remember which of my stories I began, standing by the truck at the little railroad station at Harrodsburg, Kentucky, and finished riding in the day coach of the train on my way to Louisville, I can remember only the station, each board of the station wall, the places where the boards of the station wall had pulled loose, nails pulled half out. The tail feather of a rooster stuck out of one of the crates. Once later I made love to a woman in the moonlight in a field. We had gone into the field for that purpose. There were some white flowers, field daisies, and she plucked one of them. "I am going to keep it to remember this moment," she said.

So also did I pluck a feather from the tail of a rooster at the railroad station at Harrodsburg. I put it in my hat. "I will wear it for this moment, for this glorious peep I am having into the land of Now," I said to myself. I do not remember which of my stories I wrote that evening but I remember a young girl sitting on the porch of a house across a roadway.

She also was wondering what I was up to. She kept looking across at me. When I raised my eyes from the paper on which I wrote so rapidly, she smiled at me. The girl . . . she couldn't have been more than sixteen . . . was something of a flirt. She had on a soiled yellow dress. She had thick red hair. In such moments as I am here trying to describe the eyes see more clearly. They see everything. The ears hear every little sound. The very smell of the roots, of seeds and grass buried down under the earth, seem to come up into your nostrils.

The girl sitting on the porch of the house across the road from the railroad station, had heavy sleepy blue eyes. She was full of sensuality. "She would be a pushover," I thought. "If I were not writing this story I could walk over to her.

"Come," I could say to her. "What woman could resist such a man as I am now, at this moment?"

I am trying to give, in this broken way, an impression of a man, a writer in one of the rich moments of his life. I am trying to sing in these words, put down here the more glorious moments in a writer's life.

My mind moves on to other such moments. I was in a big business office, surrounded by many people. Clerks and other fellow workers in the office where I was employed walked up and down past my desk.

They stopped to speak to me. They gave me orders, discussed with me the work in which I was engaged, or rather the work in which I was presumed to be engaged.

I had been for days in a blue funk. I had been drinking. "Here I am condemned day after day to write advertising. I am sick of it." I had been filled with self-pity. No one would buy the stories I wrote. "I will have to spend all of my life in some such place as this. I am a man of talent and they will not let me practice the art I love." I had begun hating the men and women about me, my fellow employees. I hated my work. I had been on a drunk. For several days I stayed half drunk.

I sat at my desk in the crowded busy place and wrote the story, "I'm a Fool." It is a very beautiful story. Can it be possible that I am right, that the thoughts I now am having, looking back upon the two or three hours when I wrote this story in that crowded busy place, have any foundation in fact? It seems to me, looking back, on that particular morning as I sat at my desk in a long room where there were many other desks, that a curious hush fell over the place, that the men and women engaged in the writing of advertisements in the room, advertisements of patent medicines, of toilet soaps, of farm tractors, that they all suddenly began to speak with lowered voices, that men passing in and out of the room walked more softly. There was a man who came to my desk to speak to me about some work

I was to do, a series of advertisements to be written, but he did not speak.

He stood before me a moment. He began speaking. He stopped. He went silently away.

Do I just imagine all of this? Is it but a fairy tale I am telling myself? The moments, the hours in a writer's life of which I am here trying to speak, seem very real to me. I am, to be sure, speaking only of the writing of short stories. The writing of the long story, the novel, is another matter. I had intended when I began to write to speak of the great gulf that separates the two arts, but I have been carried away by this remembering of the glorious times in the life of the writer of short tales.

There was the day, in New York City, when I was walking in a street and the passion came upon me. I have spoken of how long it sometimes takes to really write a story. You have the theme, you try and try but it does not come off.

And then, one day, at some unexpected moment it comes clearly and sweetly. It is in your brain, in your arms, your legs, your whole body.

I was in a street in New York City and, as it happened, was near the apartment of a friend.

The friend was Stark Young and I rang his bell.

It was in the early morning and he was going out.

"May I sit in your place?"

I tried to explain to him. "I have had a seizure." I tried to tell him something of my story.

"There is this tale, Stark, that I have for years been trying to write. At the moment it seems quite clear in my mind. I want to write. Give me paper and ink and go away."

He did go away. He seemed to understand. "Here is paper. And here is a bottle."

He must have left with me a bottle of whiskey for I remember that as I wrote that day, hour after hour, sitting by a window, very conscious of everything going on in the street below, of a little cigar store on a corner, men going on in and coming out, feeling all the time that, were I not at the moment engaged with a particular story I could write a story of any man or woman who went along the city street, feeling half a god who knew all, felt all, saw all . . . I remember that, as I wrote hour after hour in Mr. Young's apartment, when my hand began to tremble from weariness, I drank from the bottle.

It was a long short story. It was a story I called "The Man's Story." For three, four, five years I had been trying to write it. I wrote until the bottle before me was empty. The drink had no effect upon me until I had finished the story.

That was in the late afternoon and I staggered to a bed. When I had finished the story, I went and threw myself on the bed. There were sheets of my story thrown about the room. Fortunately I had numbered the pages. There were sheets under the bed, in the bedroom into which I went, blown there by a wind from the open window by which I had been sitting. There were sheets in Mr. Young's kitchen.

I am trying as I have said to give an impression of moments that bring glory into the life of the writer. What nonsense to mourn that we do not grow rich, get fame. Do we not have these moments, these hours? It is time something is said of such times. I have long been wanting to write of these moments, of these visits a writer sometimes makes into the land of the Now.

On the particular occasion here spoken of I was on the bed in Stark Young's apartment when in the late afternoon he came home.

He had brought a friend with him and the two men stood beside the bed on which I lay. It may have been that I was pale. Stark may have thought that I was ill. He began pulling at my coat. He aroused me.

"What has happened?" he asked.

"I have just written a beautiful, a significant story and now I am drunk," I replied.

As it happens I have not re-read the story for years. But I have a kind of faith that something of the half mystic wonder of my day in that apartment still lingers in it.

9. Man with a Book

I was in Reno, had gone there to get a divorce. It was from the sculptress and musician, Tennessee Mitchell. It seemed to both of us the best thing to do but we did not dare let it be known that we agreed. There was some queer twist to the law. If the man and woman both wanted the divorce they could not get it.

And there was a point of disagreement. We had no children and I felt her as well able to support herself as I was. I had three children from my first marriage and, when we had married, I had told Tennessee Mitchell frankly what my situation was. It turned out, that, after I had got established in Reno, she wanted me to sign certain papers, committing me to the payment of a large sum at some future time. I had gone to Reno expecting to be clear within a few months but I found myself compelled to stay more than a year. I did not too much mind. I began writing vigorously. It was at Reno that I wrote *A Story Teller's Story*.

We had been married but not really married and had been persistently unhappy together. Once, having saved a little money, I ran away from her. This was the time I went to Mobile, Alabama, and, crossing the bay, got a little house near a place called Fairhope.

She followed me. I think that, while she did not want me, she also did not want to let me go. When she appeared there at the retreat I found for myself, I was annoyed. It was then she became a sculptress. I taught her. I got clay for her.

"If you are to stay about here you will have to have something in which to absorb yourself," I said. I put the clay down before her. There was a great mass of it.

"You do not have to think of being a sculptress. Let that go," I said. I explained to her that, somewhere, within the mass of clay, there was a figure buried. "All you need to do is to release it.

"Sit down before the clay." I had made for her a few simple wooden tools. "If necessary, just sit for two or three days. Do not think of what you are to do. Think only of the figure buried away, inside the clay. When your fingers begin to itch to cut away the superfluous clay you may begin."

It worked, and afterwards I used to sit with her, telling her stories of people about whom I planned to write or about whom I had written. I kept talking of these people, planting them thus in her imagination, and presently, after I had kept it up for a time, she did cut the superfluous clay away from certain heads. Some of these I later used, as illustrations in the book *The Triumph of the Egg*.

But our marriage had been a mistake. We were both too much on the artist side and it is a mistake for two such people to marry. Our marriage, that was not a marriage, had been brought about by a curious stream of circumstance.

In the first place, my first wife, the mother of my children, had been unable to believe in me as artist and I could not blame her. She was a woman who, having married one sort of man, had awakened to find she had got another. She had married a bright young business man, one who might, had he remained as he seemed to be when she had married him, a good father, a good provider, one who would have seen to it that her children were brought up in the classic American style . . . that is to say the classic style for the well-to-do . . . who would have provided them with automobiles, sent them to the best colleges, etc.

However, I was determined, would not be turned aside, and there had been a long silent struggle, ending in a divorce.

And then, feeling as I did at the time, more or less disgraced, a man who had gone back on his own children, avoiding, for the time, old friends, constantly saying to himself that he was a complete rotter . . . at the same time a curiously and persistently determined feeling, even from the beginning, that there was in himself a something that, developed, might be of value . . . being in this mood I had met and married the woman Tennessee Mitchell.

For she had been the first to encourage me.

"Do not let them turn you aside," she had said.

As I knew that if I went along the road that seemed to me the right one I could not make money by my writing, and as it sometimes seemed that my determination to go on this road rather than to attempt to do a kind of trick writing that might bring quick success was a kind of perversion in me, I was continually questioning myself. The words of the woman who told me to go on were, at the time, golden words.

And so we had married, on the understanding that we would have one of the kind of marriages a good deal talked of at that time. She had been a strong woman suffragist and, having been named for an early suffragist, one Tennessee Claflin, was very proud of her name. We were each to lead the free life, to come and go as we pleased, to live together when in the mood and apart when in another mood.

So there I was in Reno, a strange enough city. However, there was the desert and I had got to work on a book that I very much loved doing.

And there was something else. At that time we who got divorces, and particularly one who like myself was getting a second divorce, were more or less outcasts. In Reno, however, we were all in one boat. There was a kind of comradeship, a man went about making new friends.

I had been at the public library and had got several books. I came out into the street and was hailed by a friend. It was a New York doctor, sitting in his car, and he asked me to get in and ride with him. He was in Reno for the same purpose that had brought me there.

We rode and talked and, presently, as it was a topic being much discussed in Reno at the time, we got on the subject of public prostitution. The subject had become a political issue. There was, in the town, at the edge of town, a place into which the prostitutes had been herded. It was called "the bull pen," a great enclosure, something, as I had been told . . . I had not been to the place . . . in the style of county fair grounds, at the edge of small towns in the Middle West. There was this place, a circular enclosure, with a high board fence, a row of little one-room houses along the fence and a circular sidewalk that went before the houses.

It was a place openly and frankly devoted to the one trade and, to many of the citizens of the town, many of whom had originally come for the same purpose that had brought the doctor and myself, it was too frank. They did not, they said, object to the institution of prostitution, it being perhaps a necessary evil in our civilization, etc., but this openness, this brutal frankness. . . . They could not take it. They were protesting loudly.

There was this party, struggling for political control in the town, and there was another.

"If," said the second party, the so-brutally frank ones, "we do away with our bull pen we will lose trade. Now we are dependent upon these people who come here to seek divorces. It is an uncertain business." There was, already, competition springing up. There was the possibility of getting Mexican divorces. There were other states seeking the business, while, on the other hand, there were certain men, sheepherders, and cattlemen.

"If we do away with our bull pen then the sheepherders and the cattlemen will go to other towns. They will spend their money in other places."

There was this struggle that had become a political dog fight.

"Have you ever been to the bull pen?" asked my friend, the doctor. I said I had not and that I would like to go.

We drove there and having parked the car went in. This might have been at nine o'clock at night. I had the books, some five or six of them, under my arm.

And there the place was. It was as it had been described to me. There was the high board fence and the little one-roomed houses, each with its bed, its wash basin, its wash stand and chair. I had been told that the women did not live in the place. It was, for them, a place of business. It was their Wall Street, their skyscraper.

There were men walking about. They went along the sidewalk, before the doors of the houses, a woman standing at each door, some of them speaking to the men as they passed, others remaining silent, the men, as befitted the mission that had brought them, all appearing strangely isolated from each other, going along, some of them silently, in little groups, more often singly, all with a queer and significant separateness from each other.

It was a depressing place and there were the doctor and myself, also walking. We did not go far.

There was a sudden outcry. It was startling. It was begun by one of the women who stood at the door of one of the houses near the gate and was immediately taken up by the others. It grew in volume and, presently, the women had come out of the houses and into the street. They ran to us. They surrounded the doctor and myself. The other men, who had come to the place and had been walking silently along the circular sidewalk, had stopped walking and now stood staring. The women continued the cry they had taken up, following the doctor and myself as we hurried out through a gate and to our car. Although they did not touch us, it was an assault, an assault of voices, directed, not at the doctor but at myself.

"Look! Look! A man with a book," they cried, shouting with laughter. They kept it up until we had got into the car and had driven away.

"Look! Look! A man with a book!"

We could hear the voices of the women still going on with the cry as we drove through dark little streets and toward the gay-seeming lights of the town.

10. Meeting Horace Liveright

I was in the South again, in the city of New Orleans. It was one of the old cities of my love. (If you want to see and feel something beautiful in the world go sometime to New Orleans.) New York was another. But in New York I never felt myself anything but a guest. I have lived in New York for months at a time but never said to myself, "This is my home now. I'll make myself feel at home here." Always I have arrived, even when I have expected to stay for months, with a curious feeling of uncertainty. I would leave my bag at the check room of the station and start walking. It might be in the hot summer night, in the cold winter dawn. It was all the same. I was a guest in our biggest American city, a looker-on.

I had been coming to New Orleans for two or three months during the winter, whenever my purse would permit. I had been in New Orleans during the short life of the magazine started there, *The Double Dealer,* had made friends there . . . it was there that I first saw Bill Faulkner, knew that erudite team Julius Friend and James Feibleman, Jack McClure, the poet . . . these all having a hand in the magazine.

We used to gather in the office of the magazine once a month, make a night of it, bring drinks in and go over manuscripts. When there wasn't enough to make up a number of the magazine we sat and wrote pieces to enable it to go to press.

It was in New Orleans that I wrote the novel *Many Marriages,* certainly one of my own favorites among my books, though it was even more abused than *Winesburg*. It was a book in which I had tried for a complete and absolute acceptance of flesh and, like *Winesburg,* it had been written in a peculiarly clean spirit. Yet, not only was it bitterly attacked by most of the critics, but I was told by Mr. Huebsch that some of the book stores not only refused to sell it but, because of it, refused also to sell and keep in stock any of my books. By an arrangement Mr. Huebsch had taken over the books that had been published by Lane.

Certainly there was pleasure in being with Mr. Huebsch. On my occasional visits to New York he did not try to tell me what or how to write. He was a man whose companionship I could enjoy. But he could not sell my books.

It may have been because of the sort of books I wrote but perhaps there was another reason. Was it possible, thought I, that Mr. Huebsch had no great flair for selling?

I was to do a long list of books, to be published by Mr. Huebsch. Although I was constantly being approached by other publishers, in spite of this I could not forget that Mr. Huebsch had taken my *Winesburg,* a kind of favorite child, the book in which I felt I had first come into my own, as writer . . . he had taken it when no other publisher would.

And so I had gone on, still compelled, after perhaps ten years of writing, after having been translated into several other languages, to arise every morning and go to the advertising place, there to sit, writing of toilet soap, of patent medicines.

And so the years had passed. I had not begun writing young and, many times, during the next seven or eight years, there were moments of fear.

"I shall go on thus, having I must admit a pretty good time, writing as I choose to write, paying little or no heed to the methods by which other writing men of my day are growing rich and presently I shall grow old. The ink will no longer flow from my pen. I shall be compelled to live on charity."

These moments of fear coming. Could I blame my publisher that my books did not sell? It was, I admit, a kind of satisfaction to me to do so, as thus I avoided blaming myself. It may have been all nonsense but at last, while I was at work on *A Story Teller's Story,* I made myself a promise.

"If Mr. Huebsch cannot sell this book . . . (it had been written with great joy and I thought it had the necessary elements for popularity) . . . if he cannot sell this one, I shall cut loose, try someone else."

My loyalty to Ben had gone far enough. There was a whole shelf of books written and printed. *Winesburg, Poor White, The Triumph of the Egg, Many Marriages, Horses and Men.* Now there was *A Story Teller's Story.*

And in New Orleans the chance came. There had been a morning of intense work, of utter absorption in work. I was finishing another novel called *Dark Laughter*. How easy to say "finishing." But oh, the pain of doing it.

You have the idea and you begin; but what hours and often days between the beginning of your book and its end . . . if you ever get to the end. How easy to have it slip away from you.

There are these characters, with which you start. Others come in. There is a character you thought to have play a minor role but suddenly he or she is all over your book.

And you have your theme, to which you are trying to hold. There is the necessity of a movement forward, something growing as a child grows in a pregnant woman. The whole also to be orchestrated, innumerable false starts abandoned, pages and pages, sometimes thousands of words, put down that must be thrown aside.

And then, later, something else. You have your book, your novel, at last in manuscript, and then it must go into type.

Why, here is something else again. Now, in this form, you stand a little away from it. Its intimacy with you is gone. The book is one thing in manuscript and another in type. There is this dread of seeing it thus, the trembling fear, the hope.

"Will it stand up to this?"

For hours you have been sitting at your desk, the words flowing out from under your fingers. There is something you have long been trying to get that you think you have at last got.

And then the reaction comes. There has been this intense concentration and now you are striving to come out of it. You go to walk. Sometimes I have found that drink helps at such times. You have been in one world and you are trying to return to another. Your nerves are jumpy.

And so, on this day of early spring, I was in this condition and walked in the street. I saw people, houses, cars, passing in the street without seeing. I had gone through several streets and had got down to the water front and while thus walking, half blind, trying to shake off the intense mood that had gripped me I was approached by a sailor.

He had apparently been on a long drunk. His voice was husky. He had in his mouth an unlighted cigarette. He approached me noiselessly and with a kind of supreme effort shouted in my ear.

"Hey, boss, give me a match," he said and I jumped.

It was as though someone had shot off a gun in my face. I was very angry. I turned on him. I began to curse. It is a wonder he did not knock me down.

"You damn fool," I shouted, "to so approach a man, startle him." I stood there cursing, calling him all the ugly names I could think of but he only laughed at me. Stepping a little away he eyed me with shrewd bleary eyes.

"Oh," he said, "I see, I see, a nervous proposition." It seemed to explain everything and he went away laughing and as he went he kept looking back at me.

"Oho! Oho! I see! I see! A nervous proposition," he kept repeating as he went.

Nervous or not, I wandered on. I was again nearly broke. Within a few days, I thought I would be compelled to go back again to Chicago and to the writing of advertisements . . . I was walking thus when unexpectedly I ran into a man who was to become a real influence in my life and in my affairs.

It was that strange character, much maligned, much misunderstood, the strangest man, I am sure, ever in the publishing business in America. I am speaking of Horace Liveright.

He was then and, for that matter, until the end of his life, a very handsome man, tall and erect, his hair just touched with gray. He walked with an easy swing and when I saw him that day in New Orleans, he was accompanied by a very beautiful woman.

There was an absurd mistake made. Already I knew Horace Liveright, had been with him on several occasions in New York. He was the publisher of my friend, Theodore Dreiser, and of another friend, Eugene O'Neill. He was with a beautiful woman and I had seen him with many beautiful women.

"Meet my wife," he said and, "Oh yeah?" I answered.

There was an uncomfortable moment. It *was* Mrs. Liveright. I was sunk and so was Horace.

"It may have been an uncomfortable moment for you but it was a lot more than that for me," Horace later told me.

However he forgave me. He came to see me later in the same afternoon and we went to drink together and, when he inquired, I told him that I was looking for a new publisher.

"It isn't that I am not fond of Ben," I said.

"Yes, I understand. We are all fond of Ben," he said.

He made me a proposal that took my breath away. I had spoken to him of the advertising agency. "I'll have to go back there, begin again to write of tooth paste, of kidney pills, of how to keep your hair from falling out." There must have been a note of desperation in my voice and Horace, on that occasion as always with me, was very gentle. We were at a table in the little New Orleans café and were drinking. He reached across the table and put his hand on my hand.

"So you are discouraged, eh? You think your books cannot be sold. What nonsense. You come with me." He made a proposal.

"For five years I'll send you a hundred dollars a week. I'll take what you write. I'll sell your books."

II. I Build a House

At the time Horace Liveright was the outstanding figure in the American publishing world. Having come to New York from Philadelphia he had got a job on the stock exchange and by a quick succession of speculations, run a few hundred dollars into a hundred thousand dollars.

What a place—"Horace Liveright"! Here in this publishing house was none of the dignity, the formality of the older publishing houses, the Scribners, Harpers, Century, Macmillans, etc. The place was a sort of madhouse, and I remember that when I told Ben Huebsch that I would at last have to quit him and that I was going to Horace Liveright, he was shocked.

For Horace was in and out of the stock exchange. He was in the theater. When you went to see him in his publishing house often enough the whole outer office was filled with chorus girls.

Horace, it seemed, was figuring on putting on a musical comedy and there they were. It wouldn't have surprised me when I went there to have had one of the women jump up and, with a practice swing, kick my hat off.

And there was Horace in the midst of it all. Men and women were rushing in and out, phones were ringing. Horace was talking to casting agencies in regard to players for some show he was producing; he was buying or selling stocks through some broker; authors were coming and going. It was a bedlam, a madhouse, and yet a man felt something very gratifying in it all.

Liveright had a way of trusting his authors. If at that time you went to him with a new man, and during the days of his splendor I did take both Hemingway and Faulkner to Horace with their first printed books, he took your word for it.

"Do you think they are all right, men of real talent?

"All right I'll take them on. You send them to me."

And there was his check book, always on hand, often with a bottle of whiskey on the desk beside it.

It was all rather crazy, rather splendid. Horace was a gambler and if he believed in you would gamble on you. I have always thought, since the man's death, that too much emphasis has been put on the reckless splendor of the man rather than on his never-ending generosity and his real belief in men of talent. I dedicated one of my books of verse to him and I have always been glad I did. In a way I loved the man.

As he lived he died. Certainly it was not his generosity to authors that broke him. The stock exchange did that and I shall always remember the last sight I had of him.

His publishing house had failed, dragged down by his plunges in the stock exchange, and after an attempt to find for himself a place in Hollywood he had returned to New York.

On the street I saw Tommy Smith who had been his editor-in-chief.

"Horace," he said, "is at such and such an address. He is in bad shape. Do go and see him."

And so I went to the address given and there he was. It was summer and some friend had given him the use of his apartment. He was there surrounded, as always, by people. It was morning but there had evidently been a night of carousal and Horace was in black pajamas.

As for the people about him they were of a sort you would only find in New York. They were failures in the theater, men and women who hadn't made it but were desperately keeping up a bluff. There was much loud talk, much boasting.

Horace was sitting on a couch and the morning sun was streaming through a window. He was very pale, very thin, and one of his long arms had almost withered away. I was told later that the withered arm was the result of a struggle with a woman. It was said that she had bitten him and that the arm had become infected.

And so I stood in that place, in that motley crowd. There were drinks going about. I had seen, a few weeks before, the picture called the *Cabinet of Doctor Caligari* and there he was. Horace had become that.

He was I think a little ashamed of his surroundings. He arose and went with me into a hallway. He put his good arm about my shoulder.

"Well, what the hell, Sherwood. I'm sunk," he said.

He said that and then braced. His shoulders straightened a little. I said something about his having lost control of his publishing house.

As he knew, and I knew, the house had been sold by the receivers at a low price. Its glory was quite gone. It had been something no other publishing house in America had ever been. It had put me on my feet.

"Why, I am not out of the publishing house," Horace said proudly. "It is to be reorganized on a big scale," he said.

He said he did not think that with all the other interests he had, in the theater, in Hollywood, on the stock exchange, he would be able to take any very active part in the new and bigger Liveright.

"I'll just be chairman of the board," he said, and then, with a bitter little laugh and knowing that I knew what I knew, he turned and walked away.

As for myself I took the elevator down and out of that apartment building and walked in the street below with tears half blinding my eyes.

A new, strange life again had begun for me.

I had been in New Orleans through a summer and winter. I had very little money. Having lived through one New Orleans summer, with its oppressive heat, I wanted, if possible, to avoid another.

I began to write letters to men I knew.

"Tell me, if you can, of some place to which I can go, where it is cool and where it doesn't cost much to live."

The letters brought me several suggestions, among others one from Julian Harris. Julian was at that time running his newspaper at Columbus, Georgia. He had made a fine and courageous fight against the Ku Klux Klan and I was full of admiration for him. In his letter he spoke of a Mrs. Greear, at Trout Dale, Virginia, and I have the impression that he said that Trout Dale was a place to which his father Joel Chandler Harris had often gone fishing. I wrote to Mrs. Greear, and received an answer. I could, she said, come to live in her family for a dollar a day.

"That will be for a room," I thought. I found in fact that it meant a room, my meals, my washing and mending. It meant living in a delightful family.

So I was here, where I am now, in the southwest Virginia hill country. I had come by train to the town of Marion, where I later ran two newspapers, one Democratic and the other Republican, and from there had gone on to Trout Dale by a lumber railroad.

The train, pulled by an engine geared to climb steep hills with the drive wheels apparently flying at a furious rate, sparks flying out often setting afire the neighboring woods, really crawled along at ten miles an hour.

It was a strange, a new sort of country to me. On all sides were the magnificent hills, in the Greear family a troop of boys. They all bore Biblical names, John, Joshua, David, Philip, Solomon. There was a corn field beyond a hillside apple orchard in a little hollow in the hills, and in the corn field a small one-room cabin that had not been occupied for years.

The cabin stood in the tall corn. It had no windows. For years the dust had blown in through the openings where the windows had been and through the open door. It was a foot thick on the floor.

The boys came with shovels and brooms. They cleared it out. They built in a rude table at which I could sit. They brought a chair from the house.

It was a long summer without rain in the hills and the daily train from down in the rich Holston Valley, down in the place of paved roads and prosperous farms, sent sparks into the dry woods. The engine of the train, built for hauling long trains of cars loaded with heavy logs, went slowly. It crawled painfully up wooded Trout Dale mountain sides, throwing off a stream of sparks. The little lumber town of Trout Dale was in decay. Now all the best of the timber had been cut out.

This town in the hills had tried valiantly to go on being a town; the merchants, men who had saved money working in the lumber camp, tried to establish an industry. There had been a little bank and my host, John Greear, had been the cashier.

So all of the money of the community had been put into the building of a factory and it had failed, impoverishing the little mountain village. From the Greear house I could see the remnants of the factory. All of it but a tall brick chimney had been torn away and beside the chimney lay a huge old iron boiler brown now with rust. The chimney that had furnished the power for the factory, seemed to leer at you as you went past it on the dirt road that led over the mountains to the prosperous land beyond.

I was in the corn field at work. I wrote a book there, a book of childhood I called *Tar*.

I was alone there, often all morning at my table. It was cool up there in the hills, or at least it seemed cool after New Orleans, and the sunlight came in to me through the tall corn.

The corn had begun to wither in the long drought. When there was a breeze blowing there was a sharp rustling sound. My feet, as I sat writing, were on the warm earth of the little floorless cabin. The corn seemed talking to me.

"What an ideal place for an American writer," I thought. I grew lyrical.

"The corn, the corn, how significant in all American life," I thought. I thought of all the great corn fields of the Middle West, of how when I was a small boy I had often crept into them at the edge of my own Ohio town.

I used to crawl in there and lie under the corn. It was warm and close in there. On the ground, under the tall corn, pumpkins grew. There was the singing of the insects. Little insects flew about my head or crawled along the warm ground. Then also the corn fields had talked to me. Like Henry Wallace, whom I was to know later, I became for the time, a kind of corn-field mystic.

I even tried what I had often thought of doing. When I had written a chapter of my book I went outside my cabin and read it aloud to the corn. It was all a little ridiculous but I thought, "No one knows."

And the corn did seem to talk back to me.

"Sure, you are all right. Go ahead," it seemed to say.

I had rented an old horse and buggy and in the afternoon drove by many dirt roads over the mountains.

The old horse went slowly. I had a book with me and, putting the reins on the dashboard, let the old beast take his own way. I might well have had with me a volume of George Borrow, *Lavengro* or the *Romany Rye*. They were books I loved and always carried in my bags.

I kept meeting mountain men and women who turned to stare at me. The mountaineers are like the gypsies described by Borrow. They look directly at you with a strange, fixed, somewhat disconcerting stare. For a long time after you begin to know them they say little. They are watching you.

"What sort of fellow is this?"

Sometimes, as I rode thus, often in forest roads, some mountain man appeared suddenly out of a path that led away into the deep bushes. There was an old bearded man sitting on a log with a rifle on his knees. It was not until I had lived in the mountains for several years that Dave, one of the Greear boys, told me of how I was all that summer under suspicion.

"They were watching you, quite sure you were a revenuer," he said. He explained how people came to the Greear house asking. All of this was during the time of prohibition and the business of making moonshine was flourishing.

The mountain man was poor. He lived far from the railroad. His little patch of corn, often but three or four acres, would not support his family.

The mountain families were prolific. One of my neighbors, Will Pruitt, who became a friend after I built my own house in the hills, had nineteen children by one wife. He was still vigorous, still strong. He went out on horse-trading expeditions. The farm I later bought had on it a little frame tenant house and after I had built my own house the American sculptress Lucile Swan once came to live in the tenant house.

She was young and beautiful. She bought and rode a great black horse and once Will stopped in the road.

"That woman," he said. "It's a good thing my old woman hasn't died yet. I'd never let that woman get out of this country."

But that came later. I was there in that corn field writing. Some of the mountain men had gone to the Greears to inquire.

"Why, he's a writer. He's writing a book."

It seemed like nonsense to them. One of the mountain men later told me about it.

"You didn't look like that to us," he said.

He told me of how they had sent men through the corn, creeping toward my cabin. It may be that they heard me, spouting there in the corn field. It may have saved me. They perhaps thought I was crazy.

"Well, it's a good thing you didn't get out of that old buggy and walk about much in the woods. We'd have plunked you," the man said to me.

"We thought dead sure you were a revenuer but we couldn't be sure. There were two or three men drew a bead on you but didn't shoot. You came out mighty lucky," he said.

In my wanderings with my old horse that summer I went often along a particular road out of the lumber town. It was a little winding road that followed the windings of a brook. It kept crossing and recrossing the brook by fords. I got into a little valley between the hills.

It was a sweet little valley in which there was one small farm, owned, I was told, by a widow woman. She had lost her man. He had gone off to the West Virginia mountains, to the coal mines, and had been killed there. There were two small brooks passing through the valley and beside one of the streams, crossed by a log bridge, was a mountain cabin in which the widow lived with her children.

She was a sturdy woman and was farming her own farm and doing the work of a man.

Once I stopped at the house and the widow being absent I spoke to the children. They had come down to the bridge to stare at me.

"Does your mother want to sell this farm?" I asked.

It was a senseless question. I had no money with which to buy a farm. I was indulging in a dream.

"If I had some money I'd buy this farm. I'd live here in these hills." The hunger may have come down into me from my father, who, I think, had been a North Carolina hill boy.

"If I could just buy this farm. I could live, comfortably enough, in that little cabin, over there."

My dreams ran far ahead. Sometime I might write a book that would really sell. All of that country was full of beautiful building stone. I might some day build such a stone house as I had seen in England or France.

The children, frightened by my inquiry, ran away to hide but presently one of them, a young girl, came timidly back. She stood across the creek from me and shouted a shrill voice.

"Yes, mother wants to sell. She wants to move to West Virginia," she screamed and ran away. It seemed a curious desire to me.

Fall came and I still lingered in the hills that were now covered by color. An old desire to be a painter came back to me but I did not surrender to it. I had finished my book and had written and sent off several short stories.

And then luck came my way. Two of the short stories sold and I had some money and one day, when I was again driving down through my little valley, a book in my hand, the old horse meandering along, the hills surrounding the valley covered with flowing color as though beautiful oriental carpets had been laid over them, I met a woman in the road.

Was it a woman or was it some kind of a monster? I reined in the horse and sat staring. The thing was coming down the hill toward me. It was a woman with a great brass kettle on her head, a kettle for making apple butter. I hailed the woman; she came out from under the kettle.

She was the coal miner's widow who owned the little farm in the valley below.

"Do you still want to sell your farm?"

"Yes, I want to move to West Virginia."

Again that strange desire. I bought the farm there in the road.

A number of things had happened. Chief of all was the fact that Horace Liveright had made a go of *Dark Laughter*. It was the only novel of mine that ever sold in a big way, became what is called a best seller. The sales climbed up and up. I went on a visit to New York and saw my own face staring at me from the advertising pages of newspapers, on the walls of busses and subways.

I saw men and women sitting in busses and subways with my book in their hands. They were stenographers taking it with them to the office.

"Have you read *Dark Laughter?*"

It was all very strange. It was as exciting as a young girl about to go to her first dance. I wanted to go speak to the men and women holding my book in their hands. I was in the subway and got up and clinging to a strap stood over one such woman. She was at page 181 of my book. That would be where I told of the orgies at the Quat'z Arts Ball in Paris in the year after the ending of the first World War. I remembered the American newspaper woman who had as an adventure gone to the ball and was telling of it.

She had told much that I hadn't dared put in the book. I had put in enough. I stood, in the New York subway, looking down at the woman whose eyes were fixed on the pages of my book. She was reading rapidly.

Why, she was such a respectable-looking woman. She was well dressed.

"She will be the wife of a lawyer, or a doctor or perhaps a merchant," I thought. She would live somewhere in a respectable suburb. She went to church on Sunday, belonged to a woman's book club.

I was reconstructing the life of the woman reading my book. A few years before I had written a sort of fantasy of the flesh in a book I had called *Many Marriages* and there had been, as I have said, a storm of criticism.

That the adventures told of in the book could have happened to a respectable seeming American had seemed terrible to American readers.

"That was my mistake," I told myself as I stood over the respectable woman reading my book in the subway. In the book she was reading the adventures in sex were taking place in Paris and that made it all right. That, I thought, had had much to do with the success of the later book.

I returned to my Virginia farm in the mountains. Already, during the winter, the cabin by Ripshin Creek had been torn down and a log cabin to work in had been built on a nearby hilltop. It was to be a place in which I could work while the building of a new house went on.

For I had formed rather grand plans. Money was, for the first time, rolling in. I was what is called in the South, "nigger rich." I had determined to have a house of stone to stand near where Ripshin joined Laurel Creek. There was a fine old apple orchard at that spot and my house, when built, would be protected from storms by the surrounding hills.

There was plenty of stone everywhere about but, in all the mountain country, there were no workmen who had ever built a stone house.

However they were all ready to try. I had got an old man named Ball to be my builder and he was full of confidence. Bill Spratling, who was then teaching architecture at Tulane University, in New Orleans, drew some plans for me. However we could not use the plans much, as neither the builder Ball or myself could understand the blue prints.

"But never mind," Ball said. "We'll get along."

Ball was a huge old man of near seventy who had been a builder of sawmills and it was said also that, as a younger man, he had been a famous moonshiner. I had been told that he was somewhat dangerous when crossed but he was always gentle with me.

He went about boasting of his new position. He engaged to have lumber sawed. He employed neighboring hill farmers. He set men to hauling huge stone. He stood before the store at Trout Dale boasting.

"I'm something now," he declared. "I've got into a new position in life. I'm secretary to that millionaire who has moved in here."

But I was no millionaire. I had got a few thousand as royalty on my book *Dark Laughter* and there was the hundred dollars that came every Monday from Horace Liveright.

I was intensely bothered by that. There I was. I was presumed to be a writer. "But a writer should be writing," I told myself.

And now Ball had engaged many of the neighboring hill farmers to work for me. I had built a small frame house in the valley below the hill on which my log cabin stood. It had been thrown up hastily. I thought, "When my stone house is built I'll use it as a garage."

I slept and ate down there but in the morning I arose and climbed faithfully up to my cabin on the hill. I sat at my desk by an open window and before me, stretching away, were the tops of other hills.

The hills running away into the distance were a soft blue. They were covered by forests and the trees were just coming into leaf. Here and there, on distant hillsides, were small cleared fields and men plowing. A mountain road climbed a distant hill and a man on horseback went slowly up the road.

It was all too grand. I sat in the cabin with my pen in hand and there were the blank sheets on the desk before me and down below, on Ripshin Creek, the materials for my house were being brought in.

Men were at work down there and there was I up there on that hill, my pen poised in my hand, no words coming to me.

I sprang up and went outside my cabin to look out.

"Why, I cannot write. It is too exciting down there. This is the great time in a man's life. We are all, at heart, builders. It is the dream of every man, at some time in his life, to build his own house.

"And so my house is to be built and I am to stay up here, writing words on paper. How silly."

But there was that hundred dollar check. It came every Monday morning.

Horace had said, "I will send it to you every week for five years. I'll take what you write."

"I'll not bother you," he said.

Yet each week the arrival of the check was a reminder that I was not and perhaps could not be a writer while my house was building.

"But I am under this obligation to Horace." I went again into my hilltop cabin. What really happened was that I never did write a word in that cabin. It may be that the view from the hilltop was too magnificent. It made everything I wrote seem too trivial. I had in the end, after my house was built, to move the cabin from the hill, tuck it away among the trees by the creek.

But I was still up there and down below the work on my house was under way. I had to give it up. I took a train to New York.

"Please, Horace, quit it."

"Quit what?" he asked.

"Quit sending me that money."

I tried to explain how it affected me.

"But," he said, "I have made enough on the one book—I am in the clear. Why should you worry?"

I had a hard time convincing him. He even became suspicious.

"Are you not satisfied with me as your publisher? Is that it?"

It seemed, as he said, impossible to him that a writer should refuse money.

"All right, I'll quit it, but I think you are a little crazy."

And so I was released. It is true that, when my house was half finished, I had to go lecturing. It was bad enough but it was better than having the checks come every Monday to remind me that I was a writer, not a builder.

And this suggests something to my mind. Do you, the reader, belong to some literary circle in your town or city? Do you attend lectures by novelists and poets? Would you like to know something of the financial standing of these men and women? If so, you do not need to go to Dun and Bradstreet. If they are lecturing it is a hundred to one they are broke.

We were hauling stones in from the creek for the walls of my house. We were taking stone from neighboring hillsides. Mountain men from all the surrounding hills and hollows were working for me. We sawed lumber, cut shingles, dug and laid stone walls. We built a dry kiln to dry our green lumber. Mr. Ball climbed like a squirrel over the rafters of the house. My brother Karl came and made a painting of the half-completed structure and a drawing of Ball.

Ball had his own way of life. He built heavily the stone walls eighteen inches thick, all the lumber seasoned oak.

"I'm going to build you a house that will stand here until Gabriel blows that trumpet," he said.

The small hill farmers proved to be wonderfully efficient workmen. When there was work to do on their own farms, wood to cut for their wives, corn to be cut and cultivated, or even perhaps a run of moon to be made for the West Virginia trade, they did not come.

Well, it was all right. While the money made from the sale of *Dark Laughter* held out I did not mind. Perhaps once a month old man Ball came to me. He had been, I had noticed for several days, growing a bit irritable. I thought of shootings and knifings among the hill men. There was his son Ezra working on the job. He had killed one man.

"I'm afraid," said the old man, "that I will have to lay the men off for a few days.

"I'm not feeling so well."

A slow grin spread over his old face.

"All right," I said. I knew what was coming. Marion Ball would hire a man who owned an old open-faced Ford to drive him about over the hills. He would load the car with a few gallons of local white moon, would sit sprawled on the back seat. He would drive from farmhouse to farmhouse stopping to invite men to drink with him. He would make his driver stop while he slept for an hour beside some hillside road. It was his great bragging time.

"I'm going to build that millionaire down there the finest house ever built in this country. They said I couldn't do it, that I was just a sawmill builder. Why, that fellow down there, that writer, he trusts me like a brother."

Ball's vacation lasted for perhaps three or four days and then he would reappear. He looked as fresh as a young boy.

"It rests me up to go on a bender now and then," he explained.

Old Man Ball had his own notion of me. I was more or less a child who had to be taken care of. There was a fireplace, upstairs in the house, for which a stone arch had to be cut. All of the mountain men, I had found out, were natural craftsmen. They loved stone laying. They had pride in the job they were doing.

An old man came down out of the mountain. He was driving a mule and sat in a broken-down wagon. Later I learned that his wife was dead and that his children had all moved out of the country. They had perhaps, as so many sons of mountain men did, gone off to the West Virginia coal mines. The old man lived alone in a mountain cabin somewhere back in the hills.

He stopped before my house and came to where Ball and I were standing in the yard. He was nearly bent double with disease. In truth the old man was slowly dying of cancer of the stomach.

"Do you need any stone cutters here?" he asked. He might have been Tom Wolfe's father in *Look Homeward, Angel.* This man was also a gigantic old fellow.

"And are you a stone cutter?"

"Why, I have been a stone cutter for twenty-five years," he declared.

I looked at Old Man Ball. I had never heard of any stone cutters in the hills.

"Do you know this man?" I asked Ball. "Is he a stone cutter?"

Ball looked over my head at the sky.

"Why, I'll tell you, man and boy, I have lived in this country for fifty years and some of the best men I've ever known in this country have been liars," he said.

Ball laughed and the strange old man laughed with him.

"Well, I've heard of this building going on down here," he said. "You know, Marion, I ain't got long to live. I got cancer but I want a hand in building this house."

So he got a hand. Ball took him upstairs to where the fireplace was building.

"We want an arch over that fireplace.

"You cut the stones for the arch. If they are all right, if they fit and look all right, I'll give you five dollars. Otherwise you don't get a cent."

Ball went about his affairs and I went up to where the old man was puttering about. He had got some pieces of string and was taking measurements. He kept tying knots in the string. He muttered.

"I'll show him, damn him, I'll show him," he kept declaring.

He put the pieces of string in his pocket, went painfully down the temporary stairway we had rigged up and getting into his broken-down wagon, went away.

"So that," I thought, "is the last of him. He will be dead soon now."

Very soon, after three or four weeks, he did die and we built a coffin for him. We built several rude coffins for hill men and women while my house was building. We took a day off and all went up to the old man's cabin to bury him.

And then, after several more weeks, it was time to lay up the arch over the fireplace, and Old Man Ball came to me. We drove up to that other old man's empty cabin. Ball had had a hunch.

"We might as well go up there and see," he said. He had known well the old man who had died.

"You can't tell, that old fool may have cut them stone."

So we drove up a mountain road to the empty cabin and there the stones were. They were in a little shed back of the cabin and when we brought them down they made a perfect little arch for my fireplace. The old mountain man, with the cancer eating away at him, had sat up there, slowly and painfully cutting the stones. He had managed to get a chisel and a hammer. He must have worked slowly, no doubt having to rest for long periods. He had wanted a hand in building my house. He had wanted to show Old Man Ball. He had done a fine job.

It must have seemed a very magnificent house to all the neighborhood. Their own houses were, for the most part, small unpainted shacks, often of one, two, or three rooms.

The civilization about me was not a money civilization. There was little money coming in. Moon liquor was about the only cash crop. When a man needed a new pair of shoes for his wife, a new pair of overalls, he sold a calf. Many of the people would have nothing to do with liquor making. Often they were Primitive Baptists, and devoutly religious. For the most part I found them trustworthy, good workmen and honest. If they were suspicious of strangers, slow to establish friendships, they were also, when once they had accepted you, very loyal.

One of the mountain men explained it all to me.

"We wait until we are sure we can fellowship with a man," he said.

The Primitive Baptists (sometimes called Hardshell Baptists) were also foot washers. They had several big meetings during the summer, meetings called the Big June, Big July, etc. They were really great folk gatherings, often several hundred people coming out of the hills and hollows, to gather about some church.

Whole families came, the young girls in their best dresses, the men shaved and bathed. They gathered in the road before the church and in nearby fields. All had brought food and everyone was invited to eat. Among the young men the moon bottle was passed back and forth.

It was a folk movement in which all joined. People came in wagons and on horseback. They came in Ford cars and afoot. It was a great day for courting, girl meeting boy. If there was some drunkenness it did not amount to much.

The Primitive Baptists had no paid preachers. Their preachers, like the members of the congregation, were farmers. Abe Lincoln once said that he liked a preacher who preached like a man fighting bees. He should have been there.

There was another folk meeting that was very curious. There were no Negroes in our section. For years before I came there to build my house, there had been a tradition that no Negro was to come to live in that neighborhood. It was all right for a Negro to come for a few hours but he was warned.

"Get out before dark. Do not let the sun go down on you in this neighborhood."

I was told that the prejudice against the Negro had sprung up because of labor trouble. When lumbering in that district was at its height there had been a strike and Negroes had been brought in to break it.

The mountain men had run them off with guns. It had set up a tradition.

And then, besides, my neighbors had before the Civil War never been slaveholders. Like the men of eastern Tennessee they had been Union men. Perhaps they felt that the Negro was in some way to blame for all the trouble and hardship brought on by the war. Some of the older men had been forced into a war they didn't understand. Government had long been to them a thing far off.

They got no benefit from it. Roads were poor and there were always government men interfering. They sent in men to stop their liquor making. They wanted to collect taxes.

"For what?"

What had government ever done for them?

There was this feeling about the Negro but there was a summer Sunday every year when it was set aside.

It was a Nigger Meeting Sunday. On that day the Negroes from all the low valley country to the north and south came to a neighboring high mountain top. They held services there. They preached and sang all day long.

And the Negro congregations came. They were on the mountain top with the white mountain men, women and children. All sang together. All together walked up and down in the road. On that day, Negroes and whites fellowshipped together.

Life in the hills was changing. In a few years after I came into the hills to live, a paved road was built over our hills. It passed through Trout Dale. Big cars began running over the mountains. A garage was built and there were two or three bright shining filling stations. The people of the hills had long been snuff dippers but the younger generation stopped dipping. They went down into the valley town to the movies. A few radios were bought. In the road I saw a woman of twenty-five. She had been reading some woman's magazine, had bought a cheap model of a dress of the latest New York style. Her lips, her cheeks, and even her fingernails were painted but she still had a snuff stick protruding from a corner of her mouth. It was a new world came into the hills and I was a part of it.

There was an old woman lived on a side road near my house. She had a little farm, her man was dead and she with her young daughter worked the farm. She was something rare to me and often I went to visit her, to sit with her in the evening on the porch of her little unpainted mountain cabin. She was one who proved something to me. In the South I had been hearing much talk of aristocracy. I had not heard it among the mountain people but, when I went down into the more prosperous valley town where later I ran the local newspaper, I heard much of it. It seemed to me to be always connected with the former ownership of slaves, with the ownership of rich valley land and money in the bank. To tell the truth I had grown a little weary of the talk of Southern aristocracy and had been asking myself a question.

"But what is an aristocrat?"

I thought I had found one in the hills. It was my little old woman neighbor. She had pride. She seemed to feel no one below her, no one above her. She was very poor. She worked hard. Her little thin bent old body was all hardened by toil. When I had first come into her neighborhood she had come to see me and what poise she had had.

She had heard I was a writer of books.

"Mr. Anderson," she said, "I guess we are glad enough to have you come in here and build your house. You do not seem to us an uppity man but I thought I had better come and warn you. They tell me you are a writer of books, but, Mr. Anderson, we cannot buy any books. We are too poor and besides, Mr. Anderson, there are a lot of us who cannot read and write."

It was a summer day and my neighbor, the little old woman, was going to the mill.

She was going to have corn ground for flour and went along the road past my new house half bent double with the load on her thin old shoulders.

I called her in.

"You are tired," I said. "Come and sit with me for a spell."

Now my house was half completed. Workers were scrambling up walls of stone.

We sat on a bench and I made a gesture with my hand.

"Tell me what you think of it," I said.

"Do you not think it is going to be a beautiful house?"

"Yes," she said. Her old eyes were looking steadily at me and again she said she did not think I was an uppity man.

"I guess we are glad enough to have you come in here and build your house," she said. She mentioned the fact that I was giving men work. They earned cash money working for me.

"But there is something else," she said. "We were all poor together in this neighborhood before you came."

So I had set up a new standard of life, had changed things, perhaps I was profoundly disturbing a way of life that had had its own values. I could not answer the old woman. I sat looking at the ground by my own feet. What she had said had sent a queer wave of shame down through my body.

There was another arch of stone to be built in my house. It was a puzzle to us. However we laid it out in the yard in the apple orchard behind the uncompleted house and built a wooden frame for it.

As I have said we had no tools and there were no stone cutters so my neighbors began bringing stones and trying to fit them into the arch. A man at work on the house would keep his eyes open as he came over the hills from his own cabin. If he saw a stone he thought might fit into the arch he hoisted it to his shoulder and brought it along. We gradually got the arch quite complete, lying there on the ground in the orchard and then the question arose as to which one of the men was to lay it up.

There was a good deal of controversy. Nearly all the men wanted the job but, after a good deal of discussion, it was given to a man named Cornett.

He did a good job and we all laid off work to watch him. The arch went up perfectly and when it was quite completed I went away to lunch.

Something happened. Why, I dare say the man Cornett was proud of his accomplishment. He had got hold of a chisel, may have gone off to the valley town to buy it. He carved his name in large crude letters across the face of the keystone of the arch. He did it while I and all the others were at lunch and when I returned I was furious.

I began swearing in a loud voice. I shouted. Here was something, I thought, that we had all had a hand in doing and this man had slapped his name on it. The keystone had been specially selected. It had a beautiful face. It was ruined.

I kept on ranting and raving and all the other workmen gathered about. There were shy grins on many faces.

As for Cornett, he said nothing. He went out of the room into the yard and when I came out there he stood with his coat on and his lunch pail in his hand.

"I want to talk with you. Come on down the road with me," he said.

"He is going to give me a beating," I thought. We walked in silence along the road until we came to a bridge. I had begun to be ashamed of some of the things I had said to him. When he spoke he spoke quietly enough.

"I'll have to quit you," he said. "I can't work on your house any more."

He explained that it was because all of the others would have the laugh on him.

"All right, I made a mistake. Next Sunday, when none of the others are here, I'll come back and cut my name off the stone. But I'll tell you what you should have done—if you felt you had to bawl me out, you shouldn't have done it before the others. You should have taken me aside. Then I could have stayed on here."

The man Cornett stood on the bridge looking at me. After all he had done a fine job in laying up the arch.

"Let's see, you write books, don't you?" he asked. I said I did.

"Well, when you have written a book you sign it, you put your name on it, don't you?" he asked.

He had me there. I had nothing to say, and with a slow grin on his face he walked away.

We had got near to the end of our job. The walls were up and the roof was on my house but there was the question of getting it plastered.

And then a man came, from some distant town, who was a professional plasterer.

He was quite frank.

"I'll tell you," he said. "I am a good man at my job but I get drunk and when I get drunk I stay that way.

"You'd better keep liquor away from me," he said and so I called the men together.

It was agreed that no one would give him a drink.

"We'll wait until the job is done and then we'll give the fellow a real sendoff."

So the plastering was started and presently all was done except one room. I went away to town.

It was late afternoon when I came back and there was a scene I'll not forget. Ball later explained that they had all thought they could get a start on the celebration while they were doing the last room but the moon liquor they had secretly brought for the occasion must have been very potent.

The craftsman instinct in all the men had taken control of them. There was a scaffold in the room and one by one they had all climbed up onto it. As they did this they had kept taking drinks of the moon and the plaster was already, when I arrived, a foot deep on the floor. It was in their clothes, in their hair, in their eyes, but they did not mind.

One by one they kept climbing to the scaffold.

"Now you let me try it, Frank."

Several of the men had fallen from the scaffold and when I got there two of them were lying in the soft mess on the floor. They were shouting and singing. They were boasting of their skill.

"Come on, Anderson. You try your hand at it," they shouted when they saw me standing at the door of the room.

And so I went away. There was nothing else to do. I left them at their game and, on the next day, nothing being said, they all came back to clean up the mess they had made.

My house was my house. It is true that I had to go on a lecture tour to pay for having it finished and, when it was finished, I had to close it for two years, being unable to support living in it. But there it was.

It was a place for my books. It was a place to come and to bring my friends. It was, I thought, a beautiful house and in building it I had got into a new relationship with my neighbors. They were John and Will and Pete and Frank to me, and I was Sherwood to them. I was no longer a man apart, a writer, a something strange to them. I was just a man, like themselves. I had a farm. I planted corn and kept cows. They had found out that I was far from the millionaire they had at first taken me to be and I had found my land.

BOOK V

INTO THE THIRTIES

1. A Dedication and an Explanation

I do not believe I can write of my own marriages, being fair to both myself and the women involved. Once I was speaking of them to a friend.

"What is the matter with me, Frank?"

"Such fellows as you are often strong-headed," he said. "The demands you make of life are, you know, rather terrific. Most men finally accept the harness that life puts on them. You fellows cannot. You would die if you did.

"I'll say this for you," he added. "You do take life seriously. You believe in it. Many men come to the place where they take women purely as physical facts. Intimate contact with them is a physical necessity but it is that and nothing more.

"Fellows like yourself demand more. You keep demanding this strange thing we call love. When it dies out you go. You spend your life searching for it."

My first three marriages each lasted exactly five years. I have always been sure that none of the women were to blame when our marriage failed. Any practitioner of the arts is a trial to live with.

We are never there. We go away, often for months at a time.

Well, we are there physically. We are in a house, or in a street, but we are at the same time far away.

One of us is, for example, writing a novel. For months he will be off away from the people immediately about. Inside himself he is living another life, often having nothing to do with the people with whom he is living his own physical life. Speak to him and he will answer you, but he does not really hear. You make an engagement with him. You are to meet him on a certain day, at a certain hour, in a restaurant or at a theater. Do you think he will keep it? Very likely he will not. When you made the engagement with him your words did not register on his mind. He heard but did not hear.

It was because he was not there. When you spoke to him he seemed to be sitting at his desk in a room in the house where you lived with him but in reality he was in the captain's cabin of a ship, far out in the Pacific.

There was something tense going on in the cabin of the boat. There were two men and a woman in the little room. There had been a storm and the ship, a small one, had been disabled. It was drifting.

The captain of the ship, an old man, had a young wife and the mate wanted her and she had fallen in love with the mate. It was the ancient story.

The two men and the woman are having it out, there in the cabin. You see, the ship is leaking and will soon go down. It is a question of taking to boats, the boats perhaps drifting far apart.

Is the woman to go in the boat commanded by the captain or in that commanded by the mate, the man she loves? The whole matter is to be settled now in a few minutes. It may well be that, before they leave the cabin where they now sit facing each other, one of the two men will have been killed.

See how the woman standing there by the door trembles, how white she is.

So . . . as the writer is watching all this, a fourth unseen figure in the little ship's cabin, his own wife, comes to him. She wants to make an engagement. There is something she wants him to do for her.

"Sure. All right. Certainly I will."

Why, he did not hear her at all. Her words were blown away by a wind. They did not register on his mind.

Who was that who came into this room? My wife? What is a wife? I have no wife. Did I marry someone? Where? When?

It is dreadful to live with such a man. It is only possible . . . Only a saint could do it.

There are months and months when you are merely dust under his feet. For him you have no existence. As well, during such times, be married to one of the dummies in a store window.

Almost all of my own friends, men of the theater, painters, musicians, have, in this matter of marriage, had the same experience I had had. They have tried and failed, tried and failed. Some of them, upon the break-up of a marriage, have grown bitter. They write novels making the woman the central character. They grow bitter and ugly about it all.

How absurd. When one of us makes a failure of marriage it is, almost inevitably, his own fault. He is what he is. He should not blame the woman.

The modern woman will not be kicked aside so. She wants children, she wants a certain security, for herself and for her children, but we fellows do not understand the impulse toward security. When we are secure we are dead. There is nothing secure in our world out there and, as for the matter of children, we are always having children of our own.

For example, someone is always asking me which one of my own stories I like best, which of all the characters I have put into books and stories I like best, and I have a pat answer for them.

"Go ask some mother who has had several children which one of them she likes best," I answer.

It is a changing, shifting world, this world of the imagination in which we who work in any of the arts must live so much of our lives. We have it and then we have it not. Oh, the blank days, the black despair that sometimes descends upon us.

We grow irritable. Speak to one of us at such a time and you will probably get a sharp nasty answer. Trust us and we may betray your trust.

No. Do not ask me to write of the women with whom I have lived in marriage. I respect them too much to do it. That I have found a woman who, after ten years with me, can still laugh at me, who understands my wrinkles, who is there beside me, smilingly willing to forgive my idiosyncrasies, who after seeing through the years we have lived together my worst and my best—that is my good fortune.

I am one of the lucky ones. Good luck has always been with me.

I dedicate this autobiography to my wife, Eleanor.

2. A Man Friend

A woman friend had invited me to the christening of her child. She played with me, promised me that if I would come to the christening she would name the child for me.

This was in the city of Washington. I went in my car.

I was sitting in the room where the christening had taken place and we were drinking champagne. I was a little high. I felt gay. I was happy. I was in a room with many well-dressed people. I did not know many of them. Probably they were rich.

I liked being there. I liked the feel of the people gathered about. They had christened the child and had taken it away. I remember little of that. All babies look alike to me.

I have always admired women beautifully dressed. There is something in the touch of fine fabrics that sends a thrill through my body. I love to feel, touch, see.

I was at this place with the fortunate ones. A child had been christened. I had been told that it was to bear my name. It hadn't happened.

Perhaps the woman who had made the promise had forgotten. It didn't matter.

I was a little high, full of champagne. There were many voices in the room. What seemed to me, at the moment, very beautiful women kept coming up to me. I drank with them. We touched glasses.

And then Maurice came into the room. He was a big man, an Irishman with a big head. He was a proud man, an adventurer in life.

At that time he was rich but he had been poor.

He had come to America as a young lad off some poor Irish farm. There was in him a curiously alive gay quality that I have known in other Irishmen such as George Daugherty, Paddy Welsh, and the Irish poet Padraic Colum.

Maurice as a boy had come to a certain American city and, right away, he had landed a political job.

He was in politics and then in business. He rose and fell. He was a big laughing man. He was a woman lover, a life lover.

"I am rich now," he said to me. "I have all my life been looking for a comrade. We will go look at the world."

We had planned to go together in a car. We were always making plans. We would see America first. We planned to spend a year, two years, five years, just drifting about.

"None of us know anything about people," he said to me that first time we met at the christening of the babe.

"We'll go look," he said. "Look and listen."

It was understood there was enough money, nothing financial to worry us.

It was all arranged, and then he suddenly died. I thought it was unfair.

"You are a cheat for dying," I cried.

There was, however, a period of two or three years in which he came often to see me and I went to him. When we were together, with other people, we both became wonderful.

He was a man who set me off.

I set him off.

He was a story teller and sometimes I too was good.

We knew how to feed up to each other. We made openings. There have been, during my life, some three or four, perhaps six or eight, men I have truly loved. I loved Maurice.

I remember how it came over me, a kind of gladness, that first time I saw the man. It was like being in the surf at the ocean's edge on a hot day.

A great wave came and you plunged into it. You let it carry you along. It tumbled you about, played with you. What did it matter?

Why is it that men, as males, constantly deny their greatest inheritance, the love of the male for the male? The love of man for woman is a different matter. The two passions are not alike. The whole thing has nothing to do with a man's being, or not being, a fairy.

I have always been afraid of fairies. They sell you out. They are, in some queer way, outside the life stream. They know it. The male love of the male is something else. It is something that must, some day, come back into the world.

It must be proclaimed as Walt Whitman proclaimed it. It must be understood. Upon the understanding of it, the acceptance of it with pride, hangs the chance we males have of again getting, a little again, on top of our lives.

Yes, Maurice was a man I loved. We were comrades. He had always been muddled about women, as I had been, both of us loving them, both of us wanting permanently some precious things we thought they might give. How many talks we had of it. These talks were had often, in a car, long after midnight.

The fact that he was rich and I was not, not mattering. He used sometimes to laugh at me.

"I used to think of you a great deal before we met," he said. "There are a few tales you have told in print that get down close. And now to find you—confused as I am confused."

It made a kind of open thing between us—the man, my friend, with a life so different from my own. He was so much more physically handsome than I. Wherever he went, women, like flocks of birds, were always flying about. After he died I got many letters from women.

I saw some of them, talked to some of them, and they all said the same thing.

"If he had only let me I could have given him what he wanted, what he needed—" they said.

Oh, the vanity of women.

Thinking that they can fulfill a man without allowing him men comrades.

There were a dozen, a hundred, little adventures very characteristic of the man, my friend. We were sitting on the porch of my house and there was a man walking in the road.

He was a poor man with a large family. He was in debt. He went slowly, laboriously along the road.

"That man, there," said Maurice.

"Yes," I said. "He is Irish."

He wasn't. He was just a man I knew. He has worked for me, on my farm. I was forever lying to Maurice. He lied to me. It was a kind of play that went on. "I will get from him some money for my neighbor," I thought.

"He is from your country," I said.

I began to build up my tale.

"He is a Galway man," I said.

I knew how he felt about money. Later I would tell him I had lied.

I knew little or nothing of the farmer, just that he was broke, his farm mortgaged.

"A Galway man?" cried Maurice. He sprang to his feet.

"How did you know I was a Galway man?" he asked. I hadn't known. There are moments when a man is inspired.

He got up from the porch and ran down to the man. He wrote a check. He lifted the mortgage on the man's little farm and the man was stunned. He couldn't understand. He went away, holding the check in his hands and Maurice came back to me. He sat beside me and laughed.

"He wasn't Irish at all," he said.

He went away. It was arranged that we go together to see the world. He was one who never did one dirt.

The only thing he ever did not on the square was to die.

I would like to be able to write of him, to describe him, his great head, with the mass of graying hair, his great body, his walk.

He came often to see me in the town where I lived . . . this after I had myself begun to grow gray.

The county clerk, the man who ran the drug store, a lawyer, the men who worked in my print shop . . . this was when I published and edited the two county weeklies . . . all of them spoke of him.

On my farm back in the hills there was a man who worked, a quiet man, who seldom spoke, but he spoke of Maurice.

"When will he come again?"

"When will he come again?"

The question became a refrain. Men asked the question, women, old and young, asked it.

I saw him often in my dreams. It is seldom in life this feeling comes to a man, to love wholly and without reservation another man. I am asleep and he comes into my room. It was thus, in dreams that, after her death, my mother came to me. She has not come for a long, long time.

My friend comes into the room, walking, as he always walked, with his free easy stride and he sits in the room.

He is as he was in life. He is a somewhat swaggering man. Look, how well he is dressed. He wears loose-fitting tweeds. He loves colors. He has a bright necktie. He wears gaily-colored socks.

Sometimes he sits talking to me and sometimes he sits in silence. We make plans as we were always doing when he was in life.

How many women have loved him?

How many men have loved him?

"There are too many," he used to say. "I love too many.

"I want them all."

The women flocked about him. There were tall women, short ones, dark ones, light ones, beautiful women and plain ones.

I remember sharply the day he died.

I was at the door of my home when the telephone rang. It was his son speaking.

"Father is dead. He fell down in a field."

"He had been walking in a field," the son said. He was accompanied by an old horse and a dog. The dog was a little thing. It ran whining to his house.

There was an old horse, an old gelding.

"I had been with him in the country. We were riding in his car and had stopped before a farmhouse," the son explained.

There was a sale of horses going on. There were old horses and young horses. There was an old gelding.

The gelding was old and worn out. In his youth he had been denatured. His legs were all bunged up and he had sad eyes.

The bidding was going on.

"Three dollars."

"Four dollars."

"Five dollars."

"I'll give ten," said Maurice. He got the gelding.

"I will walk home. I'll lead him home," said Maurice. He spoke of him at length.

For years and years he, the gelding, had served man. He had plowed fields. He had gone up and down over roads. Men had beaten him. They had half starved him.

In his youth they had taken his horsehood away.

"Now he shall have a home," said Maurice. "He shall eat rich grass. He shall have oats."

It was a Sunday morning, in the state of Maryland, and the sun was shining. He had sent a wire to me. "Come and we will go on a journey."

He went alone upon his journey. He walked in a field and fell down dead. The little dog whined and ran to his house. His son came and found him lying there. The old gelding, that worn-out old farm horse, that, since he had come to live with Maurice had on all such walks accompanied him, following at his heels, stood over him. The son told me.

"The old horse just stood there," he said. "He was looking down with his sad patient old eyes into my father's face."

He was a king, a lord among men. As a young man he had been married but his wife had left him. He did not blame her. "I have loved too many women," he said.

He could not help it.

He was one of the men who can give and give again. When he died and, in the newspapers, it was mentioned that I was among his friends—I was more well known than he was—the women turned to me.

For days my telephone rang. There were calls from Chicago, San Francisco, New York, St. Louis. There were calls from country towns. Old women called me. Young and beautiful women called me.

"You were his friend. Let me come to see you. Let me talk of him."

I did see some of them.

"Yes," they said. "It is true. He did love many women."

"I was closer to him than any other woman can ever be."

They all said it. They kept saying it.

"If he hadn't been so confused, if he had only accepted what I—" It was always the one talking—what she had to give.

"But what was wrong with him?" I kept asking them. To me he was O.K. "What of his confusion? Who is not confused?"

"He understood something," I said. "He understood that I loved. I understood that he loved." For a long time I was determined that I would write his life. He had been one of the greatest adventurers I have known. He was one of the rich men of my life. He was rich in money, rich in friends, in the love of women. He was rich in giving. He was a story teller. When in his house with the room filled with men drinking and going about, he began telling a story, all would become hushed.

He could touch the heart with his stories. He could make tears come to the eyes. He could make the room ring with laughter.

His life had been one of many strange adventures, and more than once, after his death, I sat down to my desk. This might have happened after one of the nights when he had come into my dreams.

He had come into the room as he used to come in life. There was the same proud half swagger. There was the half sad look that sometimes came into his eyes. In the dream he sat in the room in silence.

"It may be," I thought when I awoke, "that he wants something from me."

"He may be like all other men, all wanting their stories told."

The words would not march. There were no words with which I could tell his power over others.

3. Why I Live Where I Live

The hill people of Eastern and Middle America have begun to get into the public consciousness. The hill country runs across America, between the North and the South, taking in great chunks of Virginia, North Carolina, West Virginia, northern Georgia and Alabama, Tennessee, Kentucky and Missouri.

There have been plays, stories, magazine articles and books written about the hill people. Some of the writing has been intelligent and sensible and a lot of it has been foolish, some of it even hurtful.

There is this trick that so many writers have, of working always along broad lines. A tall lean mountain man stands at a still on a mountain side, with a rifle in his hand. He has just shot a Federal agent on the road below. Such things happen in the mountains, but not all mountain men are tall, lean and fierce, and few enough of them own rifles. It is again, as I have found in so many other levels of American life, a matter of just people. Mean ones, generous, tricky, fierce, gentle—there they are.

There still is, however, in the hill country, a way of life that is outside the tone of most America just now. The machine has not penetrated deeply into the hills. Hand weaving is still being done. Grain is still cut with a cradle. You may see oxen on the hill roads and in the fields, and when a man dies his neighbors come to his house and build his coffin in the yard before his door.

Although they call themselves Southern, the hill men are not to be confused with the men of the great coastal plains, the "crackers," so called, of the hot plains of lower Georgia, South Carolina, Florida, Alabama and Mississippi. They are alike only in that the men of the plains are also poor.

In the hills there are a good many men and women who cannot read or write, and that is confusing. There are so many smart, learned men of the richer valley towns who seem foolish enough when they come into the hills.

The hills have, however, their own fools, their beautiful women, their liars, their over-sensitive and their easily-hurt ones.

Oh, the snobbishness of men! There are prosperous towns and cities in some of the wide valleys, and in the towns and cities men live more easily than their neighbors in the hills. They grow proud and snobbish. Because their fields grow bigger corn, because they live in bigger houses, own automobiles and raise bigger cattle, they feel themselves superior.

Let them try living as the hill men must live, on the same sort of poor, often worn-out, land. Let them try to get what the poor hill men often get out of life. Last year a sculptor from New York came to live for some months in our hills and I took him for several long walks. The sculptor knew something.

We were walking on a mountain road near a mountain town and, as it was Saturday, men, women and children were coming into town for supplies. Even in the broad road they walked in single file, the man followed by his wife, the wife by the children.

"It comes from walking much on mountain trails," I explained to the sculptor.

There were mountain women and girls, some of them quite dressed up, but as is a habit of the country, many were bare-footed. The women carried shoes and stockings in their hands. They were to be put on as the women sat on a creek bank, and after they had washed their feet at the town's edge. Mountain people can't waste shoe leather. It costs too much.

The sculptor kept looking and exclaiming as we passed the women —"See how beautifully they walk." I remember one tall dark woman of thirty. But for the sculptor, I might not have noticed how firmly and beautifully her bare feet met the earth on a mountain road, or how well she carried her slender woman's body.

But I sat down this morning to write the story of the death of an old mountain man named Bill Graves. Bill died, one day last year, at the age of seventy-five. He had three wives during his long life, two of them having died of the hard work and the hard living. There had been a good many children.

He got him a new wife, a young one, when he was sixty-eight. His second wife had died two years earlier, leaving several small children on his hands.

A little mountain family—a man with his wife and daughter had come through the hills and had put up one night at his house. The daughter might have been eighteen. She was tall and dark-eyed. There often is a curious sadness in these mountain girls, a something born in them. It is like the sadness of a late fall evening when the light is fading and winds blow over the hills.

"I gotta go down this lonesome road."

Bill's new woman's father and mother were drifting through the country. We have a good many such drifters. There is a little family on a mountain farm, and the farm will no longer support it. The man has a bony horse and a wagon. He and his family become drifters, no longer attached to the soil. The man and woman who came to Bill's house were, some of the neighbors said, of the no-account sort. The man was such a fellow as Thomas Lincoln, Abe Lincoln's father. He had drifted out of the same sort of background.

The family stayed for a night with Bill and on the next day, the man and woman, with their broken wagon and the bony horse, went on their way. Bill had talked to the tall daughter during the evening before. She stayed on with him, and the next day they drove to the county seat and got married. She had four children by Bill Graves and then he died.

Bill was one of the tall, lean sort and in early life he had been a lumberjack. It was as a lumberjack, when the hill country was being timbered off, that he made the money to buy his mountain farm.

He was an impressive sort of man. None of his neighbors—at least, not the women—were surprised that the young mountain woman stayed with him and became his wife. More and more, as he had grown older, other mountain men of his mountain country had been coming to him with their problems. He was the man in his neighborhood who settled quarrels. He had got himself elected a squire and performed marriage ceremonies. With his tongue in his cheek and pen in hand, he wrote wills and agreements. It was laborious work for Bill. Two of his neighbors had got into a quarrel about a line fence but, although he was a squire, he didn't let them come into his court. He went and looked at the fence. "Put it here," he said. He had a way with men. He made his decisions stick.

Bill Graves had been a hard-drinking man all his life. Every morning when he awoke, he took a tin cupful of raw moon whiskey, and he took several more during the day. Just the same, he never got drunk. He kept his little farm in trim, and always was ready to lend a hand to others in the seasons when the farm work in the little valleys and hollows grew heavy.

There was the Widow Littlejohn, who lived on the mountain above his house. Her man died two years ahead of Bill, and in the late fall, after her man died, just when the snow began to fly, Bill drove up to her house with a load of firewood. He had cut the wood on his own land and had hauled it up the mountain side to her place. He hauled six loads, enough to keep her fires going for the winter, stopping his team in the road before her house. He threw the wood over the fence into the yard and, when she came to the door to thank him, he swore at her. He turned his team and drove away, lashing the horses and swearing.

"What the devil'd you mean, letting your man die on you—a woman ought always to die ahead of her man—that's the way to do it," he shouted.

There is some grain, mostly rye, raised in the hill country, but the hill men do not cut it with the modern self-binders. A self-binder would roll down off most of the fields. Men go into the fields with cradles to cut the grain, and when there are several mountain men working in a grain field, it is something to see. There is the long sweep of the cradles, the grain cut by the scythe and caught in the cradle. As the swing is completed, the frame of the cradler catches the bunched grain and it is laid on the ground ready for the women and children to tie into bundles. The grain cutting is something to be remembered. Often there is a group of a half-dozen men swinging across a hillside field, marching forward, the cradles swinging, the women and children following, all the men, women and children of a neighborhood gathered, the shouting and laughing, each man trying to out-march the others.

There is a jug of moon whiskey in a fence corner at the end of the field.

It is the test of the mountaineer's manhood. Can he keep up with the others? Can he lead the others across the field? Can he keep leading them, all through a long hot summer day?

The city man, that sculptor, who came to live in the hills one summer, was walking with me past Bill Graves' place on the afternoon when he died.

Bill's house was on a side road, deep in the hills.

There was the long rye field on a hillside and several mountain men, neighbors of Bill's, had come to help in the harvest. Afterwards, a doctor in town told me about Bill. He said that Bill had suffered with cancer of the stomach for two years. He hadn't let anyone know. Even his wife didn't know. There is a good deal of cancer of the stomach among mountain men. It may be the hog and hominy diet, and I dare say the raw corn whiskey doesn't help. On the day of Bill's death, the sculptor, a small blond man, walked up the road with me, and there on the sloping hillside beside the road was Bill leading a half-dozen of his neighbors across the field. We stopped and looked. I, myself, am far from a big man, and I'm a town man. What we saw in the field gripped the sculptor. There was a rail fence separating the road from the field, and he went and put his hands on the top rail, and stared.

"Look," he cried. The mountain men were swinging across the field, the sweat pouring from their faces. "Look at the rhythm of it.

"It's a dance," he cried. It was a sweltering hot day. Bill Graves was swearing at the men, taunting them as he led the march across the field and they were laughing at him. He saw us standing in the road and dropping his cradle ran down to us. He must have been full of corn whiskey—had been drinking to keep himself going.

"You! You fellows," he cried to us. "I've been waiting for this.

"You city and town fellows coming in here," he shouted. "I'm going to make you come up here into this field." He stood laughing. "I want to see what you town fellows can do with a cradle."

He had reached the fence and had put his hand on the top rail ready to vault over when something happened. Although Bill had been blustering and swearing, the little sculptor was not alarmed. He also laughed. And then suddenly the laughing died on his lips.

It was late in the afternoon. All day long Bill Graves, now seventy-five, had been leading the others in the grain field. He had kept himself going by drinking quantities of the moon whiskey. The laughing threat he threw at us was the end of him. As he stood by the fence, in the bright late afternoon sunlight, his hand on the top rail, both the sculptor and I saw the quiver that ran through his body. He died as he stood but he died laughing at us.

"I am going to get you," he cried and laughed; and then he turned and called to his young wife who had been at work among the women.

"Come here, Hallie," he called to her and she came, tall and bare-footed, down the hillside through the grain stubbles. She was very like that other woman the sculptor and I had seen in the road at the edge of the mountain town. The woman, Hallie, Bill Graves' young girl wife, came down to him as he stood by the fence, his hands behind him gripping the fence rail.

"It's come out all wrong, Hallie," he said, speaking quietly to her. "A woman should always die before her man, but I was too old when you got me."

"I'm going, I'm going to die on you," he said.

He said the words and slumped to the ground, and all the men, women and children in the field came running toward us. But Hallie, Bill's wife, didn't run.

In the road some twenty yards beyond where I stood with the sculptor from the city, there was a little bridge that crossed a stream. And while Bill's neighbors, who had been helping him in his rye field, were picking him up and carrying what was left of him over the fence and along the road toward his house, the women and children following with frightened faces, the city sculptor and I both turned and looked at Bill's Hallie.

She had jumped lightly over the fence and had walked to the bridge. She sat on the bridge and turned her back to us. She was a young but a proud woman. Afterwards the sculptor told me he would never forget her figure as she sat on the low bridge, her feet in the water of a mountain stream.

Although Bill Graves was an old man when he got his Hallie, he had done what a good many younger men never succeeded in doing with their women. He had really got her. She wanted to be alone in the first storm of her grief, and so the city sculptor and I hurried away past the house and around a turn in the road and off into the hills.

Winchester, Virginia, taken and retaken seventy-two times during the Civil War. I hadn't known that. I got the information out of a motorist guide map. I knew there had been a lot of scrapping up that valley.

Still I am like a man in a strange house. I keep finding new rooms and hallways. I walk out on little balconies and see the hills, the rivers and the plains. Many people have lived in this house. It is a large, old house. It is Virginia.

And not only Winchester. There is Manassas, Bull Run, Chancellorsville, Fredericksburg, The Wilderness, Spotsylvania, Cold Harbor, Petersburg, Appomattox, Richmond itself.

The long valleys and the mountains, the Piedmont section of Virginia, Tidewater Virginia, the Southwest.

The Southwest is over beyond the mountain. For a long time it was half forgotten by the older, more stable, more aristocratic Virginia. The people out here, where I am staying, do not really belong to the older, the aristocratic Virginia. The adventurous ones came on out here, on their way west to open up Tennessee and Kentucky, the George Rogers Clarks and Daniel Boones, that sort of fellow. Aristocrats are rarely adventurers. They are aristocrats. The fellows who came out must have been more of my own sort. I am an adventurer too. I do not know what blood runs in me. It may be the blood of kings . . . or peasants. When I have the courage to do it I try to adventure into places, into thoughts and feelings. The people of my adopted section of Virginia, the old Virginians who came out into this fine sweet western hill country to live, and were joined out here by solid Germans from Pennsylvania, and incidentally by the Lincolns. The stock that produced Abraham did not like the older colonial Virginians much in the earlier day. They felt themselves neglected, left out in the cold. They still feel that at times. Once they tried to make a state of their own—the State of Franklin, they wanted to call it. It did not come off.

Nancy Hanks' people, they say, came from just over the mountains from where I sit writing. Nancy was no aristocrat. I have seen many a Nancy Hanks in this Southwest Virginia hill country—the Blue Ridge, bluegrass country. There are many hard-bodied, easily excited, hard-working hill women here, some of them with a strange haunting loveliness of person shining through their hardness. They are getting them into the factories now. Abraham Lincoln attributed all of his own finer qualities to his mother. There is a special kind of aristocracy in hill people too.

Winchester, Manassas, Chancellorsville, Fredericksburg.

James Madison, George Washington, Thomas Jefferson, James Monroe—

Stonewall Jackson, Longstreet, Robert E. Lee.

Grant, Meade, Joe Hooker.

J. E. B. Stuart, Hancock, Early.

Sheridan.

No American of any generation could be at all alive and not be excited by these names of men and places. What men have been produced down here in Virginia, what men have come here, have fought here, have left their marks and their memories down here!

Virginia is a state with a past. There was a civilization born down here, made down here. I think Thomas Jefferson came about as near, perhaps a lot nearer than any other one man, even Washington, to making a civilization. In a sense he made the old Virginia, set it going, gave it tone and purpose. He made the University of Virginia, and Monticello and the laws and the feel of it. What Jefferson made was what Adams and others of his day, up in New England, were trying to make—that is to say a civilization on which strong individuals could leave their imprint. But Jefferson, it has always seemed to me, had a bigger, a clearer, a more complex conception than the New Englander Adams did, knew more, had felt more, was of greater stature. Adams and Jefferson both failed. Something else came into being, something they would both have fought and instinctively hated —but I will not go into that now.

The Civil War came. It was the great American War. It had to come. There was never any other war like it on our American soil and never again will be such another. It came out of the groping of men after something. I am quite sure all of the historians have missed something of the inner meaning of the story. It is perhaps brash of me to say that but I feel it. It may just be that America had promised men too much, that it always promised men too much.

There is a growing feeling among some men that America is too large, that it is too physically vast, that the whole notion of a unified America is an impossible dream.

A war full of drama, of one kind of civilization, one culture, fighting another. I myself was born and grew to manhood in the Middle West. I think the Middle West and Virginia fought out, between them, the Civil War, the great war.

New England made it and the Far South and South Carolina made it, and Virginia and the Middle West fought it. Neither wanted it. They did not understand it, or each other.

The abolitionists seemed to want it and the fire-eating Southerners from down in the cotton country seemed to want it.

The Virginians were not Southerners, never were. They were Virginians. There was a kind of integrity, a sense of wholeness growing up inside the state.

And incidentally the Middle Westerners were not abolitionists. They were Middle Westerners.

There was an empire building in the Middle West before the Civil War. There is one building there now. The Middle West fought for the Mississippi River. It fought for its place in the sun. The Middle West was, and is, the German Empire of this American Europe.

But Virginia was not England, nor France, nor Italy. It was Virginia.

And why did Virginia fight? It had to be dragged in, but once in, how it did fight! All the rest of the South quit, was licked, long before it quit.

It never did quit, was never licked. Virginia was starved out of the Civil War. Battles never did it. Virginia won the battles.

When Virginia, with Robert E. Lee at its head, had to quit at Appomattox, having no more food, having no more powder and shot, most of the rest of the South had already leaked out of the struggle. Lee was surrounded largely by Virginians that day. It was Virginia that marched out, laid down its guns, and went home horseback on the horses Grant let it keep. The rest of the South was already far on its way home by that time.

How can I help wondering how much of the old Virginia is left here? I have an odd feeling about it.

I myself came into Virginia from the South. I alighted in the southwest corner of the state and felt at home there.

Other Virginians, from the Tidewater and from the Piedmont, kept coming down. I dined with some of them, talked with others.

They were politicians out of old Virginia, come down here to get votes; university men, newspaper editors.

It made no difference to me that some of them were politicians. I remembered that Thomas Jefferson was himself a master politician.

I sought something in them—out of my own Middle-Western boyhood and Middle-Western impression, am still seeking it. With me it was like this.

They made a living stream of talk, centered about Virginia. It stirred me, stayed with me.

I read books, every book I could lay my hands on. Even as a boy I said, "Some day I may write my own history of the Civil War."

I have never in any way attempted it yet. "It is my job," I used to say to myself. "I am the man for it."

It seemed to me then that I could feel the call of the thing in my blood. Once I spoke to a neighbor of the project when I was a small boy. We were walking along a street. He was an Irishman, a storekeeper of the town. He also had been a soldier. He patted me on the head.

"You are both Southern and Northern," he said. "I respect the women of both the North and the South."

Why he threw that last in I don't know. I am quite sure my father, had I consulted him, would have felt me capable of any gigantic project, being his son.

I think I had the notion, vaguely then, that if I ever wrote my book, if I ever got leisure and money and stability enough to work on it steadily, digest the matter, visit places—perhaps for years—I would center my story about Virginia.

I would try to sense the cultural struggle that must have gone on between New England and the Middle West.

Then I would try to catch the difference between Virginia and the rest of the South.

Oh, the admiration of my own Middle-Western—may I call them my spiritual fathers? for Robert E. Lee, J. E. B. Stuart, Stonewall Jackson. It was not sentimentality in them. They were not slobbering over Lee and Jackson, as is so much the fashion now.

My father was a Jeffersonian. He was deeply that. His talk and the talk of his friends egged me on.

It comes back to me, sweeps over me again, every time I go out of my Southwest Virginia and into the old Virginia.

My heart hungers for an understanding I haven't got yet.

It may be Virginia has lost what I seek. It may have gone quite modern. I go into older Virginia now, in my car, traveling from town to town, on trains, seeing the Valley of Virginia, seeing Piedmont.

Seeing the physical University of Virginia, seeing Monticello, seeing statues of Lee, of Jackson, of J. E. B. Stuart.

I do this actually seeing these men sometimes. I sleep and dream. Robert E. Lee comes into my room. Jackson comes, Longstreet, Grant, Sheridan.

These men come into my bedroom, in dreams sometimes and talk of the war, of what got them into it, how they felt, what they think they meant by it.

They come in there, into my bedroom, talking and I know their voices.

Do I know their minds? Do I know yet what the American Civil War, the Great War, was about?

Why do I not write my own Civil War? Is it because I am too lazy, that I haven't money and leisure enough?

Or is it because I do not understand enough? Have I really come to Virginia seeking that understanding?

Will I ever attempt to write my book, and if I do write it, will I call it in the end *The Civil War*—or will I call it simply *Virginia?*

At least, every year I stay here it seems to me I am a little nearer the thing, although it may well turn out that I never put pen to paper.

This, too, of which I am going to speak is a reason why I live where I live.

The night can never be quite gorgeous, to its full possibilities, without a woman and I cannot understand those men who do not want marriage or the men and women who, being married, do not sleep together.

There are the nights that come when you are excessively alive. Now, for this one night, you do not want or need the ultimate intimacy. There is the woman beside you asleep. How quietly and softly she breathes. How excessively alive you are. Now the mind and the fancy both race. You seem to feel and hear, with her breathing, the breathing of the earth under your house, breathing of trees. There is a river just down a short hill from the house. It also breathes softly.

Now the moon is breathing, the stars breathing.

Woman. Woman. How nice to run the hand softly down over your hips, along your legs.

You get out of bed and light a candle. An electric light or lamp would make too much light. You do not want to awaken her.

What you want now is a new way of entering in. You are the male. Now she has become for you all life outside self, become quiet and very beautiful.

I remember once climbing a little hill, above a dark and dense pine forest. It was evening and the light was soft. I threw myself down on the grass. There was a soft gray sky and a new life, a new world was born. The pine forests seemed to hang suspended, downward. Airplane drivers who do stunts, loop the loop, etc., must see the world so.

The hair of the woman in bed is like the tops of dark pine trees in a soft evening light. She has got her head into an uncomfortable position and you go and change it.

Very gently now.

Very, very gently.

You do not want to disturb her dreams. You want to enter in a new way, thrust your dreams into her dreams.

Dreams thrust into skies, rivers, mountains, into Mother Earth.

Woman, you are earth beautiful.

Now I am a farmer thrusting down seed. Source of life is in you, woman.

The dream passes. The night stays. Sometimes terror comes. You have blown out the candle and crept back into bed. In her sleep she draws close to you. There is now a small woman's hand on your hips. How softly touching, softly drawing dreams into self, taking night terror away.

What fools are men who do not search and search until they find a woman with whom they may lie thus.

Once, I wrote a letter about her country and mine to a woman I loved and revered, and whose daughter I am married to as I write this book. She gave me back the letter. Here it is.

Dear Other Mother . . .

I am going to send some photographs: Dreiser, O'Neill, van Vechten and Nathan. Please put them in my little cubby-hole. They are for my house.

It was quite hot in the sleeper and Eleanor slept a little restlessly but was apparently quite O.K. this morning.

I didn't sleep much, so enjoyed lying near her and was thinking, all night, of the book I want to write now. If I wasn't very nice at home—and I've half a notion I wasn't—it was, at least partly, because, all of the time while there, I was reaching for something—a kind of tone, the middle chord of a book, what you will.

I would so like to write, before I die, one joyous book, not at all sentimentally joyous but having in it a deeper joy—such joy as I got that day when we all went to Bob's to dine on birds. I think it was just the hill before his little house.

Later on that same day I got it again when I went to walk with Eleanor by the river below Henry Copenhaver's house. There was such color in the river that day. You do have to fight hard to get a bit of this curiously elusive joy, just why, in our civilization, I don't know. Do you suppose it is because of money, and that is why Eleanor and I have to be revolutionists? These acres, down there in the valleys, among the Virginia hills . . . where in the world can be found more beautifully sensuous hills? . . . food being raised for people to eat, wheat waving in summer winds, the curious majesty of growing corn. How does it happen that money can buy or sell such acres?

Surely, Mother, there is a deeper lesson God wants us to know. I deny all who deny God . . . I insist on his acceptance of my own acceptance.

Surely we, in America, are perverse children. That is what we are—quite hopelessly children. I would so like to say it—not as an economist . . . one of your pet scientists, Mother—but as an artist should say it. I suppose I should be very happy if I can get down to a few words, a line now and then, but I am certainly impatient. If I do write the book I will dedicate it to you. I think I shall call it

OTHER MOTHER

meaning more than you, of course, as you will understand—in the sense, I suppose, that a field, a river, a hill, a town, can be my mother.

4. The Death of Lawrence

I was asked to write of the little book, *Assorted Essays* by D. H. Lawrence, published after his death, but I couldn't write of the man so. I couldn't center on one book.

The book was called *Assorted Essays,* an absurd title really for those little flashes of a man's mind, brilliant, clear little flashes of the mind of a man at work.

But why say just mind? D. H. Lawrence never wrote just with his mind. The whole sensitive male body of the man must have tingled as he wrote. You feel man flesh in his words, nerves alive, the man smelling, tasting, seeing. He must have written often with a rush.

He had a small, not-too-strong man's body.

What life there was in it! It was male life fighting for an old thing maleness once meant.

It was sweet life, too. Women should hate to see this man die. D. H. Lawrence was one of the few clean males of literature. He was a lover. He was male.

Someone told me one day that he was dead.

"What?"

"Yes, he died."

"Why, I did not think he was ready to die yet."

But you can never tell when Death will slip up suddenly on a man. He had been diseased, they say, a long time—a persistent physical disease eating away at him.

Himself burning, burning, a bright light in a murky time.

I think of other English writers of his day, of our day. Where are they? What one of them ever gave as this man did?

They are such a respectable lot . . . National Liberal Club . . . something of that sort, wanting to be English gentlemen.

What has being an artist to do with being a gentleman? Lawrence knew so much, felt so much. He must have been hurt and hurt and hurt. What did he care about being an English gentleman? Sir D. H. Lawrence. Impossible, thank God.

Now he's dead. People should begin to read him now. No one need be jealous of the man, no need now to call him dirty, ban him because he loved life so vitally that he was always wanting to touch it, bite it, put his hands on it.

Oh, thou dry-neck, here was a living man for you. Be ashamed before the life in him.

This proseman will in the end turn out to have been the most important poet of our day. Young men should read him. Begin with *Assorted Essays* if you haven't begun. Read down through him.

They'll tell you *Sons and Lovers* was his best book. Don't believe it. He wrote that long ago and the man became more and more vital until he died.

You young men . . . you want to know about the machine age . . . what it is doing to men . . . the way out. Here is a man who found a way out. He lived.

He returned to flesh . . . to living men and women, taking them close, loving, feeling with them. He put money in the right place, too. What fine contempt in him.

Oh, thou dry-neck, here was a man. Here was a man not afraid to remain loose, fluid, alive—to the last. It couldn't have been more than two or three years before he died that he wrote *Lady Chatterley's Lover*. What a clean fine book, making everything about you clean and nice as you read.

Making people clean and nice again, as Whitman at his best did, making them again feel to you as fields and trees feel.

A breath-taking piece of work. It takes common, formerly vulgar words, thoughts and feelings of everyday men and makes them beautiful. It is far ahead of Joyce's *Ulysses,* hailed as such a revolutionary masterpiece. Joyce's great work was after all centered upon death. Its aim was to make common things of life more ugly—he was trying to get out beyond desire—death.

Lawrence on the other hand went toward life always. He is the perfect antidote for the Lesbianism and homosexuality of our day. He was male, a lover. His *Lady Chatterley's Lover* should be read by every young man and woman. However, it may take a generation or two before the book can be had by people of small means. During our day it will remain a banned book only the rich can own.

You'll get the same feeling of cleanness from *Assorted Essays*—unless you also are, alas, dry-neck, in which case all of Lawrence will be just stench to you—

As Whitman has become to the dry-necks.

As are cattle in fields, women hungering for physical love and children, men puzzled and defeated, dogs, little chicks coming out of egg shells . . . all the strange forgotten loveliness of life going on . . . in spite of dry-necks . . . all the eternal wonder of Now.

I cannot write very steadily of D. H. Lawrence dead. I never knew the man personally, but his death, the news of it coming to me, was like a light going out at night in a cold strange house. It left me standing against a wall in the house, feeling along the wall for the door, wanting to get out into the night and under the stars.

A country doctor told me of Lawrence's death. He is a man who had a country practice in the hills of Tennessee, and being a lonely man he reads a lot of books.

I had gone to see this man, this country doctor, and was spending a week with him.

We drove about the country and into the hills.

On the day when he told me of Lawrence's death we had got out of his car to take a walk in a wood.

The sun was shining. There was a cold spring wind blowing.

The leaves were just starting to unfold on some of the trees. There were little red swelling bunches. As you stood looking at them the little red bunches of swelling, straining leaves, wanting to unfold, were like flesh.

They were like sweet flesh, such as the flesh of people might be, sweet flesh conscious of its own sweetness.

The doctor took a city newspaper and had read it that morning while I idled in bed. In the wood, as we walked along a path, he stopped suddenly by a tree.

He made a quick motion about the trunk of the tree with his hand. The doctor has nice hands. They are all alive. He had grabbed at something.

Life, eh?

He had caught a little gray tree lizard and held it in his hand, open before me. There in the palm of his hand the little gray creature sat . . . intensely alive. Its little throat throbbed and all its tiny body was aquiver.

How nice the gray-greenish throbbing body of the lizard against the man's flesh of the doctor's hand, a hand that had released many mountain babies into the world, that had for years been touching people, healing people.

The doctor held the tiny thing in his hand so and then, stooping down, released it in the path.

It ran quickly away, gray-green blending against the gray-green dead leaves under the tree.

"D. H. Lawrence is dead," the doctor said.

"What? I did not think he was ready to die yet."

"You can't tell about death," the doctor said . . . "Death has its own way with men."

As life has, too.

The *Assorted Essays* are quickly read. They are like little jewels, held in the hand as the doctor held the lizard, light playing on them. They are like a covey of quail at the edge of a field, little-feathered, trembling bundles of life, lying close there in the dry grass, ready to take wing and be off.

They come out of the workshop of a man . . . not a gentleman . . . an artist really . . . one of the few prose artists of our time.

There are always little nice things happening in relation to one for whom you have love.

I have felt love for D. H. Lawrence since the first sentence of his I ever read.

And so I was asked to write a review of this book of his, published after his death.

Review indeed! Who am I to write reviews?

A man I know, a critic, had already written me a letter about the dead Lawrence. It was a kind of questionnaire.

"Do you think so and so?"

A row of little questions.

"I want to get him placed in relation to the whole body of English writing."

"You do, eh?

"Three strikes. You're out."

I had thrown that critic's letter in the fire, where it deserved to be.

The book *Assorted Essays* came to me in the mail as I was going trout fishing with a man with a big mustache and big hands that can handle a trout rod with infinite delicacy.

I had got the book out of the post office.

"You read a lot, eh?" the woods boss said, seeing me put it in the door pocket of the car.

Alas, not much.

That country doctor, we both knew, would be reading ten times more books in a year.

But I read this book.

I had clambered down over rocks to a pool. I cast three times and got a trout.

The book was in my pocket and so I thought, "I'll read it here."

Such books are good to read by trout streams in the hills, in pine forests, in the presence of a woman loved. . . .

In the presence of corn fields, perhaps.

The little book of essays stood up to it, was beautiful under that hard test.

Oh, thou dry-neck!

I had read some of the living little essays down there on a rock at the pool's edge and the rest in a road above, where I am now. I can hear the roar of water tumbling over rocks as I write.

I am out of paper. I did not carry much in my pocket.

In clambering up the rocks to the road I have hurt my hand. It bleeds. There is a persistent little bleeding.

It has besmeared with my own blood some of the pages on which I write these words of Lawrence dead, to bleed no more.

Little red blotches of my blood covering the sheets on which I try to write of D. H. Lawrence, dead.

Spoiling the sheets.

Blood spoiling clean white sheets of paper.

Not quite. Blood is nice on white sheets on which a man speaks, even falteringly, of a man's man like D. H. Lawrence.

5. I Become a Protester

At Danville, Virginia, I got a picture of the futility of what might be called goodness. There was a Mr. Fitzgerald there, who is at the head of the Dan River Cotton Mills. There were two mills on strike there, the Dan River and the Riverside. Mr. Fitzgerald was the controlling man at the mills and of the town. No one doubts much that he was a good man with good intentions.

The cotton mills have been there a long time. The modern industrial town of Danville has really been made by them, but Danville is itself an old town. It was once, for a brief passing moment, the capital of the Southern Confederacy. Mr. Davis, with his Cabinet, fled to Danville when Grant took Richmond. There must still have been some hope, a feverish kind of uncertain hope. "We may win yet. Something may happen," the men there must have been saying to themselves, whistling in the dark to keep up courage, like the strikers when I was there.

I went down to Danville from Richmond, driving down in the rain, and at Richmond I had told several men where I was going. They all said the same thing. "Why do these men strike now? There are so many men out of work everywhere. It will be too easy to whip them now."

We went puddling through the rain and drove down past one of the mills. There were pickets scattered about. They had built up temporary shelters. One group had got an old piece of canvas, such as farmers use to cover haystacks, and had propped it up on sticks. Two men and a girl were huddled in under there and as we passed slowly the girl put out her head. We waved our hands and she grinned, a girlish grin. "Hello," we called and "Hot stuff," she replied. There was that American thing. These youngsters. They get you by the throat. I wasn't in the late war myself, but I get a picture, gathered from young fellows, friends of mine coming back, a picture of just such young Americans as you will find there on strike, at the cotton mills at Danville. A kind of gaiety going on, in spite of hell. To the average man in the trenches—I mean the common soldier, let him be English, American, German, French, what not—I dare say there wasn't much thought of winning or losing the war. They must have been quite willing to let the heavy thinkers, the Wilsons, Clemenceaus, the Lloyd Georges, figure out the purposes of the war and all that. What I fancy about them is that they had consciousness only of the thing in front of them. "It's no use grouching," they must have said to themselves, "I may be dead tomorrow. But there are these others here, Jim and Bud and Joe and Frank. If I can get a grin out of one of them it will help just that much."

There is always this feeling when you (being a man like myself . . . a middle-class man really, although you are a writer and do not buy or sell anything) come into a hall where there are a lot of workers, strikers congregated. They cheer.

There they are, sitting or standing in the room. It is always such a gloomy room, somewhere on a side street. The men and women, the strikers, packed in there. At Danville they had got a hall that had been used by the Ku Klux Klan and in a corner, propped against a wall, there was a huge cross, all arranged like the lights you see put up over movie theaters, wired to make a fiery cross. They propped it against a wall in a corner and the people crowded in, some standing, as there were not seats enough. We went in.

I had been in town some three or four hours. I had met a lot of newspaper men . . . bright fellows . . . talk of the strike and of the town. They took me out of town to a country estate, of Laurence Stallings, who collaborated on *What Price Glory?* He had just had his tonsils cut out and we sat and looked at each other. "So that's you?" "Yes." "That's you, eh?"

It would have been much better if the newspaper men had not taken me out there. A man who has just had his tonsils out doesn't want to see a fellow writer. Seeing fellow writers isn't such great shucks anyway, any time. We know each other too well. It would have been better if I had gone down there in the rain to the picket lines, stood around in the little temporary shelters, looking out at the great stone mills. I might have got more a sense of something I was after down there. I was sore at the people who were managing the strike that they had not arranged it in that way.

We did get to the hall finally.

You come into such a place. Let us say, just to make the point, that they have been told something about you. One of the amazingly charming things about Americans, and in particular about American workers, is a kind of humility in them that makes you ashamed. Why, they believe in you. They believe you can do something to help them. In Danville they believe in Mr. Fitzgerald. You ask one of the strikers down there, "What about Mr. Fitzgerald?" "Oh, he's all right. He's a good man," he'll say. These workers, mill hands, men and women, are like poets really. They believe it will happen. They think it may happen at any time, any minute.

What do they believe?

They believe in people.

It may be because they are poor. They believe that in some queer way, some man having come along, let's say some fellow like myself, he having made a speech . . . something of that sort . . . they believe all will change.

I dare say they have a sense of something. At Danville I was told something about cotton mills. They came in there a long time ago and the mills have been well managed. Let us say there was, originally, a million dollars invested. The mills have prospered and there have been big dividends made, stock distributed. Let's say the valuation has gone up to fifteen millions. There have been big salaries paid, too, a president getting seventy-five thousand a year and other officials as high as fifty thousand. What a lot of money really. Sometimes it seems to a man like myself that working people, who haven't any money and never expect to have any, do not really believe that our American civilization is a money civilization. They believe vaguely that there is just some kind of misunderstanding, and the queer part of it all is that they are right.

At any rate, at Danville, Mr. Fitzgerald and his fellows on their side have tried, from their point of view, to be decent. They own the houses in which the workers live and the strikers have been out for two months now. They might have thrown the strikers out into the streets but they haven't. A few have been thrown out recently.

At Danville the workers were striking simply for the right to organize. That is the main, the central idea. They have been told over and over how it is. "Look here," the labor leaders say to them, "capital is organized against you, all modern life is organized. No one of you has much chance, standing alone."

They know that is true. Modern people who so seldom go into any of our great American mills should go in oftener. The mills are terrifically well organized. They overpower you with the organization that has been built up.

You know well enough that, as an individual, a worker, you can't stand up against that. You are such a tiny little thing, such a minute cog in the great machine. "Stand together," the labor leaders say. "Let us stand together," the workers repeat.

There is so much confusion. You talk to almost any employer of labor about the right to organize. "How can you deny the right?" you ask.

"I can't. I don't," he replies.

He doesn't, either; that's the joke of it. "Why, I'll organize them myself," he says. "I'll let them have meetings. They can even make suggestions to me. All I want to do is to run the thing. I know more about running things than these fellows do."

The workers agree to that, but it doesn't work out. They get restless. What I myself fancy is that the average worker, having worked for one man for a long time as have so many of these people at Danville, Virginia, has a vague notion that if some fellow would come along and say just the right thing everything would clear up.

They are really modest people—these workers. "I can't talk myself," they say. They look about, hoping to find someone to do their talking for them. If someone would just get to the boss, say just the right thing to him. "I'm sure he is a good man," they say. "He doesn't understand how we feel."

So it goes on. The workers in such a mill go on strike. I said a moment ago that more people should go into modern factories but, when it comes to that, more people should go to strike meetings, too.

There is a way in which people, workers, when they go on strike, even when they are pretty sure to lose, get something, and it should be borne in mind that there isn't much these people get out of life. Labor hours are long. Life is a grind for them. Youth doesn't last long in a mill.

It is like this—modern men and women, modern workers in the modern big mills, when there is no strike on, when things are just running on as usual, get very little feeling of each other. They are in the presence always, all days, every day, of a big, tightly organized thing. It makes them feel small. They lose the sense of each other.

Then a strike comes and, for a time at least, they get a rather fine feeling of each other. A man or woman, a worker, in ordinary times, is just a man or woman, but in a hall, while a strike is going on, he is, at the moment at least, a part of something like an army. He is, for a time at least, as big as the mills. He gets sharply the sense of others. Something grows warm in him. Hands reach out. Any American who has really been in at a strike while it is going on, before it wears out, while the spirit of it is at fever heat, will have an experience he won't forget.

He has perhaps been told by the newspapers that these people are dangerous. Why, they are people in love with each other, for the moment anyway. The feeling of isolation, so universal nowadays in our modern industrialized America, is gone. These people want only to stand shoulder to shoulder. They want to keep this feeling for each other. In a case such as that at Danville, they wouldn't mind really having the boss belong to their union, his running it, if they could feel he was one of themselves.

They can't feel that. Can you blame them? Should Mr. Fitzgerald expect that? Can any man, running a factory, really feel that a company union is a real union?

You come into such a place, an outsider. You are to make a speech. How futile really. What can you say?

You can say you hope they will win.

What?

Why, just the right to go on being as they are at that moment, all one, organized, feeling close to each other. You feel the struggle of all men against the control of all life by the machine.

They are men and women and, while I am on this matter, I would like to say something for the men and women who run these strikes. It is a heart-breaking job. You are always going about to little halls, seeing people such as I saw at Danville, people struggling for some right to live. You feel them almost inevitably doomed to defeat just now. It gets you.

There they are. They crowd into the little halls. They cheer you when you come in. Faces peer up at you. There is hope, love, expectation in the eyes of the people. At Danville, in the front row, there was a young fellow with his girl. He reached over stealthily and took her hand. Old men, heads of families, were there, and tired old women workers. A thousand eyes looking up at you. A kind of love grips you at the throat, but how utterly futile you feel, how ashamed. They so believe in you, or in someone like you, some talker, some writer, some leader, some poet who is to come and make what they want understood to their boss, to all bosses.

Well, you do nothing. You say a few words. You go away. You go back to your hotel. Some man comes in and offers you a drink. It is a pretty heart-breaking matter—this situation of most industrial workers in America.

They had got me again. There was another protest to be made. The bonus soldiers had marched on Washington and were driven out by guns and gas. When I was asked to go with other writers to protest to President Hoover I went.

I thought it was all a sad mistake, that had the president had the courage and more understanding of the everyday man he would have gone to the bonus soldiers and spoken directly to them. It seemed shameful to me to drive them away with guns and gas.

I was told that there would be a crowd of writers going down from New York. We were to meet at the Pennsylvania Station.

"There will be newspaper men and photographers."

When I got to the station there were but three of us, Waldo Frank, Elliot Cohn, and myself.

"However I'll stick it out," I thought.

Had notice been sent to the President? Had he been asked if he would see us?

Yes, a telegram had been sent and a reply received. He would not see us.

"But then, why go?"

It was for the sake of publicity, that was it. Our going would call attention again to the injustice done to the bonus soldiers.

I had my doubts. I had been given to understand that reporters would crowd about us at the railroad station in New York, that we would be interviewed and photographed. A man gets himself worked up on such occasions. He thinks of snappy things to say. He begins to feel that what he has to say is of importance to the nation.

But there were no reporters in sight, no photographers. We got on the train. We were joined in Philadelphia by a Negro writer.

So there we were. We got to Washington and went to the President's office. There were newspaper men and others sitting about.

There we were, we four American writers, in that place to make our protest. It was, we were told, the President's birthday. Newspaper men, who were evidently not fond of Mr. Hoover, kept coming to whisper to us. They said he was getting birthday presents.

We were in a long room with chairs down each side and, at the end, a desk back of which sat a gray-haired dignified-looking man.

On the train we had selected Waldo as our spokesman. He seemed to be willing. We others were all a little shy. It may have been an old feeling, come down from childhood.

"Well, the President."

I am sure I would have stammered. He would have seemed so high up there.

We were kept waiting in the room. An hour, perhaps two hours passed. Waldo kept going to the gray-haired man at the desk. The President would not see him but we would presently be seen by one of his secretaries.

I had my own reason for being embarrassed. Once before I had gone to see Mr. Hoover. That was when he was in Mr. Coolidge's cabinet.

I had been sent there by one of the popular magazines. All had been arranged. I was to be well paid.

"Go to the office of the Secretary of Commerce. You will receive then a wire telling you what questions to ask."

I had gone.

"All right," I had thought. I had never talked to a man who was likely to become President.

"It will, at any rate, be an experience," I thought.

I had gone to Washington on that occasion and had received my instructions.

"So you sat in President Harding's Cabinet. You sat cheek by jowl with Fall of New Mexico.

"Do you mean to tell me you did not know that there was stealing going on?"

There were a dozen such questions and I could not ask them. I had however been escorted into Mr. Hoover's office. There had been, at that time, great floods in the valley of the Mississippi and he had been sent down there. "There are these questions I am instructed to ask you but I do not ask. The questions are too impertinent. I cannot ask them."

Mr. Hoover seemed to be pleased. "We will talk then of the Mississippi River," he said.

I said that would be nice.

And so we did talk and I thought him a little too cocksure about the river. He said that the control of the Mississippi was all very simple, but when I had lived in New Orleans I had talked to many river men, had traveled up and down the river with them.

I thought Mr. Hoover a shy and rather sensitive man. We did not talk long. I thought him the soul of respectability. I did not write the piece for the magazine. I told them I couldn't ask the questions they had sent me.

So that time I was free, for the day, there in Washington. I went about the city. I visited the Freer Galleries.

I wrote a piece about my day that was later published. It was republished in several large newspapers and in the London *Times.* In the Freer Galleries I had seen the Whistlers collected by the rich man Mr. Freer and I saw also some old Chinese paintings.

There was one that had particularly taken my eye. It was a painting of a Chinese emperor walking in the evening in a garden with his concubines and in the piece I wrote I tried to assure people that if Mr. Hoover were elected President he would never walk in the evening in the garden of the White House with his concubines.

I was remembering that on this other occasion as I sat waiting with the others in the President's office, Mr. Hoover was President now. I had laughed at him for taking the Mississippi River so lightly. I had made that crack about his solid respectability. If by chance he did see us I would be embarrassed.

However, he did not see us. We were seen finally by one of his secretaries. He lectured us. He said we had no business there, bothering the President. He said, "I do not speak to you for the President nor as the President's secretary but as a fellow craftsman," but what he meant by that I did not know.

"I wonder if he also writes books," I was thinking. I was wondering if a man could do that and be also the secretary to a President.

We were there in the office of the secretary. We were not asked to sit. We had filed in and stood with our backs against a wall. When we had come in, the President's secretary had not, for what seemed a long time, paid any attention to us. He sat writing by a desk. He sat there writing.

And then, at last, after what seemed to me at least a half hour, he arose and delivered his lecture.

I was embarrassed. I wanted to leave.

"We are getting nowhere," I thought.

However Waldo had something to say. He began to say that we were there as representatives of the writers and artists of America but I did not think that was true. He was suggesting that we exerted a wide influence on the public mind and I did not believe that we did. I thought it made no difference who we were.

"If we had been four laboring men or clerks in stores it would have been the same," I thought.

An injustice had been done.

"Any American should have the right to come here and protest an injustice," I thought.

We were, at that time, in the midst of the depression. Mr. Hoover had come into his Presidency during the Coolidge boom days and then had come the crash. I was a little sorry for the man. I was remembering that other time when I had come to interview him and the impression of a rather sensitive and puzzled man I had carried away.

So I went, after the attempt to protest about the wrong done the bonus marchers, to a hotel. I had said good-by to the other writers. They were taking a train back to New York. I went to Norfolk and wrote a letter to Mr. Hoover, an open letter that was later published in the *Nation*.

Norfolk, Virginia, August 11

Mr. Herbert Hoover
President of the United States
Washington, D. C.

DEAR MR. PRESIDENT:

I am an ex-soldier, an ex-laboring man, a native American, now a professional writer. Yesterday I came to Washington with a group of writers to protest the treatment given the bonus army in Washington. Coming to a President of my country to voice such a protest isn't a thing I like to do. With me it is like this: I am intensely interested in the lives of the common everyday people, laborers, mill hands, soldiers, stenographers, or whatever they may be. It may be because I, myself, come out of the laboring class. I was born in a poor family, I am still poor. I understand that you also were once poor.

Being a writer I am inclined to lead a quiet life, going about and peering into the corners of life. It happens that for the last four or five years I have spent most of my time in a small car going about to factory towns in America, going into the homes of poor farmers, into the houses of workers in mill villages. I haven't been doing any kind of propaganda. I have been looking, watching, finding out what I could about American life.

I came yesterday to Washington to speak to you, came as a delegate from a group of American writers and intellectuals. I did not want to come. I had no desire to make you uncomfortable. It was your birthday. You were receiving friends. You were preparing your speech of acceptance of renomination as President. Political advisers were, I dare say, flocking about. That is your life—perhaps it has to be your life. I am not criticizing it. I came with the other writers because I was myself uncomfortable.

Mr. President, I've been seeing at first hand the condition of men out of work in America. I have been walking about with them, talking with them, sitting with them. To me, although they are men and women out of work, they remain fellow-Americans. I have been seeing things with my own eyes: men who are heads of families creeping through streets of American cities eating from garbage cans; men turned out of houses and sleeping week after week on park benches, on the ground in parks, in the mud under bridges. The great majority of these men are eager enough to work. Our streets are filled with beggars, with men new to the art of begging.

I came to you with the other writers because I was ashamed not to come. When men are trying to assert their rights to live decently in America, trying to organize to assert more effectually their human rights—when these men are brutally put down by police or soldiers—bear in mind I have seen these things with my own eyes—when that happens something within me hurts and bleeds.

What I am trying to say to you is that men like me do not want to be radicals. I am, myself, a story teller. I would like to give all my time and thought and energy to story telling. I can't.

I am wondering, Mr. President, if men like you, men now high in our public life, captains of industry, financiers—the kind of men who seem always to be closest now to our public men—I am wondering if all of you are not nowadays too much separated from the actuality of life. Everything has been very highly organized and centralized in America. Perhaps you have been organized and centralized out of our common lives.

I have an idea. It may amuse you. I think we Americans ought to elect two Presidents. For example, let you and Mr. Roosevelt both be President, for the next four years. They may prove to be eventful years. Let you serve, say for three months, and then let Mr. Roosevelt have his turn. In the interval you come out of your White House and away from your political advisers, industrial magnates, and bankers, and spend the time with me. We will get into my cheap car and live for a time as millions of Americans live now. Together we will walk at night in city streets, into homes of workers, into parks and camps where the unemployed gather, into a thousand places you have never seen. When you go back into your Presidency I will then take Mr. Roosevelt for his turn. It will be educational to you both. I swear it. Incidentally it may turn out to be the most interesting three months of your life.

As it happens, Mr. President, not all of my friends are poor or unemployed. I know personally a good many rich and powerful Americans, and I know that something quite dreadful does happen to all of you rich and powerful men. You do get horribly separated from actuality. I guess you can't help it. Recently I was staying in the house of a rich man, a friend—as kind-hearted a man as I know. One evening I heard him talking. Do you know, Mr. President, that he did not think that the present depression was so bad? He spoke of it as a passing thing, not of really great importance. I remember how I felt as he talked. There was no personal dislike of the man. I love him, but he did not know, does not himself feel what life has made me feel. Several times I went out of his house to walk alone, and often within a few blocks I saw men, often young men, eating from garbage cans, sleeping on benches, always tired, always hungry. Seeing nothing in the future but more of the same.

I have seen and talked to many poor farmers who are now losing their little bits of land, who are now poor, destitute, and discouraged. There are little things that happen to a man. I spoke of my heart being made to bleed. Your heart would be made to bleed also, seeing what I have seen. Recently, within the year, I was walking one day in a wood. It had rained. The ground was wet. I went silently. Suddenly I heard a voice. I crept forward. There was a little Virginia farmer kneeling by a fence at the edge of the wood and praying. Tears ran from his old eyes. I crept away without being seen, but afterward I inquired. He was just a hard-working poor American farmer who had a big family and who had got into debt, and whose little farm was to be sold. He did not know where to turn. He was frightened, hurt, and perplexed, kneeling there and crying to God. He is not an isolated figure. He represents, as I have pictured him here, millions of Americans now.

You, Mr. President, and myself have a good deal in common. We were once both poor boys, both came from poor families. You went the road of money-making, of power-getting, and I went another road. Just the same, if I know anything at all, I know that we are both perplexed. When the group of American writers of whom I was one went recently to Washington to try to speak to you personally of all these things, it is true that we made a point of the treatment recently given to the perplexed soldiers who have been camped down there. That is what they were—perplexed men. Think of the promises we Americans made those men but a few years ago.

This is my own attitude. Before going on this fruitless mission to Washington to try to see and talk to you personally, hoping perhaps to take to you a little cry out of the masses of people, I went to see some of the Communist leaders. The idea that they had any effect on the mass of soldiers in Washington is absurd. It is a joke, Mr. President. It is true that some of them went to Washington to try to work there among the soldiers, but they, themselves, told me that they could do nothing. "We couldn't touch those men." I think they told me the truth. Newspaper men and many citizens of Washington have told me how, all the time they were there, they went about flag-waving and begging. They demanded so little from their government, after all the things that had been promised them, that the situation was laughable.

When we writers came to Washington you would not see us. A Mr. Theodore G. Joslin, one of your secretaries, I believe, did finally see us. He told us firmly and finally at once that you would not bother to see us. Then an amusing thing happened. He was a bit nervous and pale. He said he did not speak to us for you or as your secretary, but as a fellow-American and a fellow-writer. He seemed to me a rather pathetic figure at the moment. He lectured us like a lot of schoolboys. The import of what he said was that the trouble at Washington, in regard to the bonus army, was that the men weren't soldiers. We were given the idea that the distraught men that had come to Washington were really Huns. They went about attacking police and trying to tear down government. They threw stones at harmless soldiers. You would have thought that the soldiers and police were unarmed rather than these distraught, puzzled men out of work—the same men who but so short a time ago were our national heroes.

Mr. President, after this absurd incident in Washington, on your birthday, we writers separated. I went to see a friend. We had a talk. He is not an unsuccessful man as I am, but is very successful. He said that, even in Washington, you were utterly separated from the reality of life in America now, so surrounded by yes-sayers that nothing touched you. He suggested to me an idea. He said that when you were in the Far East, when you were making your fortune, you handled coolies. He said that you had come to think of most of us here in America, who happen to be poor or out of work, as coolies. He thought you believed in the whip. That is what we came to Washington to protest against, Mr. President—the whip. Its lash is falling across the backs of millions of Americans. It is the lash that is making radicals in America.

I return to my suggestion. If my notion that we elect both you and Mr. Roosevelt is absurd and you are re-elected I suggest that you take that vacation. Sneak out of the back door at the White House some evening. Let me take you with me for a few weeks so that you may see with your own eyes what is happening to millions of Americans, what American life is becoming.

SHERWOOD ANDERSON

My piece was published. I have sometimes thought since that the expedition of protest by us writers was got up by the Communists. If it was, I didn't know it then.

At any rate, later, when I was in New York I was asked by some of the leaders of the Communist party to come have a talk with them, and I went.

I went to a building in 13th Street in New York and I was told then that my open letter to the President was a mistake.

"You should not have done it," they told me.

"And why?" I asked.

"It may arouse some sympathy for the President."

"Yes?" I said.

They thought that shouldn't be done.

But I am sympathetic. I understand what power does to a man, what he is up against.

They declared that it was all wrong. They scolded me but I only laughed.

"Fortunately, I was expressing my own point of view, not yours," I said and so walked out of their presence.

Meanwhile in New York the New York papers were playing up a phase of Waldo Frank's new book on Russia that spoke of the difficulty the artist must meet in a civilization devoted to giving new life and health to workers. I had not read Frank's book yet but he would agree with me in this—that any difficulty the artist may meet in a civilization under the dictatorship of workers could easily be capped in any money civilization.

One of the saddest experiences to be had by any writer in America was at this time to go into the office of almost any American book or magazine publishing house. Lord, what gloom, what deep despair.

Why? No advertising, book sales dropping off, subscriptions to magazines almost impossible to get.

I went about the city, stopping often to listen to young Communist men and women speaking on street corners, and was a bit ashamed of my white suit, my panama hat, my walking stick. A little girl Communist speaking at Ninth Street and Second Avenue came to me as I stood listening. This at night. "Are you a comrade out of work?" she asked with charming innocence. I swear to God I was ashamed.

The white linen suit, the panama hat, the swagger walking stick.

"My dear child, men out of work are not rigged out like this."

As for American writers—God help the new man out now with a new book having poetic strength. He'll find restrictions enough, God knows.

Among the young fighting Communists I found poverty, youth, no gloom.

My own feeling now is that if it be necessary, in order to bring about the end of a money civilization and set up something new, healthy and strong, we of the so-called artist class have to be submerged. Let us be submerged. Down with us. A little poverty and shaking down won't hurt us and I believe in my own class, the artists' class. I believe in our ability to survive. The world is old. Changes have swept over the world before. If new worth-while and significant men are to arise in America the chances are a hundred to one that they will come up out of the masses. It's in the air.

If the movement to free all men from the rule of money means the submerging of our class, let us be submerged. Down with us. Let's have no starving workers to save us. We'll survive. We'll swim. We will in the long run be healthier and better if we get it in the neck now along with the workers.

6. Backstage with a Martyr

I was in the city of San Francisco. This was when my friend Lincoln Steffens was still alive and he asked me to go see Mr. Fremont Older. As everyone on the Coast knows, the late Mr. Older had made a long fight for the release of Tom Mooney. Older had been, for many years, the best-known and, I'm sure, the best-loved newspaper man on the Coast.

He was very insistent that I go out to San Quentin to see Tom Mooney.

But why?

What could I do for him?

However I went and Ted Lilienthal went with me. He drove me out. Ted, with Leon Gelber, runs a delightful book store in San Francisco and they are also interested in young painters, showing their works in the store. Ted belongs to a family that has been very powerful, I'm told, in banking and financial circles on the Coast but is himself not interested in finance.

So we drove out to San Quentin. We went to the office of the warden.

I told him who I was, that I had been sent to him by Older, that I had come to see Tom Mooney.

The warden was a large heavy-looking man. When I had told him my mission, he sat for a long time looking at me. Then he made a little motion with his hand.

"Another one to see Tom Mooney, eh?" he said.

He leaned forward, pointed a finger at me. Ted, a shy man, had gone into a corner by himself. What the warden said made me feel a little foolish.

"This Tom Mooney," he said, "I know nothing about it. I don't know whether he is guilty or not. I didn't try him. I'm the warden of this prison. People keep coming and coming to see Tom Mooney.

"Hell, man," he said, "I got a lot of other boys in here. Some of them would like to have people coming, now and then, to see them."

It was something to think about. It was no doubt true. What could I do for Tom Mooney?

Then I thought of something. At the time, during the same labor war on the Coast, when they had convicted Tom, there had been two others also convicted.

There was a man called "Smitty" and there was one of the MacNamara brothers. They were in the prison for life. Not much chance of their getting out.

They had blown up a newspaper office down in Los Angeles. There had been people killed.

It hadn't been planned that way. There was this bitter labor struggle. They had planned to blow up the building when it was unoccupied but things had gone wrong.

"Sure we're guilty. We did it."

When I mentioned the names of the two men, the warden's face lighted up. He smiled.

"Sure you can see them. They're a couple of swell eggs."

They were brought in, two healthy-looking, quiet men and we began to talk, pulling shy Ted into the conversation, the warden leaning forward to listen.

They were both curiously alive, intellectually alive. They had done something terrible enough earlier in their lives and were paying for it.

They knew my books, the books of other men of my time. They discussed them with me, asked questions, were filled with intellectual curiosity.

They mentioned some of our outstanding writers. What sort of guys were they? What about Hemingway, Faulkner, Dos Passos, Dreiser? How did these fellows live? What did they look like? Did I know them?

Ted and I both were taken into what seemed to me a kind of warm friendliness, the warden leaning forward to listen, apparently warming himself in it.

They were there and they were gone.

"Well, so long, men."

A kind of warm heartiness. The warden weakened.

"Oh, I guess I'll have them bring in Tom. Why not?"

He seemed to give the order for Tom's coming a little wearily, like a bartender humoring a drunken man.

And then Tom came. He was dressed in white, with a black flowing tie.

He marched in. I cannot help what I felt. To me he was a bit the bad actor, let's say playing the part of Napoleon.

So I was Sherwood Anderson, eh? He strode across the room to me, a finger pointed at my face.

"So you are Sherwood Anderson?" he said again. His finger seemed about to run into my eye and I drew away, but he followed.

"You quit what you are doing," he said. "You be the American Zola. I'm the American Dreyfus."

That was about all. We didn't stay long. I tried to introduce him to Ted Lilienthal but he dismissed poor Ted with disdain.

"A Lilienthal? One of my enemies," he said.

As I have suggested, that is about all I can remember.

He had come into the room and he went out, striding out as he strode in. He left us curiously flat.

It wasn't that we doubted his innocence. Why should we? There was apparently plenty of evidence that he was innocent.

But had his innocence, his martyrdom, done that to him? We had no way of knowing.

There were the other two who were guilty. Two guilty men who knew they were stuck.

So warm and friendly.

And then Tom—the innocent one.

"I'm the American Dreyfus. You be the American Zola."

Well, you who read this, figure it out if you can.

7. The Feeders

Morning at my farm. I have received a letter from ——. So he is still there. He is one of the most lovable men I have known.

He is one of the thousands everywhere who aspire to be writers. He has written two or three long novels.

They never quite come off and I do not believe he has ever submitted them to a publisher. He declares they are too intimate. Well, I dare say people very close to him, his wife perhaps, others who live in the same house with him, have been brought into the novels. He has got a certain satisfaction in writing them. Something is got off his chest, things he wants to say have been put down.

He was for years a newspaper man and his writing is filled with newspaper cliché. He is what Mrs. Petolengro, in George Borrow's *Romany Rye,* called "a newspaper Ned."

I set great value on my friend. He has been one of my own best feeders. When you are with him you are always a little amused. He is a big man and very awkward. He stumbles over chairs, stumbles, knocks against you.

At one time he made a good deal of money, let us say some six thousand a year. He has always been very fond of women and has had several intense affairs during the time I have known him. When he is in love he is in it with his whole being. It is a kind of insanity of love.

That also gives him the impulse to write. He is not very successful or fortunate in love. He relieves himself by writing.

That, however, also stands in the way of his sending his novels to a publisher. He has none of the real writer's abandon. He has written of his love for some woman, perhaps employed in the office where he is employed, has let himself go in writing of her. He describes her, the way she walks, the clothes she wears, the color of her hair and eyes, the shape of her nose and mouth. Alas, he has never been permitted to kiss that mouth. He kisses it in his book.

But if the book were published his wife would read it.

"There would be hell then. I couldn't stand it. As it is she is always suspicious," he says.

"Now and then she comes to the office. She looks about. Let us say that, on the occasion of such a visit, I am dictating letters. There is a woman, not bad-looking, taking my letters.

"I am not in love with her. She is one of the employees of the office, that is all, but immediately when I arrive home in the evening she begins making accusations."

"Well, I saw the way you looked at her. You can't tell me."

That sort of thing, carried on endlessly.

My friend decided that, for a time, he would escape his home. His work compelled him to do a certain amount of traveling.

He came to see me. At the time I was in New York. I had saved a little money and was living in a cheap room, engaged in writing a book, making my money go as far as it would.

"Could you get me a small room, very cheap?" He had managed to save a little out of the lunch money allowed him by his wife.

If his wife knew that he had taken a room in the city she would be suspicious. She would think he was living with some woman. However he did get the room, a very small one at a low price. To save money he cooked his own meals. He bought himself some kind of small tin outfit and cooked with canned heat. His food, for the most part, was fried eggs.

"I've eaten so many eggs that I awaken myself in the night by cackling like a hen," he said.

He sat in the room at a small desk writing away at a novel. That was twenty years ago and I am quite sure he is still at it. He writes the same novel over and over. Once I read one of his novels.

"Let me try my hand at it," I said.

I was quite sure that with some editing, a touch here and there, some of the characters of his book more developed, I could make it at least publishable. I thought, "Now he has been at this for a long time. It will do him good to see his efforts in print."

He was indignant. He was hurt. He took my suggestion as a sort of insult.

Or it may be that he was afraid the book might be published. There was in every book he wrote a certain woman. I had never seen his wife but was quite sure she was the woman of the book. He was getting even with her, that was it. Sometimes he made her tall, with red hair, again a small black-haired woman, but there she was. She was fat and lean, tall and short, but always she was the same woman.

In conversation he was wonderful. He came into my room and sat. He spoke of his youth, told stories of his childhood, of his young manhood, of his courting of his wife. There was in all his talk a curious naïve honesty and I listened, filled with joy. He had, in conversation, a way of suddenly dropping a sentence that illuminated perfectly the scene or person he was describing and as he talked thus my own fingers itched to get a pen in my hand. It may be that my affection for him was largely due to this. He was a feeder. He fed me. Often, after an hour with him in my room, I put aside the story I was working on to put down his story just as he told it. Some of the best stories I ever wrote I got from him thus, using often his very language. Once or twice, when he had told me one of his stories I sent him off to his own room.

"Now go and write that story just as you have told it to me," I said and he tried.

It never came off. With the pen in his hand he became again the "newspaper Ned."

What clichés, what flatness. I grew unscrupulous. I let him feed me. I used him. In my life I have known several such people, feeders to others. Their talk is wonderful. There are sentences dropped into their talk that make you want to shout with joy. With pen in hand they become self-conscious.

"Now I am writing."

It may be they are conscious of a possible audience for what they write. What is in them will not flow down their arms and into their fingers. The pen in their hand kills for them all spontaneity, all free expression.

Annoying things were always happening to my friend and how well he told of them.

He had an affair with a woman somewhat older than himself. She was living with her father and mother in a house on the East Side. This was when he had a room near my own.

He used to go to her, perhaps twice a month. Her father and mother, he told me, were quite old. "So I go there. If they have gone to bed the window shade of her room is fixed in just a certain way. The front door of the house has been left unlocked. She has crept down and unlocked it.

"So I go up. I have taken off my shoes. I go up softly and there, I am in her arms."

It was hard to imagine my friend in a woman's arms. He was so big and awkward, so like a huge bear, but there he was. He had loved the woman for a long time and there was something sad about the story. From all he told me she must have been a very gentle one, a contrast no doubt to his wife. She believed in his writing.

"She thinks I am a genius," he once said to me, smiling sadly. For all of his continuing to write he was always sharply aware of his own deficiencies.

"I'll never make it, but what do I care? It gives me great satisfaction," he once said to me.

It was a winter night and snowing, and being restless in his little cramped room he had gone to his love. He had already told me that she had a weak heart.

He had gone there at perhaps two in the morning. He crept up to her. In the ecstasy of love she died in his arms.

He must have been horribly frightened.

"So I arranged everything in the room and then I crept out," he said.

He was on the stairs of the house and the stairs creaked. He did not know whether in creeping away thus he was trying to protect himself or her. She had always, he said, been what is called a good woman. No breath of scandal had ever touched her. "I wanted her old father and mother to find her there, thinking her innocent as they had always thought of her," he said.

He got out of the house and into the street. It was snowing and there was a heavy fall of snow on the ground. With his shoes in his hand he ran. He ran through the street. There was a kind of wild ecstasy of running. He stumbled and fell. He got up and ran again. In some way he got through Central Park and to the West Side unnoticed.

"Once I was noticed," he later told me. Some men shouted at him but he dodged into a side path and kept running.

He arrived in my room (it might have been at three in the morning) with his shoes still clutched in his hand. He lay on the floor and sobbed. It was one of the strange sort of things that were always happening to him.

His whole life, as I knew it and as he told it to me, was filled with strange, sometimes terrible, sometimes amusing adventures but he could not write of them.

I had a letter from him this morning. No doubt as I write this he is sitting somewhere in a room writing. He has started another novel. He has read a novel, let us say, by H. G. Wells. He tries his hand at one rather like that. His writing will still be flat and rather meaningless. It will be full of newspaper clichés. Strange, amusing and sometimes terrible things will still be happening to him but he cannot really tell of them except in talk.

It is his fate. He is not a writer. He is one who feeds writers. There are a good many such in the world.

8. The Sound of the Stream

I have already mentioned that my house stands by a mountain stream. It is a stream of sounds and at night, ever since I had completed the building of my house and had moved into it, the stream has talked to me.

On how many nights have I lain in my bed in my house, the doors and windows that faced the stream all open and the sounds coming in.

The stream runs over rocks. It runs under a bridge and somewhere I have written telling how, on dark nights, the sounds change and become strangely significant.

There was the sound of the feet of children running on the floor of the bridge. A horse galloped, soldiers marched. I heard at night the footsteps of old friends, the voices of women I had loved.

There was a crippled girl I have spoken of to whom I had once made love, in the rain, under a bush in a city park. She had cried and I heard the haunting sound of her feet, the curious broken rhythm on the bridge over the stream by my house at night . . . the voices of Fred, of Mary, of Tom, of Esther and a hundred others, loved and lost in what I called my real life and, always, above these voices, the sound also of the footsteps and the voices of those of my imaginative world.

The long slow stride of Hugh McVey. These mingled let us say with the footsteps of Carl Sandburg or Ben Hecht. My friend John Emerson or Maurice Long walking beside my Doctor Parcival. The footsteps of the naked man in the room with his daughter in *Many Marriages* soft beside the footsteps of some dear one in the life I had led away from my desk.

These sounds from the stream whispering to me, sometimes crying out, through many nights, making nights alive . . .

It was in the early summer and I had gotten a letter from my literary agent. It may be that I had been writing to him. He had certain stories I had sent him to sell.

"Can't you, sir, sell one of the stories to some magazine? I am needing money."

He answered my letter. He is a sensible man, knows his business.

"I admit that the stories you have sent me are good stories. But," he said, "you are always getting something into all of your stories that spoils the sale."

He did not go further but I know what he meant.

"Look here," he once said to me, "why don't you, for the time at least, drop this rather intimate style of yours?"

He smiled when he said it and I also smiled.

"Let us say, now, that you are yourself the editor of one of our big American magazines. You have yourself been in business. When you first began to write, even after you had published some of your earlier books, you had to go on for years, working in an advertising place. You must know that all of our large American magazines are business ventures. It costs a great deal of money to print and distribute hundreds of thousands of copies. Often, as you know, the price received for the magazine, when sold on the newsstand, does not pay for the paper on which it is printed."

"Yes, I know."

"They have to have stories that please people."

"Yes, I know."

We had stopped to have a drink at a bar. But a few weeks before he had written me a letter. "There is a certain large magazine that would like to have a story from you. It should be, let us say, a story of about ten thousand words. Do not attempt to write the story. Make an outline, I should say a three- or four-page outline. I can sell the story for you."

I made the outline and sent it to him.

"It is splendid," he wrote. "Now you can go ahead. I can get such and such a sum."

"Oh!" The sum mentioned would get me out of my difficulties.

"I will get busy," I said to myself. "In a week I will dash off the story."

Some two or three weeks before, a man friend had come to me one evening. He is a man to whom I am deeply attached.

"Come and walk with me," he said, and we set out afoot, leaving the town where he lived. I had gone to the town to see him but, when I got to his town, there was a sudden illness in his house. The man has children and two of them were in bed with a contagious disease.

I stayed at a hotel. He came there. We walked beyond the town, got into a dirt road, passed farmhouses, dogs barked at us. We got into a moonlit meadow.

We had walked for a long time in silence. At the hotel I had noticed that my friend was in a tense, excited mood.

"You are in some sort of trouble. Is it the children? Has the disease taken a turn for the worse?"

"No," he said, "the children are better. They are all right."

We were in the moonlit meadow, standing by a fence, some sheep grazing nearby and it was a delicious night of the early summer.

"There is something I have to tell to someone," he said. "I wrote to you, begged you to come here."

My friend is a highly respected man in his town.

He began talking. He talked for hours. He told me a story of a secret life he had been living.

My friend is a man of fifty. He is employed as an experimental scientist by a large manufacturing company.

But I might as well confess at once that I am, as you the reader may have guessed, covering the trail of my friend. I am a man rather fortunate in life. I have a good many men friends. If I make this one an experimental scientist working for a large manufacturing company, it will do.

His story was, on the whole, strange. It was like so many stories, not invented but coming directly out of life. It was a story having in it certain so-called sordid touches, strange impulses come to a man of fifty in the grip of an odd passion.

"I have been doing this.

"I have been doing that.

"I have to unload, to tell someone.

"I have been suffering."

My friend did unload his story, getting a certain relief talking to me of a turn in his life that threatened to destroy the position he had achieved in his community. He had got a sudden passion for a woman of his town, the sort of thing always happening in towns. "Three years ago," he said to me, "there was another man here, a friend, a man, as I am, of standing in our community, who did what I am doing now. He became enamored of a woman here, the wife of a friend, and began to meet her secretly.

"At least he thought, or hoped, he was meeting her secretly.

"He did as I have been doing. In the evening when darkness came, he got into his car. She had walked out along a street and in some dark place along the street he picked her up. He drove with her out along little side roads, went to distant towns but soon everyone knew.

"And how I blamed him. I went to him. 'What a fool you are being,' I said to him.

" 'Yes, but I cannot help it. This is the great love of my life.'

" 'What nonsense,' I said. I pled with him, quarreled with him, but it did no good. I thought him an utter fool and now I am being just such another."

I had taken the man with whom I talked in the field, and his story, as the basis for the story I was to write for one of the popular magazines, had made an outline that was pronounced splendid by my agent.

But what rough places I had smoothed out.

"No, I cannot say that such a figure holding such a respectable place in my life did that. There must not be anything unpleasant. There must be nothing that will remind readers of certain sordid moments, thoughts, passions, acts, in their own lives if I am to get this money—and, oh, how I need it."

I am no Shakespeare, but did not even Shakespeare write a play he called *As You Like It?*

"When you are writing to please people you must not touch certain secret, often dark little recesses, that are in all humans.

"Keep in the clear, man. Go gaily along.

"It will be all right to startle them a little.

"You must get a certain dramatic force into your story."

But that night the man, upon whose story I have based the story I am about to write, was, as he talked, simply broken. He even put his face down upon the top rail of the fence, there in that moonlit meadow, and cried. I went to him. I put my arms about his shoulders, said words to him.

"This passion that has come to you at this time in your life, that now threatens to tear down all you have so carefully built up, that threatens to destroy the lives of others you love, will pass.

"At our age everything passes."

I do not remember just what I did say to him.

And so I began to write, but alas. . . .

Our difficulty is that as we write we become interested, absorbed, often a little in love with these characters of our stories that seem to be growing here, under our hand.

I have begun this story, taking off, as it were, from the story told me in the meadow by my friend; but now, as I write, he has disappeared.

There is a new man, coming to life, here. He seems to be here in this room where I work.

"You must do me right now," he seems to be saying to me.

"There is a certain morality involved," he says.

"Now you must tell everything, put it all down. Do not hesitate. I want it all put down."

At this point there was a series of letters concerning a story to be written that lay on my desk. I had had them brought to me from my files.

"If you are to write the story for us it would be well for you to keep certain things in mind.

"The story should be concerned with the lives of people who are in what might be called comfortable circumstances.

"Above all, it should not be too gloomy.

"We want you to understand that we do not wish, in any way, to dictate to you."

I had sat down to write the tale, for which I had made an outline, in bitter need of the money it might bring. After twenty-five years of writing, some twenty to twenty-five books published, my name up as one of the outstanding American writers of my day, my books translated into many languages, after all of this, I was always in need of money, always just two jumps ahead of the sheriff.

"Well, I will do it. I will. I will."

For two days, three, a week, I wrote doggedly, with dogged determination.

"I will give them just what they want. I had been told, it had been impressed deeply upon my mind that, above all things, to be popular, successful, I must first of all observe the 'don'ts.' "

A friend, another American writer, came to see me. He mentioned a certain, at present, very popular woman writer.

"Boy, she is cleaning up," he said.

However it seemed that she, one who knew her trade and was safe, occasionally slipped.

It may be that here, in telling of this incident, I have got the story of what happened to the woman writer confused with many such stories I have heard.

However it lies in my mind that the writer was making, for the movies, an adaptation of a very popular novel of a past generation. In it there was a child who, eating candy before breakfast, was reproved by his mother.

"Put that stuff aside. It will ruin your health."

Something of that sort must have been written. It was unnoticed, got by. What, and with the candy people spending millions in advertising! What, the suggestion that candy could ruin the health of a child, candy called "stuff"!

My friend told some tale of a big damage suit, of indignant candy manufacturers.

"Why, there must be thousands of these 'don'ts,'" I said to myself.

"It would be better, in your story, if your people be in what might be called comfortable positions in life."

I had got that sentence from someone. I wrote it out, tucked it up over my desk.

And so I wrote for a week, and there was a great sickness in me. I who had always loved the pile of clean white sheets on my desk, who had been for years obsessed with the notion that some day, by chance, I would find myself suddenly overtaken by a passion for writing and would find myself without paper, pencils, pens, or ink so that I was always stealing fountain pens and pencils from my friends, storing them away as a squirrel stores nuts, who, upon going for even a short trip away from home always put into my car enough paper to write at least five long novels, who kept bottles of ink stored in all sorts of odd places about the house, found myself suddenly hating the smell of ink.

There were the white sheets and I wanted to throw them all out of the window.

Days of this, a week. It may have gone on for two weeks. There were the days, something strangely gone out of life, and there were the nights. Why, I dare say that to those who do not write or paint or in any way work in the arts, all of this will seem nonsense indeed.

"When it comes to that," they will be saying, "our own work is not always so pleasant. Do you think it's always a joy to be a lawyer, wrangling over other people's ugly quarrels in courts, or being a doctor, always and forever with the sick, or a factory owner, with all this new unrest among workers, or a worker, getting nowhere working your life out for the profit of others?"

But there I was, having what is called literary fame. And I was no longer young. "Presently I will be old. The pen will fall from my hand. There will come the time of long afternoons sitting in the sun, or under the shade of a tree. I will no longer want to write. It may be that I will have my fill of people, their problems, the tangle of life, and will want only to look at sheep grazing on distant hillsides, to watch the waters of a stream rolling over rocks, or just follow with my aging eyes the wandering of a country road winding away among hills," I thought.

"It would be better for me to turn aside, make money now. I must. I must."

I remembered the advice always being given me when I was a young writer. "Go in for it," my friends said. At that time the movies had just become a gold mine for writers.

"Take it on for a time," my friends were saying to me. "You can change. Get yourself a stake. Make yourself secure and then, when you are quite safe, you can go abroad. Then you can write as you want to write."

"It may not have been good advice then but it is now," I said to myself. Formerly when I was writing all of my earlier books, I was very strong. I could work all day in the advertising place or in the factory I once owned. I could go home to my rooms. I took a cold plunge. Always, it seemed to me there was something that had to be washed away. When I was writing the Winesburg tales and, later, the novel, *Poor White,* I couldn't get tired, and often after working all day wrote all night. I have never been one who can correct, fill in, rework his stories. I must try, and when I fail must throw away. Some of my best stories have been written ten or twelve times.

An odd thing happens to a man, a writer. Perhaps I am saying all of this, not at all for those who do not write but for the young American writers. Nowadays they are always coming to me. They write me letters. "You are our father," they say to me.

"One day I picked up a book of stories of yours, or it was one of your novels, and a great door seemed to swing open for me."

There are such sentences written to me by young writers in letters. Sometimes they even put such sentences into the autobiographical novels with which almost all new writers begin.

And it is so they should begin too. First the learning to use the experiences, the words and hungers of their own lives and then, gradually, the reaching out into other lives.

And so I am addressing here our young American writers, the beginners, but what am I trying to say to them?

Perhaps I am only trying to say that the struggle in which we are engaged has no end, that we in America have, all of us, been led into a blind alley. We have always before us, we keep before us, the mythical thing we call "success," but for us there is, there can be, no success, for while this belief in the mythical thing called success remains among us, always in the minds of others about us, we shall be in danger of infection. I am trying to prove all of this to you by showing here how I, a veteran now among you, for a long time thinking myself safe from the contagion, was also taken with the disease.

And so I sat in my room, trying and trying.

I was in one of my frightened moods. Soon now my money would all be gone. I am a man who has always had, in the matter of finance, a line that, when crossed, made me begin to tremble. Anything above five hundred dollars in the bank has always seemed to me riches, but when my bank account goes below that amount the fears come.

Soon I shall have but four hundred dollars, then three, two, one. I live in the country on a farm and in the house built by my one successful book. Bills come, so many pounds of grass seed for a field, a ton of lime, a new plow. Great God, will I be compelled to return to the advertising agency?

I have three or four short stories in my agent's hands. Once a magazine called *Pictorial Review* paid me seven hundred and fifty dollars for a short story. I had given the story the title, "There She is, She is Taking Her Bath," but after the story had been got into type and illustrations made for it the editor of the magazine grew doubtful. "We are doubtful about the title," he wired. "Can't you suggest another?" and I replied, saying, "ROLL YOUR OWN," but got from him a second wire, saying that he didn't think that that title fitted the story and in the end he never published it.

"Will he be demanding back my seven hundred and fifty dollars?" I asked myself, knowing nothing of my own legal rights. But then a thought came, a very comforting thought.

"He may demand but how can he get it?" I had spent the money for an automobile, had got a new overcoat, a new suit of clothes.

"Just let him try. What can he do? I am dustproof," I muttered; but I had misjudged the man. He must really have been a splendid fellow, for in the end and without protest, and after some four or five years, he sent the story back to me saying nothing at all of all that money given me for it. He said, if I remember correctly, that, while he personally liked the story, in fact thought it splendid, a magnificent achievement, etc., etc., also that he had always greatly admired my work, this story did not really fit into the tone of the magazine. There was in it, as I now remember, a little business man, timid and absurdly jealous of his wife. He had got it into his head that she was having affairs with other men and had determined to have it out with her but, when he worked himself up to it and rushed home, always fearing he would lose his courage, it happened that invariably she was taking her bath. A man couldn't, of course, stand outside the door of a bathroom, his wife splashing in the tub, and through the door accuse her of unfaithfulness.

In my story the wife was, to be sure, quite innocent. As a detective he hired to watch her assured him, she was as innocent as a little flower . . . if I remember correctly that was the expression used . . . but, also, as in so many of my stories, there was a business man made to appear a little ridiculous.

Why, I am told there are men and women who receive, for a single short story, as much as a thousand, fifteen hundred, even two thousand dollars. I am also told that I have had a profound effect upon the art of short-story writing.

"And so, what's wrong?" I more than a hundred times have asked myself; but at last I have come to a conclusion.

"You are just a little too apt, Sherwood, my boy, to find the business man a little ridiculous," I have told myself.

"Yes, and there is just your trouble, my boy. The business man, as he is represented in our picture, as he must be represented, is, above all things, a shrewd and knowing man. It would be better to represent him as very resolute, very courageous. He should have really what is called 'an iron jaw.' This is to indicate resolution, courage, determination.

"And you are to bear in mind that earlier in life he was an athlete. He was a star football player, a triple threat, whatever that is, or he was of the team at Yale.

"He is older now but he has kept himself in trim. He is like the first Roosevelt, the Teddy one. Every day he goes to his club to box. The man who is to succeed in business cannot . . . keep that in mind . . . let himself grow fat. Do not ever make him fat, watery-eyed, bald. Do not let him have a kidney complaint.

"The trouble with you," I told myself, "is just the years you spent in business," and I began to remember the men, hundreds of them, some of them known internationally, often sensitive fellows, at bottom kindly, who were puzzled as I was puzzled, always breaking out into odd confessions, telling intimate little stories of their loves, their hopes, their disappointments.

"How did I get where I am? What brought me here?"

"This is something I never wanted to do. Why am I doing it?"

Something of that sort and then also, so often, something naïve, often wistful and also a little ridiculous.

I could not shake off the fact that, in the fifteen or twenty years during which I was in business as advertising writer, as manufacturer, five men among my personal acquaintances killed themselves.

So there was tragedy too, plenty of it.

"But, my dear fellow, you must bear in mind that this is a country ruled by business. Only yesterday, when you were driving on the highway, you saw a huge sign. 'What is good for business is good for you,' the sign said.

"So there, you see, we are one great brotherhood."

All of this said to myself, over and over. "Now you are below the line, the five-hundred-dollar line. Keep that in mind."

There were these days, my struggle to write in a new vein, to keep persistently cheerful, letting nothing reflecting on the uprightness, the good intent, the underlying courage of business, creep into my story.

"Above all do not put into your story a business man who is by chance shy, sensitive, who does occasionally ridiculous things. Even if, at bottom, the fellow is gentle, lovable, do not do that."

"But, you see, my man is not in business. I have made him a judge.

"But, you fool, don't you see . . . my God, man, a judge.

"Is there not also a pattern, a mold made, for the judge?"

And so you see me arguing, fighting with myself, through the days, through the nights. The nights were the worst.

"But can't you sleep, my dear?"

"No, my darling, I cannot sleep."

"But what is on your mind?"

You see, I cannot tell my wife. She would rebel. She would begin talking about a job. "We can give up this house, this farm," she would say. "You are always spending your money on it," she would add. She would call attention to the absurd notion I have that, in the end, I can make our farm pay. We would get into an argument, with me pointing out that it is a dishonorable thing to live on land and not work constantly to make it more productive.

"It would be better for me to surrender everything else before my love of the land itself," I would say, and this would set me off. As she is a Southern woman I would begin on the South, pointing out to her how the masters of the land and the slaves of the old South, claiming as they did an aristocratic outlook on life, had been, nevertheless, great land destroyers; and from that I would go on, declaring that no man could make claim to aristocracy who destroyed the land under his feet.

It is a favorite subject of mine and it gets us nowhere.

"I think I have been smoking too many cigarettes," I said and she agreed with me. She spoke again, as she had so often, of her fear of the habit-forming danger of a certain drug I sometimes take; but—"You had better take one," she said.

And so I did but it did not help.

"But why should you be afraid?" I asked myself. Even after I had taken the drug I was wide awake and remained so night after night.

But why go on? We story tellers, and I am writing all of this solely for story tellers, all know, we must know, it is the beginning of knowledge of our craft, that the unreal is more real than the real, that there is no real other than the unreal; and I say this here because, first of all, I presume to re-establish my own faith—badly shaken recently by an experience—and I say it a little because as a veteran story teller I want to strengthen the faith in other and younger American men.

Now I have remembered that once, some five or ten years ago . . . I was living in New Orleans at the time . . . I had been in the evening to the movies and had seen a picture, written by a man of talent, who had once been my friend, and having seen it had been shocked by what seemed to me a terrible selling out of all life, and, having got out of the movie theater and into the street, I went along, growing constantly more and more angry, so that when I got to my room I sat down at my desk and wrote for the rest of the night, and what I wrote was a kind of American "I Accuse."

I had written the words, "I Accuse," at the head of the first of a great pile of sheets on the desk before me and, as I wrote that night, I called the roll. I made a great list of the names, of American actors, American writers, who having had a quick and often temporary success in New York or who having written a novel or a story that had caught the popular fancy, had walked off to Hollywood.

There was the temptation and I knew it must be a terrible one: . . . five hundred, a thousand a week.

"I will do it for a time. I will store up my money.

"When I have got rich I will be free."

"But, my dear fellow, do you not understand that the complete selling out of the imaginations of the men and women of America, by the artists, of the stage, by the artist story tellers, is completely and wholly an acceptance of harlotry?"

I had written all of this very bitterly, on a certain night in New Orleans, naming the men who had done it, some of them my personal friends. A good many of them were also radicals. They wanted, or thought they wanted, a new world. They thought that a new world could be made by depending on the economists . . . it was a time when the whole world was, seemingly, dominated by the economists. A new world was to arise, dominated by a new class, the proletariat. A good many of them had turned to the writing of so-called proletarian stories. It was the fashion.

"If I go to Hollywood, write there, get money by it, and if I give that money to the cause?"

"But please, what cause?"

"Why, to the overthrowing of capitalism, the making of a new and better world."

"But, don't you see that what you are doing . . . the suffering of the world, the most bitter suffering, does not come primarily from physical suffering. It is by the continual selling out of the imaginative lives of people that the great suffering comes. There the most bitter harm is done."

I accuse.

I accuse.

I had accused my fellow artists of America, had named names. I wrote for hours and hours and when I had finished writing, had poured out all of the bitterness in me, brought on by the picture I had seen, I leaned back in my chair and laughed at myself.

"How can you accuse others when you yourself have not been tempted?"

Once, being in California, I had gone to Hollywood to see a friend working in one of the great studios; and as we walked through a hallway in one of the buildings, now often a row of little offices like the offices we used to sit in in the advertising agency, I saw the name of a writer I knew; the writer came out to me.

"And have they got you too?"

"No," I said, "I am just looking about."

"Well, they have not got you yet but they will get to you."

I had even written two or three times to agents in New York or Hollywood.

"Cannot you sell, to the pictures, such and such a story of mine?"

There had been no offers. I had not been tempted.

"Let us say," I remarked to myself that night in New Orleans after the outbreak of writing against others, accusations hurled on their heads, "that you had been offered . . . let us be generous . . . let us say twenty-five thousand for the best of all of your Winesburg stories, or, for that matter, for the whole series.

"Would you have turned the offer down? If you did such a thing everyone who knew you and who knew of your constant need of money would call you a fool. Would you do it?"

I had to admit that I did not know and so, laughing at myself, I was compelled to tear up, to throw in the wastebasket, the thousands of words of my American "I Accuse."

You were, on that night in New Orleans, asking yourself whether you, the pure and holy one, would have the courage to turn down an offer of twenty-five thousand just to let someone sentimentalize one of your stories, twist the characters of the stories about; yet now, because you are again nearly broke, because you are beginning to fear old age, an old age perhaps of poverty, you are at work doing the thing for which you were about to publicly accuse others and doing it for a few hundred dollars.

The above thought jumping into my head at night, I got out of bed. The moon was shining and sending so bright a path of light through an open door into the room that I thought a lamp must have been left burning in a nearby room. I went to look.

I returned to where my wife lay, curled into a little ball at the bed's edge, the light coming through the door falling on her face. I had told her nothing of the new temptation that had come to me. She was one who, like my mother, would have gladly worked herself into the grave, as my mother had done, rather than that I should be trying to do what I had been trying to do.

And what was the fear that had come upon me, the fear of old age, an old age of poverty?

But you will not starve. At the worst you will have more than your mother ever had during her whole life. You will wear better clothes, eat better food. You may be even able to retain this beautiful house a book of yours built.

I stood that night by my wife's bed, having this argument with myself, the whole matter being one that will interest only other artists, realizing dimly as I stood thus, that the fear in me that night, of which my wife knew nothing . . . it would have shocked her profoundly to be told of it . . . the fear perhaps came up into me from a long line of men and women . . . I remembered that night how my father, in his occasional sad moods . . . he was, most of the time rather a gay dog . . . used to go sit in the darkness of our house in a street of workingmen's houses, and sitting there, the rest of us suddenly silent, sing in a low voice a song called "Over the Hill to the Poor-House."

The fear in him too, perhaps into him from his father and his father's father and on back and back, all perhaps men who had lived as I had always lived, precariously.

It is what gets a man. In the artist there must always be this terrible contradiction. It is in all of us. We want passionately the luxuries of life, the things we produce—our books, paintings, statues, the songs we make, the music we make—these are all luxuries.

We want luxuries, for who but his fellow artists can really love the work of the artist while at the same time knowing, deep down in us, that if we give way to this passion for the possession of beautiful things about us, getting them by cheapening our own work, all understanding of beauty must go out of us.

"And so why all this silly struggle? Why this absurd fear?"

I left the moonlit room where my wife lay asleep . . . there is something grows very close between people who have lived long together, who have really achieved a marriage . . . as I had stood at the foot of the bed in which my wife lay I had seen little waves of pain run across her sleeping face as waves run across a lake in a wind. . . .

Barefooted I went out of my house, clad in my pajamas . . . they are of silk . . . my wife insists on buying them for me with money she herself earns . . . she is constantly, persistently buying me expensive shirts, expensive ties, shoes, hats, overcoats . . . I speak here of poverty but, on a rack in a closet off my sleeping room there are dozens, perhaps even a hundred ties that have cost at least two dollars each.

Absurdity and more absurdity. What children we are. I went and stood by an apple tree in the orchard back of my house and then, going around the house, climbed a little hill where I could see the front of the house.

"It is one of the most beautiful houses in all America," I said to myself and for a time that night I sat absorbed, forgetting entirely the absurd struggle that had been going on in me for a week, for two weeks, my eye following the line of the wall rising out of the ground and then following along the roof. "Oh, how perfect the proportion; and there is where beauty lies."

Only a few of the many people who had come to visit me had been able to realize the extreme beauty of my achievement in building the house. It was true that there had been an architect who had made the drawings for me but I had not followed the drawings. For two years and while the house was building, all the money made for me by Horace Liveright going into it, myself once having to stop building for two years while I went delivering silly lectures to get more money, I had done no writing. It didn't matter. A friend had once walked up the hill with me, to sit with me on the top of a cement tank that went down into the ground, where I sat that night in my pajamas, it also being a moonlight night, had said that my house was as beautiful to him as a poem. "Cling to it," he said. "Live all the rest of your days in it." He went on at length, saying that the house was as beautiful as my story "Brother Death." He named those other stories, "The Untold Lie," "The New Englander" and "A Man's Story." "It has the quality they have."

He said that and I giggled with pleasure, enjoying his praise of the beauty of my house more than any praise I had ever got from my writing.

On that night I walked down the hill past my house and to a bridge over a stream and stood still arguing with myself.

"But I have a right now to put money first. I have got to begin now thinking of money. I have got to begin making money. I will—I will. These people of my story shall behave as I wish. For years I have been a slave to these people of my imagination but I will be a slave no longer. For years I have served them and now they shall serve me."

Here I was, standing in silence on the bridge over the stream. . . . And there again were the sounds in the stream. They crept into me, invaded me. I heard again the sound of the feet of children, horses galloping, soldiers marching, the sob of that crippled girl. I heard the voices of old friends. The sounds went on for a time. Of a sudden the sounds all changed.

There were no more voices, only laughter. The laughter began. It increased in volume. It seemed to become a roar.

"See, the very stream is laughing at me," I cried and began to run along the country road that goes past my house. I ran and ran. I ran until I was exhausted. I ran up hill and down. I hurt my bare feet. I had come out of my house wearing bedroom slippers but I had lost them. I ran until I was out of breath, exhausted. I had hurt one of my feet on a sharp stone. It bled. I stopped running that night at the brow of a low hill, after all not far from my house . . . a man of my age, who has spent so much of his life at a desk, who has smoked so many hundreds of thousands, it may be near millions, of cigarettes, does not run far.

I ran until I was exhausted and then, hobbling along, as once a crippled girl in Chicago had hobbled sobbing beside me in a rain-swept Chicago street, I went back over the road along which I had been running and to my cabin by the creek.

I let myself into my cabin and getting the manuscript on which I had been at work I took it out to a little open grassy place beside the stream and sitting there on the grass I burned it page by page.

The burning took a long time and it was a job. It was, I knew, an absurd performance; and I knew that I was, as all such men as myself must ever be, a child. But later, as you see, I have wanted to write of it, to see if in words I can catch the mood of it.

"It will be a joy to other writers, other artists, to know that I also, a veteran among them, am also as they are, a child," I thought.

I did all of this—as I have here set it down, going at great length, as you will see, to catch the mood of it, to give it background—and then, being very careful with my cut foot, I went back to my house and to my bed.

However I went first to the bathroom. I put disinfectant on the cut on my foot and my wife awoke.

"What are you doing?" she asked me, speaking sleepily, and, "Oh, I just got up to go to the bathroom," I said. And so she slept again and before again getting into bed I stood for a time looking at her asleep.

"I dare say that all men, artists and others, are as I am, children, at bottom," I thought; and I wondered a little if it were true that only a few women among all the millions of women got, by the pain of living with us, a little mature.

I was again in my bed and I thought that the voices in the stream by my house had stopped laughing at me and that again they talked and whispered to me; and on the next morning my shoe hurt my foot so that, when I was out of my wife's sight, I hobbled painfully along. I went to my cabin and to the black spot on the grass by the creek where I had burned the attempt I had made to impose my own will on the people of my imaginative world. I began to laugh at myself.

It had, I thought, been an absurd and silly experience through which I had passed but, God knows, I told myself I may have to pass through it again, time after time. I knew as I sat down at my desk that morning, determined again not to impose myself, to let the story I was trying to write write itself, to be again what I had always been, a slave to the people of my imaginary world if they would do it, making their own story of their own loves, my pen merely forming the words on the paper . . . I knew that what I had been through, in such an absurd and childish form, letting myself again be a victim to old fears, was nevertheless the story of like experiences in the life of all artists, no doubt throughout time.

BOOK VI

LIFE, NOT DEATH—

1. The Other One

He comes to you suddenly. But wait. That is hardly true. You are aware of him. He seems to go away. He comes again. He stays longer. You become most fully aware of him, let us say, at the age of fifty.

You were a man who, from the age of twenty-five and until you had touched forty-five, weighed a hundred and fifty. You didn't vary much. You were five feet ten.

There was this man to whom you had become accustomed. You were no athlete but you went along, on the whole a cheerful sprawling figure, living and loving, sometimes hating. You slept, you worked, you ate, you went to see your friends.

And then this other one came. His face and body were both heavy. He was inclined to stumble. He got fussy about his clothes, was always trying to appear what he was not.

He seemed to have crowded yourself, as you had always thought of yourself, out of the picture. He brought a new strangeness into your life. By yourself, you were as you had always been.

You stood sometimes before your glass.

"Where have I gone?" you asked yourself.

This one who has now taken possession of you has thin hair. Your own hair was thick. It was black. This one has gray hair.

He wears glasses. When he gets out of bed in the morning and leans over to tie his shoes he groans. He is always making these unpleasant noises.

It is all very strange. There you are, lying in your bed. It is morning and outside your house the sun is shining. As long as you lie very still, do not move, your old self seems in possession of you.

"Now to leap out of bed, dance, shout, embrace the day."

"Ha! You will, will you?"

This other one has driven your real self back and back, into some dark hidden corner of yourself. Your real self, what you have always known as your self, is now crouched in the darkness, far back in there. He is trembling with fright.

This other one, the heavy awkward lumbering one, is in possession again.

Hear him groan. Watch him stumble about. Where did he come from?

Can this be yourself, growing old? How terrible!

Now you avoid looking in your glass. You keep denying him, trying to push him away but, in spite of his groaning, his awkwardness, he is very strong. He has got possession. He hangs on. The other one, you knew so well, so long, is gone.

Now he can only come back to you in your dreams.

2. Work Fast, Man

It is an old saying that no man knows himself but surely there is much concerning the self that only the self can know.

What of this secret life we all lead, the secret thoughts we have, secret acts we do?

There is this man, of whom I have again proposed to write. I have been with him since he came from the womb, have walked with him, slept with him, worn his clothes, thought his thoughts. Never has he been able to escape from me or I from him.

Will I dare tell all I know of him?

No. I am quite sure I cannot do that, would not dare do that.

He has too often done things, mean ugly things he did not quite know he was doing. At such times, often I whispered to him, "Do not do it," but he went ahead, driven by some dark impulse.

Then he began justifying his acts, defending himself. An ugly enough act became something almost noble. It would all be quite laughable if it were not so sad.

And why tell all of this, or any part of it? Why bother?

But are we not now suddenly passing into a new phase of general life? Individuality is to pass away now. Not the individual but the state is to become all-important. Presently we will all be soldiers. We are to become like a swarm of bees in a beehive or like ants in an ant hill. Every act, every impulse in our lives will be directed.

So, you see, such books as the one I here propose to write will become historical documents. I am writing of a man, now rapidly becoming an old man. When he was a boy there were no automobiles, no airplanes, no radios. He spent his boyhood in a Middle-Western town where there was but one telephone. There were no chain stores. The great trusts that were to exert such a powerful influence on American life were just forming.

Men were free.

It is true that they were free to lie, to cheat, to gouge one another as well as to live. I shall not try, in preparing this historical document, to set the old life against the new. I shall try instead to be a true historian.

There is something deep down within me that laughs when I say that.

But never mind, I shall try. Courage, man! Soon there will be no such thing as individuality left. Hear the soft purr of the new thousands of airplanes far up in the sky. The bees are swarming. New hives are being formed. Work fast, man.

3. I Went with Eleanor

So I went along a Chicago street with my wife, Eleanor. She had on a black dress with a white front and sleeves, two long white wings thrown over her shoulder—

Small delicate feet, a big head, covered with blue-black hair, large eyes—

A quick sensitive face, always changing—small delicate hands too.

We were walking on sacred ground—sacred to me.

"Here," I said to myself as I walked along, "I have led so much of my life." We had gone from the Auditorium Hotel up Michigan Boulevard—wind whipping in the street—slender young girls passing—will I ever lose my eye for, my love of, these Middle-Western women—?

Ghosts too in the street—ghosts of women Eleanor had never known. Jane Heap, Margaret Anderson, Mary, Marietta—that queer assertive little one—Tennessee Mitchell—what sweet dignity there was in your stride, Tennessee—someone away back in your childhood had done you a great wrong. You could never quite tell of it, although you wanted to.

Or perhaps it was some man later—some poet—you had a passion for poets.

I remember Alys Bentley once shouting at you—

"Let go of it, Tennessee. Let go of it."

You couldn't, could you?

And yet you walked sweetly and with firm tread.

Thoughts rushing in me as I walked with Eleanor.

"Where are we going?"

"Well, never mind—come on."

Now every building along the street crying to me. Van Buren Street, Jackson, Adams, Monroe, Madison, Washington.

Big names, eh? Men who have been President.

Would you—Sherwood—have liked to be a big man in this American world?

No. No.

For this life of my own I would not trade any life ever lived here, on this American soil.

Eleanor sweetly, "Of what are you thinking?"

Myself. Don't talk. Come on. Give me this day, this hour.

Be silent, walk in silence with me.

A thought—you are an American woman and I love American women. They are our finest product so far. We haven't measured up to them yet.

There have been at least a dozen American women to whom I for example have tried to measure up and I have always failed.

In the shops—women's gowns, men's clothes. This is a rich street. I have always been a clothes lover, lover of fine fabrics.

I have always been wanting to take beautiful women into expensive little shops—"Here, have this. Take home this hat, this gown." Once little Anita Loos told me—it was at a time when she was rich—she told me how when she went to Paris she put aside one to three thousand dollars and spent it on little French shop girls met on Paris streets. "Here, come into this shop. Here's a hat for you. Here's a gown for you."

As fine as anything ever done, from woman to woman. American woman to French woman, that.

I myself—once—with a rich and beautiful American actress. She was going to the shops. This also in Paris. "Let me have your money. Let me put it in my pocket," I said.

I want to play, for this one afternoon, that I am a very rich American and that you are my mistress.

She was splendid, that actress.

Sherwood, you almost tempt me to take you for my lover.

No. No.

I want only to go to the shops with you. You are no sweet young virgin, are you?

No—alas.

Well, never mind. Let us imagine you are. I am rich. I am a poetic American banker.

Or a dreaming manufacturer of automobiles.

I have ruined you. I found you a simple country girl and led you astray.

Now I am going to try to make you happy.

I want to go into shops with you, stand about, looking rich and stupid.

Suddenly I will amaze the shopkeeper. She will be trying to sell you a hat or a gown not fitted to your type of beauty and I will step forward. And then to the amazement of the shopkeeper I step forward—I select the most beautiful hat for you—the most beautiful gown. I pull your money out of my pocket and pay for it.

And "Oh," cries the little shopkeeper. "What marvelous knowledge, what infallible, exquisite taste the American man has."

Oh, gorgeous actress. She let me do it.

"Of what are you thinking?" said Eleanor again that day in Chicago as we passed Monroe Street.

"I was thinking of the Monroe Doctrine and of how it has affected American international relations," I said.

"Liar," said she.

And so—

In the dark night,
  In the dark days
Martin Van Buren
  James Monroe
George Washington

Do you wish you were a big powerful man and lived in the White House?

It is said—any American boy, born in America, may be President.

(*Soft feminine voice*) "Why don't you come back from where you are?"

(*Answer*) "But I am here. I am walking beside you.

"Do you wish me always to be admiring you, seeking out your own little touches of beauty—

"In this great Middle-Western place of beautiful women—"

✦

They kept passing—walking in the wind-swept street. It would not do not to make conversation about the street—

On how many great streets have you walked.
Let's think
Avenue de l'Opéra
Unter den Linden
Royal and Canal Streets in New Orleans
The Strand
Cheap Street
Halsted Street
Euclid Avenue

Do you remember the day when you sat weeping in the Tuileries in Paris, tears running from your eyes, Sherwood, because you thought everything around you so beautiful—

Paul Rosenfeld coming to you as you sat weeping—wanting to sob—

"What's the matter, Sherwood?"

"Why, I have only got dust in my eyes."

Paul had got some money. Some forgotten aunt of his had died and when the will was read there was a little round sum for Paul and he had wired me—"Let's go to Paris and spend it."

"What do you suppose his aunt was like?" I said to Eleanor that day when we walked in Michigan Boulevard in Chicago.

Evening of a fall day.
Nights go on.
And days go on?

"Whose aunt? What are you talking about?

"I might as well have stayed in my hotel."

"My dear, you are mistaken about that. It is quite true that, often as I walk with you—as I am now doing—I do for the time—fleeting moments, thoughts passing my head.

"I am trying to tell you, dear, that I lose often all sense of you and your presence."

However—far back in me, sweet sense of how nice it is that you are here.

What a great lover I am. When I die a great lover will have gone out of the world.

It is quite true that often I do not love you—as an individual.

You get lost in something.

The larger synthesis, my dear.

Damn such a lover.

Wait, my dear. It is not only tall young women who walk here at evening. Let me look at my watch. It is just five. See them pouring into this street from other west-going streets.

"You shouldn't sing it in the open street; attracting attention to yourself—don't begin again, as you did a moment ago—singing

Washington
Monroe
Madison
etc.—

"Don't, dear."

What I was trying to say was that as I looked at strong young Middle-Western women—their arches, legs, shoulders, breasts, sweetness of mouths—there were strong young Middle-Western men looking at you, my dear.

4. Writers Sweet and Sour

I went for two or three weeks to the University of Colorado at Boulder. It was in the summer and I was to have four hundred dollars for going. I was to be the "star" of a sort of summer school for writers but was told that I would not have to teach. I was to deliver two talks, perhaps look at a select few of the manuscripts turned in, but, as it turned out, I was asked to conduct two classes. In one of them I talked of Ring Lardner and in the other of race horses. I got out pretty easily.

There were other writers also engaged. The two novelists, John Peale Bishop and Evelyn Scott, the poet John Crowe Ransom, the critic Howard Mumford Jones, but the most fuss was made over me. Ransom was one of the Southern group of poets, formerly connected with Vanderbilt University, at Nashville, Tennessee. He was one of the group calling themselves agrarians. They published a book called *We Take Our Stand.* The whole industrial civilization was to be done away with, that is to say in the South. For a time the group went about debating in other colleges and universities. They came to Richmond, Virginia, and I was asked to be the chairman of the meeting there. They debated with certain professors from the Virginia University. I thought the whole thing rather pathetic. A great host of people had come, the meeting was held in a large hall while these professors lost themselves in what seemed to me rather complicated academic theory. I was most amazed by the patience of the audience.

I made a suggestion to the agrarians. "Do not go about debating with other professors," I said. "Get some big industrialist to take you on."

They did that. There was a debate held at Atlanta, Georgia; an industrialist, from Macon, Georgia, one Anderson, came to Atlanta. He brought with him a troupe of young girls. They were employed in his cotton mill. He had them well trained. In the midst of the debate they marched in. They stood before the audience.

"Who do you love?" a leader asked.

"Anderson! Anderson!" they shouted.
"Who is the greatest man in the South?"
"Anderson! Anderson!"

At Boulder, Ransom talked of a new attitude taken by many of the former agrarians. It seemed they had dropped agrarianism. There was a sort of fascist program, that seemed, as Ransom spoke of it, to involve continual subjugation of the Negro and hatred of the Jews. There was something about adopting the feeling of the community in which you lived. If hatred of the Jews, for example, was a characteristic of the community you did not oppose it. You gave yourself to it.

However, the two talented novelists, Bishop and Scott, definitely held themselves open to sympathetic understanding of all sorts of people. I was particularly struck by Bishop, a man I thought as true and real a gentleman and thoroughbred as any man I have ever met.

It was a severe test, for there was I, being constantly played up, treated in a particularly special way while Bishop was often neglected. He did not seem to mind. In spite of it he could, seemingly without effort, accept me as a friend. I have known few other writers who could have commanded in themselves this fineness.

Figures of many writers are marching through my mind—some of them part of the Chicago summer when we all felt the world was our oyster. Henry Fuller. I saw him sometimes and remember him as a very reticent, sensitive-looking man, sitting in a small room filled with people. He had quit writing at an age when a writer should be at the height of his power and told Dreiser that he could not go on. The two men must have been sitting in a room together or perhaps they had gone for a walk and it pleases my fancy to imagine them so, perhaps walking about in the Chicago street, the small, shy, sensitive Fuller beside the bulky form of Dreiser. Dreiser for all his rough exterior would be as sensitive as the other man. His seeming brutality was always to be aimed against injustice, unfairness, the lie. Fuller has been telling Dreiser a story. It would be a simple, perhaps tragic, story of some family. The family would be friends of Fuller. "It is a strange, a little terrible, but quite wonderful story," he says, "but you see I cannot tell it."

"Why not?" says Dreiser.

"Oh, no, no, no. You see I know these people."

"But can you not cover them up? Put your story in another city. It is the kind of story that needs telling. Why not write it?"

"But I can't, can't. Alas, the new daring is not for me."

Fuller might even have laughed a little bitterly. "After all, I dare say I belong to the school of Dean Howells. You know what he said about presenting only a pleasanter aspect of our human existence." A roar from Dreiser that did not stop.

"I know, but it is not for me. I am at bottom a Victorian. It got into me when I was a child. I can't escape it. I have a mind and an imagination. I have eyes to see, ears to hear. The wall we are all building about ourselves must be broken down. We have come out of an age when we have all presumed, for example, that all women, that is to say good women, never have any impure thoughts, never have any impure desires. I know it is all wrong, that it would be sweeter and better, healthier for us all, to have more of the reality of life come into our writing, but I cannot do it."

"Nor can I go on writing the everlasting cheerful meaningless stuff we are expected to write.

"Therefore I quit. I have told you this story. I know a thousand such stories. America is full of wonderful material for stories. You may have it if you want the story."

Jack Reed. I can't remember when I first met him, although it must have been during one of the early trips I took to New York. I would have been sent East by my advertising agency. There were accounts to be written, the agency having established a New York office. Already some of the men of the world of writers I had known in Chicago had gone on to New York. I saw Floyd Dell, who had joined the editorial staff of the old *Masses,* Lucian Cary, who was later to become a successful *Saturday Evening Post* writer, and many others, met through them. It must have been at the time that I first saw Max Eastman, the cartoonist Art Young, Griffin Barry, and a dozen others. There had been this sudden outbreak of the little magazines, the highbrow magazines.

I remember a hot summer night in the apartment of Edna Kenton.

She had gone away somewhere for the summer and had left her apartment in the hands of Griffin Barry, and on a certain night we foregathered there.

It was a very, very hot night. It was so hot that as the night went on, as the drinks were passed, and the literary discussion grew hotter, we began to strip. More and more clothes were taken off. We were at last in our underwear and I remember the occasion so vividly because mine was so ragged.

It was an old fault of mine, this wearing underwear until there was nothing left but rags, but what was I to do? The others were stripping, so strip I did and there was a great shout.

"For God's sake . . . will you look at him?"

I remember my mother had always been afraid of this.

"You will get caught yet," she was always saying to me. She begged me to let her patch my underwear but I refused.

"But there will be an accident. You may be struck by a train." She thought it would be a reflection on herself, on her motherhood; and here I was caught. After the night in the Kenton apartment . . . we came near wrecking it before the night was over . . . I kept meeting men who had been present.

"Oh, yes," they said, "you are the man of the ragged underwear."

Was Jack Reed there on that occasion? I can't remember. However I remember breakfasting with him a short time later. He was married then to Louise Bryant, who wrote the so sobful book about him after his death, a great fellow, big of body, warm, and with, I remember, a fine joyousness in him.

I had the impression of him, then and later, as a playboy.

He had already made a reputation for himself, was a well-known reporter, had been all over Europe looking at the various wars, and had been with Villa in Mexico.

He was a reporter, but was also a poet, and on the occasion when I breakfasted with him, over our coffee he read some of his verses.

We had a talk then, and a good deal of talk later, and I remember, in particular, a certain winter evening in New York, snow flying, and Jack and I walking on Fifth Avenue. On that occasion he said something to me that I remembered sharply later, when he had gone to Russia, taken part in the revolution there, sickened and died, and been buried in the Kremlin, the American hero of the revolution, hero also of all the young American Communists.

This man walking with me in the snowing night.

"And it is your first love, the revolution?" I had asked him and he laughed.

He was big of body, loosely built. He kept pulling up his pants.

"If I could be sure," he said.

"Of what?"

"That I had it."

He stopped walking and put his hand on my shoulders. This at the corner of Fifth Avenue and Fourteenth Street, in New York.

It would have been just at the hour when mobs of people were pouring out of buildings and lofts, homeward bound. There was an ocean of people about us.

"If I thought I was a real poet."

"A man must do what he can."

"If I thought I was a real poet I would let everything else go."

This impression of the man, and another. I was in the city of Chicago and the World War came on. There I was, still marooned in the advertising office, and there was a telephone call. It was from Jack.

"I want to see you," he said and gave an address and I went to him.

He was in a hall, somewhere on Chicago's West Side, and there was a meeting being held in the hall. I have a notion that it was the beginning of the organization of the American Communist Party and I remember a speaker standing up and myself at the door. There must also have been secret service men about. I was told afterwards that certain men later given twenty years by Judge Landis, were at that meeting, and it may be because of my presence there that day that I also became a suspect. During the rest of my stay in Chicago my mail was opened. It came to me marked "Opened by Censor."

I asked for him at the door and he came.

"Come on," he said and led me down a flight of stairs and into a toilet. It was a big toilet, with a trough at which many men could stand. He stood and I stood.

And then suddenly he was as I remember him best. He was no more the revolutionist. I remember that I asked him what they were doing above. "To hell with that," he said.

He said that they had got to a resolution stage in the meeting above and that he was sick of it.

"I am afraid it will always turn out so," he said and there came to his face the curious boyish wistful look by which I remember the man. He had asked me to come because, he said, he had written some verses he thought were good.

"They have the toughness I want," he said and gave them to me.

I remember that I later thought they were indifferent verses.

"All right, take them. You read them and we'll have a talk," he said, and I left him.

It was the last time I ever saw him, but if later I thought the verses indifferent enough and the man but half a poet in words, I did feel that he was, in a very real sense, a poet of living.

I was filled with admiration for D.M. I was also very grateful to him but in the end something came between us.

It is a thing that may be very old in the world. To my mind . . . the realization came to me slowly . . . it is about the most destructive thing in life.

As to D.M. he seemed to me when we met, to be very warm and alive. He had so much that I wanted for myself. D.M. was a college man. He had, as a young man and after college, gone to live in Europe. He had acquired languages, spoke French, Spanish, Italian. He was one of several men who, when I had begun to write, was struggling to get something within myself out to others, had put out a hand to me.

I had written some stories about people I had seen.

But no, they were not that. They were people who had come to life in a special world of my own.

These people had become very real to me. Had I actually plucked them out of life? I never knew.

They were in me for a long time. I felt them, had their thoughts, passions, fears, lusts, moments of hope and despair.

In my stories I had tried to let them be born out of myself and when the stories were at last printed I was terribly shocked and hurt to find that the stories offended others.

It was D.M. who had used a curious phrase about me. He had spoken of me as a great man.

"A great man being born into the world, eh?" There was a shock. Something ugly has happened again. There had been in what D.M. had written this warmth, enthusiasm, fine generosity.

"But why that about greatness?"

It was some time later that D.M. and I became friends and for a time we were much together and my admiration for D.M. for a time kept growing.

"Oh, that I could know so much, could speak languages, have this man's familiarity with the literature and thoughts of the world." It was, for a time, something wonderful for me that I could have, as a friend, such a one as D.M. I went to my friend's house, went to dine with him, went with him into the country. For hours often I sat, filled with wonder and admiration, while D.M. talked.

There was this seeming ocean of knowledge. D.M. had read all of the great masters in their own languages. He had traveled over the world, had talked intimately with men who had written notable books. He was the son of a rich man and knew the cities of the world, how to order wines, how to live richly and well.

D.M. was also a writer. He wrote books and stories. His talk began to take on a new tone. There was again that talk of greatness.

Will our names go down to posterity?

There were pictures made for me—of statues to be built for us when we were dead. Once we were walking on a bridge that crossed a river and I later remembered gulls flying in the air over the river. I remembered the color of the water of the river. In the distance there was a ship tied to the dock and I began to think it was like a gull alighted there in the distance on the water but at that moment D.M. spoke to me of something. He spoke of what a tragedy it would be to literature if the bridge on which we walked should go down.

It is true he said it with laughter but nevertheless it hurt me.

It was as though a black cloud had descended, hiding the ship in the distance, the gulls flying, the river flowing.

So I began to see less and less of D.M., but one day I got a letter.

The letter again spoke of greatness.

"Do you not think, Sherwood, that you and I . . ." he named a third ". . . that we are the great men of our time?" I did not answer the letter but one day D.M. came to my room. I was living at that time in New York. It was when the World War was on and I had hidden myself away. I had got a room in a workingmen's quarter of the city.

It was a time of too much greatness.

Great generals.

Great statesmen.

Great hatreds sweeping through the world.
Great writers glorifying war.
Great diplomats at work.

It was a flood. It was, to me, terrible, unbearable. I had hidden myself away. More and more I had retreated into an old life I had known before the war came. I wanted passionately now to think not of great soldiers, statesmen, writers, but of being first of all little.

I wanted again the little life—in streets, on farms, in towns, in little frame houses in towns and cities. I was fighting to live in that life, in spite of the great war and hubbub going on everywhere about me, to keep that old life alive in myself.

I was there, in that place, when one day D.M. came to me.

He came into my room; he sat in a chair. He was as he had always been. There was warmth in him.

This was after my first marriage. I did not live with my wife but I had become the father of children as had D.M. For the time we had both escaped the draft. In the end we did escape.

The man was sitting in my room and I was angry. I got up from my chair and walked to a window. I did not face my friend. I talked.

I was very bitter. I spoke of the letter I had received. "It was vile," I said. I asked D.M. to leave my room and not to return.

"There is this talk of greatness. It is your disease and you are trying to give it to me." I declared that no such thing as a great man could exist. I said, "I am trying here, in this room, to hang onto something, and you come to destroy it.

"It is hard enough," I said, "for me to keep myself, occasionally, out from between myself and what I am trying to do.

"The struggle is hard enough without you and your greatness."

I had begun to shout. I wanted to run to D.M., strike him in the face, throw him down, kick him down the flight of stairs that led to the street and when I turned from the window there was D.M. in tears.

D.M. had gone very pale. He had moved from his chair. He was on my bed. He was lying on the bed, his face buried in a pillow, his shoulders shaking, and when he had recovered a little he began to thank me for all I had said.

He sat up on the bed and talked. He wiped away his tears and coming across the room took my hand.

"You are the only friend I have ever had. You have spoken truth to me. Your words have been like knives. They have entered my heart.

"What I have been I shall never be again."

There was this moment between us. We stood holding each other's hand. The warmth in D.M. seemed to flow over me. I also felt like crying.

We left my room and went for a walk. We were walking just as darkness came in a city street.

It was a poor section of the city and children were laughing and playing in the street. There was for me on that evening as I walked with D.M., for a time, for five minutes, ten, perhaps twenty minutes, something very wonderful in the city street, in the sight of wives of workers going in at the doors of little stores, in the shouts of children.

The war seemed for the moment very far away. We were walking in silence.

"I have got my friend back," I thought. I was thinking that, just at the time, more than anything else in the world I was wanting such friends.

"I have been mistaken in him. He is not what I had begun to think and fear. This talk of greatness, himself great, me great, or to become great, is only something superficial in him.

It has passed now. There will be no more of it. It may begin now.

Two men friends.

Then four.

Then more and more.

Man to man.

No more greatness nor talk of greatness.

A beginning. A new passion loose in the world, to want to be little, not be big.

I had got into a kind of exaltation. I was walking thus with D.M., thinking these thoughts when D.M. spoke. He spoke of the fact that he had money.

"You have never been to Europe, have you, Sherwood?

"You see this war will not always go on.

"We must go together, but not yet.

"Not yet," he said. "We must wait.

"We must wait until our names have rung through Europe, until we are known, appreciated, until all Europe is standing with open arms waiting for us." D.M. had said this to me. We were still walking together. Yes, I had wanted to strike D.M., to choke him, kick him, hurt him, but now I only smiled. We had come to a street corner and I put out my hand. I took D.M.'s hand. I smiled. "Well, good-by, D.M.," I said, and smiling went back to my room.

I was with Frank Swinnerton and Arnold Bennett at a club in London. I had met Swinnerton on the boat and had found him charming company. Swinnerton was a great admirer of Bennett, and I thought Bennett's *Old Wives' Tale* one of the richest novels I had ever read.

At the club I was rude. I thought that later Bennett had gone too obviously into cheap romancing. Someone had told me that Bennett was hungry for money and position. He wanted to become Sir Arnold Bennett.

The club to which we went seemed to me also a heavy, ponderous place and I thought that Bennett had become ponderous. I got a little nasty and could not resist the impulse to remind Bennett of what we were.

"You know what we are," I said, "we are all whores."

Perhaps Bennett was not as shocked as I hoped. Later Bennett wrote his autobiography (We all do it. We are doing it all our lives) and in it he spoke kindly enough of the meeting.

I was on the boat with Swinnerton and there were two other American writers on the boat. Swinnerton spoke of them.

"They would like to meet you but they are afraid of you."

At first I didn't understand.

"Afraid? I do not understand."

It was explained that they were afraid I would have contempt for them.

They both wrote detective stories. They were men who made twenty, thirty thousand a year by their trade.

"But, Frank—that is something, twenty, thirty thousand . . . how wonderful."

I was thinking of all the things I could do with all that money. All my life I had had a passionate desire.

With that much money coming in I would buy a stable of race horses.

I would not buy runners. I would buy trotters and pacers.

In the winter I would go, say, to the Old Glory sale of colts. At that time the sale was held every winter in an armory in New York City. Whenever the sale was on and I was in New York I went there.

But I had no money to buy colts, and what glorious creatures they were. They were being bid off at four, five, six hundred; two, three, four thousand dollars each.

I had to sit down among the buyers.

Oh, what fortunate men. How passionately I wanted to buy four, five, six, a dozen of the beautiful creatures. And then to train them, patiently, sitting day after day in one of the little carts, some such highly bred colt between my legs.

The stroke of the colt to be perfected, the perfect balance caught. The man, the driver, myself, to become more and more a part of the horse.

Oh, what had man sacrificed when he had given up the horse, the daily companion, for the automobile!

The trotter or the pacer so different from the runner. Here was discipline. I would train the colts to hold and perfect the stroke of the trotter pace as I was always trying to train my hand to march across the pages on my desk.

The sentences to march, to be disciplined, to hold a balance, and yet to go at speed.

More and more speed. There are so many stories to be told.

But never mind the sentences, the sheet of paper, the books.

I would be first a horseman, nothing more. I would take my colts off in the winter to some little Southern town where there was a race track. There would be Negro grooms, one for each colt, and all day they would train the colts, living in that world of delicately adjusted horseflesh.

At night sitting over a little stove, with the Negro men.

Perhaps they would sing songs, tell stories. That would be a life.

And then, later, when the colts were trained to go at speed, not to lose their stride, to go off to the races, to go to country homes, all over America, the common folks, farmers and small towners gathered in, men who still understood the delicacy and balance of the finely trained pacer or trotter.

Myself driving daringly, taking my life in my hands, darting my colt through narrow openings where the wheels of racing carts just touched on either side of me.

The other drivers such hearty fellows, swearing at me, cursing me.

It all was in the game. Later, when I had won the race the same men coming to slap me on the back.

"Boy, that was glove-hand driving you did."

No puny artist man here—artists instead in horseflesh.

Given twenty, thirty thousand a year, for one or two years, I would disappear into the ranks of the harness horse drivers.

An old dream out of my boyhood, coming back one day as I sat on the deck of an ocean steamer with Frank Swinnerton, hearing him tell me that two other writers aboard the ship were afraid to meet me because they were making twenty to thirty thousand a year by writing romances and detective stories.

I sat staring at Swinnerton. I was puzzled.

"If I could write detective stories, and make that much money, surely I would do it." This thought in my mind.

It was surely a gift, this fabricating of such stories. It was a special talent. You worked it out like a mathematical problem.

I had myself no talent for solving problems. It happened my mind did not work that way.

My own stories were picked up from observing people, from my own experiences of life, my own feelings.

Often my stories shocked people, challenged them.

Did I want to do that?

I certainly did not.

There was no reformer in me. Often I had said to myself that, if the power were suddenly given me, as Omar said—to break life into bits and then remold it nearer to the heart's desire—if the power were given to me to smash and remold all society by the turning over of my hand, no power on earth could induce me to turn it.

I had wanted to tell the story of things seen, felt, tasted, heard, nothing more.

And it was possible, I had afterwards thought, that the thing I was always trying to do, to get the smell, the taste, the sound, the feel of life into my tales, was really immoral.

After all, life as I had known it in myself and others wasn't so sweet, and these others, the romancers, the writers of detective stories, movies, etc., did at least, for a time, take people away from the pain of living.

I had quite worked myself up that day on the boat with Swinnerton, was ready to cry "all hail" to the successful writers of detective stories.

Earlier in life I had happened to pick up a detective story by the Englishwoman, Dorothy Sayers, and what joy it had given me.

Oh, how perfectly she had got the place, the English advertising agency, so like its American counterpart.

I had run about giving the book to everyone.

"Read it. Read it. It is wonderful."

I had begun to urge upon Swinnerton that he bring one of the successful detective story writers to me.

"Please do. I want to talk with him."

And then I met one of the men and together we walked about on the deck of the boat.

How strange. Why was this thing always happening?

It is bad for the writer to associate with the kind of writers we now produce. To associate with their wives is even worse. The men sometimes have moments of being ashamed. The wives never. These men have made a business of writing. They speak and talk of nothing else.

They call it "work." Such conversations as this always go on.

"I am at my desk at night."

"I work until twelve."

"How are things going with you?" says one.

He means, how are your pencils holding up.

Their wives chatter endlessly—always about writing.

Such men make money and collect things—old furniture, rare editions. They are like bankers trying to prove their culture. A worried, nervous, useless crew.

I would rather be a Negro deck hand on a steamboat.

Give me for associates, farmers, cattle buyers, railroad men, sailors, small merchants, taxi drivers.

How can a man grow rich writing who has good taste?

Good taste is as necessary to friendship as breath to the body.

When I have been a long time away from the haunts of writers I forget what they are like. I go to New York or Paris. God only knows how gladly I escape these places.

Bertrand Russell and the Negro Women. I used to see Bertrand Russell at Horace Liveright's apartment in New York, and I found him a very friendly and charming man. He sat amidst all of the hullabaloo going on in the Liveright apartment smoking his pipe and with a dry smile on his face.

Some man had an idea. He engaged Russell and me to debate on the subject of the care of children. We were to have five hundred each, but, in the end, had to settle for something like three hundred each. It seemed that the populace wasn't sufficiently interested. The man who gambled upon our drawing a crowd was disappointed.

We went to debate the question as to whether it was better for the children to be raised by the state or by the parents of the children and I was on the parents' side.

My daughter made an amusing remark. She had come to see me.

"I hear you are to debate with Bertrand Russell."

I admitted that there was some such plan afoot.

"And what is the subject of the debate?"

I told her.

"And what side are you on?"

I told her that too.

"What, you?" she said.

I rather think I did Russell dirt. I went through his books. I remembered the old saying, "Oh, that my enemy would write a book," and Russell had written many books. As I was to have the floor during the last ten minutes I planned to take the time reading sentences of his that would refute all he could say on the other side of the question.

Russell was entirely fair and of course I was not. As we stood together in the wings, before going on the stage, he warned me.

"You won't mind if I am a bit rough with you?"

I said I wouldn't mind.

"I am going to be a bit rough myself. I'm going to do you dirt."

My wife, who was present, was bitterly disappointed by my appearance, so disappointed that I am sure she did not hear the debate. I had put on evening clothes but had forgotten to change my socks. I had on red socks. I am very fond of red socks and neckties. I forgot.

Later I was unable to convince my wife that I had been very brilliant, had annihilated poor Russell.

"I didn't hear you," she said. "I was so ashamed. You looked so grotesque."

Tommy Smith, who was at the time Horace Liveright's editorial chief, wanted to give a party for Russell. It may be that Russell had expressed a desire to see the life of Harlem.

At any rate, we went there, had dinner, and Tommy, to make the dinner quite complete, had invited two very charming Negro women to dine with us.

There must have been two or three other men and I remember that the poet Genevieve Taggard dined with us and was very beautiful and the life of the party.

And there were the two Negro women who were no doubt from the very upper crust of Harlem's social and intellectual set. They were very quiet and took part in the dinner conversation and it was evident that they were what is called well read. No doubt, they were the daughters of wealthy men. They had been students in one of the more fashionable Northern woman's colleges, Bryn Mawr or Smith.

They were also very beautiful, with the strangely soft brown eyes of their race, both slender and tall, both with rich high brown skins and both beautifully clad.

So we dined and went on to a cabaret where there was dancing.

It was a brown and white place. It was the thing you find in Harlem. The men of our party danced but they did not dance with the two Negro women, and so I did.

We had dined with them. They were our guests. Tommy Smith had arranged it so and it seemed to me rather a shabby thing that, under the circumstances, the two young Negro women should be left sitting at the table while man after man of our party danced with Genevieve.

Besides they were wonderful dancers.

And so all evening I danced with them and what amazed me was that Russell was shocked.

He came and spoke to me about it.

"It isn't done, old chap."

He shook his head over my extraordinary behavior.

But they were our guests. Tommy had invited them. "They have dined with us. They are, as you can see, very beautiful; and they dance wonderfully."

However, he kept insisting that what I was doing was in some way wrong, not the proper thing to do. He was being very English, very upper-class that evening. In spite of all of his radicalism I could feel old Lord John Russell very much taking command of Bertrand for at least that evening.

✦

Of Faulkner and Hemingway. The two most notable writers, it seems to me, who have come on in America since the World War are these two men. I knew them both rather intimately just after the war, before either had published. I had a quarrel with each. Both men were terribly injured in the war. One is a Northern man, the other Southern. Hemingway, who was, I believe, with the Italian army, drove an ambulance, and Faulkner was with the English, in the air.

If you want to know what happened to Hemingway and how magnificently he recovered, read *The Sun Also Rises* and then read *A Farewell to Arms.* Then, if you do not get his story, I shall never tell it.

Hemingway is a large man and Faulkner is small. I remember Hemingway most vividly as he came one evening in Chicago to my apartment. He had just got married and had got a job as a Paris correspondent, I believe, for a group of Canadian newspapers. He was leaving for Europe the next morning and had packed into a huge army knapsack all the provisions left over at his place.

That was a nice idea, bringing thus to a fellow scribbler the food he had to abandon. The big knapsack was filled with canned foods. I remember his coming up the stairs, a magnificent broad-shouldered man, shouting as he came. Why, there must have been a hundred pounds of perfectly good rations in that knapsack.

I first saw Bill Faulkner when he came to my apartment in New Orleans. You will remember the story of Abraham Lincoln's meeting with the Southern commissioners, on the boat, on the Potomac in 1864. The Southern commissioners had come to try to negotiate some sort of peace and among them was the Vice-President of the confederacy, Alexander Stephens. He was such a small man and wore a huge overcoat.

"Did you ever see so much shuck for so little nubbin?" Lincoln said to a friend.

I thought of the story when I first saw Faulkner. He also had on a big overcoat, it being winter, and it bulged strangely, so much, that, at first glance, I thought he must be in some queer way deformed. He told me that he intended to stay for some time in New Orleans and asked if in the meantime, while he was looking for a place, he could leave some of his things with me. His "things" consisted of some six or eight half gallon jars of moon liquor he had brought with him from the country and that were stowed in the pockets of the big coat.

Faulkner is a man of great talent who has one fault. He is too talented, too clever. He can write you any sort of story you wish, but, at the same time, his work has been tremendously healthy. For one thing he exposed a lot of Southern bunk. After all, there is a lot of insanity in the South. Everywhere there are those decayed families making claim to aristocracy, often living very isolated lives in lonely, run-down Southern towns, surrounded by Negroes. There is a kind of cruelty thought necessary to keep the Negro, as they say, "in his place."

In these isolated towns and on the plantations there are no books. Many of the towns are so small that there are no movies. Nearly all of the young people, men, begin their sex life with Negro girls.

Faulkner has got hold of the queer sort of insanity that results. He understands and draws clearly the little white business man, the small white farmers; still, at the same time, there is in him also a lot of the same old bunk about the South. I remember, when I first met him, when he had first come from his own little Southern town, sitting with him one evening before the cathedral in New Orleans while he contended with entire seriousness that the cross between the white man and the Negro woman always resulted, after the first crossing, in sterility. He spoke of the cross between the jack and the mare that produced the mule and said that, as between the white man and the Negro woman, it was just the same.

However, there never was any doubt in my mind about Faulkner. From the first he was a real writer. He had the touch—and in the novel *The Sound and the Fury* he finally produced a beautiful and sympathetic piece of work. Here is a story of Southerners as remote from the South most people think of—the South of romance that doesn't exist, thank God—as J. J. Lankes' lovely Virginia woodcuts are remote from the Virginia of "The Valley," the place to which come the rich from New York, trying to make themselves believe they are Virginians.

There was always something finer and certainly more generous in Faulkner than, for example, in Hemingway. I speak of the two men together, also, because it was through my efforts that both first got published. I'm not certain Hemingway was pleased. When he began to write, he began with the short story and I had already published my *Winesburg, Ohio*. I had published also my *Horses and Men* and my *Triumph of the Egg,* and, I dare say, more than one critic, in speaking of his work, attributed his impulse to me. They had even perhaps intimated that I was a strong influence.

It is a thing that happens to every writer when he begins. My own impulse had been attributed to Dreiser, to the Russians, whom I had, at the time, never read. Anyway it is sure that if others said I had shown Hemingway the way, I myself had never said so. I thought, as I did in the case of Faulkner, that he had his own gift, which had nothing particularly to do with me.

In the case of Hemingway there may have been something else. Absorption in his ideas may have affected his capacity for friendship.

At any rate I had taken our friendship for granted when he went off to Paris. I am told, he attributed what happened to the influence of a friend. I am referring to the attack upon me in the form of *The Torrents of Spring,* the parodistic book which might have been humorous had Max Beerbohm condensed it into twelve pages.

I got a letter from Hemingway. This after he had written and published *The Torrents of Spring*. It was certainly the most self-conscious and probably the most completely patronizing letter ever written.

He spoke of the book as something fatal to me. He had, he said, written it on an impulse, taking only six weeks to do it. It was intended to bring to an end, once and for all, the notion that there was any worth in my own work. This, he said, was a thing he had hated doing, because of his personal regard for me, and he had done it in the interest of literature. Literature, I was to understand, was bigger than either of us.

There was something in the letter that was gigantic. It was a kind of funeral oration delivered over my grave. It was so raw, so pretentious, so patronizing that in a repellent way it was amusing, but I was filled with wonder. Just what I said to him, in return, I don't remember. It was something to the effect that I thought it foolish that we writers should devote our time to the attempt to kill each other off. In the letter he had used a prize-fighting term, speaking of the knockout blow he had given me, and in my answer I think I did say that I had always thought of myself as a pretty good middleweight and I doubted *his* ever being able to make the heavyweight class.

However, I can't be sure. I kept no copy of my letter.

I did not see Hemingway for a long time after the incident. When he had gone to Paris I had given him a note to my friend, Gertrude Stein, with whom he was also friends for several years. Later she told me, in speaking of the ugly matter, that Hemingway's grievance flowed from my having written two stories, "I'm a Fool" and "I Want to Know Why"; she suggested that he had, in his own mind, staked out the whole field of sports for himself.

I had given Hemingway letters to other friends in Paris and among others, one to Ralph Church. Church, who was at that time a student at Oxford . . . he was specializing in philosophy . . . ran over to Paris often and, for a year or two, he and Hemingway were much together.

And then, after several years, I came to Paris and there was Church and there was also Hemingway, and Church was amused. He used to go to Hemingway saying, "Sherwood is in town. Why don't you go to see him?" and, when he had said it, he told me that Hemingway always declared his real friendship for me.

"I am going to see him today," he said each time the matter was brought up, but he did not appear.

It came to my last day in Paris and I was sitting in my room, having packed. Church had told him of my plan to depart and there was a sudden knock on the door of my hotel room, and there Hemingway was.

He stood in the doorway.

"How about a drink?" he said, and I followed him down a stairway and across a street.

We went into a small bar.

"What will you have?"

"Beer."

"And you?"

"A beer."

"Well, here's how."

"Here's how."

He turned and walked rapidly away. He had, I dare say, proved his sportsmanship to himself.

But what about Faulkner? After the New Orleans days and after I had made a fight to get his book published, as I had with Hemingway, going personally to Horace Liveright to plead for the books, I did not see him again for years.

It is true that Bill had dedicated a book to me and he had written me no patronizing letters speaking of knockout blows, of his sorrow over my death as a writer, etc., but he had caused me to remember an old story. It is the story of the politician who, finding a certain man fighting him, speaks to a friend.

"What is the matter with Bill?" he asks. "Why is he so against me? I can't understand his hatred of me. I never did anything to help him."

Not that my going to bat for either of the two men, mentioned here, was personal. They were both men of ability. I went to bat for that ability.

But I did remember the story of the politician and, when, after a good many years, I was one day in New York at a cocktail party and saw Faulkner there, I avoided him.

"It will be better," I thought. But presently, as I did not approach the man, he came to me. He took hold of my coat sleeve and pulled me aside. He grinned.

"Sherwood, what the hell is the matter with you? Do you think I'm a mucker?" he asked.

Tobacco Boy. The playwright, Paul Green, told me a story. He was raised as a boy on a farm in eastern North Carolina. It was in the great coastal plain.

He was ambitious, eager, strong. He wanted to go to college.

His father gave him a chance. There was a certain field.

"It's yours. You take it. Raise yourself a crop of tobacco."

Paul Green, as a young boy, must have been very much alive. He is still that way. Life bubbles and boils in him.

So he went to it. He did raise himself a crop of tobacco. It is a job.

First you must make your seed-bed. The best plan is to go find yourself a bit of new ground. You go, perhaps, to the edge of a wood. For a long time leaves have been falling and decaying. The ground is rich.

You put some litter on it. You burn it over. This is to kill the insect life in the ground.

You prepare the ground. You put in the seed. You go to town and get a thin kind of cloth. It is called mosquito netting. You stretch it over your seed-bed.

The plants come up.

You have prepared your field, plowed it, harrowed it. You set out your plants.

But, for all their strength, it seems the tobacco plants are delicate.

You must cultivate the ground. There is a certain worm. Look out for him. Every day you must go, lift the leaves, look.

"Ah, there you are."

You keep after the worms, you cultivate, you pinch out the buds that will grow into blossoms.

You are not raising seed tobacco. You are raising tobacco to sell.

The tobacco grows. It puts out broad leaves. The tobacco plant is a magnificent plant. In all nature there is nothing more gorgeous than a field of tobacco.

So it grows strong and big. You cut it. There are some who cure the tobacco on racks in the field. Others take it to a barn.

You must have a special barn. You must let the breezes blow through. You must not let too much dampness in.

Your tobacco must be cured properly. It may become spotted. Look out. You must know how to do it.

You make it into bundles. They are called "hands."

You pile it on a truck.

Now you are going to the tobacco market. Your tobacco is to be auctioned off.

Paul told the story of his experience. He went through it all. All summer he worked. He had no truck and his father had none.

He had to hire a truck. He went off with the truck and his tobacco to the tobacco market. The owner and driver of the truck was a neighbor.

He was at the market. Farmers had gathered in. Paul's tobacco with that of many others had been put into great baskets. It was on the floor. The floor was huge. There were long rows of tobacco.

There were farmers walking up and down. They were experienced men. The sale was going on. A group of farmers came to Paul's baskets.

Paul said he was leaning against a wall. He said his heart was thumping. Soon the auctioneer would come to his basket.

There was a group of farmers idly walking. Paul said they came to his basket. They stopped. They inspected his tobacco. They looked at it. They pulled out "hands."

They laughed.

"Well, for God's sake, look at this trash."

Paul said he sat down on the floor near the wall.

"I wasn't thinking of the money," he said. "I was so ashamed I wanted to cry."

He said the auctioneer came and sold his tobacco.

"I didn't listen much," he said. He said he got for his whole summer's work just enough to pay for the truck.

He said he rode home with the man who owned the truck.

He rode a long way and "he didn't say a word, nor did I. Night was coming on," he said.

He said that he and the man who owned the truck had got almost home before the man spoke.

"And what did he say?"

"He said that life was hell all right, and I agreed with him.

"And then," said Paul, "we both laughed.

"What else was there to do?" he said.

Ford Madox Ford was a true literary man. He was always generous, particularly to young writers, often too generous. A thin trickle of talent became to him a flood. A talk with Ford would send a young writer floating away into feathery clouds. Publishers and editors would clamor for his work. When he awoke in the morning there would be a dozen of them camped on his doorstep.

Indeed, in Ford's imagination they did camp there. I once heard him tell a tale of such an incident. He had found a young writer. He had proclaimed him. Now there were a dozen publishers after him. Only the other day he came home from a walk and there were three publishers waiting for him. Ford was telling the tale as a fact, and to him it was a fact. Later I saw the young writer and spoke of it. A sickly smile came to his lips. "You see Ford wanted it. He wanted it so much that it became a fact to him," he said. At least he understood Ford, the depth and sincerity of his generosity.

Once, in the city of Paris, I met Ford at a party. It was before disease had begun to punish his poor body. He took my arm and led me into a corner.

"You are just the man I have been waiting to see." He began to speak of a house he had in the hills of Pennsylvania. There it was. He described the house, the view from a terrace at the front, the garden, the apple trees that grew on a nearby hillside. The house was beautifully furnished and there was a retinue of servants. The pity was that he had built the house, intending to go there to work, but had never been able to do so.

And what was a man to do? He could not bear the thought of discharging the servants and closing the house. And why should I not take the place, go there to live, Ford wanted to know? It would cost me nothing. The house had been built having in mind some writer who wanted to retire to some such quiet and secluded spot to work.

"Please," he said, "you take it. You go there. At least promise me that you will spend your summer there." His voice was rich with fervor. There was an eager light in his eyes.

Only those who knew Ford well will understand how sincere the offer was, how real and tangible the house had become to him.

At the time I did not know Ford well. "He is a rich man who has houses scattered about the world," I thought.

During the course of that evening, Ford offered me two other houses, one in Florida and another in California. They were there waiting. "A man can't go about discharging servants. It upsets him too much, gets his mind off his work."

As I was nearly broke at the time, I took all of this with entire seriousness. Now I know that, in offering the houses, Ford was himself entirely serious. The houses existed for him. He was a man who lived in a splendid world, created in his own imagination, and the world he had created was gloriously real to him.

A Famous Man. In Mexico in the city of Acapulco, I met a man with whom I had formerly been associated. He was the advertising manager for one of the greatest of America's industries for which, at one time, I wrote advertisements. I had not seen him for some twenty years. He rushed up to me, began to introduce me to his friends.

"Here," he declared, "we have one of America's great writers."

He began speaking of my great success, evidently convinced that I had become rich. He kept speaking of my greatness as a writer but gradually, as he talked on, a puzzled look came into his eyes and into the eyes of the friends with whom he was traveling. He was on some sort of tour and with him and his wife were several other American business men with their wives. He drew me away from them.

"I know you are a great writer," he said. "I have heard that, but, you see, when I am again alone with them, my friends will be asking me what you have written.

"I think you had better tell me," he said.

5. Mexican Night

Since they have built the new paved road from Laredo on the border down over the mountains to Mexico City, the tourists in their cars come always in greater and greater numbers. They come from the cities and from the small towns. Sometimes the cars come singly and sometimes in cavalcades. There is the fascination of being in a strange foreign place and of getting what seems such a lot of Mexican dollars for, say, a ten-dollar bill. We tourists buy guide books and dictionaries. Some of us . . . bring cameras and take thousands of shots of the straw-thatched huts in Mexican villages, of the little naked boy babies, of the arrieros, with their pack trains . . . the little shuffling burros with their half dance step under their great loads, followed by their Indian drivers, also shuffling softly, softly along.

We tourists are like an army in that we all seem to congregate in certain towns, in certain hotels. On the way down and back we stop at the same towns. We go to the Xochimilco, to Taxco, where we buy silver of Bill Spratling. We gather together in groups and, as it is in the army, strange and often unfounded rumors run about among us.

There is, for example, always the idea that a revolution may start at any moment. That and the question of holdups, or people kidnapped, carried off by bandits into the hills. It all gives a thrill, adds a touch of spice. You'd really think there had never been such a thing as a kidnapping or a holdup in our own beloved land.

This or that happened to a man from Des Moines. "There was a man, one of the natives, came right up to him. I got this straight. He asked this man a question and because he couldn't answer, didn't know the lingo, the fellow drew a knife and stabbed him. Of course it wasn't in the papers. They don't let you know such things.

"And they say that the soldiers you see . . . they say they'll hold you up as quick as a bandit."

These and other stories, running among us tourists. I've an idea that most of us, the males among us, would much rather be at home or, if we have to take the wife for a trip, we'd much rather have gone to California, say to Hollywood. We tell each other so. "But, you see, there's the wife," we say. We explain to one another how it is, how, just because certain women from our towns have been down here and have brought home a lot of baskets and these serapes and things and maybe made talks before the Women's Clubs about Mexican art and this Diego Rivera, we have to be dragged down.

We had got into this little Mexican town, Fred and I and the two newspaper men. It was when the President of Mexico took over the oil companies, American and British, and the newspaper men were going down by train but, as we had space in the car, they said they would come with us.

So we were in this town off the big highway and it was night and, when we had been there for an hour or two, one of the newspaper men who spoke Spanish, having got us well fixed up in the town's one hotel, these other people arrived. They were like us in that they were in a town where few tourists stopped. They had got out of the main stream, had perhaps lost their way. There was a small, nervous man of, say, fifty-five, with two women, his wife and another . . . his wife's sister, Fred said. He said that the sister had been a schoolteacher and had retired on a pension. He said they were from North Dakota . . . he could have got that from their car license . . . and he went on, in a way he has, describing the lives of these three people after the first glance as though he had come from their town and had known them all his life. It is exasperating to hear Fred go on in this way about people he doesn't know at all, and what is most exasperating is that so often he is right.

Anyway there we were in this town and it was night, just after dark, and these people came. They drove up in front of the little hotel that had a patio into which, if you were skillful enough, you could drive your car through a very narrow driveway . . . you had to go down a steep stony side street to the driveway . . . and there we were, just loafing and looking, and, as we had all agreed it might be better not to drink water, we had been hitting the Scotch. We were on a little veranda above the patio and, when the man had unloaded his women, he tried to drive down the steep side street and into the patio and he jammed his car.

He got it caught in the narrow driveway and couldn't move it and, as always happens in a Mexican town, at least since we tourists have been coming down in such flocks, the car was literally covered with Mexican kids.

They were on the running boards of the car, they were perched on the hood, they had run on ahead, they were giving directions in Spanish, they were grinning and waving their arms, they were like a freight train crew making up a train in a railroad terminal. One kid motioned for the man to back the car, another to come ahead. They kept it up, grinning, dancing and waving arms until the car was hopelessly jammed and the man, who Fred declared was a manufacturer of washing machines . . . (you'd have thought, to hear Fred talk later, that he had been in business with the man, or had married into his family or something) . . . had got out of the car. He had to crawl over one of the mudguards and he slipped and fell. He was in the patio below us, his two women having come out to join us. We were all standing and looking down at him and, naturally, he was furious.

He was blaming Mexico. He was blaming his wife and his wife's sister. He was there in the patio, as I have suggested, a somewhat small, obviously nervous man, bald and with a little mustache. As he stood looking up at us and scolding . . . he kept waving his arms and hopping about . . . the ends of his mustache also seemed to be hopping up and down.

And he had the Mexican kids on his hands. As he hopped about, they hopped. They had begun a chant that all we tourists in Mexico have come to know. There were many pairs of small brown hands thrust out and, as the man addressed us from above, telling us that it was the kids that had got him into the trouble with the car, saying that, anyway, he had never wanted to come to Mexico, blaming his wife and his wife's sister, they carried on the chant. They made a kind of chorus to his shrill sharp voice.

"Ten cents. Ten cents. Ten cents," they chanted. They had made a circle about him and, as he grew more angry, shouting and scolding more and more shrilly, they, like all the kids in the world, began to enjoy the situation. They kept chanting the two words, the only English words they knew; they danced about him; they kept thrusting the little brown hands at him.

Then something else happened. The man below had appealed to us, asking if any of us could speak what he called their lingo, wanting us to tell the kids to vamoose, and the one of our party who might have helped, the newspaper man who spoke Spanish, had answered, saying, no, that we didn't know a word of Spanish . . . the particular newspaper man is named Lindsey . . . Jake Lindsey . . . and I had seen him, but a moment before, step aside and whisper something to the hotel proprietor, a Mexican with a big mustache, explaining, as I later found out, the situation, putting it up to him to help carry on the show, being thus as malicious as the kids. The hotel proprietor, like many Mexicans, was not averse to seeing an American in a ridiculous position . . . this thing always being carried on between peoples who do not speak the same language, do not live in the same sort of civilization . . .

All this going on, the Scotch, I dare say at work in us . . . it had come out of Jake Lindsey's bag and the hotel man had been in on it . . . the man's wife and his wife's sister begging him to come on up out of the patio, pleading that a man could be got to get the car out of the driveway, reminding him that every time he got excited he was sick afterwards, the man protesting, the kids dancing about him and carrying on their chant, the hotel proprietor grinning, the great racket going on attracting the attention of people in the street outside.

As suggested it was already night, and dark, but there was light in the patio and outside, in the village street, there were men coming home from their work in the fields. They were the sort of men we had been seeing all that day in the road. They were Mexican farmers, some afoot, some mounted on their little burros and, in the hand of each, the inevitable machete.

It is a long knife. It is the sort of knife used by the American farmer to cut corn but the Mexican, being a Mexican, has glorified it. Sometimes he has it in a leather sheath like a sword, sometimes it is curved at the end and sometimes straight. They all carry machetes. They wear them as they wear their shoes, when they have shoes. They carry them into town, into the fields. Fred says they sleep with the machetes in their hands.

The men were coming from the fields and, hearing the racket in the patio, they were curious. They began climbing over the car jammed in the driveway. They advanced toward the excited man and the circle of kids and, up above, the two women seeing them advancing so, the long knives in their hands . . . the truth was that they were all grinning . . . the two women began to scream and, turning and seeing the men with the knives, the man below fled up a flight of stairs to us.

"Ten cents. Ten cents. Ten cents."

They followed the man, now gone white, up the stairs to the veranda above but stopped there. The man had already engaged rooms and the hotel proprietor, thinking no doubt that the show had gone on long enough, went and threw open a door to one of the rooms. They ran in and the door was slammed and the newspaper man, that Jake Lindsey who might have helped the man and wouldn't, began to shower ten-cent pieces among the kids. He threw them into the patio below and the kids dashed down, the Mexican men with the long knives standing and laughing. They began waving the knives about.

"Viva America," they shouted. Laughing, they crawled away, over the jammed car that the two newspaper men later released and got back into the street of the town.

It was a night of sounds. It was a night of plots. I have an idea that I did not succeed, in spite of patient inquiry, in getting at the truth of it all. Fred says he wasn't in on it but I think he lied and I am sure that the two newspaper men and the Mexican hotel proprietor were in it up to their eyes.

As for myself, as I had been driving all day, I slept; but before sleeping I did get the feel, the sound, the smell of the Mexican village at night. For one thing, wanting to wear down the Scotch, I went for a walk, but how long and how far I walked I don't know. I was in many little dark streets. I was in a market crowded with people. The brown, bare-legged Mexican kids kept calling to me. There were two or three words of English they had learned. "Allo! Good-by!" they said and laughed. Now and then one of the kids varied it a bit. "Allo! O.K.!" he said.

As I have said, it was a night of sounds, and it is everywhere the same on such a night. There are these nights when the world seems suddenly filled with strange and unnatural sounds. I have known them in America but in Mexican towns the night sounds are all so new. The border between the two countries is such an absolute border. There are these strange people . . . certainly to the American, strange . . . who do not seem to want our way of life, who are continually holding fiestas, who do not build skyscrapers in their cities, who hold dances in their churches, who use primitive wooden plows in their fields, who adore bull fights and passionately desire pistols with inlaid ivory handles. There are these Spaniards, Mestizos, Indians, Africanos, all seemingly living happily together.

There was all of this on this particular Mexican night, and there was the man in the room with the two women. As I learned later they did not come out to dine but they stayed in the room into which they had fled. Fred said that when the newspaper men were getting the car out of the driveway and were driving it into the patio, he did see the door to their room open a crack. He said that the man looked out, put his hand to his forehead, moaned and shut the door again.

And then the long night came with its sounds. Have you ever slept alone in a strange house when the wind blew, when windows rattled, when doors seemed to open and close mysteriously, when strange shadows ran across the floors?

There must have been a company of Mexican soldiers marching in a road. There was the steady rhythmic sound of marching feet and, somewhere in the distance, a drum began to beat. There was the distant sound of cheering.

These sounds for a time, and then others. Even in the heart of Mexico City the cocks crow all night. It must be that Mexican city men keep fighting cocks. They were crowing in the town, and men shod in the sort of soft leather sandals called "huarachos," were going up and down the street outside. They walk softly. Then they run a little, then walk again. There is a soft rhythm. Occasionally a group of them stopped in the street. They may have been farmers who had come into town. They carried machetes. I myself, awakening once in the night, saw a group under my window. I heard the soft footsteps of other men in the street and the continual crowing of the cocks. The men in the street, outside my window, spoke softly together. They kept looking up and down the street and as I stood watching and wondering, before I threw myself on my bed to sleep again, I heard, first a sudden outburst of the town cocks crowing, and then, in the silence, a voice. It was the voice of the man with the two women. "Look! Listen!" he moaned. "It is a signal. We will be murdered and robbed." He spoke of his car in the patio below. "It isn't locked. We'll lose our things," he said, and when he had stopped speaking there was the sound of low laughter. That, as I found out later, came from the Scotch. It had died in me but it was alive and at work in Fred, in the two newspaper men and in the man with the big mustache who ran the hotel.

It was, however, the crowing of the cocks that was to drive at least one American tourist out of Mexico, release him, free him from the necessity of visiting with his wife and his wife's sister innumerable Mexican churches, from going to the Xochimilco to ride in a boat, from seeing all of the Diego Rivera murals.

The man from North Dakota was in his room with the two women and they had not undressed. He had seen his car brought into the patio but it was not locked. He must have heard the marching of the soldiers and seen the men with the machetes standing under his window.

And then the cocks began crowing and Fred and the two newspaper men, who were in an adjoining room . . . they had got the hotel proprietor in there . . . they still were drinking the Scotch and when the cocks kept crowing, they also began to crow.

It began and they kept it up. There was this outburst of crowing. Fred said that one of the newspaper men, a little high, went down into the patio. There was a little old Mexican man, a kind of guard, on post in the patio, to watch the cars of such occasional tourists as came that way, and the newspaper man, that Jake Lindsey, the one who spoke Spanish, had got him into the plot. He may have taken him some of the Scotch.

He also began to crow. He stood in the patio and crowed. The two newspaper men and the hotel proprietor in the room above crowed and the Mexican cocks, scattered about over the town, crowed lustily.

It was a bedlam. It was too much for the man from North Dakota. It convinced his two women. No doubt it seemed to them that signals were being given for another Mexican revolution. It became connected in their minds with the men with the machetes under the window and the marching of the company of soldiers. Fred said that if he and the others hadn't been spiffed, they would presently have chucked the fun . . . they kept hearing the moans and the prayers of the three people in the adjoining room . . . but that, spiffed as they were, it had all seemed innocent enough.

They kept it up, Fred, the two newspaper men, the hotel proprietor and the guard, down in the patio, until the Mexican night was almost gone and the three tourists could stand it no longer. They made a dash for it. Fred said that he and the others came out of the room where they had been holding wassail and stood on the balcony above the patio. He said that the man from North Dakota had a pair of scissors in his hand. They were, he thought, a contribution of one of the women . . . and that he stood before the little old Mexican guard and waved them back and forth trying, Fred thought, to pass them off as a gun, and then, when the women had got into the car, he sprang in and made a dash for the driveway.

He made a dash for it and this time, there being no Mexican kids to confuse, he made it all right. He was in the street outside and there was a streak of morning light in the east. He was making for the border, and as he drove rapidly away the three Americans and the two Mexican men, the hotel proprietor and the little old guard from the patio—he with the serape about his old shoulders, ran into the street and stood together, sending up a chorus of crows. Fred, in telling of it, said that they were all a little ashamed but that on the other hand they all felt that in getting one male American tourist thus out of the country they were doing a rather high class favor to him.

6. Dinner in Thessaly

"Not life but the good life." Didn't Socrates say something like that? It seems to me moral nonsense to go on, in old age, in pain, in uselessness to others . . . to say nothing of self.

I have always wondered about this whole notion. "Why . . . if you take your own life you won't go to heaven."

But it's this heaven that I must wonder about. What monstrous egotism . . . that I, who have lived as I have, so often cruel and brutal to others, selfish, self-centered, only occasionally losing self, becoming impersonal, only at rare, rare moments doing any work that means anything to others—

The thought that this life of mine should be perpetuated, go on forever. . . .

By what terrible mischance does it deserve that?

There is this woman, whose death by her own hands I take it inspired this discussion. It was, to my sensing, so nice, so clean—what she did, and her reasons given—so sensible. It happens that I once met her, sat dining near her, heard her talk. She was one of the living people I have met, full of intense life, energy, of works.

I have, you see, to make this personal, thinking of my own life, grown old, perhaps diseased, thinking of myself become a burden on others.

Do you remember Socrates, condemned by the state to die? I remember that his friends came to him. A way of escape could be found. He could flee to Thessaly. There would be friends and admirers in that distant place.

But Socrates had lived in Athens in the day of the glory of Athens. At least it must have seemed so to him. What! . . . To flee all that, friends, comrades, the good talk, the wine of that life, for a few more years in the distant place . . . surrounded perhaps by a few disciples? There was probably a Ladies' Literary Club out there.

What! for a dinner in Thessaly? Bring on the hemlock.

What! for an assurance of this heaven no man has ever been able to describe satisfactorily, even to imagine satisfactorily.

I have nothing but respect for the woman Charlotte Perkins Gilman. My hat is off to her. I wish I also could be assured of the same sort of clean departure, of the courage and sanity for it.

For to me it seems quite clear that all of this clinging to life, giving it so often this vast over-estimate . . . granting always disease . . . perhaps some quite incurable and loathsome disease. . . let the gods explain the existence of such evil in the world . . . I'll not attempt it . . . the gods' business for the gods . . . my business under such circumstances for myself.

Friends who perhaps have loved me, to have this load put on them . . . coming into my sickroom, myself lying there, old and helpless—the stink of that place, the low misery, the mind losing its clean clearness . . .

"Oh, my friends, dear ones . . . with whom I have walked, talked, made love, seen days and nights. . . .

"To do this to you. . . ."

I think, I must think, that it is past all words moral nonsense to say that I must go on, under such circumstances, bringing that much more evil into other lives.

For to me disease is evil, old age, decrepitude, with incurable disease the final evil.

Springs coming, walks in the forest, love, comradeship . . . these all gone.

Who took these from me?

Thanks be to those, scientists or others, who have invented or discovered these poisons—perhaps for an almost quiet exit, the door somewhat softly opened.

An end to my being a nuisance to others. Do I want them all to rejoice when I at last die . . . that sort of rejoicing?

7. After a Conference

Again I have come from a writers' conference. I was there with several other professional writers. We lectured. We read manuscripts. After reading the manuscript of a novel, or of several short stories submitted, it was part of our job to take the young writer aside, have a talk with him or her.

That, we all found, was the hardest part of it all.

I think we were all eager to hand out words of praise and encouragement. We professional writers went from one to another.

"Have you read Miss Smith's manuscript?

"Well?"

There was the hope that the other had found something you had not found.

Among ourselves we talked big.

"Ah, tell her to quit writing. It's hopeless. Tell her to chuck it."

It is so easy to talk big when you are not in the actual presence of the young writer.

But wait. They are not all so young. There are men and women of forty and even fifty who have been at it for years. How patiently they have struggled. Evidently there is something corked up in such a one that needs uncorking. Life has hedged him about.

There is a woman who has made, let's say, a bad marriage but she is one who does not believe in divorce. She is grimly determined to stick it out, but something within her keeps wanting to run away.

Or a man is hedged about by a family. He is, we'll say, a clerk who has all his life, dreamed of a life of adventure.

They are both trying to get through words what they cannot or dare not try to get in life.

How can you help being sympathetic? It is something we all do. All of us no doubt spend a large part of our lives living in impossible dreams.

So there you are, in the presence of such a one. What are you to say? The manuscript you have been reading was bad enough. People in the novel or story were pushed ruthlessly about. They were made to fit into a crudely conceived plot.

But there is the writer sitting with you. I am quite sure that almost always such a beginner knows in his heart, or wherever a person does know such things, that his manuscript is bad, but he has this queer belief that a word from you will make it good.

So he sits with the expectant, hopeful light in his eyes.

And what are you to do, what are you to say? To say what you are really feeling would be like striking a child with your fist.

"Ah, go on home. Be a good wife, or a good husband. Go join the army. Get a job in a sawmill."

You can't do it. You hedge. In spite of yourself, when you see no hope, you begin saying hopeful words.

"Keep at it," you say. "Write more and more.

"The way to learn to write is to write."

You get off these old sayings. Let us say that there were, in a long novel you have waded through painfully enough, a few passages.

There was a description of an evening's walk, by a tree-lined road, just as darkness was coming on. At least that was felt. It was a little oasis in the desert of words. You cling to that, praise it, make much of it. You make too much of it.

And all the time there are the eyes looking at you. They are accusing you.

"You could tell me if you would," the eyes are saying. There is this belief that you have, concealed somewhere in your pocket, a key that, if you would but pass it out, would open all doors.

It is all very discouraging, very sad, except that now and then when you have grown most indignant with yourself, something sometimes happens.

"Why have I let myself be put into this position?"

It isn't only at writers' conferences that these things happen to you. Young writers come to your house, bringing manuscripts, or they send them by mail.

You grow furious.

"What right have they?"

You flee from them. You take it out on your wife. You are like a fish, hooked, that cannot escape.

And then—now and then—at long intervals—the thing happens. You remember a day, long ago, when you picked up and read a story by a man you knew, a Bill Faulkner or an Ernest Hemingway.

And, even at a writers' conference, it sometimes happens.

You have picked up another manuscript, feeling the hopelessness of it all, swearing to yourself that you will never again let yourself be persuaded to come to such a place, and there before you, on the white sheets, it is.

People in the story or the novel you hold in your hand become a little alive, really moving through the story, something really felt, a little actually put down.

It seems to justify it all, all your past embarrassment, your annoyance and anger.

There is someone really doing it. Again the sun warms you, the rain wets you. There is no gladness like the gladness that comes with the finding of another real writer just beginning to really throw the ink.

8. The Dance Is On

It is, just now, a crazy dance. It is in your mind, in your imagination, on the sea, on land, in the air.

We do not come close any more, even to kill another man, or a thousand men, women and children, or to destroy a town or a city. We are far up in the air when we do it, or we are at the breech of a huge gun, forty or fifty miles away.

Houses, towns and cities are built slowly. What plans men make, how men and women labor, plan, save, dream, to build a house, to plant a garden, to a little beautify a street; all of this to pull us all a little more up out of savagery, something achieved beyond bare want, ugliness, brutality.

And then, with a crash, a great column of black smoke filling the spring air, flying bits of wood, brick, stone, human bodies. It is all gone.

Who has done this thing? Whose bodies are those so mangled, so blown to bits?

There was a young man, there at the breech of a gun. Or he was far up in the sky, in a plane, when he dropped the bomb. Do you think he is some casual brute, caring nothing?

He is the young man with whom you dined one evening last summer. He is that other young man you see there, thoughtfully helping an old woman across the street in city traffic. He is the victim of some blind force loose in the world.

Can the dance of death be stopped? It seems a long slow road back to sanity.

There is something loose in the world—a monster. It is in every factory. Go into a cotton mill, into a silk mill. Go look at the press that printed this book.

The thing is not a monster here. It is even beautiful. There is a gay dance, a purposeful dance. See the many-colored cloth rolling out of the flying machines in the cloth mill. Here is beautiful cloth to clothe all the world. See the newspapers dropping as thick as snowflakes in a snow-storm. See the graceful stream-lined cars, coming off the belt in the huge automobile plant.

It is something to make the heart sing, man's amazing skill in destroying distances, making all the world a next-door neighbor, man to live richly, proudly, in a grand rich new world that man's brains and hands have made.

And now turn the page to the other, this horror. Can it be stopped? Can the dance be made, not a dance of death but of joyous new life?

Can men come out of themselves to others?

What a long road to be traveled.

Years ago I wrote some stories of life in American Middle-Western towns. They were, as best I could make them, studies of little lives, everyday small people in a small town, their reactions to one another; and for years afterward I got letters from England, Germany, Turkey, Japan, from South American republics, from France, from many other nations, all saying the same thing.

The stories, they all said, might have been written about people in their own South American, European, Asiatic towns.

So there is this common thing we all have, our lives, so essentially alike, deep down the same dreams, aspirations, hungers.

And then the power hunger, hunger to command other men's lives that has now changed, perverted, the thing we have made—the machine.

The machine that can be so beautiful, that can do such wonders for us.

Must the power hunger, also in man, defeat us all, pervert, make horrible all our lives?

It is a dance.

Man never intended it to be the dance of death. He dreamed of making it a great new dance of life.

Life to be larger, richer, sweeter.

The test of man and the thing he calls "civilization" is upon us. There is this inanimate monster loose in the world. It can make life richer. It can destroy all we have built up. It is up to man, who made it, to control it. Will it all end in a dance of death or in a dance of new and richer life?

The dance is on.

9. One by One

A certain man has built up a national reputation as a lover of humanity. He is forever suffering with peoples. Something dreadful has happened to the Spanish people, to the Finns, to the Dutch, to the Belgians. The man of whom I am speaking weeps with these peoples. He writes articles, attends meetings, makes speeches. There are a good many such men.

I have been sometimes in the company of the man spoken of above. I have walked with him in city streets. I have known others like him. Often, when I am in the company of such men, or women, and when I hear them pouring out this sympathy for distant peoples or for certain classes so-called among our own American people, the workers, the unemployed, etc., etc., I have dreadful moments of doubt.

I keep wondering if it can be done. Can a man, any man, really pour out his sympathies so? Can a man understand hunger who has never been hungry? If you have not walked, day after day, from door to door, seeking employment, can you really comprehend the curious hopeless feeling that presently comes? Do these words we have grown so accustomed to, the workers, the masses, the French, the Dutch, mean anything? I keep remembering impressions got during the first World War. At that time, as now, there were many meetings being held. I was a good deal in New York and in Chicago then and I was continually meeting men and women who had just come from such meetings.

The meetings were concerned with suffering Belgians, suffering Poles, etc., etc. Often the men and women attending these meetings had never been either in Poland or Belgium. It may well have been true that they had never known an individual, a native of these countries. Often such a one had attended three or four such meetings during an afternoon.

He went then to a cocktail party where I saw him. It was very strange. After several such meetings concerned with people starving, being driven from their homes into fields, families broken up, disease rampant among them, such a one, having come from all these meetings, appeared at the cocktail party as chipper as a spring robin hopping across a green lawn in a peaceful land.

I was quite sure that had one of these people been brought into the actual presence of one starving man or woman his day would have been wrecked.

A good many years ago I wrote a novel that was concerned with the workers. I had been among them, had been a factory hand. I tried to make the figures of my novel human. Some of the men with whom I had worked had been liars. Others were sneaks and cheats. A good many were fine fellows, men you were proud to have as friends.

And then, after the book was published, I got a letter from a well-known socialist. He scolded me.

"Even if some of the workers are liars and sneaks you shouldn't show them up. Workers have a hard time. You shouldn't tell on them."

Nowadays there is all of this talk of giving up individuality. It seems nonsense to me. If I give up my individuality, what have I left? It is my own firm belief that all of us, and in spite of all the modern talk of giving up individuality, remain individuals, and that all of this thinking and attempting to feel toward others in the mass is an attempt to think and feel in a vacuum.

I am one man. I go about. I have friends, people loved.

Often as I walk about, either in city streets or on a country road, I see things that do touch me deeply.

I have seen, for example, a man, no doubt out of work, destitute and starving, fingering the refuse in a garbage can in an alleyway in a city. He is one man to me and seeing him thus I am deeply hurt, but my mind cannot multiply the man indefinitely. He remains a solitary figure to me. I identify myself with him personally, not with a whole class of men. I have stopped in a city street and am staring at him and he looks up from the garbage can and sees me standing and looking. Shame sweeps over him and over me. Suddenly thus we have something in common, our shame.

Or I see a tenant farmer with his family, after a year of failure on some poor farm, who has loaded his few poor belongings on a half broken-down wagon and is about to try his luck on another poor farm.

He is walking along a country road beside a lame mule, his thin wife and children following in the road.

I cannot identify him in my mind with an entire farming class. He is the one man there in the road, after the year of failure, facing his seemingly hopeless future.

Surely I can feel all of that, in him, in me.

Save by the grace of God, that is me there in the road. How I have escaped that destitution I do not know.

All of life has for me this queer accidental quality. I turn a corner out of a city street and meet a man, or a woman, who gives me a shove up or down. Every man or woman who crosses the doorstep of my house brings something into my house. We are all of us all the time giving off either health or poison. To surrender individuality, if it could be done, would be also to shirk all the responsibility of living.

I must get all people so—one by one, as I come to them. Is it a shallowness in me that I cannot think in terms of a French nation but only of individual Frenchmen I have known? The Germans have gone into Holland, the guns blasting a road for them, and my mind stays on one individual, a woman, known well, who lives in the city of Amsterdam. As I read the newspapers or hear the voices on the radio my mind stays on her. All of the rest is too big for me, too vast.

I see only the one figure running from the guns, a slender tall woman. She runs through fields, along roads, past people. I see her white frightened face. I see her fall and rise again. I hear her sobs. Her figure remains thus, in my mind, in my imagination, it may be will always remain so.

But she is not to me the Dutch people. She is that one woman I have known.

And so also with certain other individual figures I have personally known in Paris.

They are not to me all France. I cannot picture them so. When I get to these big words, describing or attempting to describe whole classes or nations of people my mind goes blank.

Is it a fault in me, something left out of my nature or am I like all people? If we were honest with ourselves would we not, all of us, have to take all others so—one by one? For myself I have found it difficult enough to try to understand a little a few other men and women. I have to take them one by one—one by one—otherwise I am lost and cruelty becomes easy to me.

10. God Bless the Americas

There must be thousands, even hundreds of thousands like her in America. They are of German, Polish, Italian, Spanish descent. Their parents or grandparents came here from any one of fifteen or twenty European nations, now all, in some way, involved in the second World War. She is now a woman of thirty with the dark eyes, the dark skin, the shining blue-black hair characteristic of so many of her Spanish people. She is certainly beautiful.

There is a kind of hardness in her. She had come to my hotel to see me, this in a Florida city where there is a large Spanish population, for the most part working people, makers of cigars, and where she has lived since childhood.

The matter that had brought us together having been settled, we sat in the hotel lobby and talked. We began speaking of the new effort of our own country to draw closer to the South Americans and the point of view she expressed was absorbingly interesting to me.

"I am speaking now as a Spaniard," she said. She laughed.

"Oh, yes, I am a Spaniard all right. I am a Spaniard, and at the same time I am very American too."

She said that she was very anxious to explain a certain feeling she had.

"It is a somewhat nervous time for us," she said. She thought there must be hundreds of thousands of people like herself, living here in the United States, born here, of Spanish, Italian, German parents, loving intensely something the life here had meant to them and their people and, at the same time, as they well knew, now somewhat subject to suspicion.

"It is such a mistake to think that all of us, or for that matter many of us, are thinking and feeling as Spaniards, Italians or Germans," she said. "We are just people. We eat, we sleep, we try to find work, we want to try to live a good and a happy life. We know that our fathers and mothers, or our grandfathers and grandmothers, came here to escape something. They came here to find something for which they hungered." It was true enough, she said, that many had come simply because they had heard it was easy to grow rich here. She laughed when she said that. It certainly hadn't worked out for most of them, she said.

In her effort to make me understand what was in her mind she began speaking of her own childhood and girlhood. Her father had come here as a boy and being a shrewd and capable man had got into business. He had married a Spanish woman but he wanted very much that his children learn to think of themselves as Americans.

"So I went to the public school. It was here, in this city where there are many Spaniards. They are for the most part poor. They are working people.

"I was in the public school but was set apart from the other Spanish pupils because my father was more well-to-do. I dressed better than they did. I could play the piano, had taken dancing lessons. I dare say I was somewhat snobbish. I looked down upon the poor Spanish children, many of them Mestizos, half-Indian, and the children of the older American families did the same to me.

"So I was set apart. I was lonely. When I went home I went into my own room and cried. I wanted very much to be what I was, the daughter of my own father and my own mother, but at the same time I wanted to be taken in by the others. I knew I was bright, that I had talent. I presume I wanted to be admired.

"Oh, I know it was snobbish of me to look down upon the other children, the daughters and sons of poor Spanish and Mestizos, but there the others were, doing the same thing to me.

"I was in my room at home, crying about all this, confused and hurt, and my father came in. In such families as ours, people of Spanish descent, the family life is very close and intense. In such a family as ours the father is king. We both love and fear him.

"But my father was very tender with me. I tried to explain and he understood at once. It may be that, as a boy here, he had gone through the same thing. He was a small child when the Spanish-American War was fought. More than once I had heard him speak of it to his friends who came to our house. He had spoken of how he and mother felt. There was, you see, the rejoicing at the easy victory of the Yankees, and over the humiliation of the Spaniards, and there were his people, wanting intensely to be thought of and to feel as Americans and at the same time, inevitably you see, feeling also the humiliation of the people of their own blood.

"My father thought of something he felt might be a way out for me. He sent me to a convent school where there were only girls, of our so-called Spanish upper class, but I was unhappy there too."

"And why?"

"Well, I hardly know why. I was being trained into a way of life foreign to the life about me. You see, I had got something else from my father. We Latin people are dreamers. We are what you might call hard-boiled dreamers. I dare say that you Americans, whose people have been here for many generations, cannot know what the word America has meant to many generations of Europeans. Oh, how they dreamed of coming here or of having their children come here, of having a chance here to rise a little in the world, get education, position, standing; to live, you see, in a free land, with free men, not as strangers but as brothers, as fellow Americans.

"So I did not stay in the convent. I begged my father to take me out. I begged him to send me away, to some place where there were few or no Spanish people and he, understanding, sent me to a college, one of the big state universities of the North."

The American woman of Spanish blood laughed again. It was a hard little laugh. No, there was no joy in it.

"Oh, it was quite different there," she said. "There I was something, well, I dare say, a little exotic. I was taken up, courted, made much of. I was, you see, again set apart. I was not just a person, one among all of the others, standing on my feet, admired for some superior quality in myself, but was treated always as something again a little strange and apart, courted, you see, for the very thing that, when there were many others of my blood about, had led to my being snubbed."

The Spanish woman who had come to see me was now very earnest. She began trying to tell me that it was possible for many people like herself, people whose fathers or grandfathers had come here from one of the countries now at war with the democratic way of life, to themselves love passionately the country they had come to think of as their own country, to believe even more passionately than the older Americans in the democratic way of life, without being too fond of many of the Americans they daily came into contact with.

"It may be because we know, with a kind of blood knowledge born in us, what dictatorships mean," she said. She said that she was forced to admit that among her own people, as among the Germans, the Italians, and others, whose people in Europe were now bound by fear, like slaves, to the dictators, that there were some ready enough to betray the democracy in which they lived.

"And you have Americans of families who have been here for many generations, who are no better," she said.

"There are betrayers among all peoples," she said, but, at the same time she added there would be so much gained if Americans in general, everywhere, would keep trying to throw off suspicion of all such people as herself, she being so obviously Spanish as well as American, as hundreds of thousands of Italians and Germans were obviously Italian and German as well as American.

As she was Spanish she spoke particularly of the Spanish here. Now we were trying suddenly to win the affection and friendship of South Americans, who were nearly all of Spanish blood. It was a quick and sudden courtship. There was much to be forgotten before we would be accepted as lovers. In the past there had been too much ridicule, too much misunderstanding of the problems faced by the people in the countries of South America. What had to be slowly and painfully learned was that people down there, the Spanish Americans, the Indians, the Mestizos, were at bottom as we were, just people. They wanted, as we here wanted, a quiet and peaceful way of life, to be accepted as equals, not patronized.

"It is by the way of fear and suspicion that the dictators have come into power in Europe," she said. "Our people, the Spaniards, as well as the Italians and the Germans here know that old fear and suspicion," she added. "It has come down into us with our blood and many times, here among you Americans, we have felt it in our daily lives.

"They will be trying to do it here and in South America. They will be working to set one class against another, one race against another.

"It isn't so easy to be really democratic, is it?" she asked, getting up to go.

She laughed again, the same quick hard little laugh I had noticed before.

"You have now a popular song, 'God Bless America,'" she said.

"You had better change it," she added.

"Why not make it 'God Bless the Americas'?" was her parting shot as she went out at the door.

II. The Fortunate One

I was in the country, having taken a room in the house of a certain family. There were many children. There was no place to work. There were young boys in the family.

There was a low shed, that had formerly, I believed, housed pigs. It had no doors or windows. It stood in the midst of a corn field.

The boys cleaned it and I helped. We shoveled dirt from the floor until we got down to the hard clean clay. We whitewashed the walls.

I moved my desk in there. I could not stand erect. While I worked in that place . . . again a madness of writing had seized me . . . the corn about me grew tall. The stalks pushed through the open windows, through the low doorway. A broad green corn leaf lay across the corner of my desk.

I wrote a book of childhood, an American childhood. It was in that place that a certain sentence came into my head. I was hoping that if, after my death, there were any who wished to do me honor they would honor me, not for what I had written, but for the full rich life I have lived. I was craving to be known as one man who had never saved, never provided for the morrow, as a man who had wished only to live in the Now.

"Life, not Death, is the great adventure," I wrote.

For years I have been jotting down these impressions, memories, things seen and felt during what has continued to seem to me a very good life. On all sides now I hear complaints of the quality of life in our times. Possibly in years to come men will look back upon our time and speak of it as another dark age. Any civilization absorbed in economics, in war, in the economic interpretation of history, etc., can but be a savage and brutal civilization. It may be that I was born one of the lucky ones.

To be sure as a writer I have had endless miserable days. Black gloom having settled upon me often has stayed for days, weeks and months and these black times have always been connected with my work. I have been too eager. I have wanted to create constantly, never stopping. Yet what man at all sensitive to life doesn't have these weeks and months of gloom? And there have come these rich glad times. In a perhaps muddled time I have lived fully.

Has any man of my time approached me in richness of living? Perhaps Lawrence; but in my own experience of men I have never met another who has smelled, tasted, felt, seen as I have. I have been all my life a wanderer but my wandering has been to some purpose. America is a vast country. I have wanted to feel all of it in its thousand phases, see it, walk upon it—its plains, mountains, towns, cities, rivers, lakes, forests and plowed lands. I have been a true son of God in my eager love for and appreciation of nature. It is only through nature and art that men really live.

Women to me are related always to the world of nature, the male to the spirit. To me they have been, when not trying also to be male, the good earth. I am very male and do not believe in women artists—and these men feminists, how they bore me, how they make my bones ache with boredom. To me women are as a flowing stream in which I bathe and clothe myself. They are rich wine drunk, fruit eaten. They have washed me as summer rains wash me. It is because I am so very male that I can be a real lover of women. But although I am essentially male I am not particularly lustful. There has been too much of the male energy in me gone into the effort to produce a beautiful art, to permit that. I have succeeded sometimes, failed often. But I believe in art. It is my only central purpose to produce, now and then, a flash of beauty in work. Not only because in the end nothing lives on but art.

The male desires not to be beautiful but to create beauty, and no woman can be beautiful without the help of the male. We create their beauty, fertilize it, feed it. In reality women have no desire to do. Doing is for them a substitute. Their desire is to be BE. There was never a real woman lived who did not hunger to be beautiful. Woman is not man: I have had to write a book about this and it went unnoticed. If we were a strong race our women would be more beautiful, our land and our cities more beautiful. Because Americans have no understanding of women America has become a matriarchy.

All evil, all ugliness is a sign of weakness. The men in America who build ugly cities, ugly factory towns, who make fields and forests ugly, who make wars, cry out constantly the word progress, progress, to cover the fact of their ugly work—these are all weak men.

Strong men are always gentle. To them a field is as a woman loved. O women, women, how we have defeated you!

But I have lived here. I have been all my life a poet here. The matriarchy in which I have lived, the vulgarity of men seeking their so-called success, the difficulty of going on living as a poet in the midst of this has only drawn me to shrewdness. It is that that has made me a proseman. I write prose only to conceal song, the music of living.

Having a little money I went to the country and built a cabin on a high hill and every morning I climbed the hill.

"Oh, what a magnificent view." The few people who climbed the hill to my cabin all went into ecstasies. "What a place in which to work.

"You should do magnificent work up here."

Day after day I climbed the hill. The hills, going away into the distance, were like the waves of a vast sea. Clouds floated across the hills. Little fragments of clouds crept down into hollows in the hills. My eye could follow a pale yellow dirt road that wound around and up over hills. Horses in a distant hill-top pasture stood silhouetted against a pale blue sky.

I sat on some steps before my cabin and the hours passed. Nature, so on parade, was too much for me. Nature seemed to be mocking me, laughing at me. The hills laughed. Trees on a nearby hill thumbed their noses at me. I kept going back to the cabin on the hilltop. Formerly, when I first began to write, I used to tell myself that a good test for anything I had written would be reading it aloud in a corn field. Now I thought of going into a silent wood, of standing under tall trees, my manuscript in my hands, reading to the trees.

"If I am not too much ashamed it should be a sign," I said to myself. I never tried the experiment. It was one of my poetic notions.

I, however, have had times of being very pagan. It has seemed to me that formerly, when man believed in wood gods, in fairies dancing in the grass, in giants living in castles hidden in mountains, life must have been richer. I have tried to re-create these. When I have been living in the country and have gone to my place of work at night . . . usually in some isolated building I have lighted candles and carried them outdoors.

I put the candles under two trees. I went indoors and sat at my desk near a window. I prayed to the old gods. There was some difficulty. I had got together certain characters. How did this woman, created in my imagination, affect the life of this man? I had got lost in some way and wanted the old gods to come back and lead me out of the maze.

I used to take little things to worship. Now I am talking about a time when I was a young man. It might be just a young tree. I remember once a man gave me a little wooden figure. I was working all day in an advertising agency, writing advertisements.

I kept the little figure in a box. Sometimes at night, when I was depressed, I crept out of bed and knelt by a table. I felt about in the darkness until I had got out the figure; then I caressed it with my hands.

The figure was of no importance. I did not dare look at it in the daytime. At night, when my fingers played over it, my imagination was aroused. As I never looked at it in the light, it became for me a marvelous thing. I was all the time quite conscious that the arousing of my own imagination was the important thing. Any loveliness in the absurd doll was my own creation. I was like a farmer compelled to plow the land, sow seed, and grind the grain before he could get bread to feed himself.

Once, when I was in love and could not find a woman who satisfied me, I bestowed my love on a young tree that grew in Chicago, in Jackson Park.

I used to walk there in the darkness, never going too near the tree. One night when I was very sad and lonely I did approach the tree. I touched it with my fingers. A thrill ran through my body. It was almost as though the tree had been a lovely woman and I had lain with her.

There still is something sought after and never touched. I write as to a dear friend, a comrade, a being neither man nor woman.

Women with their flesh, their breasts, hips, eyes, legs, drive me from the point.

All men feel that.

I seek a companion without sex, ageless, silent, beautiful.

It is the kind of conception out of which Christ was born.

I accept Christ. I become a Christian—one who loves Christ.

Christianity has become corrupt. Perhaps it has never been pure, but once a poet conceived the figure of Christ. For just the moment—when the conception was born in the mind of the poet, Christ was pure.

I do not ask Christ to save me. I ask him to save himself.

It is only in the moment of my own hunger I can be a Christian.

If I love Christ, thinking that as a reward of my love I shall be given another life, I do not love.

Love seeking a reward is no love.

So I have been a writer now for thirty years and on too many days I still write badly. I have been panned and praised by critics, have been called a genius, a pioneer, a heavy-thinker, clear-headed, muddle-headed, a groper. That last has stuck more persistently than any of the others. If it is meant, by groping, that I do not know the answers, O.K. During most of my life, to date, I have been healthy and strong. I am no prize fighter, no athlete, but I enjoy thoroughly my friends, women, food, drink, sleep. There is a kind of persistent youth in some men and I am one of that sort. I rebound quickly from disaster, laugh a good deal, make rather quick and easy connections with others . . .

And I say that when I die I should like this inscription put on my grave . . .

LIFE, NOT DEATH, IS THE GREAT ADVENTURE.